D1454319

'So clean'

MANCHESTER
1824

Manchester University Press

'So clean'

Lord Leverhulme, soap and civilization

BRIAN LEWIS

Manchester University Press
Manchester and New York

distributed exclusively in the USA by Palgrave Macmillan

Published by Manchester University Press
Oxford Road, Manchester M13 9NR, UK
and Room 400, 175 Fifth Avenue, New York, NY 10010, USA
www.manchesteruniversitypress.co.uk

Distributed in the United States exclusively by
Palgrave Macmillan, 175 Fifth Avenue,
New York, NY 10010, USA

Distributed in Canada exclusively by
UBC Press, University of British Columbia, 2029 West Mall,
Vancouver, BC, Canada V6T 1Z2

British Library Cataloguing-in-Publication Data is available

Library of Congress Cataloging-in-Publication Data is available

ISBN 978 0 7190 8913 8 paperback

First published by Manchester University Press in hardback 2008

This paperback edition first published 2012

Printed by Lightning Source

For my parents

Contents

List of illustrations   *page* viii
Acknowledgements   ix

1 The Napoleon of soap   1

2 Soft soap and soap operas   56

3 Sunlight for the unwashed   93

4 Sunlight for savages   154

5 Twilight   199

   Select bibliography   226
   Index   241

Illustrations

1 William Hesketh Lever, *c.* 1901. (Reproduced with kind permission of Unilever from an original in Unilever Archives) *page* 13

2 Mr and Mrs Lever and their son outside Thornton Manor, *c.* 1905. (Reproduced with kind permission of Unilever from an original in Unilever Archives) 17

3 Map of Rivington. In Thomas H. Mawson, *Civic Art: Studies in Town Planning* (London: B. T. Batsford, 1911), fig. 270 32

4 Sketch of the pigeon tower and a shelter and lookout at Roynton Cottage, Rivington. In Thomas H. Mawson, *Civic Art: Studies in Town Planning* (London: B. T. Batsford, 1911), fig. 269 34

5 Lever Brothers' advertisement 'Why does a woman look old sooner than a man?' (Reproduced with kind permission of Unilever from an original in Unilever Archives) 75

6 Port Sunlight cottages, Park Road, *c.* 1913. (Reproduced with kind permission of Unilever from an original in Unilever Archives) 111

7 Lunch hour at the main gate, Port Sunlight works, 1907. (Reproduced with kind permission of Unilever from an original in Unilever Archives) 114

8 Gladstone Hall dining room, Port Sunlight, 1895. (Reproduced with kind permission of Unilever from an original in Unilever Archives) 115

9 Map of Port Sunlight with proposed Beaux-Arts additions. In Thomas H. Mawson, *Civic Art: Studies in Town Planning* (London: B. T. Batsford, 1911), fig. 239 138

10 The projected causeway, Bolton. In Thomas H. Mawson, *Civic Art: Studies in Town Planning* (London: B. T. Batsford, 1911), fig. 1 139

11 Map of the Belgian Congo showing the concession areas of the 1911 Convention. Derived from a map in Charles Wilson, *The History of Unilever: A Study in Economic Growth and Social Change*, vol. I (London: Cassell and Co., 1954), p. 171 172

12 'Stornoway of the future'. Sketch by Raffles Davison in *Academy Architecture and Architectural Review*, 52 (1921), 7 207

Acknowledgements

I am indebted to many people in the research and writing of this book. I would like to thank the staff at Unilever Archives and Records Management (UARM), Bolton Archives and Local Studies, the Sydney Jones Library of the University of Liverpool, the British Library of Political and Economic Science at the London School of Economics, and the McLennan, Blackader-Lauterman, Osler and Howard Ross Management Libraries of McGill University. At UARM, Jeannette Strickland, the Head Archivist, was particularly helpful in accommodating my research and, after reading the manuscript, saving me from a number of factual errors, while Lesley Owen-Edwards gave me much assistance in providing photographs. I am very grateful to Unilever for permission to quote from the archives and for the use of several illustrations. I should point out that the company did not, in any way, seek to influence the contents of this book or exert editorial control.

I am grateful to Xiaoying Ni for bibliographical help, to Irene Pugh for showing me around Thornton Manor (by permission of the late Lord Leverhulme), to Geoff Foote for acting as 'chauffeur' and companion on trips to Harris and Lewis and Bournville, to William Foulger of the Stornoway Historical Society for answering queries, to Lisa Jorgensen for sharing her knowledge of publishers, to Bob Tittler and Marilyn Berger for help with illustrations, to Hassan Mian of McGill's Digital Collections Program for preparing a number of images, to Tom Brydon for help compiling the index and to Kate Desbarats for verifying a translation. Colin Duncan, Nancy Partner and Andrea Tone read the entire manuscript, and Myron Echenberg read chapter four, providing invaluable feedback and much advice and encouragement when it was most needed. Thanks also to the three anonymous reviewers for Manchester University Press, whose helpful suggestions I have attempted to incorporate, and to the prompt and efficient staff at the press. John Hall, then Dean of Arts at McGill, kindly allowed me some relief from teaching at a critical juncture during the writing. A McGill internal Social Sciences and Humanities Research Council of Canada grant and, in part, a Québec FCAR *programme établissement de nouveaux chercheurs* grant made the research possible.

This book was written while I served a busy but rewarding five-year term as Chair of McGill History Department. To my colleagues, students and support staff who have made the department such a congenial environment in which to work, and for compensating for me when my concentration on administrative tasks wavered, a sincere thank you. Family and friends, in and out of McGill – it would be invidious to single any one out, but they know who they are – have striven mightily to keep me (relatively) sane by providing excellent company and joining me for good food and fine ale. I owe special thanks to my parents, Val and Frank Lewis. They have provided unfailing support and a home and a research base in Blackburn, Lancashire, for my trips from Canada to England. As far back as I can remember they took me on rambles around Lever Park and the terraced gardens at Rivington, sparking my initial interest in Lord Leverhulme and his story. Rivington is still one of their favourite outings today, and I hope that in particular they enjoy the relevant section in chapter one. The book is dedicated to them, once again, with love and gratitude.

B.L.
Montréal

1

The Napoleon of soap

Et lux perpetua

He died from pneumonia on 7 May 1925 at his home on Hampstead Heath, aged seventy-four. 'The career of Lord Leverhulme bristles with dramatic values that will prove an embarrassment of riches for his biographer,' wrote an obituarist in the *New York Evening Post*.

> His career from obscurity to industrial command and affluence has challenged and allured Americans. They liked his rapid-fire, militant decisiveness, the extensive sweep and intensive development of his far-flung enterprises, the wide range of his hobbies outside his vested interests, the lavish, open-handed hospitality he dispensed after he had 'made his pile', his genuine concern for the welfare of the workmen, his Co-Partners, combining a general philanthropy with a shrewd doctrine of productive efficiency.

The *Toronto Globe* saw him as 'one of the world's greatest industrial leaders. His name was linked with those of Carnegie, Rockefeller, and Ford.'[1]

Other newspapers, piling on the awestruck praise, celebrated him as the supreme devotee and exemplar of the gospels of hard work and self-help according to Thomas Carlyle and Samuel Smiles. He personified, they said, capitalism at its best and the repudiation of socialist doctrines: 'He was no half-hearted apologist for the Capitalistic system. He believed in it with all the fervour of his ardent soul.' He was, they contended, a great British imperialist – 'the kind of man who made the British Empire possible' – and an enlightened autocrat: 'in him were the qualities of that ideal ruler of whom Aristotle wrote – a man with almost absolute power blessed with the mind of a philosopher.'[2] *The Times* said of him, striking an oft-repeated ambivalent note, 'He will be remembered not least for the kind of paternal rule which he established over his numerous employees, for, although he was theoretically an old-fashioned Liberal, he possessed in practice some of the characteristics of a despot – benevolent, it is true, but still a despot.'[3] 'Lord Leverhulme was a just man,' wrote an obituarist in the *Liverpool Post and Mercury*, 'but also on certain sides of his character a hard man; without that hardness he could never have reached the position to which he attained.'[4]

Lever greatly admired strong-willed, decisive, Great Men. Abraham Lincoln and William Ewart Gladstone were his political heroes. David Lloyd George's 'amazing energy and personal forcefulness', in the words of Lever's son, 'his determination and ability to "get things done" and his power to inspire others' naturally appealed. Lever met Theodore Roosevelt in 1902 and wrote, 'He wore a riding suit, jackboots, spurs and a slouch hat – looked the very picture of the brave, strong man he is.' Cecil Rhodes he met in Cape Town in 1895. 'In later years the one has often been likened to the other,' his son wrote, 'and in many ways their characters and achievements were similar. Courage, organizing ability and breadth of vision were their outstanding qualities, and each did a great work for Africa.'[5]

The most frequently recurring comparison during his life and at his death, however, was with Napoleon. If he had not built up the Lever Brothers soap business, wrote the radical journalist and editor of the *Daily News*, A. G. Gardiner, in 1914, 'he would have been the Napoleon of tea or of oil or of sugar. For he is of the Napoleon breed, born to marshal big battalions and win empires, if not in war, then in peace.'[6] A writer in *Town Topics* in 1912 rather less charitably declared that Lever was 'more ruthless, more autocratic, more dogmatic than Napoleon'.[7] The landscape architect Thomas Mawson described his first encounter with Lever in 1905:

> William Hesketh Lever was, I quickly realised, a man of strong personality, who had absolute control of himself and all his interests, in which I include those interests which absorbed his few leisure hours. At this our first interview he struck me as a veritable Napoleon in his grasp of all the factors dominating any problem he tackled, in his walk and pose, and in his speech, which contained the concentrated essence of thought. There were all the characteristics which we associate with the 'Little Corporal'.[8]

In an address at a memorial service in 1925 the Rev. Dr J. D. Jones, Chairman of the Congregational Union of England and Wales, opined, 'There was something Napoleonic about him. He had vision. He had the big mind…. He could form vast and daring plans. He thought not in terms of cities or towns but of continents. He was a born leader of men.'[9] Lever himself admired Napoleon, and in collecting Napoleonic memorabilia, which he put on display in a special Napoleon Room in the Lady Lever Art Gallery in Port Sunlight, he invited the comparison. He even bought around the turn of the century for one of his principal residences, Thornton Manor, the twenty-four-seater dining-room table used by the deposed Emperor Napoleon III in his final exile in England, at Camden Place, Chislehurst, and a couple of Napoleon III armchairs.[10]

With the death of this electrifying coil of energy, this 'great and overpowering personality',[11] this 'whirlwind of a man',[12] this Napoleon of soap, it was up to his biographers to try and make sense of his life. Lever refused to sanction the publication of a biography during his lifetime. He wrote in 1921 to Stanley

Unwin of the George Allen and Unwin publishing house, 'I have not in any way changed my opinion that a book on myself, either Biography or Autobiography would be of the slightest interest to more than a very limited circle and, therefore, I have no intention of approving of either.' Unwin reproved him in 1924, 'You have had an extraordinarily interesting life and I am afraid you will have to pay the penalty! A biography will appear sooner or later.' One of Lever's secretaries, Rowland Evans, did complete a biography in 1924, without the Old Man's assistance, negotiated with Unwin, but declined to publish in deference to Lever's wishes during his lifetime. After Lever's death, his son, the second viscount, moved swiftly to buy the manuscript and copyright from Evans for £250 and to promise George Allen and Unwin an official biography if they abandoned their plans to publish the unauthorized version.[13]

Evans was disappointed; 'on the other hand I shall always have the satisfaction of knowing that I have not opposed the wishes of the son and the Executors and Trustees of the man whose life I so greatly admire and whose memory I revere'. But self-denial turned to anger when both Evans and his wife were dismissed from the firm's employ as superfluous to requirements. Evans lashed out, 'I was prevented from being the author of one of the late Lord Leverhulme's "Lives" for purely undemocratic reasons ... there is no moral justification for either the son or the Executors ... desiring me not to write such a "Life" merely because I occupy a humble niche in this world.' It was too late to do anything about it, because the son had the rights to the manuscript. The second viscount in private claimed that Evans's manuscript was not as useful to him in writing his own biography as he had hoped, but in the foreword he gave a brief acknowledgement of 'the help I have derived from reading Mr. Evans's manuscript'. There appears to be no trace of the Evans manuscript today.[14]

There have been four book-length studies. The first was indeed by his son, a couple of years after his death. It remains a useful quarry of information but is a period piece, lacking critical distance (in time and from the subject), and is heavily dated in tone, style and conclusions. The second, the first volume of Charles Wilson's monumental history of Unilever (1954), a pioneering work in the field of business history, still stands out as by far the best study of Lever, and my debt to it is apparent in the notes. But, insightful as it is, it principally deals only with the economic aspects of his life and the building of Lever Brothers. The third is a 1976 popular biography by W. P. Jolly, which is a straightforward and fair-minded run-through of Lever's life from womb to tomb, largely devoid of historical context and secondary scholarship. The last is Adam MacQueen's breezy and entertaining 2004 biography.[15]

A number of authors have, in addition, drawn on unoriginal sources to include Lever as a chapter in compilations on thrusting industrialists – men or, more decisively, 'heroes' who 'deserve careful study ... as an example and an inspiration.[16] The titles speak for themselves: A. G. Gardiner's *Pillars of Society*, Mrs Stuart Menzies' *Men of Mark*, William Henry Beable's *Romance of Great Businesses* and H. Maitland Crichton's *The Romance of Million Making*.[17] These were almost unreservedly adulatory. By the mid-century, Harley Williams's *Men of Stress* and W. S. Adams's *Edwardian Portraits*[18] were more critical. In the 1980s Ian Campbell Bradley's *Enlightened Entrepreneurs* reverted to little disguised admiration for his cast of characters, but James Bellini's *Rule Britannia* used Lever as a scapegoat for Britain's industrial decline, an argument we shall return to below.[19] These chapters tend to fit preconceived notions and are scarcely fair to the complexities of Lever's character and motivations. The rest of Lever scholarship is fragmented, focusing on certain aspects of his life and work, notably Nigel Nicolson's *Lord of the Isles* and Roger Hutchinson's *The Soap Man*, which are detailed accounts of his abortive attempt to make inroads into the Scottish fishing industry towards the end of his career, and an important collection of essays edited by Edward Morris on Lever as a collector.[20] A contextualized biography, fully informed by contemporary historical scholarship, is lacking. My biography of Lever aims to fill this void.

This is not a conventional biography. Any reader interested simply in a chronological trot though his life and work should consult one of the studies above. What I find most fascinating about him is that he unites within one person so many intriguing developments of the late nineteenth and early twentieth centuries. Hence my plan of campaign, to use a suitably Napoleonic metaphor: chapter one sketches out his life, the rise and triumph of his business, and explores his homes, his gardens and his collections. Chapters two to four contain essays on Lever in the context of the history of advertising (chapter two), of factory paternalism and town planning (chapter three) and of colonial encounters (chapter four). The concluding chapter resumes something of the narrative and summary format and looks at Lever's extraordinary activity in his final years.

William, Mr Lever, Sir William, Lord Leverhulme of Bolton le Moors, Viscount Leverhulme of the Western Isles, the Chairman, the Chief, the Founder, the Old Man, Uncle Billy: Lever was called all these and more, a reminder that a subject is never stable, always performing different roles for different audiences.[21] Perceptions of his personality depended on the angle from which he was viewed, the play of the light, his age, the status of the person with which he was interacting; straightforward linear narrative is a profound simplification in all biography. Any biography, just like any history, is partial and provisional, twisting a story out of all the biased fragments that have survived, conscious or not of how and why some of this evidence was created and preserved and everything else ignored or lost, self-conscious or not of how the end product has been filtered through the author's own upbringing, influences and prejudices.[22]

These caveats aside, most biography, if not merely prurient, voyeuristic or iconoclastic, justifies itself by the belief that, somehow, digging deep into the personal and private will help us understand what made these people tick, which will help us understand why they did what they did, which will help us understand the march of History. This brings us to that old chestnut, beloved of introductory historical methods classes for undergraduates, the role of the individual in history. At one end of the spectrum are those who subscribe to the 'Cleopatra's nose' version of history, the classic suggestion of the ancient historian J. B. Bury that it was because Mark Antony was so distracted by the physical beauty of Cleopatra that he was unable to pay full attention to the job at hand and lost the battle of Actium in 31 BCE to Octavian, which explains the downfall of the Roman Republic, with incalculable consequences for world history.[23] At the other end of the spectrum are those who deny the role of accident, chance, luck or contingency in history and concentrate on the great economic and social forces that, they say, determine the world's trajectory. For them a focus on the individual and on human agency utterly trivializes historical causation.

This is a caricature, of course. Most historians find themselves somewhere in the middle, adopting a variation on Karl Marx's formulation in one of his less deterministic moments: 'Men make their own history, but they do not make it just as they please; they do not make it under circumstances chosen by themselves, but under given circumstances directly encountered and inherited from the past.'[24] But the dilemma is particularly acute for economic and business historians. Economic historians, Marxist and non-Marxist alike, have tended to argue against the 'Great Man' thesis, suggesting that if the supposed giants of the industrial revolution like Richard Arkwright, James Watt, Samuel Crompton and their successors had never existed, the favourable times would have thrown up other, comparable agents who would have performed similar tasks. Eschewing the notion of the indispensable individual has, in the words of F. M. L. Thompson, 'freed historians to concentrate on the apparently more objective tasks of investigating and explaining the preconditions of economic growth in terms of markets, the supply of capital and labour, and the availability of technology, without the need to incorporate the awkward imponderables of unusual or extraordinary human talents into their theories'.

Many business historians, on the other hand, have built careers out of the close examination of particular companies or entrepreneurs and, up close and personal, in discovering how particular people made momentous decisions that might revolutionize an industry or cause it to collapse, they find it hard to imagine that the role of the individual is so unimportant.[25] This, for example, is what Charles Wilson has to say:

> No one who has examined the progress of his firm can fail to comprehend the influence which Leverhulme's driving personality exercised over its growth....

There is a view of economic history which regards the capitalist as only a cork bobbing on the economic tide. To regard a phenomenon such as the Lever business merely as an inevitable result of the tendency towards large-scale organization and the destruction of competition would be to court ridicule. Without Lever there would have been no Lever Brothers, and the whole structure of a national industry and a by no means negligible section of British world economic interests might have borne a very different aspect.[26]

But what is obvious and commonsensical from one perspective blends into nuance from another. To put the conundrum in its crassest form: if William Hesketh Lever's mother had had a miscarriage and the boy had not been born, would the world have been substantially different? (Already, by inserting 'substantially', I am hedging my bets.) To which my answer is: in its essentials, no; in its particulars, maybe. There is no doubt that Lever was a remarkable character who had a direct impact on thousands of lives and who helped channel the direction of growth of the soap industry, not to mention his myriad other undertakings. This I hope will emerge in the following pages. But more interesting to my mind is the context that allowed such a man to flourish, and that will form the major part of this book.

This was the era of the so-called 'second industrial revolution', based primarily on chemicals, electricity and the automobile, and the times were peculiarly propitious for a breed of entrepreneur who could take advantage of the take-off of mass consumer industries and the dramatic transformation of the global economy. Take Lever out of this environment and he is a whale without an ocean. For Lever and his ilk to flourish, many preconditions had to be in place: a population that was expanding rapidly and becoming more urban and marginally more prosperous so that more and more people could afford commodities like soap; technological innovations to allow the mass production and mass marketing of such commodities; a reliable supply of and ready access to water; a national and international market facilitated by the spread of communications networks; successive governments friendly to expanding commerce, both at home and in the empire; and sufficient capital to allow firms to increase from the merely large to the truly colossal by internal diversification and the swallowing or elimination of rivals.

Lever and his fellow plutocrats fitted into a particular phase in the development of Western capitalism. Before them, the family firm dominated. With the expansion of joint-stock companies, however, aided by statutes of the 1850s and 1860s that legalized limited liability, entrepreneurs had access to significantly bigger pools of finance, albeit giving shareholders a say in the running and fortunes of their firms. For a relatively brief period, in the bigger firms, entrepreneurial titans retained control and amassed fabulous wealth, but, as these firms expanded, impersonal corporate management became the norm and the role of the founder's family receded. This transition to an economy of large corporations was taking place at the same time as the transition to mass democracy and greater state provision for social welfare and economic management. Just as in the boardroom, so in society as a whole and in relation to the work force, the brief era of the plutocrats and the social and economic power they wielded was going to fade in the inter-war period.[27]

James Bellini, in his polemical book *Rule Britannia*, provided a fine example of the confusion between the (in this case baleful) role of individuals and the contexts in which they are embedded. In this, the harshest critique of Lever, Bellini picked up on the then fashionable notion, propagated by the Thatcherite Right and some on the Left, that Britain's relative industrial decline during the twentieth century could be ascribed principally to a failure of entrepreneurial drive. Businessmen, according to this thesis, once they had made their fortunes and reputations, sold out. They abandoned mass-production industry, accepted titles, bought country estates and mansions, put their money in land or high finance. Bourgeois industrial potential was neutered by this process of feudalization: 'If the death of British industry can be explained by any social mechanism, then the perennial hankering for escape from industry into the pastoral peace of aristocratic gentility, so typical of the successful British entrepreneur, must come top of the list.'

Bellini called this the 'LeverPearson effect'. From the 1880s, Weetman Pearson had built the Pearson family fortune in making concrete, building harbours and dams and extracting oil; but he bought Cowdray Park, West Sussex, in 1908 and was raised to the peerage in a similar fashion to Lever, first as a baron, then as a viscount; and by the 1980s the company had given up on industry in favour of financial services, land and amusement parks. Lever's career was no better, degenerating into 'benevolent despotism, egocentric lunacy and a craving for the lordly powers of a Norman ruler'. Far from creating a promising base for a competitive industry for the future, his 'megalomaniac tendencies' drove him to implement gigantic projects for his own gratification. He was a product of Britain's 'feudal subconscious'; 'Almost every brick laid by Lever in his years of construction carried the imprint of a man who had created industry only in order to condemn its filth, who took the wealth it produced for him only in order to re-create the lifestyle of the Middle Ages.'[28]

This is enjoyable, rollicking stuff, and quite an indictment. That Lever loved selected and superficial elements of a pseudo-feudal past is clear; that he sent his son to Eton and Trinity College, Cambridge, is undeniable; that his grandson, the third and last viscount (also Eton and Trinity), a staunch Conservative, avoided involvement in industry, and spent his time in horse racing, hunting and shooting,[29] is also true: but much of Bellini's case is unpersuasive. This was indeed a period when international plutocrats and home-grown industrial or commercial millionaires were diluting the aristocracy, but only a handful went the whole hog and built up large landed estates. For most, the mansions and the honours were merely cosmetic affectations, quite compatible with business.[30] There is no compelling evidence that British entrepreneurs of the period made worse or more irrational decisions than their predecessors or than those in rival countries. As many historians have pointed out, the buying of 'aristocratic' accoutrements was not 'a bizarrely British phenomenon' but something broadly practised by plutocrats at the time, witness for example the Krupps in Germany or the Vanderbilts and Rockefellers in America. It is a phenomenon that needs to be accounted for and contextualized rather than used as a simplistic explanation for Britain's alleged industrial failings. Using Lever as a case study is particularly strange, given that his legacy, the huge manufacturing and retailing concern of Unilever, counts as one of British industry's great, continuing success stories.[31]

Steady application and perseverance day by day – that's all

William Hesketh Lever was first and foremost a Victorian. He deviated little from the script: a profound belief in progress, free trade, capitalism, the liberal empire and its 'civilizing mission', the work ethic, self-help, energy, movement, technology, the appliance of science, moral rectitude, emotional reserve, self-improvement and patriotism. With typical Liberal Nonconformist optimism, he professed to believe that anyone could succeed; it just took 'steady application and perseverance day by day – that's all'. Self-sacrifice, hard work early in life and denial of pleasures and comforts were the keys to later success. Better, though, to start out with nothing, because those who began with something often lost it; for example, 'Mr. Ford, who, it is said, has made fifty millions out of motor cars, had no capital to start with.'[32]

Lever was self-made in the sense that he climbed from the ranks of the Lancashire middle classes to unimaginable plutocratic heights, but he hardly started with nothing. The hard facts and brass tacks of his life and career can be summarized briefly. He was born on 19 September 1851 at 16 Wood Street, Bolton, the seventh of ten children (and the first of two boys) born to James and Eliza Lever. The story of the business began with his father. James Lever was a partner in a grocer's shop known as 'The Lower Blackamoor' but moved out of retail in 1864 to set up on his own as a wholesale grocer. William, educated mainly at the Bolton Church Institute, entered the business at the age of sixteen and became a partner at twenty-one. He married Elizabeth Ellen Hulme in 1874. They had known each other for years, first meeting at the small school in Wood Street that Lever attended between the ages of six and nine.

Under James's careful guidance, Lever and Co. became a thriving concern, so much so that the family entered the ranks of the local haute bourgeoisie and moved into Harwood Lodge, a large Jacobean house with a Georgian extension, two miles from Bolton. But it was the initiative and energy of his son that caused the business to expand further. William organized the creation of a branch in Wigan by buying up a wholesale grocery business, as well as the introduction of intensive advertising and trips to Ireland and Holland to buy butter and eggs direct, eliminating the middleman.[33] William became solely responsible for managing the new Wigan branch. By the time he was in his early thirties he was prosperous and contemplating semi-retirement, including maybe even the purchase of a small Orkney island.

Instead, he began to explore the greater possibilities of soap. With money gathered from the business and loans from family members, Lever rented a Warrington factory in 1885 and started to manufacture soap. After moving to the greenfield site of Port Sunlight in 1888 the business continued to grow rapidly, from 1890 as a private company with an authorized capital of £300,000 and from 1894 as a public company – Lever Brothers Ltd – with an issue of Cumulative Preference shares and of Ordinary shares and an authorized capital of £1.5 million. Soon Lever became the sole Ordinary shareholder, which helped him to be the sole policy maker for much of the rest of his life, with minimal input from the directors.

At that stage the firm had only two leading brands – Sunlight (1884) and Lifebuoy (1894) – but added Lux Flakes in 1900 and Vim in 1904 in a steady expansion of the products manufactured at Port Sunlight. These remained Lever Brothers' bedrock. The development into a leading multinational corporation, however, required several more momentous steps. One involved the setting up, taking over or merger of subsidiaries, daughter companies or 'associated companies' in foreign countries. Lever had worked hard at opening agencies and selling his soap abroad since 1888, but if import drives proved unsatisfactory, logic dictated that soap should be manufactured and sold locally, both to reduce the price by vaulting tariff barriers on imports and to cater for idiosyncratic local tastes. As D. K. Fieldhouse points out, Lever Brothers was one of the first generation of capitalist concerns to manufacture in a number of countries.[34] The company opened or started building factories in America (Lever Brothers Company in Cambridge, Massachusetts), Switzerland, Canada, Australia and Germany in the late 1890s, and then spread to most western European countries and the other white settler colonies of the empire, as well as more tentatively to Asia and Africa. In his bid to sell his soap and oversee his growing concerns he travelled extensively, often accompanied by his wife. Business was to take him around the world on five separate occasions. These were the only times he visited Australasia, Asian countries and parts of the Pacific, but on numerous additional occasions he travelled to North America, Africa and Europe.

A second significant factor in the expansion of the business was the takeover of rival soap companies in Britain, part of the broader trend towards monopoly in the period as capitalists sought to dominate their industries by reducing or eliminating competition. In 1906 Lever tried to establish a soap combine in an attempt to avoid cut-throat competition during a difficult period of high prices for raw materials. This 'Soap Trust' collectively decided, among other things, to reduce newspaper advertising. The press, and in particular Lord Northcliffe's *Daily Mail*, partly in retaliation and partly echoing ferocious attacks on robber-baron monopolies in the United States, chose to regard the combine as an unwarranted attempt by ruthless fat-cat capitalists to defraud the customer. Such was the negative publicity that the combine collapsed and sales of Sunlight plummeted. Lever estimated his losses at over half a million pounds, and he sued the Northcliffe press for libel in 1907. In court, Sir Edward Carson for Lever bested Rufus Isaacs for Northcliffe, and Lever received unprecedented libel damages of £50,000. A trial in Scotland against some of the defendants' Scottish newspapers brought the total to £91,000.[35] Lever had won, but he did not attempt a similar combine again, preferring to pick off the competition one at a time, taking over such noted and well established soap companies as Vinolia in 1906, R. S. Hudson in 1908, Pears in 1914, Joseph Watson in 1917, both Crosfield's and Gossage's in 1919 and John Knight's in 1920.

A third major factor in the expansion of Lever Brothers was entry into the business of planting, harvesting or gathering raw materials (see chapters four and five) – coconut oil in the Solomon Islands (Lever Pacific Plantations Ltd, 1902), palm oil in the Congo (Les Huileries du Congo Belge, 1911), whale oil in the South and North Atlantic (1919 and 1922 respectively) – and processing some of them in oil mills at Port Sunlight and in Sydney, Australia. The acquisition of some sizeable mercantile concerns, notably the Niger Company (1920) with its huge raw materials and shipping interests in West Africa, was part of this drive for vertical linkages, the control of each stage from the ingredients to the finished product. With the exception of margarine, horizontal expansion into the food industry – the fourth significant element in the company's growth – came unexpectedly as a by-product of Lever's creation of Mac Fisheries and acquisition of forty-seven associated companies after the First World War, bought up by Lever Brothers in 1922 (chapter five).

The fifth factor, entry into the margarine business in 1914 under the name of the Planters Margarine Company, was at the behest of a government worried by wartime disruption of supplies of butter and margarine from Denmark and Holland. The company began building a factory at Bromborough Port, next to Port Sunlight, in 1916. A French chemist, Hippolyte Mège Mouriès, had invented margarine, a concoction of beef fat and milk, in 1869. Jurgens and Van den Bergh's, two rival families of butter merchants in Oss, Brabant, Holland, developed it in industrial quantities, particularly when Chicago meat packers began flooding the markets with huge amounts of animal fat from the late 1870s. Both firms deployed similar marketing techniques to Lever Brothers, and thrived principally by exporting to Britain and setting up factories in Germany. Still, while the industry was dependent on beef tallow expansion was restricted. The breakthrough came in 1902 after a German research scientist, Wilhelm Normann, invented hydrogenation – the process of adding hydrogen to fluid oils in the presence of a nickel catalyst to harden them into solid fats. This meant that margarine makers could now use vegetable oils more extensively, and soap makers could use 'softer' oils like whale oil. It also meant that they were both in competition for similar raw materials and could, without stretching too much, also begin manufacturing either soap or margarine on the side, in addition to their main products.

The stage was set both for some major corporate clashes but also for eventual mergers. One clash, in part involving hydrogenation patents, occurred between Lever and Brunner Mond and Co. Ludwig Mond and his sons and John Brunner were Liberal paternalists like Lever, but that did not prevent them falling out over alkali – caustic soda – which Lever needed for his business and which Brunner Mond supplied. Lever's bid to free himself from this monopoly led to his purchase of the 1,700 acre Lymm estate in Cheshire with its extensive salt deposits in 1911. This prompted Brunner Mond to venture into the soap business in retaliation, buying out Crosfield's and Gossage's. In what W. J. Reader described as the biggest corporate quarrel in the history of British business, the two sides found themselves in court in 1913 (a test case over whether Crosfield's claim to a hydrogenation patent was valid, which would have given Brunner Mond a monopoly in fat hardening; Lever won), and then again in 1916, 1917 and 1918.

An agreement hammered out in 1919 sold Crosfield's and Gossage's to Lever Brothers for £4 million (about £1 million too much, Lever reckoned), and Lever renewed his exclusive alkali contract with Brunner Mond. He was assured that the rival Co-operative Wholesale Society would not be getting alkali at a discount. Four years later he discovered that this was not true, and that through various accounting subterfuges CWS had being paying less. To lessen the damage to its reputation, and to keep the affair as private as possible, Brunner Mond agreed to an out-of-court settlement by paying Lever Brothers £1 million. It was sweet revenge for Lever after the previous 'overcharging'. The chairman, Roscoe Brunner, resigned. When the company merged with the three other largest British chemical firms to form ICI in 1926, he was excluded from the new company's board of directors. The wound to his pride was deepened when his wife hawked his grievance around various newspaper offices. In a tragic and sensational murder-suicide denouement, he shot her, then himself.[36]

As free-market logic saw the biggest and fittest swallowing up weaker fry and a few giants coming to dominate their respective industries, ICI was one of the great 'efficiency combines' created in the 1920s, Unilever another.[37] The constituent companies of the future Unilever underwent a quarter of a century of intense rivalry, suspicion and wrangling over hydrogenation patents before they were ready to talk about merger. Lever, as we have seen, took advantage of wartime disruption of Dutch trade to launch Planters Margarine. Jurgens in turn bought a number of British factories in the post-war boom, as well as control of the Home and Colonial Stores, to create, like Lever Brothers, a very large vertically and horizontally integrated company. Van den Bergh's was more cautious, but still took control of the Lipton's chain of grocers' shops in 1927. By then, stung by the collapse of the post-war boom of 1920 and the reduction in demand, the two Dutch companies were taking steps towards forming a defensive alliance. They merged into one entity, the Margarine Union/Margarine Unie, in 1927.

Meanwhile, on the Lever Brothers side, a merger was engineered in 1929 between its Niger Company and the other large mercantile group in West Africa, the African and Eastern Trade Corporation, to create the United Africa Company. In September of 1929, over four years since Lever's death, all of these elements were brought together in a fusion between the Lever Brothers companies and the Margarine Union to establish a dualistic corporate structure: two parent companies, Unilever Ltd in Britain, chaired by the Lever Brothers chairman, Francis D'Arcy Cooper, and Unilever NV in Holland, with identical board memberships, separated only so as to avoid paying tax twice, once in each country. As Charles Wilson points out, this was one of the biggest industrial amalgamations in European history, producing a business that employed nearly a quarter of a million people, that bought and processed over a third of the oils and fats in world commerce, and that traded in more places and in more products than any other concern on the planet.[38] In 1930 Unilever was the largest company in Britain in terms of market value (£132 million), slightly ahead of its nearest rival, Imperial Tobacco, and well ahead of third-placed ICI.[39]

Unwrapping the man

What kind of a man helped create this colossus? Commentators described him as 'a bit of human granite': short (but, at 5 ft 5 in., probably not for someone born into a mid-nineteenth-century industrial town) and thick-set – he was stout even in middle age, turning to corpulence later on. He had, they said, a sturdy and very upright body; small hands and feet and a quick, short step; very little neck, a massive head and a thin-lipped, wide, expressive mouth. His head looked big both because of his cockatoo crest of thick, curly, upstanding hair, which turned white but did not recede as he aged, and his habit of wearing a hat half-way between a bowler and a top hat. Different writers,

1 William Hesketh Lever, *c.* 1901

searching to convey the same idea, described his eyes as impassively cold, or as piercing, or as 'of a brilliant, gleaming, arresting blue', or as humorous but blazing when angry, flashing with challenge; 'the light blue eyes looking out at the world with fearless directness; tenacious mouth; a chin that will stand no nonsense', wrote A. G. Gardiner. He wasted no words, being eloquently silent on committees and possessing 'the Lancashire man's faculty of saying "No" without circumlocution'. But even those who experienced his wrath spoke of him with great respect, extolling his keen sense of humour, his 'lovable friendliness' and his personal magnetism. The 'Old Man was and has remained the hero of my life', wrote Andrew Knox, a Unilever director, fifty years after his death. Lever had charisma, and he knew how to deploy it.[40]

Even as he ascended the ladder into the plutocratic elite and acquired titles his northern Nonconformist roots continued to show through. He delighted in describing himself as a mere soap maker and larding his writings and speeches with stories, blunt home truths and pragmatic homilies, delivered in his flat-vowelled, Lancashire accent. He came late to public speaking – not until he was nearly forty – and he was visibly nervous and uncomfortable during his first attempts. But with practice came fluency, and late in life one commentator said of him, 'Leverhulme speaks well, with a flow of language of a homely order, no great rhetoric, rather fatherly expoundings, mixed with endless anecdotes.'[41]

He repeatedly ascribed all his success in life to parental influences and the support of his wife.[42] But the people around him are marginalized by the historical record, black-and-white background figures to his gloriously Technicolor leading role. His father has left little imprint, his mother scarcely registers, his sisters appear in the story from time to time (particularly those who did not marry and kept house for him), but are silent. Even his brother, James Darcy, the other half of 'Lever Brothers', gets very little attention. In one of the sparse mentions of him in his biography, Lever's son remarked, 'William Lever had always been the dominant partner, the originator, the directing mind, the controlling force; but his brother, until illness overtook him, gave him loyal, competent and unstinted support. With an equal in dynamic energy William Lever could never have worked on the same terms of partnership as he did with his brother.' This is a strange formulation: James Darcy's very secondary role alone made the 'partnership' succeed. He retired through ill health in 1895, apparently a mental breakdown that may have been associated with diabetes, and remained unwell almost continuously until his death at his house in Thornton Hough in 1910.[43]

As for Lever's wife, Elizabeth, she was described as 'a gracious, kindly and gentle little woman'.[44] We rarely hear her voice. At the ground breaking at Port Sunlight in 1888, for example, she was introduced by William Owen, architect, who handed her a silver spade, and the newspaper report read:

> 'Every step we have taken,' he said, 'has been watched with the greatest care and interest by Mrs. Lever. I have pleasure in presenting her with this implement of peace with which we, as Lancashire men, invade Cheshire.' After cutting the first sod, Mrs. Lever made a brief speech wishing success to the new works.[45]

The brief speech was not recorded. This is what her son had to say about her:

> My mother never pretended to be a business woman. Her contribution was sympathy and understanding – an unquestioning belief in the rightness of all that her husband undertook. She never asked for any altered mode of life which might have distracted him from the work he had in hand. She could, with good reason, have demanded more of his time away from business, but she was unselfishness personified, and that is why, without her, Port Sunlight could never have been realized, and the success of her husband's business – at home and overseas – achieved.[46]

This, again, is a curious way of expressing things. Lever's success is ascribed to the fact that his wife did not interfere with, contradict or distract him – did not act as the power behind the throne in any conventional sense, but merely absorbed his ego. Lever seems to have agreed. He later said of her, at the opening of the Lady Lever Art Gallery, 'She was essentially a womanly woman, and her knowledge of business was nil. A wife need not be an inspired genius in guiding and directing her husband – genius might be a handicap and not a help – but she can be an inspiration and source of confidence.'[47] She died of pneumonia in July 1913; it was 'the greatest sorrow of his life'. He buried her beneath the west window of Christ Church, Port Sunlight, added a recumbent bronze effigy of her with two children at its base 'to symbolize my mother's love for children and theirs for her'. The stained glass he added to the west window included 'The Good Housewife' and 'Ruth and Naomi' with its text, one of her favourite quotations, 'Whither thou goest, I will go.' This seemed to sum up their joint understanding (and her acceptance) of her subservient role.[48]

At home and outside the office, by all accounts, Lever was warm, affectionate and approachable, a generous host to his executive and staff, an expert at working the room to make each guest feel special, twinkling and avuncular to children, apparently never happier than when playing leapfrog or other such games with the kids of Port Sunlight on the lawns at Thornton Manor.[49] He loved ballroom dancing (he 'usually chose the wallflowers to dance with and it is recalled that at Port Sunlight he always had a dance with Ethel Williams, the hunchback') and rekindled a fondness for it later in life (after he grew too deaf for the theatre, a long-standing passion) because it was good exercise and he could enjoy the company of young people.[50] 'I wish I could convey to you the atmosphere of his beautiful home life,' wrote Angus Watson, a friend and business associate, 'of his bounteous and constant hospitality, of the little thoughtful courtesies that he loved to show his guests, of the wonderful affection that existed between him and his wife and sisters, and the admiration that the working members of his household had for him.'[51]

At work Lever played the autocrat, used to getting his way and having his word obeyed: decisive, impatient, inexorable, resolute, brisk, keen, electrifying, restless, a hater of idleness, ruthless and (on occasion) wounding were the words used about him. 'At very first glance I would put him down as a rather insignificant little fellow,' wrote one civil servant. 'That impression lasted for a shorter time than it takes to write it. Charm, tact, decision, power radiated from the man's every word, look, and gesture. I had never met a man who was so obviously a megalomaniac and accustomed to having his own way.'[52] 'Mr. Lloyd George once remarked to me,' wrote the journalist and author Harold Begbie, 'that the trouble with Lord Leverhulme is that he cannot work with other men.'[53] As his son phrased it, 'Lever's strength of will and originality made him unsuited to any sphere of activity other than one in which his could be the sole deciding voice.'[54]

Lever wasted no time, his own or anyone else's; he made decisions rapidly, once and once only; the pace he set in the firm was furious, and his staff were expected to follow. He sought advice from others, but not unsolicited opinions from subordinates. 'I am always glad to have your free expression of opinion on all matters that I may discuss with you,' he wrote to one underling who had had the temerity to recommend a strategy for a shareholders' meeting,

> but until I do discuss a matter with you, I think you will agree with me that it is not within your province to lay your views before me. I hope that this will be the last time on which you will venture an expression of opinion as to what course I should take at a Meeting unless in response to a request from myself that you should do so.[55]

Stories of his work habits and the phenomenal amount and detail of his correspondence abound. He would dictate letters at a steady, conversational pace without pause to two or three female stenographers, 'so that what one missed another might pick up'. One of these women would often accompany him to take dictation on the train to and from London, so that precious minutes were not wasted.[56] On his overseas trips, after leaving a company, the officials of that firm would accompany him on the train for a final discussion and would be dropped off at some prearranged point, where the officials of the company he was about to visit would be picked up. If he were travelling by car, there might be a moving conference, with those he wished to speak to next following in a car behind, both cars periodically stopping so that his passenger could be changed.[57]

Harley Williams, a Scottish medical officer who encountered Lever on the isle of Lewis, wrote a book shortly after the Second World War comparing and contrasting three 'Men of Stress': Lever, Andrew Carnegie and Woodrow Wilson. His essay on Lever was an interesting speculation as to why the man was so pathologically energetic. Lever's 'abnormal', 'monstrous' activity came from conquest of fear, said Williams. He was afraid of himself, knew he was possessed of a devil, knew that he had to ride the tiger, to tame the terrible

2 Mr and Mrs Lever and their son outside Thornton Manor, *c.* 1905

power within, or the result would be psychological ruin. His choice of a career in soap was no accident. '[W]as soap the outward expression of a desire to cleanse away guilty thoughts?' Williams pondered. 'Guilt in the mind of such a man there must have been and he would not be the first idealist who drew energy for noble purposes from such inward compensations.'[58]

Williams had no evidence to back this up, and his speculation arose from the vaguely plausible but ultimately unhelpful notion that Lever's pace of life derived from unspecified inner demons. Which inner demons might these have been? And guilt about what? Unclean thoughts about sex, perhaps? Pop psychology might hypothesize the rechannelling of a powerful sex drive into the world of work (without explaining why it should take that particular form). Lever was apparently faithful to his wife and there is not a hint of impropriety in the surviving records: 'In his private life there were no scandals connected with wine and women,' as Williams pointed out.[59] The couple suffered the frustration of producing only one surviving child, in 1888, after nearly fourteen years of marriage. There were suggestions of multiple miscarriages and maybe stillbirths, but nothing definite. Did this impact on his sense of virility and did he subconsciously feel the need to prove his masculine identity in other avenues?

Did he perhaps have same-sex desires? He had a number of long-term, close male friendships, in particular with the architect Jonathan Simpson, who, from boyhood onwards, according to Lever's son, 'played "Jonathan" to my father's "David" all his life'.[60] This is a reference to passages in the Book of Samuel telling of the love between David and Jonathan, notably David saying to the slain Jonathan (2 Samuel 1:26), 'thy love to me was wonderful, passing the love of women'. Although men could use this as a cover for sexual relationships, we can safely assume that in his pious biography of his father the second viscount was not remotely hinting at anything of the kind. The ideal of platonic love between males, a component of the concept of 'manliness' as developed by the late Victorians, held that same-sex love was superior to love for the opposite sex because it was assumed to be non-sexual and spiritual.[61] Without any supporting evidence of unstated sexual frustrations the best we can manage is a succession of perhapses and maybes.

That there *is* something to be explained comes out most strongly with regard to his eccentric sleeping habits, a fact widely known at the time and much discussed, inconclusively, ever since. He built himself an open-air bedroom on the roof at Thornton Manor, his bed only partially protected from the elements by a frosted-glass roof, and slept there throughout the year and whatever the weather. After he had arisen and performed twenty minutes of physical exercises on his electric horse or other machines,[62] he took a cold bath in a stone tub, also on the roof. He subsequently added comparable bedrooms at each of his residences. To give another example, the bedroom at his isle of Lewis residence, Lews Castle, was on asphalt flooring, the high-up window had no glass and there were holes in the roof tiles. But these alfresco sleeping and bathing arrangements were not lifelong obsessions. Describing an incident of swallows nesting on the roof at Thornton Manor in 1910, his son indicated that the open-air bedroom was 'newly constructed'. This, remember, was the first, and Lever was nearly sixty. Whether his wife joined him in the roof-bed in the final three or so years of her life is not clear. Some biographers have confidently asserted that she did – Nigel Nicolson, for example, wrote, 'It was not unknown for Leverhulme and his uncomplaining wife to wake up under a coverlet of snow' – but the son made no mention of this.[63]

'A prisoner of hygiene' is how Williams described him.[64] There was certainly something of the faddist or health fanatic about him: no tobacco after the age of forty-five (he enjoyed a cigar two or three times a day until then); never any spirits; champagne or light wines only two or three times a year; no coffee; lots of tea; much fruit; regular exercise, including horse riding and calisthenics; simple and plain meals when eating alone; vegetarianism for a short period; going to bed at nine if possible and rising very early (half-past six in the 1890s, as early as four o'clock in the 1920s), compensating with power naps during the course of the day. It all sounds like a mixture of contemporary concerns about good, wholesome, clean living – the healthy mind in the healthy body propagated by Muscular Christian public schools, Baron Pierre de Coubertin's revival of the Olympics in the 1890s, the Boy Scout movement in the 1900s and a myriad other such moralizing initiatives focused on the body – and a later twentieth-century obsession with health clubs and dietary regimes. But he took none of this behaviour to extremes, and his corpulence indicated that on other occasions he liked his food. Many similar 'enlightened entrepreneurs' of his generation, who subscribed to the gospel of hard work and self-help, also embraced self-discipline, temperance or teetotalism, early rising, wholesome physical exercise and cold baths.[65] The only thing that really stands out is the outside bed and bath: if he believed in the benefits of fresh air at night, he could simply have kept the window open and still slept in some comfort. So this might suggest he was somehow testing himself, or hardening his body for the daily struggle, or self-mortifying the flesh in an attempt to combat 'illicit' desires. Gardiner perhaps came closest when he wrote that Lever:

> is all moral purpose. He reminds one of Benjamin Franklin. I can see him putting himself though the same hard moral discipline, taking himself in hand with a certain grim joy, and subduing himself to his own maxims with relentless firmness. He is a moral athlete who has trained himself down to the last ounce, and wins the race by first winning the victory over himself.... he preaches self-conquest as the path to happiness, like the old-fashioned Puritan that he is.[66]

Lever, God and Mammon

Lever's father, James, had converted in his youth from Anglicanism to Congregationalism. This meant that young William grew up in a typical Victorian Nonconformist household – not rigid in its puritanism, since the father enjoyed concerts and tolerated the theatre, but certainly without wine, tobacco or cards. Any form of gambling was strictly taboo. As we have seen, there are many indications that Lever continued to be influenced (but not bound) by this tight morality. He clearly did not wallow in the silk-sheeted, sensuous luxury of the idle rich and it seems that he was sexually continent, but he loved the theatre (the whole gamut from highbrow, particularly Shakespeare, down to music hall), and although he despised gambling and lotteries, it was notably not on religious grounds but because the winners 'would be undergoing the demoralizing experience of possessing fortunes which they had not, in any remote sense of the term, earned'.[67]

In conformity with his Nonconformist upbringing and the dictates of a deeply engrained, ambient Christianity, Lever was a man of the strictest probity in his commercial dealings. But he was ruthless in exploiting legitimate business openings and opportunities and a harsh litigant when he felt wronged or slighted. Some of this was, as we have seen, vital to his business interests, some of it was trivial. He threatened to sue G. K. Chesterton in 1913, for example, because of derogatory comments in a speech reported in the *Christian Commonwealth* newspaper ('it accuses us of introducing slavery in Port Sunlight'). 'I would like to have a whack at this windbag, Mr G. K. Chesterton, if it is possible,' he wrote to his solicitor. After a year Chesterton settled out of court.[68]

Lever was a regular churchgoer (until his deafness prevented him from hearing much of what was going on) and a strong supporter of Congregationalism: he built four Congregational churches and contributed frequently to the Congregational Union.[69] He was no hidebound conformist, however. He professed belief in a Supreme Being, but never joined a church and felt that he could not be bound by any one creed.[70] According to his son, he consistently avoided religious argument, had a respect for all sincere forms of belief and felt 'little attraction towards rigid expressions of creed and any system of Church government which restricted personal liberty of thought'. Christ Church, the Gothic church he built at Port Sunlight, reflected his distinctly Anglican architectural tastes, and the introduction of surplices, organ and a peel of bells his love of ceremony and ritual. But although its governance and minister came under the Congregational Union, it was in practice an experiment in non-contentious, interdenominational cooperation, attracting worshippers of many Protestant creeds. His ecumenism was also reflected in his substantial benefactions to Cheshunt College, the nondenominational training centre for theological students at Cambridge, and in his support for the missionary

Catholic Fathers in the Congo (see chapter four). His latitudinarianism even took him as far as the Christian Scientists for a time. He consulted a Christian Science 'healer' about his deafness, before drawing back, unpersuaded. After seven 'treatments' he wrote to one believer, 'It seems to me that there is more than a germ of truth in your method, but, unfortunately, germs to increase require a proper soil, and I don't appear to be proper soil for their cultivation. I am a "doubting Thomas", and I am afraid I shall continue one.'[71]

Lever may have been a Doubting Thomas in a more fundamental sense. In public he cultivated his image of bold, swift, imperious, Napoleonic decisiveness, quite lacking in any form of doubt. Beneath the surface there is little surviving sense of his interior self – there are few revelatory moments of introspection; no surviving diaries, only a handful of personal letters – so it is difficult to be certain about his inner beliefs. But Angus Watson alleged that Lever talked of the presence of God being with him in all his activities while doubting that there was any immortality for the individual. '"When he has finished his task," he said, "I am not sure that he does not also come to the end of his journey. Who knows, and what matter, if he has done his best."'[72] This was far removed from conventional Christian notions of toil in this vale of tears being merely preparatory for the afterlife. It throws an intriguing light on Lever's rather curious and unorthodox defence of money making.

It was a question he could scarcely avoid. One cannot worship both God and Mammon: the familiar biblical injunction. The Sermon on the Mount, along with a variety of equally admonitory passages about rich men, camels, eyes of needles and the like, appeared to be unambiguous on this score. Stricter Christian commentators held that worshipping Mammon implied not only covetousness but also a love of and desire for the world, for its own sake, seeking happiness herein, losing sight of the hereafter. How, then, could one of the filthy rich reconcile his faith with his wealth?

Lever believed that 'Every successful business has been founded on the principles laid down in the Bible, laid down in Shakespeare's works, and laid down in many other great books.'[73] 'If a businessman has not read the Book of Proverbs,' he said on another occasion, 'I will never believe that he can be a true, careful, sound and cautious business man.' He read some of the Bible every day – but as literature and, especially, 'as a book of practical advice', his son relates, rather than for its religious message. For him there was no contradiction between Christian morality and business: they were, in fact, synonymous terms.[74] He addressed the alleged conflict between God and Mammon directly in a talk in Mawdsley Street Congregational Church, Bolton, in 1915. 'You will find that money is required for every good work that is done in the world,' he told his audience. 'I hear someone ask, "Can anyone, as a Christian, devote his mind to making money?" I say, "Yes!" "But surely not a religious, Christian young man?" I say again, "Yes!"'[75]

Lever was being deliberately provocative, and his argument as it unfolds is rather more subtle than appears at first blush. In an era of barely fettered capitalism, biblical sanction for money making was of course very convenient, but Lever's was not an invocation of the creed that greed is good and, praise the Lord, divinely blessed. 'It is our duty,' he continued, ' – every one of us – to make money, as much as it is our duty to worship God and love our fellow-men.' He conceded that without money one could still do good, but money certainly helped. According to the Bible it was not money *per se* but the *love* of money that was the root of all evil. Holding on to money, hugging it close, fetishizing it: *that* was wicked. But striving hard to accumulate it for the good of others, *that* was truly Christian.[76]

This did not mean charitable doles or good works in any Catholic sense of succouring the poor in order to chalk up credit in the divine ledger against the Day of Judgement. He despised charity. One of the striking things about his speech at the Mawdsley Street church was his contempt for individual weakness. He peppered his talk with phrases like 'Let us learn ... to hate pity and sympathy and coddling,' 'Religion is not a sickly sentimentality or the practice of a maudlin mutual admiration society,' 'A strong belief in God and the Bible, and the everlasting struggle to live a better life, are the mark and sign of true manhood.'[77] This was a muscle-bound, testosterone-fuelled Christianity, focusing on the self-reliant, striving, resolute individual carving out his own path to success. Adopting the familiar language of Poor Law guardians and charity commissioners, anyone who was unduly coddled would become demoralized.

The accumulation of money for the good of others boiled down to a philosophy of service. In his words, 'The fact is that the foundation of business success and of Christianity are the same, and that foundation is service to others. In rendering service to others, money is the most effective means of removing our limitations.' One example was Henry Ford, who started as a simple mechanic but rendered a service to humanity by producing a cheap car; another, by implication, was himself, who in producing a quality affordable soap enabled the greater cleanliness of the greater number.[78] Presumably his notion of service also included the factory village he built at Port Sunlight, the building of improved housing and provision of greater welfare for African labourers in his palm oil concessions in the Congo, and his scattering of initiatives on Harris and Lewis in an attempt to revolutionize the lives of crofters.

In this idea of service, God had receded. Lever justified his paternalistic ventures in secular terms, as shrewd, calculated self-interest. A happy, healthy, loyal work force was a more productive, contented work force, less liable to strike or be swayed by the rhetoric of socialism. He did not believe in an interventionist God, one who was involved in the day-to-day running of the world. For example, far from subscribing to the Calvinist belief that business success was a sign of special favour, he explicitly stated his faith in an equal-opportunities God. 'It would be grossly monstrous and unfair,' he said, 'and I would not myself believe in a Deity who could treat His children so unjustly and unfairly as to make money-making possible to some and impossible to others.'[79]

It is difficult to avoid the conclusion that his true Bible was Samuel Smiles's *Self Help* and his true god Liberal Progress. His father gave him *Self Help* for his sixteenth birthday. In later years Lever frequently donated copies to promising young men and, when he was president of the Institute of Certificated Grocers, to every student who qualified for membership.[80] On the front page of one copy, which he inscribed near the end of his life and which found its way into Unilever Archives, he wrote, 'It is impossible for me to say how much I owe to the fact that in my early youth I obtained a copy of Smiles' *Self-Help*.'[81] Smiles taught him, he said, that successful business was honourable, and that if it failed to be honourable it would not succeed.[82] The foundation of all progress, he wrote elsewhere, was the 'universal law of self-interest of the individual' – 'the persistent, consistent, and uninterrupted effort of every right-thinking man to better his condition' – a principle 'as unvarying as the law of gravitation'.[83]

Lever contended on many occasions that the ultimate goal in life was the achievement of personal happiness. He recounted the story of a man who experienced true happiness when he introduced his bride to their home: '"Darling, every piece of furniture in this house I have worked hard to buy, and it has been bought with my savings, the result of my work, darling."' This was less an ode to the joys of a modest Pooterish competence than the suggestion that such a home, 'the living temple of the soul, in which nothing vile or unworthy can endure', was an essential building block for wealth creation and for opportunities to provide service for others.[84]

What, then, are we to make of Lever and religion? A set of beliefs that extols the virtues of money making while rejecting covetousness can just about be reconciled with biblical injunctions against worshipping Mammon. But a creed centring on earthly happiness and doubting in an afterlife is a form of Mammon worship, in its broader interpretation, and comes perilously close to rejecting the main tenets of Christianity. The fact that one of the leading industrial magnates of the age felt the need to explain himself in religious terms is a testimony to Christianity's enduring importance in framing business discourse well into the twentieth century, but even the most conventional-seeming religiosity could be intriguingly hollow. Lever was undoubtedly strongly influenced by a rigorously moralistic, Christian-based mind set in his personal conduct; he followed the outward forms of his faith; but his daily business practices and philosophy owed little to religion.[85] His was but a pale shadow of the faith of the early Victorians.

Xanadu

As his wealth grew, Lever increasingly indulged a passion for building or transforming houses and gardens. A residual puritanism did not constrict him here. For him the restless pleasure was in the creation, not the finished product, and through most of his life his homes remained works in progress. Three stand out – Thornton Manor, his residence on the Wirral close to Port Sunlight; The Hill, on Hampstead Heath, his London home; and Roynton Cottage, or The Bungalow, at Rivington, his escape into the airy countryside. Towards the end of his life he made further residences in Lews Castle on Lewis and Borve Lodge on Harris. In passing he acquired but did not live in Rivington Hall with the purchase of the Rivington estate, plus large houses in Cheshire that came with the estates he purchased from 1911, and he bought two of London's great family palaces. The first of these was Stafford House in 1912, from the Duke of Sutherland, and the fact that a grandee was selling up to the son of a Bolton grocer provoked comment. He renamed it Lancaster House in honour of his home county and donated it to the nation to serve as a home for the London Museum and a site for government receptions. The second was the Duke of Westminster's Grosvenor House in 1924, vaguely intending to build on the site a public centre for the arts, but he died before any steps could be taken.[86] He also bought the 3,000 acre Moor Park estate in Hertfordshire from Lord Ebury in 1919 as a business proposition, turning it into a country club with three golf courses.[87]

The first of his big houses was Thornton Manor, where the Levers moved in 1888. He found it a Victorian Gothic building and left it Tudorbethan. The metamorphosis would have continued were it not for the First World War, because the architect James Lomax Simpson had drawn up plans for additional wings, facades and an arched entrance lodge to create a fantasy Elizabethan manor house.[88] Not content with rendering the house unrecognizable, Lever also decided to transform the neighbouring village, Thornton Hough, from a mangy collection of cottages into a mock feudal, olde-worlde ensemble with all mod. cons. After his mother's death in 1893, his father (who died in 1897) took up residence in a large house close to the village. His brother and several of his sisters likewise moved into capacious dwellings in the neighbourhood during the 1890s. At the heart of the revamped village stood the Congregational church, designed in Norman style by Lomax Simpson, and surrounding it a picturesque collection of 'traditional' Cheshire cottages, an inn, a village school and a half-timbered smithy. The smithy came complete with a chestnut tree to evoke Henry Wadsworth Longfellow's poem 'The Village Blacksmith', which had obvious appeal to Lever:

> Under a spreading chestnut-tree
> The village smithy stands;

The smith, a mighty man is he,
With large and sinewy hands;
…
His brow is wet with honest sweat,
He earns whate'er he can,
And looks the whole world in the face,
For he owes not any man.[89]

It was at Thornton Manor that Lever first met Thomas Hayton Mawson. Lever became Mawson's principal client and Mawson in turn was the greatest influence on Lever's property development in his final two decades. Mawson had started a nursery and landscape gardening business with his brothers in Windermere in the 1880s, and expanded from a local practice designing private gardens to a sought-after national concern that also included in its portfolio public parks and town planning schemes. He went solo in 1900, the year he published his manifesto, *The Art and Craft of Garden Making*, and established a reputation as the foremost contemporary landscape architect. Notable clients included Andrew Carnegie and Queen Alexandra; notable commissions included the design of the gardens for the Peace Palace at The Hague (1908–10), a major re-landscaping of the royal gardens and a park system in Athens for King Constantine and the Greek government in 1913, and several schemes for Canadian universities and cities from Ottawa to Vancouver. His second major book, *Civic Art*, came out in 1911, and he propagated his ideas through lecture tours in North America and by serving as a lecturer in town planning at the new School of Civic Design at the University of Liverpool. His influence was rewarded with the presidency of the Town Planning Institute in 1923 and the inaugural presidency of the Institute of Landscape Architects in 1929, by which stage he was in a wheelchair and largely incapacitated by Parkinson's Disease. Throughout his career triumphs it was work for Lever that was the mainstay of his business.[90]

The two first met after Mawson was summoned to Thornton Manor in 1905. They got down to work at a quarter past six the morning after Mawson's arrival, once Lever had returned from his morning canter. Lever presented him with plans he had drawn up for the improvement of the Manor gardens, with the caveat that:

> I must not allow myself to be too much influenced by these plans, as they were merely the work of an amateur. As the work of an amateur they were truly remarkable…. His scheme outlined a formal garden of heroic proportions, adapted to the changing levels of the site, and I have never met a man, layman or professional, who could reckon up so rapidly the amount of 'cut and fill' required to form the levels he planned.[91]

Lever encouraged Mawson to criticize freely, and by breakfast they had thrashed out an agreed scheme. From that point on, Lever was to hire Mawson not only for his major work at Thornton Manor, at Rivington and at The Hill (a balanced trio of landscape studies, as Mawson described it: the country house garden, the mountainside garden and the suburban garden), but also for the design of the gardens at Hall i' th' Wood (see below) and for visionary schemes for the redevelopment of Bolton and of the isle of Lewis.

It is not surprising that the two were attracted to each other. Lever was a study in motion; he liked long, unimpeded lines. 'When indulging in concentrated thought or talking with a friend, he liked to walk to and fro along a straight and level garden-path or up and down a conveniently large room,' wrote his son.

> Looking back upon the most memorable conversations which I have had with him – those intimate and companionable talks between father and son which remain indelibly engraven on the mind – I see as their setting the garden at Thornton, the terrace at 'The Hill', the verandah at 'The Bungalow', or the deck of a ship; they are associated with movement, not with rest.[92]

'I do not want a garden so much for rest as for promenades and walks,' Lever wrote to Mawson. 'I cannot rest in [the retreats and garden shelters] two minutes ... and a number of breaks and levels, I find to be irritating and annoying.'[93] Mawson too liked straight lines and provided them for him. In the summary of Myles Wright, a later holder of the Lever Chair in Town Planning and Civic Design at the University of Liverpool, who thought Mawson too rigid and unimaginative, Mawson loved axial lines, avenues, terraces and balustrades, turning his back on the informal landscaped English garden that had reigned supreme for much of the previous two centuries.[94]

Mawson designed the thirteen-acre lake and attached ornamental canal at Thornton Manor. The idea was partly to provide space for the entertainment of the children and workpeople of Port Sunlight, so he also created a bathing pavilion (Italianate, so as not to spoil the views from the vicinity of the house) and a bathing pond at the top of the canal; a ferry and two Italianate shelters on each side at the bottom of the canal at the junction with the lake; wet and dry docks for boats on the lake; and a large room for the children to have tea.[95]

Lever bought The Hill on Hampstead Heath in 1904. Through much of the nineteenth century the original 'Hill House' had been home to members of the Hoare banking family, but the house Lever bought was nearly new, rebuilt in the 1890s. He immediately set about extending it, with the addition of two wings, one for a music room, the other for a succession of picture galleries. Here, as in his other properties, he established a series of period rooms and, as at Rivington and Lews Castle, added a ballroom late in life to indulge his rekindled interest in dancing. Although 'one of the largest private ball-rooms in London' (140 ft by 27 ft), he slotted it inconspicuously underground, beneath the verandah along the west side of the house. His final additions, completed just before he died, consisted of galleries for modern pictures, watercolours and sculptures in an enlargement of the south wing.[96]

One of the things that attracted Lever to The Hill was the prospect across west Hampstead Heath and the open countryside beyond, but this meant there was little privacy in the garden from strollers on the common. The solution – again the work of Mawson, with considerable input from his client – was to raise the ground of the garden by twenty feet or more and to run an Italianate pergola along the top, creating a substantial measure of privacy but retaining the open view. Finding so much filling material would normally have proved well nigh impossible but, Mawson explained, 'by the great good fortune which seems to follow some men's enterprises, the Hampstead Tube Railway happened to be in course of construction at the time, and instead of Sir William having to pay for the filling required, he was actually paid a small fee per load for the tip.'[97]

In 1911 Lever purchased Heath Lodge, the property next door separated by a sunken lane (a public footpath), knocked down the mansion so that he could use the entire grounds for garden parties, built a connecting bridge between the two gardens and extended the pergola to screen his new garden from the common as well. In perhaps his only negative comment on Lever's life and work, A. G. Gardiner grumbled that 'he extends the outer ramparts of his house at Hampstead so that they dominate and despoil the most sylvan beauty-spot of the wonderful Heath.'[98] But the pergola, a Grade II listed structure, is nowadays a prized feature of the West Heath. It is open to the public and was meticulously restored by the Corporation of London in the 1990s.[99] It looks out over London's most popular gay cruising ground where, according to one source, up to 3,000 men can be found looking for sex among the trees and undergrowth on a warm summer's evening.[100]

Of all Lever's house-and-garden schemes, Rivington near Chorley in Lancashire is the most intriguing. Stretching from Rivington Pike, topped by a squat stone tower, down to picturesque reservoirs owned by Liverpool Corporation, the Rivington Hall estate was predominantly moorland. In 1899 Lever's solicitor, maintaining the anonymity of his client, approached the trustees of the estate and offered £40,000. There was a suggestion that the Crompton family, who owned the estate, were experiencing financial difficulties and might be disposed to sell at a very moderate price; but the answer came back that they wanted at least £70,000. At this point Liverpool Corporation entered the scene. The original statute of 1847 that allowed the construction of the reservoirs had neglected to appropriate the watershed to protect the purity of the water feeding the lakes (something that became a regular feature of later legislation). Here was an opportunity for the corporation to remedy this, and they put in a bid. Lever apparently withdrew, deciding that, in the public interest, he would not compete against the city. But Liverpool Corporation, mindful of ratepayers' money, would bid no higher than £50,000, and this was rejected. Lever thought that the field was now clear and increased his bid to £60,000. It was accepted in 1900, and the deal sealed.[101]

Lever had no intention of living in the Georgian Rivington Hall, which he rented to the Cromptons. Instead he carved out forty-eight acres for a private residence for himself high up on the hillside, replaced moorland tracks with twenty miles of metalled access roads, built three entrance lodges with thatched roofs around his new enclave, and in the middle put up a large wooden bungalow, Roynton Cottage (designed, transported and constructed by the Portable Building Company of Manchester), with sweeping views out over the Lancashire plain, fringed by Snowdonia, the Lake District and the coast.[102] 'If you build it of stone it would, perhaps, be more monumental,' he said of his new cottage, 'but if you build it of wood it is more comfortable and cosy.'[103] Damp, windy, misty days are not infrequent in these parts, and before he began to plant his garden around it the cottage in sour weather must have been exceptionally bleak. But as he was going to demonstrate again later on in the purchase of Lewis and Harris, bleakness did not serve as a deterrent.

In 1901 he publicly announced his intention to donate four hundred acres at the bottom of the hill, running close to the reservoirs, as a park for his native town of Bolton. He would demolish the various farmhouses and scattered villas, put the land out of cultivation and provide public access from the park to Rivington Pike, all on the understanding that he retain control: a free hand to do whatever he liked at his own expense, construct whatever paths, roads and buildings he deemed appropriate, 'and generally deal with the land as may appear to me to be desirable for the purpose for which the Park is intended, viz., its free and uninterrupted enjoyment by the Public'.[104] As a Liverpool newspaper put it, the park would form 'the most magnificent municipal domain in the kingdom, and constitute one of the most splendid gifts ever made to the public'.[105] According to his son, Lever's motivation in this and all his other donations to Bolton – Hall i' th' Wood, a Congregational church as a tribute to his parents, the buildings and endowment of Bolton School – should be seen as the repayment of a debt: 'the debt which every man owes to his native town, not because he happens to have been born there, but because, in most cases, it has provided the influences and opportunities of his early and formative years'.[106]

The projected Lever Park was just a tram ride from Bolton and even closer to Chorley. There was every indication that it would be popular. Members of Liverpool Corporation instantly imagined hordes of proletarians paddling and piddling in the city's water supply, and they now sought to wrest the watershed from Lever's grasp by introducing a Bill for the compulsory purchase of 6,000 acres, 2,200 of them Lever's. Lever resisted vigorously. During the hearings, Ralph Littler, acting for Lever, ridiculed one of the corporation's chief fears:

[B]eing a descendant of Bolton myself, and knowing something about the habits and manners of the Bolton people, some of them are a rough lot, but they are not a people who defy all laws of public decency and go out into the open of a public park for the purpose of discharging the functions of nature.... It seems to me as if they [the corporation] contemplated the population of Bolton taking the tramcars out to this park for the express purpose of using it for that part of our business which our ancestors used to describe as being done in a privy-house or office.[107]

The corporation won this battle, but it turned out to be a partial and expensive victory. The Liverpool Corporation Act of 1902 stipulated that the land be transferred to the corporation but that Lever could keep his forty-eight-acre enclave, that he could continue with his plans to lay out the park at his own expense 'for the use and enjoyment of the inhabitants of the county borough of Bolton and generally of the public for ever' (except for a strip of land between an unclimbable fence and the reservoir), that the corporation could divert or culvert over any streams on the land to protect them from pollution, and that the corporation was obliged to maintain and manage Lever Park. The question of compensation for Lever went to arbitration. Thus far he had spent over £133,000, including the £60,000 purchase money and nearly £13,000 on buying up adjoining properties, nearly £11,000 on roads with more to come, and a similar figure on the cottage (the wooden building, the lodges, the roads within the grounds, bringing water to the property and installing dynamo-generated electric lights). But his claim for compensation was £457,000.

At the arbitration hearings his legal counsel, H. H. Asquith (the future Prime Minister), explained that, all along, Lever intended to develop the rest of the estate for building purposes, since he was a man who always took a great interest 'in the laying out and development on what he conceives to be both businesslike and public spirited lines, of property'.[108] What had once been fit for nothing beyond a grouse moor was now prime real estate because of the improved roads and the proximity to a beautiful park. This was a reversal of arguments from the hearings over the Bill, and unwittingly the corporation's fault. Part of the corporation case had been that if Liverpool did not own the land, at some point it could be built on and the water contaminated with household effluent. Lever does not seem to have mentioned the possibility of building. His agent, Francis Thompson, a solicitor and chairman of the Bolton Waterworks Committee, explicitly stated, 'I know Mr. Lever has not the slightest intention of doing any building ... I have been in his confidence a great deal in connection with the matter.... I know he had not the slightest intention of doing anything in the way of development'.[109]

In contrast, at the arbitration hearing Lever stated baldly that 'to let the surrounding land for building purposes was part of my scheme'.[110] He argued that his plan for Rivington was consistent with his theories developed over the years, partially implemented at Port Sunlight, that the best way to develop an estate was not to cram it full of houses but to create attractive public open space, to the benefit of both residents and landowner. He built the bungalow, he said, 'so that I might have a place where I might go and always have a foothold there at week ends, or whenever I could go, for the development of the estate'.[111] This is not entirely implausible. Lever liked to develop grand schemes in unlikely places and did not let nature stand in his way. His donation of a park to increase the value of the surrounding land, rather than merely an act of philanthropy, would also have been in character with his shrewd business brain. But it seems improbable that the well heeled local bourgeoisie could have been induced to rent houses in such an exposed, elevated setting open to the elements, and the suspicion is that Lever was being economical with the truth, determined to turn the tables on Liverpool Corporation by using their argument against them and gouging them for all he could get.

The arbitrator, Reginald Middleton, awarded Lever £138,449 plus costs of around £10,000. Liverpool Corporation and press were outraged. The *Liverpool Courier* noted that according to this ruling the city was to pay for Lever's bungalow and forty-eight acres, give him a profit on top 'and the more intangible advantage of considerable popularity at Bolton gained by reason of his gift of a public park to that borough – a gift for which the ratepayers of Liverpool not only have to pay in the first instance, but the maintenance of which will be a perpetual charge upon this city'. One angry letter writer to the press demanded, 'May I now ask Sir Charles Petrie, as the leader of the dominant party in the City Council, how he can explain a policy which has resulted in our having to pay £138,000, to practically provide a 400 acre park for Bolton, and to maintain it for all time, all of which could have been obtained for the £60,000 which Mr. Lever paid for it a few years ago?'[112]

The corporation, for its part, voted forty-eight to seven to contest the award, on the grounds of Middleton's 'impaired mental vigour' – he allegedly had a nervous breakdown at or around the time he visited Rivington. (One councillor 'remarked that he had no sympathy with men like Mr. Lever. A great capitalist who would burden a city like this with an extraordinary debt and then pose as a friend of the people – there was something wrong about him.')[113] Lever rubbed in the salt when he pointed out that the corporation had no reason to be surprised at the award: if the councillors had not made the case that the estate was potential building land and not simply farm and moorland, Parliament might well have decided against allowing ratepayers' money to be locked up in it; if the case were not well founded, they got their Act on false pretences; if it were, they got the land at a very moderate price. The appeal failed, and the corporation by a forty-six to forty vote decided to let things rest. Lever and his lawyers had taken Liverpool Corporation and ratepayers to the cleaners.

'It is not to be a park on the ordinary lines,' said one newspaper in 1901 of this pioneer country park, 'but a free, extensive, grassy space where parties may wander about, have picnics, games, etc., and hold high festival in the green heart of the country.'[114] 'Here may be enjoyed the exhilaration of the open country and the peculiar refreshment which comes from the contemplation of scenery,' Thomas Mawson later wrote, ' – a want which the rich can fill by fleeing from town at certain seasons, but which is seldom procurable by the toiler unless it is made reasonably accessible.' Lever Park was officially opened in May 1904, followed by luncheon in the Rivington Hall barn. This and another, larger, cruck barn, the Great House or lower barn, were thought to be medieval but date mainly from the early eighteenth century. Jonathan Simpson reconstructed these magnificent structures for Lever, retaining the cruck frame but creating side aisles, adding entrance porches and stone-flagging the roofs, so that they could serve as refreshment rooms.

Over the next few years, in harmony with their love of straight lines, Lever and Mawson created a series of broad, radial, tree-lined avenues in the park, planted clumps of trees, removed buildings and hedges, fenced in woodland spaces for herds of red deer and generally managed things 'to develop the many natural beauties of the park with as little artificiality as possible'. Only the fearsome iron railings protecting the reservoir and the watercourses (the Liverpool Water Committee was taking no chances) struck a false note amidst this carefully crafted 'natural' display.[115]

Lever stocked a small zoo next to the hall with exotic animals. At his death in 1925 the list of animals and birds in the zoo and the park consisted of an emu, an Indian cow, a Chartley bull, four Chartley cows and four Chartley calves, eight Old English sheep, seventeen deer, two llamas, nine Scotch cattle, two zebras, five wallabies, three swans, three African cranes, a peacock and a peahen and around 200 pigeons, plus a further 120 wild duck, six swans, 450 pigeons and a flamingo in the Bungalow grounds. (Lever's lion cub, meanwhile, a gift from his visit to Nigeria, was on loan to the 'Temple of Neptune' at Wembley.)[116]

Because he had the money to run riot with his imagination, he began a full-scale replica of the ruins of Liverpool Castle as a further attraction for visitors. 'One associates such a quaint exercise as the building of a ruin with America rather than England,' wrote his son, 'and amongst Englishmen Lever was one of the few men – perhaps the only man – whom one can imagine carrying out such a scheme.' He had read an illustrated book by E. W. Cox (1892) about the castle, which had been severely damaged during the Civil War and was completely demolished in 1725, and saw a resemblance between its site and a spot on the edge of the reservoir. In 1912, with the collaboration of Mawson and Lomax Simpson, he set about recreating the ruins. To his mind, they would serve as a tribute to the city that owned the land, an experiment

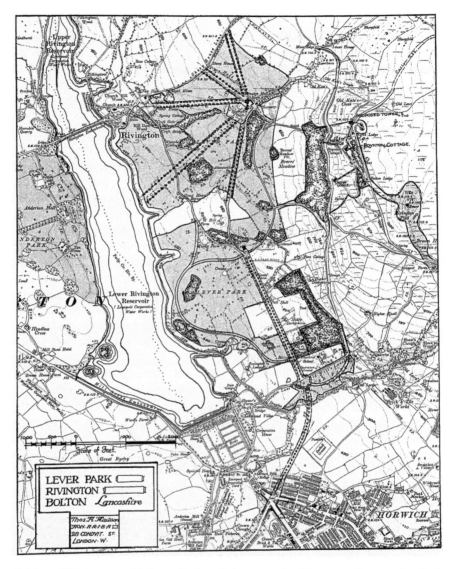

3 Map of Rivington, with Lever Park and the grounds of Roynton Cottage sketched in by Mawson, 1911

in landscape design, a celebration of the romantic and picturesque sentiments that had held sway for over a century and a practical lesson in English history. Hauling the massive blocks of stone into place proceeded slowly, with only a few stonemasons and labourers engaged at a time, and the structure still did not resemble the desired ruinous look by the time Lever died, when all work on it ceased.[117]

Even more ambitious was the work on his own enclave up on the hillside. More than one writer has referred to this as his Xanadu,[118] drawing on Samuel Taylor Coleridge's opium-induced reverie-poem *Kubla Khan* ('In Xanadu did Kubla Khan/A stately pleasure-dome decree'), and on Orson Welles's appropriation of the idea for his barely disguised portrait of the American press baron William Randolph Hearst in *Citizen Kane*. Hearst's Xanadu – Hearst Castle, in San Simeon, California – came later than Lever's in Lancashire, and it was vastly more extravagant. He inherited a quarter-million-acre ranch in 1919, and within it created Casa Grande, a palatial house of 165 rooms modelled on a Spanish cathedral, which he lavishly adorned with some of the finest European and Mediterranean art treasures, plus three Mediterranean Revival-style guest houses and 127 acres of gardens, terraces, pools and walkways.[119] Though Lever's site was more improbable, his creation was considerably more modest.

Mawson described Rivington as his most congenial commission because it provided an unusual challenge and scope for originality. Over the years he and Lever experimented at length on this hillside, figuring out what would and would not grow in the peaty soil and harsh weather. They planted hundreds of varieties – rhododendrons, azaleas, kalmias, broad-leaved hollies, ericas, berberis, cotoneasters, Scotch and Austrian pines, Alpine rock plants, to name but a few – and many of them flourished. 'Everyone interested expressed the decided opinion that nothing whatever except the native heather and bilberry would grow by any means whatsoever,' wrote Mawson. 'These wiseacres have been abundantly proved to be wrong, and now considerably over one hundred and fifty thousand trees and shrubs in great variety have been planted and are doing well.'

In keeping with the rugged landscape, Lever and his architects used local stone and a heavy style of building. Jonathan and James Lomax Simpson designed most of the buildings, but the terracing, lawns, ponds, crazy-paved paths, pergolas, shelters and loggias with flat, concrete roofs as viewpoints – all loosely based on an Arts and Crafts vision of ancient Italy – owed most to Mawson in collaboration with Lever. Below the house Mawson laid out in 1906 the 'Great Lawn' with its two garden shelters. Lever himself provided the initial plans, worked up by Simpson and Mawson, for a seven-arch footbridge designed like a Roman viaduct, crossing over Roynton Lane to connect with the western part of the grounds, which were landscaped in five terraces with winding stone steps and miniature waterfalls. A third wave of construction came in 1909–10, when Robert Atkinson, part of Mawson's practice, designed the Arts and Crafts lookout tower or 'Pigeon Tower', with terraces connecting it with the 'Swimming Pool'; and the fourth and biggest lodge (the Stone

SKETCH OF TOWER
AND GARDEN HOUSE
ROYNTON COTTAGE

4 Sketch of the pigeon tower and a shelter and lookout at Roynton Cottage,
Rivington, 1911

House) was added. Mawson's son, Edward Prentice Mawson, was primarily responsible for the construction from 1920 of the Ravine, a series of receding ledges and cascades quarried into the sandstone and crossed by two arched stone bridges. The pond in the Japanese garden above acted as a compensation reservoir, augmenting the water flow in dry weather.[120]

This Japanese garden at Rivington came last, in 1922 – an imagined Orient of Asian plants, overhanging trees, stone lanterns and three shelters in the style of Japanese tea houses, all surrounding an ornamental lake, with small waterfalls and a landing stage for punts. It sounds, and was, unlikely in such a setting, but the idea and practice of Japanese gardens were already well established in Britain by this date (albeit in more favourable locations). A strong Western taste for all things Japanese had begun after 1854, when American Commodore Matthew Perry forced Japan to end its insularity and open up to Western trade and consular relations. Japanese objects and prints began to be exhibited at major international exhibitions, but it was tourists and diplomats in the 1880s and 1890s who really developed the notion of establishing Japanese gardens in Europe and America. Josiah Condor's *Landscape Gardening in Japan* (1893) proved to be the seminal work of guidance. 'At best they were a distillation of Eastern influence within a Western framework,' according to Amanda Herries, 'and at worst they simply displayed a Japanese "touch"' – failing to take account of the role of Shinto or Buddhism, asymmetry and a balance between the *in* and the *yo* (the Chinese *yin* and *yang*) that were essential for a true Japanese garden.

In Britain an important influence was the Japan-British Exhibition at White City, London, in 1910, which featured two large Japanese gardens: a Garden of Peace and a Garden of the Floating Islands. Gardening journals reported on these in detail and wrote extensively about the introduction of Japanese plants. By the 1920s English nurseries routinely stocked an extensive range of Japanese plants, from azaleas to aucubas. By the mid-twentieth century, around sixty significant Japanese gardens had been created in Britain. Among the best were Friar Park near Henley on Thames, designed for Sir Frank Crisp in 1906 (alongside his miniature Matterhorn and alpine plants); Hinching-brooke, Huntingdon, Cambridgeshire, for the Earl of Sandwich after his return from the Far East in 1906; Tatton Park in Cheshire, inspired by a visit of Alan de Tatton to the 1910 exhibition (this was restored in 2001); and the Japanese gardens for a clutch of businessmen keen to demonstrate their fashionable tastes: Gatton Park, Surrey, for the mustard maker Jeremiah Colman; Gunnersbury Park, West London (1906), for the banker Leopold de Rothschild (his son, Lionel Nathan de Rothschild, planted a prized collection of azaleas and rhododendrons at Exbury, Hampshire, in the 1920s, but did not create a garden); and Lever's Rivington.[121] Lever's chief influence is not clear, but he had himself briefly visited Japan in 1913.

In the midst of Lever's part fantasy-Italian, part quasi-Arts and Crafts, part pseudo-Asian, part eccentric 'mountain garden' sat Roynton Cottage or The Bungalow. On the evening of 7 July 1913, while he and his wife were dining with King George V as guests of the Earl of Derby at Knowsley House, an arsonist struck. Edith Rigby, daughter of one Preston doctor and wife of another but gloriously unconventional by the standards of her class and gender, was an early member of the Independent Labour Party and a militant suffragette. She had already been convicted a number of times for public order offences when, at the height of the suffragettes' property-damaging campaign in 1913, she targeted both Liverpool Cotton Exchange and Roynton Cottage within a couple of days of each other. The bomb in the basement of the Exchange was a symbolic attack on the power and wealth of the cotton industry, which was largely built on female labour in the mills, but women were not recompensed with the rights of active citizenship. It did little damage; 'I wanted to place it where there was the least possible risk, where it would hurt neither myself nor anybody else,' she later said in court. As for Lever, he publicly favoured women's suffrage, but Rigby apparently did not realize this, and in any case, as far as she was concerned, he was both a supporter of an obdurate Liberal government that refused to give way on the issue and more broadly the personification of the capitalism she despised. 'I want to ask him whether he thinks his property on Rivington Pike is more valuable as one of his superfluous houses to be occasionally opened to people and used occasionally,' she was to tell the magistrate, 'or as a beacon lighted for the King and country to see that there were some insupportable grievances for women.'[122]

With the help of an accomplice, she lugged a keg of paraffin up the hill on the night in question, checked that the house was indeed empty, and laid and lit the paraffin trail. The property, to which Lever had recently added a second storey, was razed to the ground. Rigby gave herself up to the police. 'No doubt she will get a sentence of a long term of penal servitude and be out again in three days,' Lever predicted.[123] He was right. Stung by bad publicity about the force-feeding of suffragettes who went on hunger strike after their imprisonment, the government had introduced the 'Cat and Mouse' Act: hunger strikers were to be released, and then rearrested at a later stage to serve some more of their sentence. At Liverpool City Sessions at the end of July, Rigby was sent down for nine months' hard labour, and the 'game' of cat and mouse began. According to her niece, the poet Phoebe Hesketh, Rigby absconded to Ireland during one of her releases. Such tactics played by suffragettes, and the campaign of militancy, continued up to the outbreak of the First World War.[124]

Lever began rebuilding The Bungalow in 1914 as a substantial stone structure with a concrete and asphalt roof to deter another would-be arsonist, and in his usual fashion tacked on additions, only completing it in 1923. By then it

commodes. He collected English embroideries for Hall i' th' Wood, Thornton Manor, The Bungalow at Rivington (one set was lost in the arson attack) and The Hill, in the new Stuart Room built after the First World War.

Most of his Chinese porcelain collection he accumulated from the mid-1890s until the end of his life, principally blue-and-white and enamelled pieces from the Kangxi period, for no better nor worse reason than that they were popular and readily available at the time and they appealed to him more than other specimens. Only later, when his thoughts turned from collections for his own houses to displaying them for public benefit, did he broaden his acquisitions, but expert opinion holds that the fine collection in the Lady Lever Art Gallery is still narrowly defined. In 1911, for £275,000, the dealer Edgar Gorer sold him the entire collection – 395 items – of Chinese porcelain built up by Richard Bennett of Thornby Hall, Northamptonshire, who had made his fortune as a Lancashire bleacher and cotton spinner. Or at least that was the plan. Lever requested anonymity and was to pay in twenty monthly instalments, with the stipulation that he could backtrack on the deal if his name leaked out. It did. Lever backtracked. Gorer said he had told only Queen Mary, and sued. Sir Edward Carson (for Gorer) and F. E. Smith (for Lever) fought the ensuing courtroom dual. The final settlement saw Lever keeping fifty-one pieces for the £55,000 that he had already paid.[141]

Lever also built up his Wedgwood collection of 2,700 items through dealers, often buying *en bloc*. He started it by purchasing the collection of D. C. Marjoribanks, Lord Tweedmouth, in 1905 for over £15,000, placing it in a specially created 'Wedgwood Room' at The Hill, and a decade later became the most important client of Frederick Rathbone, the leading Wedgwood dealer of the time.[142] Using a reputed dealer was convenient, saved him time and – he hoped – ensured quality and value for money. As he wrote in a letter to Rathbone in 1916, 'If I were to begin examining pieces at Christie's, I am of opinion that I should do more harm than good. It is quite sufficient for me to take a hurried glance, and then communicate with yourself and others whose judgement in any case would be better than my own in the article in which they had specialized.'[143]

Once again following a trend – the vogue for period rooms that was especially popular at the turn of the century, and which Lever introduced at Thornton Manor, The Hill and the Lady Lever Art Gallery – Lever insisted on the appropriate furnishings for particular styles, all set out in perfect, symmetrical order.[144] The result was a kind of stuffy and somewhat uncomfortable formality, something to admire visually rather than to touch or feel at home in, fine for grand entertainments but not for relaxing in, snuggled up with a good book. Such an approach, while internally consistent in each room, produced the kind of mishmashed eclecticism and lack of sustained, holistic vision (the interior failing to reflect the exterior) that was to invite the ridicule and disdain of architectural critics in succeeding decades. In an oft-quoted letter to Thomas Mawson in 1910 he wrote:

> I feel that in the course of centuries we have gradually gained experience in the type of architecture suitable for each room. For instance, I prefer Georgian dining-rooms as the rooms in which to give large dinners; for small dining-rooms I prefer Tudor. For drawing-rooms I prefer what is called the Adams style; for entrance halls the Georgian. For a large room, such as a music-room, I prefer the period which I should call the Inigo Jones type of Renaissance.[145]

Lever's lasting legacy for the art world is the Lady Lever Art Gallery. In 1913 he bought all the paintings of George McCullough, a mine owner, and some of them, such as Frederic Leighton's *The Daphnephoria*, were of such generous proportions that he felt the need for a purpose-built gallery to house them.[146] By this time and until the end of his life he was buying on a prodigious scale, and the choicest items – amounting to three or four times the value of the rest of his collection, according to his son's estimate – ended up in the gallery. King George V laid the foundation stone of this stone-clad concrete building in 1913, but because of wartime delays the gallery did not actually open until 1922. The structure had to be capacious enough to house not only the British Old Masters, the English watercolours and the Pre-Raphaelites, the sculptures and the tapestries, the Chinese pottery and porcelain, the Tweedmouth Wedgwood and the English furniture arranged into four period rooms, but also the Napoleon Room of assorted Bonaparte memorabilia and a Masonic collection. (Lever took a keen interest in freemasonry, founded numerous lodges and rose to become the Provincial Senior Grand Warden of the Provincial Grand Lodge of Cheshire. The books, documents, regalia, glass, pottery and porcelain in this collection are reputedly the finest in any public collection, and again they were mostly bought from one dealer, Albert Calvert.) Although the Lady Lever Art Gallery is the culmination of the stylistically jarring Beaux-Arts transformation imposed on the rustic village (see chapter three), it also had to be relatively squat so as not to look entirely incongruous in a village of workers' cottages.[147] Even so, as one writer puts it, it 'stands among Port Sunlight's English-vernacular terraces like a grande dame at a village fête'.[148]

Segar Owen was the architect and inevitably Lever was deeply involved in the design, especially of the interior, bringing to bear his trademark micro-managerial style and sense of detail. For instance, here are his thoughts on the projected Tapestry Room in 1914:

> Respecting the dado height, I shall have to go very carefully into this, not only in regard to the Tapestries but for the furniture. It seems to me to be rather high than low, if I am able to scale it correctly, in doing which it seems to be about 3 ft 6 in. There are very few side tables, commodes, etc. that are higher than 34 ft. I would suggest that what I call the chair rail be omitted entirely. It would

only confuse with any pieces of furniture I might put in, and probably with the hanging of the tapestries. I would rather have a free hand above the skirting. The skirting ought to be a good depth – 15 in. to 18 in., but that is all.[149]

Lever 'arranged the whole collection himself', wrote his son, 'devoting many long and happy hours to the task'. After the gallery opened, he fixed even more of his formidable energies upon it, in effect acting as its curator. His son, speaking of his father's final visit to the gallery, recalls him inspecting the Adams Room which was nearing completion and 'telling the craftsman who was carrying out the work to tone down the rich "Wedgwood" blue of the walls until the right degree of mellowness was reached'.[150]

Why did Lever collect? He was not given to incessant introspection, so we have to speculate. One answer could be financial: collecting made sound economic sense. Given the demand, any items purchased could be expected to appreciate in value – whether as much as investment in other areas was difficult to say, given the vagaries of the art market, but presumably a shrewd businessman like Lever did not consider his collecting to be a losing proposition. A second answer could be psychological. On one of the rare occasions when his thoughts on collecting were recorded, a speech at the opening of the Lady Lever Art Gallery in 1922, he remarked that art for him was 'a stimulating influence', 'an inspiration' – and so it is plausible that his selection of items fulfilled various unanalyzed psychological needs. He surrounded himself with objects of personal meaning and remembrance, of beauty to give him a spark of pleasure and fleetingly lighten his mental load, and of monetary value to prove to himself his own self-worth, that he had arrived and could hope to incite the envy of others.[151]

This segues into a third reason. Lever's contemporary, the American economist Thorstein Veblen, had an answer in his mischievous put-down of social snobbery, *The Theory of the Leisure Class* (1899). 'The basis on which good repute in any highly organized industrial community ultimately rests is pecuniary strength', he wrote, 'and the means of showing pecuniary strength, and so of gaining or retaining a good name, are leisure and a conspicuous consumption of goods.' The utility of both these factors for the purposes of reputation, Veblen went on, lies in the element of waste: 'In the one case it is a waste of time and effort, in the other it is a waste of goods.'[152] No one could ever accuse Lever of wasting time and effort; but in terms of conspicuous consumption of goods, Veblen may have been on to something.

Lever grew up in the world of the Victorian bourgeoisie, a culture that valued a fulsome display of material possessions as a marker of wealth, discernment and status. Members of the bourgeoisie liked to show off their domestic interiors to their peers in the well established ritual of house calling. Cramming as many goods as he reasonably could into his houses would have seemed obvious and natural to Lever, his appetite whetted as his pocketbook expanded along with the number of residences upon which he could inflict his imagination. Wealthier northern industrialists had long since emulated members of the aristocracy and gentry in building up substantial fine art collections, sometimes housing them in specially built galleries attached to their houses.[153] Again, all this followed contemporary fashion.

Lever was emulating not only the British plutocratic elite but also some of the great tycoons in the United States – Henry Clay Frick, J. Pierpont Morgan, John D. Rockefeller, Andrew Mellon, Andrew Carnegie, Samuel H. Kress, William Randolph Hearst – who were constructing their collections with blank cheques during the same period, using their Croesian wealth to buy up the art treasures of Europe. Lever was a great admirer of America and its business dynamism, and his decision to create a purpose-built gallery to display a portion of his collection mirrored both contemporary American examples and the fashion for the creation of national and municipal galleries in Britain in the late nineteenth century and beyond. Some of the most prominent examples are the Walker Art Gallery in Liverpool (1877) with money from the brewer, Sir Andrew Barclay Walker; the City of Manchester Art Gallery (1882); the Whitworth Gallery in Manchester (1890), thanks to the donation of Sir Joseph Whitworth, who made his money in armaments and machinery; the National Portrait Gallery in London (1898), with funds from the property dealer William Henry Alexander; and the Chorley-born sugar refiner Sir Henry Tate's eponymous gallery ('the National Gallery of British Art', to give it its proper name) at Millbank in London (1897).[154]

Another set of motivations fuelled Lever's decision to make his collections public. Like many before him who organized public exhibitions of art, he believed strongly in the didactic function of art: its power to moralize, civilize and spiritually uplift the masses.[155] During their hours of leisure, he believed, if they were not tending to their allotments there was no better place for the working men and women of Britain than in an art gallery, contemplating the skill and message of renowned artists. In 1917, while advocating a six-hour day, he was asked what men over thirty would do with their time, and he replied that they would 'in all probability, like to have the time in their garden or for some hobby of their own. Some would visit Picture Galleries.'[156]

Whether this civilizing function worked or not is a different question. Whenever someone makes a case for appreciators of arts being more civilized than the rest, someone else is sure to mention that Adolf Hitler was a watercolourist and Hermann Goering an art connoisseur, and the argument rapidly deflates. In our anti-elitist and post-paternalist times, as the distinguished art historian E. H. Gombrich pointed out in a Leverhulme Memorial Lecture in 1981:

[É]litism is alleged to pride itself in the possession of a superior culture, and paternalism adds to this charge the arrogant belief that members of the elite also know better than common mortals do what is good for them…. How can anyone claim to know the needs of the mind and allege that the vast majority of men and women here on earth who have little contact with the beauties of nature and none with art are short of mental sustenance? How can we be sure that we, who have enjoyed some of these benefits, have thereby improved our minds beyond the level of those who have not?[157]

Lever harboured no such doubts and would have found the question incomprehensible. In his moral earnestness he was echoing widely held assumptions. 'Art tells us that it is only the true and honest work of life that will survive, and, therefore, Art can be to everyone an inspiration,' he said in his speech at the opening of the Lady Lever Art Gallery. 'It is within the reach of all of us, however humble we may be, for with modern inventions and the genius of printers' reproductions all the finest works of art are within the reach of all, and a visit to the art galleries in our large centres will take us to the originals.'

Lever was intent on bringing the originals to the people, whether in Hall i' th' Wood, the Free Library and Museum at Port Sunlight (from 1903), the art gallery he created at Hulme Hall (formerly a dining room for women workers) from 1911, Rivington Hall (which he opened up to the public as an art gallery and museum in 1911) or, a decade later, the Lady Lever Art Gallery. And one of his major goals was strongly nationalistic. To be sure, he had a wide curiosity about other cultures. He amassed a collection of over a thousand ethnographic items – weapons, clothing, masks, bowls, canoes, native costumes and the like – which he purchased from collectors, dealers or missionaries on his travels in Africa, Asia and the Pacific, and he housed them sequentially in the Free Library and Museum and Hulme Hall, moving the best pieces for display at the new London headquarters, Lever House at Blackfriars, in 1922. He also bought the extensive shell collection of John Simpson Tyerman, once a curator of Liverpool Botanic Gardens, intending them for an unrealized science museum as part of the Lady Lever Art Gallery, and had a collection of more than three hundred archaeological objects thanks to a couple of digs he helped sponsor in Egypt and the Sudan carried out by the distinguished Egyptologist John Garstang.[158]

There were foreign components to Lever's art collection, but it was overwhelmingly British. To quote once again from his speech at the opening ceremony of the Lady Lever Art Gallery, he said:

Another object I had in view in establishing this Gallery was to show that English Art throughout the centuries had not been second to the art of any nation in the world. We British are sometimes too fond of depreciating ourselves, but I venture to say that if you will look at the last two centuries you will find that English Art – the Art of the home, not of the palace – transcends in beauty of outline, form and colour that of any of our neighbours, however famous they may be.[159]

This 'art of the home', housed in the classical splendour of the Lady Lever, made a claim to a sense of British national superiority. But as well as the proud patriot (British, English and, later in life, pseudo-Scottish) one of Lever's layers of allegiance was as a northerner with a no-nonsense Lancashire accent, proud of his roots. He opened up Hall i' th' Wood, the half-timbered manor house where Samuel Crompton had invented the spinning mule, as a museum to the memory of Crompton and to the history of the textile industry and as a show-case for English vernacular furnishings. He bought it in 1899, presented it as a gift to the town of Bolton and it opened in 1902. The endeavour spoke not only to a wish to celebrate the spirit of Smilesian progress in the guise of a humble figure who was one of the industrial revolution's great inventors, but also to a desire to preserve a certain nostalgic sense of regional history and identity, a pre-industrial 'old Lancashire' of 'traditional' values of a bygone era of greater harmony and brotherhood – the ideals, as we shall see in chapter three, that he was attempting to put into practice at Port Sunlight. In a speech at the opening of the Hall he said that 'He came of a Bolton family, he was proud of his connection with the town, and he tried to be as true to Bolton principles, its hatred of humbug, love of hard work and thoroughness, and loyalty to the town as one who travelled about a good deal could be.'[160]

Like Rivington, the Lady Lever Art Gallery and Hall i' th' Wood remain popular with visitors today. But the last of the private collection was dispersed after the death of the third viscount in 2000. The auction by Sotheby's of the contents of Thornton Manor in June 2001 fetched £9,555,551, breaking the record for a British house contents sale. Among the bidders were Britain's glamour couple and style trendsetters of the moment, Posh and Becks – Victoria and David Beckham, the former Spice Girl and the metrosexual England foot-ball captain – who flew in by helicopter from their nearby Cheshire mansion and spent more than £2 million.[161] Doubtless some blanched at the thought of footballers and pop musicians, the latest additions to Britain's plutocratic elite, buying up the nation's heritage, just like their predecessors when a mere soapboiler did it a century ago.

Notes

1 'In memoriam: William Hesketh Viscount Leverhulme', *Progress* (the Lever Broth-ers magazine), 25:168 (July 1925), 154.
2 *Ibid.*, 147–52: first quotation, p. 147, Harold Spender, political journalist, in *The Contemporary Review*; second quotation, p. 137, F. A. Countway, president of Lever Bothers in Cambridge, MA, in *The Lever Standard* (the local house organ); third quotation, p. 138, Thomas Dreier, editorial in *The Lever Standard*.
3 *The Times*, 8 May 1925 (in Bolton Archives and Local Studies (hereafter BALS), B920 B LEV, newspaper cuttings on Lever).
4 T. P. O'Connor, in *Liverpool Post and Mercury*, 8 May 1925 (in BALS, B920 B LEV,

newspaper cuttings on Lever).

5 William Hulme Lever [second Viscount Leverhulme], *Viscount Leverhulme* (Boston, MA, and New York: Houghton Mifflin, 1927), pp. 17, 236 (first quotation), 66 (second), 67 (third).

6 A. G. Gardiner, *Pillars of Society* (London: James Nisbet, 1914), p. 199.

7 16 November 1912. Quoted by Jamie Camplin, *The Rise of the Plutocrats: Wealth and Power in Edwardian England* (London: Constable, 1978), p. 70.

8 Thomas H. Mawson, *The Life and Work of an English Landscape Architect: An Autobiography* (New York: Charles Scribner's Sons, 1927), p. 116.

9 Excerpt from *Liverpool Daily Post* in *Progress*, 25:168 (July 1925), 116–17.

10 See the Sotheby's catalogue for the sale of the Leverhulme Collection at Thornton Manor (June 2001): Lot 165: 'Imperial: A massive colonial solid sissoo dining table' (sold for £322,500), http://search.sothebys.com/jsps/live/lot/LotDetail.jsp?sale_number=L01703&live_lot_id=165, and Lot 30: 'A pair of Napoleon III carved giltwood armchairs' (sold for £7,200), http://search.sothebys.com/jsps/live/lot/LotDetail.jsp?lot_id=3CDKW, accessed 16 August 2006.

11 Unilever Archives and Records Management, Port Sunlight (hereafter UARM), Lever Business Correspondence, LBC 196, Joshua Hacking in Minutes of Soapmakers' Association, London, 13 January 1911.

12 Earl of Birkenhead [F. E. Smith], *Contemporary Personalities* (London: Cassell and Co., 1924), p. 284.

13 UARM, Small Deposits Collection, SDC 9/3/14, Lever to Stanley Unwin, 8 April 1921; Unwin to Lever, 1 May 1924; copy indenture between R. B. Evans and second viscount, 25 June 1925; C. D. Medley to John McDowell, 26 June 1925.

14 *Ibid.*, Evans to Unwin, 26 June 1925; Evans to Field, Roscoe and Co., 26 June 1926; Hulme Lever to Edgar Sanders, 18 June 1926; Lever, *Leverhulme*, p. 5.

15 Charles Wilson, *The History of Unilever: A Study in Economic Growth and Social Change*, vol. I (London: Cassell and Co., 1954); W. P. Jolly, *Lord Leverhulme: A Biography* (London: Constable, 1976); Adam MacQueen, *The King of Sunlight: How William Lever cleaned up the World* (London: Bantam Press, 2004).

16 Rt Hon. Lord Riddell, 'Foreword' to William Henry Beable, *Romance of Great Businesses* (London: Heath Cranton, 1926), vol. I, p. 7.

17 Mrs Stuart Menzies, *Modern Men of Mark* (London: Herbert Jenkins, 1921); H. Maitland Crichton, *The Romance of Million-Making* (London: George G. Harrap and Co., 1931).

18 Harley Williams, *Men of Stress: Three Dynamic Interpretations: Woodrow Wilson, Andrew Carnegie, William Hesketh Lever* (London: Jonathan Cape, 1948); W. S. Adams, *Edwardian Portraits* (Secker and Warburg, 1957).

19 Ian Campbell Bradley, *Enlightened Entrepreneurs* (London: Weidenfeld and Nicolson, 1987); James Bellini, *Rule Britannia: A Progress Report for Domesday 1986* (London: Jonathan Cape, 1981).

20 Nigel Nicolson, *Lord of the Isles* (Stornoway: Acair, 2000; 1st edn, 1960); Roger Hutchinson, *The Soap Man: Lewis, Harris and Lord Leverhulme* (Edinburgh: Birlinn, 2003); Edward Morris (ed.), *Art and Business in Edwardian England: The Making of the Lady Lever Art Gallery* (Oxford: Oxford University Press, 1992, for National Museums and Galleries on Merseyside; reprinted from *Journal of the*

History of Collections, 4:2 (1992)).

21 John Griffiths, '"Give my regards to Uncle Billy ...": the rites and rituals of company life at Lever Brothers, *c*. 1900–*c*. 1990', *Business History*, 37:4 (October 1995), 29, 32.

22 See Kali Israel, *Names and Stories: Emilia Dilke and Victorian Culture* (New York: Oxford University Press, 1999), pp. 13, 16–18.

23 J. B. Bury, 'Cleopatra's nose' (1916), reprinted in his *Selected Essays* (Cambridge: Cambridge University Press, 1930).

24 Karl Marx, *The 18th Brumaire of Louis Bonaparte* (Beijing: Foreign languages Press, 1978), p. 9.

25 See, for example, Howard Archer, 'The role of the entrepreneur in the emergence and development of UK multinational enterprises', *Journal of European Economic History*, 19:2 (fall 1990), 294, 296, 307; F. M. L. Thompson, *Gentrification and the Enterprise Culture: Britain 1780–1980* (Oxford: Oxford University Press, 2001), pp. 4–6 (quotation p. 5); Alfred D. Chandler Jr, 'Comparative business history', in D. C. Coleman and Peter Mathias (eds), *Enterprise and History: Essays in Honour of Charles Wilson* (Cambridge: Cambridge University Press, 1984), pp. 7, 10.

26 Wilson, *Unilever*, pp. 290–1.

27 Bradley, *Enlightened Entrepreneurs*, pp. 1–9; Camplin, *Rise of the Plutocrats*, pp. 35–7, 71, 282; Chandler, 'Comparative business history', pp. 24–5, and W. J. Reader, 'Businessmen and their motives', pp. 42–3, 51, in Coleman and Mathias (eds), *Enterprise and History*; Leslie Hannah, *The Rise of the Corporate Economy* (London: Methuen and Co., 1976), pp. 1–3, 16–17, 21–6; Harold Perkin, *The Rise of Professional Society: England since 1880* (London and New York: Routledge, 1989), pp. 256, 294–5. For Lever's take on this see Lord Leverhulme, *The Six-Hour Day and other Industrial Questions* (London: George Allen and Unwin, 1918), pp. 262–3 (speech to Port Sunlight Men's Meeting, 11 January 1903).

28 Bellini, *Rule Britannia*, chap. 13 (first quotation, p. 152; second and third quotations, p. 144).

29 Obit. of Philip William Bryce Lever, third Viscount Leverhulme, *Guardian*, 11 July 2000.

30 David Cannadine, *The Decline and Fall of the British Aristocracy* (New Haven, CT: Yale University Press, 1990), pp. 356–9; Martin Pugh, *State and Society: A Social and Political History of Britain 1870–1997*, 2nd edn (London: Edward Arnold, 2000), p. 100; Perkin, *Rise of Professional Society*, p. 366.

31 For the historical debate see, for example, Martin J. Weiner, *English Culture and the Decline of the Industrial Spirit 1850–1980* (Cambridge: Cambridge University Press, 1981); W. D. Rubinstein, *Elites and the Wealthy in Modern British History: Essays in Social and Economic History* (Brighton: Harvester Press, 1987); W. D. Rubinstein, *Men of Property: The Very Wealthy in Britain since the Industrial Revolution* (London: Croom Helm, 1981); P. J. Cain and A. G. Hopkins, *British Imperialism*, 2 vols (London: Longman, 1993); Martin J. Daunton, '"Gentlemanly capitalism" and British industry 1820–1914', *Past and Present*, 122 (February 1989), 119–58; Geoffrey Ingham, 'British capitalism: empire, merchants and decline', *Social History*, 20:3 (October 1995), 339–54; Raymond E. Dumett (ed.), *Gentlemanly Capitalism and British Imperialism: The New Debate on Empire* (London:

Longman, 1999); Simon Gunn, 'The "failure" of the Victorian middle class: a critique', in Janet Wolff and John Seed (eds), *The Culture of Capital: Art, Power and the Nineteenth-Century Middle Class* (Manchester: Manchester University Press, 1988); Thompson, *Gentrification and the Enterprise Culture*.

32 'Day by day – that's all' (address at Wigan and District Mining and Technical College, 1 December 1915), in Sir William Hesketh Lever, *Three Addresses* (Port Sunlight: Lever Brothers, n.d.), pp. 9–10.

33 UARM, LBC 8362C, Lever to H. F. W. Bousfield, 2 December 1921.

34 D. K. Fieldhouse, *Unilever Overseas: The Anatomy of a Multinational 1895–1965* (London: Croom Helm, 1978). This summary of Lever's biographical details and business-building is derived from Wilson, *Unilever*, the biographies already cited and Fieldhouse.

35 Edward Marjoribanks, *The Life of Lord Carson*, vol. I (Toronto: Macmillan, 1932), chap. 30; Wilson, *Unilever*, chap. 6; Lever, *Leverhulme*, chap. 17; Jolly, *Leverhulme*, pp. 45–57; Perkin, *Rise of Professional Society*, p. 294.

36 W. J. Reader, *Imperial Chemical Industries: A History*, vol. 1: *The Forerunners 1870–1926* (London: Oxford University Press, 1970), pp. 232–9, 293–8, 373–5; A. E. Musson, *Enterprise in Soap and Chemicals: Joseph Crosfield and Sons, Ltd 1815–1965* (Manchester: Manchester University Press, 1965), pp. 243–4, 248, 251, 283–6; Andrew M. Knox, *Coming Clean: A Postscript after Retirement from Unilever* (London: Heinemann, 1976), p. 72; Wilson, *Unilever*, chap. 9; *The Times*, 5 November 1926, pp. 9, 11; 9 November, p. 11.

37 Perkin, *Rise of Professional Society*, pp. 293–4.

38 W. J. Reader, *Unilever: A Short History* (London: Unilever House, 1960), pp. 9–41; W. G. Hoffmann, '100 Years of the Margarine Industry', in J. H. van Stuyvenberg (ed.), *Margarine: An Economic, Social and Scientific History 1869–1969* (Toronto: University of Toronto Press, 1969), pp. 15–16; Fieldhouse, *Unilever Overseas*, pp. 37–9; Wilson, *Unilever*, p. xvii.

39 Hannah, *Rise of the Corporate Economy*, p. 120.

40 *Progress*, 25:168 (July 1925), 145 (first quotation: Sydney Walton in the *Yorkshire Evening News*); Birkenhead, *Contemporary Personalities*, p. 277 (second quotation); Gardiner, *Pillars of Society*, pp. 197 (third quotation), 201 (fourth quotation); Angus Watson, *My Life: An Autobiography* (London: Ivor Nicholson and Watson, 1937), pp. 140–2, 144, 145, 152, 155, 216 (fifth quotation), 219; Knox, *Coming Clean*, pp. 40 (sixth quotation), 57, 69, 77; Arthur Geddes, *The Isle of Lewis and Harris: A Study in British Community* (Edinburgh: Edinburgh University Press, 1955), p. 257; Williams, *Men of Stress*, p. 304; Menzies, *Modern Men of Mark*, pp. 148–9. On the question of height see Roderick Floud, Kenneth Wachter and Annabel Gregory, *Height, Health and History: Nutritional Status in the United Kingdom 1750–1980* (Cambridge: Cambridge University Press, 1990), pp. 305–6, 319 and *passim*.

41 Menzies, *Modern Men of Mark*, p. 147 (quotation); Lever, *Leverhulme*, pp. 259–60.

42 *Progress*, 25:168 (July 1925), 87, 113, 117, 123; BALS, ABZ/37/1/6, *Presentation of the Honorary Freedom of the Borough to William Hesketh Lever, Esq. and John Pennington Thomasson, Esq.* (Bolton, 1902), p. 22.

43 Lever, *Leverhulme*, pp. 79 (quotation), 150; MacQueen, *King of Sunlight*, chap. 11. MacQueen mistakes hyperglycaemia for hypoglycaemia but his point about the possible impact of diabetes is plausible. I am grateful to Dr Frank Lewis for this clarification.

44 Knox, *Coming Clean*, p. 45.

45 *Liverpool Echo*, 3 March 1888.

46 Lever, *Leverhulme*, p. 30.

47 Quoted *ibid.*, p. 179.

48 *Ibid.*, pp. 177–8.

49 Knox, *Coming Clean*, pp. 2, 4, 43; Colin MacDonald, *Highland Journey* (Edinburgh and London: Moray Press, 1943), p. 151; UARM, LBC 4271, Madge Duckworth to Lever, 17 September 1923.

50 Knox, *Coming Clean*, p. 54.

51 Watson, *My Life*, p. 221.

52 MacDonald, *Highland Journey*, p. 140.

53 'A Gentleman with a Duster' [Harold Begbie], *The Mirrors of Downing Street: Some Political Reflections* (London: Mills and Boon, 1920), p. 155.

54 Lever, *Leverhulme*, p. 82.

55 Quoted by Wilson, *Unilever*, p. 49.

56 Lever, *Leverhulme*, p. 80.

57 *Ibid.*, pp. 301–2; Nicolson, *Lord of the Isles*, pp. 63–6.

58 Williams, *Men of Stress*, pp. 273 (quotation), 304–7.

59 *Ibid.*, p. 305.

60 Lever, *Leverhulme*, p. 15.

61 Jeffrey Richards, '"Passing the love of women": manly love and Victorian society', and J. A. Mangan and James Walvin, 'Introduction', in Mangan and Walvin (eds), *Manliness and Morality: Middle-Class Masculinity in Britain and America 1800–1940* (Manchester: Manchester University Press, 1987); Harry Cocks, '*Calamus* in Bolton: spirituality and homosexual desire in late Victorian England', *Gender and History*, 13:2 (August 2001), 191–223.

62 For diagrams and descriptions of the types of machine that appealed to him – 'Horse Rider', 'Camel Rider', 'Massage vibrator', 'Tripod pulsator', non-electric rowing machine, fixed cycles and the like – in this case the machines that he took with him on his yacht, the SY *Albion*, on his trip to West Africa in 1924, see the correspondence in UARM, SDC 9/3/44.

63 Lever, *Leverhulme*, pp. 101–3, 268–71, 292; Williams, *Men of Stress*, p. 357; Nicolson, *Lord of the Isles*, pp. 8 (quotation), 63.

64 Williams, *Men of Stress*, p. 357.

65 Bradley, *Enlightened Entrepreneurs*, pp. 5–6.

66 Gardiner, *Pillars of Society*, pp. 195, 201.

67 Lever, *Leverhulme*, pp. 13–16, 276 (quotation).

68 UARM, LBC 735, Lever to George Harley, 15 April 1913, and subsequent correspondence.

69 Lever, *Leverhulme*, pp. 253–5.

70 'Each other's burdens' (New Year address at Gladstone Hall, Port Sunlight, 2 January 1916), in Lever, *Three Addresses*, pp. 14–15.

71 Lever, *Leverhulme*, pp. 95 (first quotation), 96, 253–5, 274, 275 (second quotation).

72 Watson, *My Life*, pp. 143, 218, 221 (quotation).

73 Lever, 'Each other's burdens', *Three Addresses*, p. 21.

74 Lever, *Leverhulme*, p. 276.

75 Lever, 'Fast asleep on a gold mine' (address at Mawdsley Street Congregational Church PSA Brotherhood, 5 December 1915), in Lever, *Six-Hour Day*, p. 214 (also reprinted in *Three Addresses*).

76 *Ibid.*, p. 215.

77 *Ibid.*, pp. 211 (first quotation), 214 (second and third quotations).

78 *Ibid.*, pp. 214 (quotation), 217.

79 *Ibid.*, p. 215.

80 Lever, *Leverhulme*, pp. 21–2, 257.

81 Quoted by Bradley, *Enlightened Entrepreneurs*, p. 201.

82 *Bolton Evening News*, 8 March 1923.

83 Lever, *Six-Hour Day*, p. 98 (speech in Birmingham, 8 November 1912).

84 Lever, 'Fast asleep', *Six-Hour Day*, pp. 218–20.

85 See Callum G. Brown, *The Death of Christian Britain* (London and New York, 2001); David J. Jeremy, 'The enlightened paternalist in action: William Hesketh Lever at Port Sunlight before 1914', *Business History*, 33:1 (January 1991), 58–81; David J. Jeremy, *Capitalists and Christians: Business Leaders and the Churches in Britain 1900–1960* (Oxford: Clarendon Press, 1990).

86 Cannadine, *Decline and Fall*, p. 116; Lever, *Leverhulme*, pp. 252–3, 267, 298.

87 Lever, *Leverhulme*, pp. 229–30.

88 *Ibid.*, pp. 100–1, 290.

89 Thomas H. Mawson, *Civic Art: Studies in Town Planning: Parks, Boulevards and Open Spaces* (London: B. T. Batsford, 1911), p. 50; Lever, *Leverhulme*, pp. 103–6. For the poem see Palgrave's *Golden Treasury of English Songs and Lyrics* (London: J. M. Dent, 1906 edn), p. 344.

90 David Mawson, 'T. H. Mawson (1861–1933): landscape architect and town planner', *Journal of the Royal Society of Arts*, 5331:132 (February 1984), 184–99; Harriet Jordan, 'Mawson, Thomas Hayton (1861–1933)', rev., *Oxford Dictionary of National Biography* (Oxford: Oxford University Press, 2004; online edn, May 2005, www.oxforddnb.com/view/article/37748, accessed 19 September 2005).

91 Mawson, *Life and Work*, p. 117.

92 Lever, *Leverhulme*, pp. 289–90.

93 Quoted *ibid.*, p. 291.

94 Myles Wright, *Lord Leverhulme's Unknown Venture: the Lever Chair and the Beginnings of Town and Regional Planning 1908–1948* (London: Hutchinson Benham, 1982), p. 84.

95 Mawson, *Civic Art*, pp. 180–2, 196–9.

96 Lever, *Leverhulme*, pp. 292–6 (quotation p. 295).

97 Mawson, *Life and Work*, pp. 129–30.

98 *Ibid.*, pp. 179–80, 189; Gardiner, *Pillars of Society*, p. 200.

99 Stanley Unwin, *The Truth about a Publisher* (London: George Allen and Unwin, 1960), pp. 208–9; *The Pergola: The Birth, Decline and Spectacular Renaissance of*

a Unique Edwardian Extravaganza (London: Corporation of London, n.d.). The shipowner Andrew Weir, first Baron Inverforth, bought The Hill on Lever's death in 1925, renamed it Inverforth House and lived there until he died in 1955. It then became a convalescent home for Manor House Hospital and was subsequently converted into up-market flats.

100 See the documentary, 'The truth about gay sex' (2001), directed by Kristiene Clarke.

101 The story of the sale negotiations and subsequent battle can be found in BALS, Lever Papers, ZLE/2, miscellaneous correspondence with Messrs Joseph Jackson and Son, agents for the Rivington Park estate; ZLE/5/1, House of Commons, Session 1902: petitions of Lever and of Bolton Corporation against the Liverpool Corporation Bill; *Liverpool Daily Post*, 29 April 1902; Minutes of Evidence, Select Committee of Commons on Liverpool Corporation Bill; ZLE/5/2, Lever and Liverpool Corporation arbitration, 1904; *Liverpool Corporation Act*, 2 Edw. 7, c. ccxl; ZLE/2/16/10, F. W. Thompson, 'Rivington Hall Estate. Short History of the negotiations, previous to the purchase by W. H. Lever, Esq'.; ZLE/4/1, Newspaper cuttings book: Lever and Liverpool Corporation, 1901–05.

102 Malcolm D. Smith, *Leverhulme's Rivington (The Story of the Rivington 'Bungalow')* (St Michael's on Wyre, Lancs.: Wyre Publishing, 1998), pp. 22, 33–5.

103 ZLE/5/2, In Arbitration, Lever and Corporation of Liverpool, 11 July 1904, p. 31, q. 232.

104 Lever to J. Simpson, F. W. Thompson and Messrs Hulton, Son and Harwood, 6 September 1901, in Minutes of Evidence, 13 May 1902, p. 404.

105 *Liverpool Daily Post*, 29 April 1902.

106 Lever, *Leverhulme*, p. 132.

107 Minutes of Evidence, pp. 362–3, 13 May 1902.

108 ZLE/5/2, In Arbitration, Lever and Corporation of Liverpool, 11 July 1904, p. 5.

109 Minutes of Evidence, pp. 322–3, examination of Francis William Thompson, 13 May 1902, q. 3520.

110 ZLE/4/1, Newspaper cuttings book, report of arbitration proceedings in cutting of 12 July 1904.

111 ZLE/5/2, In Arbitration, Lever and Corporation of Liverpool, 11 July 1904, p. 23, q. 89.

112 *Liverpool Courier*, 7 November 1904, including letter of Edward Evans, Jr.

113 ZLE/4/1, Newspaper cuttings book, report of Liverpool Corporation meeting.

114 *Ibid.*, cutting of 3 December 1901.

115 Mawson, *Civic Art*, pp. 346–8 (quotations p. 346).

116 UARM, SDC 9/3/16, Edward Hart to second viscount, 29 June 1925; second viscount to Edgar Sanders, 29 June, 2 July.

117 Lever, *Leverhulme*, pp. 131–2 (quotation p. 131).

118 For example, Bellini, *Rule Britannia*, p. 146; Phoebe Hesketh, *My Aunt Edith: The Story of a Preston Suffragette* (Preston: Lancashire County Books, 1992; 1st edn, 1966), p. 62.

119 Hearst Castle brochure (California State Parks, 2001).

120 Thomas H. Mawson, *The Art and Craft of Garden Making*, 5th edn (London: B. T. Batsford, 1926), p. 408 (quotation); Mawson, *Life and Work*, pp. 128–9, 179,

339–40; Michael Shippobottom, 'Unmatched for drama: Lord Leverhulme's Rivington estate', *Country Life* (13 September 1984), pp. 678–80; Lever, *Leverhulme*, pp. 297–8; BALS, B914.728 LEV, The Bungalow, Rivington: auction catalogue, 1925; Smith, *Leverhulme's Rivington*, pp. 18, 50–70.

121 Amanda Herries, *Japanese Gardens in Britain* (Princes Risborough: Shire Books, 2001), *passim* (quotation p. 5).

122 *The Times*, 11 July 1913, p. 11. See also *ibid.*, 9 July, p. 8; *Manchester Evening News*, 10 July 1913, quoted by Smith, *Leverhulme's Rivington*.

123 UARM, LBC 114, Lever to John Hope, 11 July 1913.

124 *The Times*, 18 July 1913, p. 14; 31 July, pp. 7–8; Hesketh, *My Aunt Edith*, chaps 5–6; *Guardian*, 3 March 2005 (obit. of Phoebe Hesketh); Lever, *Leverhulme*, pp. 176–7; Laura E. Nym Mayhall, *The Militant Suffrage Movement: Citizenship and Resistance in Britain 1860–1930* (Oxford: Oxford University Press, 2003), p. 107; Andrew Rosen, *'Rise up, Women!' The Militant Campaign of the Women's Social and Political Union 1903–1914* (London: Routledge, 1974), pp. 189–202. Hesketh's vivid account needs to be treated with caution. For example, she claims (pp. 67–8) that it was in December 1913 that Rigby attempted to bomb Liverpool Cotton Exchange and that she was arrested before she could detonate it, whereas the event took place on 5 July, the bomb did explode, and Rigby surrendered to the police on 9 July (two days after the Roynton Cottage fire).

125 BALS, B914.728 LEV, The Bungalow, Rivington: auction catalogue, 1925; Smith, *Leverhulme's Rivington*, pp. 102–13.

126 UARM, LBC 4271, Lever to Harold Odling, 10 June 1920; Lever to Myrtle Odling, 29 June 1921.

127 Entry of 5 October 1928 in John Vincent (ed.), *The Crawford Papers: the Journals of David Lindsay twenty-seventh Earl of Crawford and tenth Earl of Balcarres 1871–1940 during the years 1892 to 1940* (Manchester: Manchester University Press, 1984), p. 527.

128 Smith, *Leverhulme's Rivington*, pp. 119–22; George Birtill, 'The park that Lever built', *Lancashire Life* (July 1973), p. 31.

129 See Chorley Borough Council's publicity brochure, 'Rivington terraced garden project: re-awaken the oasis'.

130 Lever, *Leverhulme*, p. 277.

131 Morris, 'Introduction' to Morris (ed.), *Art and Business*, p. 172.

132 Alex Kidson, 'Lever and the collecting of eighteenth-century British paintings', in Morris (ed.), *Art and Business*, p. 201.

133 Lever, *Leverhulme*, p. 273.

134 Morris, 'Introduction' to Morris (ed.), *Art and Business*, p. 170–1 (quotation p. 171); Lever, *Leverhulme*, p. 279.

135 James Henry Duveen, *Collections and Recollections: A Century and a Half of Art Deals* (London: Jarrolds, 1935), pp. 114–17 (quotation pp. 116–17).

136 Christopher Beetles, 'Orrock, James (1829–1913)', *Oxford Dictionary of National Biography* (www.oxforddnb.com/view/article/39344, accessed 8 September 2005); Lucy Wood, 'Lever's objectives in collecting old furniture', in Morris (ed.), *Art and Business*, pp. 211, 216–17; Lever, *Leverhulme*, pp. 279–80.

137 Morris, 'Introduction' to Morris (ed.), *Art and Business*, p. 170.

138 Michael Shippobottom, 'The building of the Lady Lever Art Gallery', in Morris (ed.), *Art and Business*, p. 175.

139 BALS, BO69 Lev, Catalogue to *The Lady Lever Collection, Port Sunlight* (1977), p. 1. See also www.liverpoolmuseums.org.uk/ladylever/collections, accessed 8 September 2005.

140 *The Art Collections of the late Viscount Leverhulme: To be Sold by Order of the Executors* (New York: The Anderson Galleries, 1926).

141 Oliver Impey, 'Lever as a collector of Chinese porcelain', pp. 227–8, 232–5, 237, Wood, 'Lever's objectives in collecting old furniture', pp. 212–14, Xanthe Brooke, '"The art of the home, not of the palace": Lever and his collection of embroidery', pp. 257–60, in Morris (ed.), *Art and Business*; Lever, *Leverhulme*, pp. 123–4, 278–81, 284–7; Percy Macquoid, 'Furniture of the XVII and XVIII centuries: Sir W. H. Lever's collection', *Country Life*, 28 October 1911, pp. 635–9, and 4 November 1911, pp. 673–8; Adrian Levy and Cathy Scott-Clark, *The Stone of Heaven: Unearthing the Secret History of Imperial Green Jade* (Boston: Little Brown and Co., 2001), p. 149.

142 Ann Eatwell, 'Lever as a collector of Wedgwood and the fashion for collecting Wedgwood in the nineteenth century', in Morris (ed.), *Art and Business*, pp. 239, 246–8, 252.

143 Lady Lever Art Gallery Archive, Rathbone correspondence files, Lever to Rathbone, 21 February 1916, quoted by Eatwell, 'Lever as a collector of Wedgwood', p. 252.

144 Wood, 'Lever's objectives in collecting old furniture', pp. 219–20.

145 Lever, *Leverhulme*, p. 295.

146 www.liverpoolmuseums.org.uk/ladylever/collections, accessed 8 September 2005.

147 Shippobottom, 'The building of the Lady Lever Art Gallery', pp. 181–2, John M. Hamill, 'The Masonic collection at the Lady Lever Art Gallery', pp. 285–8, in Morris (ed.), *Art and Business*.

148 Peter Campbell, 'In Port Sunlight', *London Review of Books*, 27:2 (20 January 2005), p. 28.

149 Lady Lever Art Gallery Archives, letter of Lever, 13 November 1914, quoted by Shippobottom, 'The building of the Lady Lever Art Gallery'.

150 Lever, *Leverhulme*, pp. 287–8; Morris, 'Introduction' to Morris (ed.), *Art and Business*, p. 171.

151 See Werner Muensterberger, *Collecting: An Unruly Passion: Psychological Perspectives* (Princeton, NJ: Princeton University Press, 1994).

152 Thorstein Veblen, *The Theory of the Leisure Class* (Boston: Houghton Mifflin, 1973; 1st edn, 1899), pp. 70–1.

153 Brian Lewis, *The Middlemost and the Milltowns: Bourgeois Culture and Politics in Early Industrial England* (Palo Alto, CA: Stanford University Press, 2001), pp. 361–2; Cornelius P. Darcy, *The Encouragement of the Fine Arts in Lancashire 1760–1860* (Manchester: Chetham Society, 1976), pp. 143–58.

154 Philipp Blom, *To Have and to Hold: An Intimate History of Collectors and Collecting* (Woodstock, NY, and New York: Overlook Press, 2003), pp. 127–8; Shippobottom, 'The building of the Lady Lever Art Gallery', pp. 177, 181; Thompson,

Gentrification and the Enterprise Culture, pp. 117–21; Roger Munting, 'Tate, Sir Henry, first baronet (1819–1899)', *Oxford Dictionary of National Biography* (www.oxforddnb.com/view/article/26984, accessed 1 November 2005).

155 Lewis, *Middlemost and the Milltowns*, pp. 284–5.

156 UARM, LBC 809, Lever to John Cheshire, 23 April 1917.

157 E. H. Gombrich, 'Nature and art as needs of the mind: the philanthropic ideals of Lord Leverhulme (1851–1925)', in *Tributes: Interpreters of our Cultural Tradition* (Ithaca, NY: Cornell University Press, 1984), p. 72.

158 Andrew West, 'The history of the ethnography collections of W. H. Lever', pp. 273–83, Nora McMillan, 'Lever and his shell collection', pp. 297–9, and Angela P. Thomas, 'Lever as a collector of archaeology and as a sponsor of archaeological excavations', pp. 267–71, in Morris (ed.), *Art and Business*.

159 Quoted by Lever, *Leverhulme*, p. 288. See also *The Times*, 18 December 1922, p. 9.

160 BALS, ZLE/4/1, Newspaper cuttings book, cutting on the opening of Hall i' th' Wood.

161 Mike Storry and Peter Childs (eds), *British Cultural Identities*, 2nd edn (London: Routledge, 2002), pp. 24–5; Sotheby's auction results, Leverhulme Collection, Thornton Manor (http://search.sothebys.com/jsps/live/lot/LotResultsDetailList.jsp?sale_number=L01703&event_id=21661, accessed 16 August 2006). Thornton Manor is now used for lavish weddings and corporate entertaining. See www.thorntonmanor.co.uk.

2

Soft soap and soap operas

There's no damn difference between soaps

In *The Hucksters*, his 1946 potboiler about the American advertising industry, Frederic Wakeman created the character of 'Beautee Soap' magnate Evan Llewelyn Evans. At one point, Evans, known as the Old Man by his subordinates, lectures newly recruited ad man Victor Norman:

> I'll tell you a secret about the soap business, Mr. Norman. There's no damn difference between soaps. Except for perfume and color, soap is soap. Oh, maybe we got a few manufacturing tricks, but the public don't give a damn about that. But the difference, you see, is in the selling and advertising. We sell soap twice as fast as our nearest competitor because we outsell and out-advertise 'em.[1]

Old Man Evans's recipe for success was crudely, not to say offensively, straightforward: 'One, a good simple idea.' This might include a catchy tag line ('Beautee is as Beautee does') and/or association with glamour ('Eighty-one percent of Hollywood's loveliest Beauties use Beautee soap'). 'Two, repetition. And by repetition, by God, I mean until the public is so irritated with it, they'll buy your brand because they bloody well can't forget it. All you professional advertising men are scared to death of raping the public; I say the public likes it, if you got the know-how to make 'em relax and enjoy it.'[2]

Our Old Man, William Hesketh Lever, would have concurred at least in part. He always emphasized the power of advertising in bringing about his business success. 'People already in the soap business could have put rings round me on manufacturing soap,' he wrote in 1923, looking back to the early days of his career, 'but none of them understood how to sell soap, and therefore I concentrated on the selling side of soap, advertising, agencies, etc., and left others to look after the works.'[3] More pithily, the chairman of A. and F. Pears, Thomas J. Barratt – dubbed 'the father of Modern Advertising' by the press baron, Lord Northcliffe[4] – allegedly remarked, 'Any fool can make soap, it takes a clever man to sell it.'[5] Deciding on what does or does not work in advertising, however, is notoriously difficult. An oft-quoted line in business circles, usually attributed to Lever but sometimes to the Philadelphia department store magnate John Wanamaker, to F. W. Woolworth or to other contenders, reads, 'I know that at least half of my advertising money is being wasted. My problem is I do not know which half.'[6]

This was optimistic. Shelves of books and myriad courses in management and business schools provide analysis and promise answers. Advertising is supposed to be one of the glamour industries of our time, recruiting some of the brightest and best, paying them lucrative salaries. But still the overwhelming majority of ads shrivel and die, unsung and unmourned. By the end of the twentieth century, when global advertising expenditure had reached $300 billion a year – $16.5 billion in Britain alone – and every adult in the West was bombarded with well over 2,000 advertising images per day, finding a way through the visual and aural clutter was increasingly challenging.[7]

Yet, with few exceptions (such as Marks and Spencer and the Body Shop), market leaders of brands – in the United Kingdom: Unilever, Procter and Gamble, British Telecom, Mars, Dixon's stores, General Motors and Nestlé – spent appreciably more than their rivals and 'exercised' their brands regularly to keep them in the public eye. Simply reciting a short selection from the 900 brands in the Unilever food, home care and personal hygiene inventory more than hints at how the well advertised, ubiquitous brand is part of the average shopper's mental furniture: Becel, Ben and Jerry's, Bertolli, Bird's Eye, Blue Band, Brooke Bond, Comfort, Country Crock, Domestos, Dove, Findus, Flora, Hellmann's, Knorr, Lipton, Lux, Omo, Persil, PG Tips, Pond's, Pot Noodle, Signal, Slim Fast, Sunlight, Sunsilk, Surf, Wall's.[8] Advertising in some sense clearly works: corporations staffed with savvy people would not be so rash as to throw their corporate billions around if it did not. But, equally with few exceptions, people are not entirely gullible, they do not take claims in ads at face value, and even the best advertised product will not survive long if its quality is poor or if public interest has switched to a supposedly better alternative. Soap is a case in point. As liquid soaps, shower gels and bodywashes, with their greater convenience and superior moisturizing properties, caught the imagination in the 1990s, the humble toilet soap bar shrank to just 20 per cent of the market. Lever Brothers' sales of bars dropped by 75 per cent in five years, and they stopped manufacturing Lux and Lifebuoy at Port Sunlight in October 2001.[9]

According to marketing theory, consumer behaviour is determined in a different mix for each item by the 'Four Ps': pricing, promotion, product and placement (meaning sales networks, targeting and distribution). Goods produced by heavy industry generally serve limited markets and do not need mass promotion. Consumer durables, such as cars and washing machines, tend to rely more on technological and design innovations if they are to succeed. But cheap, everyday, household, packaged items depend much more thoroughly on marketing. This is not to downplay innovation, even here. Looking back, Bryant and May, for example, leapfrogged ahead of the competition in the 1870s when they introduced the safety match; W. D. and H. O. Wills's adoption of the Bonsack rolling machine in 1888 allowed them to launch Wild Woodbine and to dominate the market for cheap, packeted cigarettes for thirty years, with no need for heavy promotion; and the discovery of hydrogenation allowed the Dutch firms to make strides in the margarine industry. In soap, Lever Brothers' Sunlight and Procter and Gamble's Ivory established the vegetable-soap standard that all other manufacturers felt obliged to follow. P and G were to do it again with the introduction in 1946 of Tide, the first synthetic detergent, gaining two years on the competition, who then came up with comparable products – Colgate-Palmolive's Fab and Lever Brothers' Surf.[10]

Most of the time, however, there is very little to differentiate products. All soaps wash the body and all detergents clean clothes. In these circumstances, marketing is critical. But teasing apart all the variable factors – quality, cost, the competition, packaging, distribution – and assigning a value to the advertising (with its own sub-category variables of timing, audience targeting, research and planning) defeats all but the most optimistic.[11] One recent celebration of the history of Procter and Gamble, rather overconfidently drawing out lessons for successful brand management, claims that the company recognized at an early stage that building brands was not primarily a marketing activity. Each stage of the process – research and development, product innovation and improvement, market research, purchasing, manufacturing, financing, marketing, sales, human resources, public relations – had to pull together to produce a better brand that customers would value.[12] A noted commentator on marketing really only restated Lever's (or Wanamaker's, or Woolworth's) point when he wrote, 'only the very brave or the very ignorant ... can say exactly what advertising does in the marketplace.'[13]

Packaged proprietary products

Lever and his company were part of a merchandising revolution during the late nineteenth century. For the first time the majority of the population could aspire to own more than mere necessities. Much of the marketing of commodities was aimed at middle-class consumers, an increasing number of whom could afford to dress fashionably and furnish the home more fancily. In the lower ranks, at the turn of the century around 30 per cent of the population still remained too poor to be a part of a 'consumer revolution';[14] but skilled workers and those in steady jobs did have a little disposable income to spend on such things as more efficient soaps, starches and polishes; teas, cocoas and chocolates; jams, biscuits and syrups; sauces, potted meats and pickles: all increasingly bottled, canned or packeted and branded.[15]

As one British advertising writer summed it up in 1927:

Tea, cocoa, and oatmeal … are no longer shovelled out of dusty bins, weighed in insanitary scales, poured into bags blown open by the breath of the shopkeeper, the last crumbs being swept in with scrupulous honesty, if doubtful cleanliness, from off a littered counter: they are packaged in hygienic, air-tight containers, as fresh and clean and wholesome as when they left the factory.

'The American of [the] day before yesterday asked for a pound of crackers,' wrote two American counterparts a year later. 'Today his grandson demands a box of Uneeda. Grandmother took the familiar stone jug to the grocery and had the grocer fill it up with vinegar. Granddaughter consults her shopping lists and asks for a quart bottle of Heinz's vinegar.'[16]

Branding was scarcely new. Elite, quality articles like Stradivarius violins and Chippendale furniture were brands in all but name, and during the first so-called 'consumer revolution' of the eighteenth century the concept expanded as some resourceful London entrepreneurs marketed with proprietary trade names commonplace goods such as razor strops and candlesticks. Josiah Wedgwood went further with the distinctive earthenware pottery manufactured in his Etruria factory. He turned himself into a household name across the country and abroad, first by stamping his name into the pottery clay, and then through aggressive marketing, notably the distribution of catalogues and the deployment of platoons of travelling salesmen.[17]

But branding and advertising of everyday products accelerated with innovations in packaging. One such was the invention of metal containers for canning. In the 1790s Nicolas Appert, a French chef and confectioner, pioneered the heat-processing method of food preservation, selling his soups, vegetables and meats in glass jars sealed with pitch. In 1810 a London broker, Peter Durand, patented a similar technique and quickly sold it to an engineer, Bryan Donkin. Donkin, with his partners John Gamble and John Hall of the Dartford Iron Works, turned from glass to tin, inaugurating the world's first food canning business.[18] A series of other packaging experiments followed: the bottling and labelling of patent medicines; John Horniman first selling his tea in packets rather than loose in 1826; Thomas Beecham putting his pills in boxes in 1848 rather than wrapping them in paper; John Player pre-packing his blends of tobacco in his Nottingham shop, rather than measuring them out from large jars and selling them in small screws of paper. Pre-packaging gave space and opportunity for labelling and branding. The Wills family of Bristol first gave brand names to two of their tobaccos, Best Bird's Eye and Bishop Blaze, in 1847, helping begin a shift away from the specialist retail tobacconist. In 1877, in the same year he bought a tobacco factory, John Player registered his first brand name – Gold Leaf – and his first trade mark – Nottingham Castle – and printed them on the packets. The company adopted the familiar picture of a bearded sailor framed by a lifebelt alongside the slogan 'Player's please' in 1882 to market Player's Navy Cut. Both John Player and the Willses added collectible coloured cards to their packets, which served as stiffeners and fostered brand loyalty.[19]

In the United States the building of the transcontinental railroads after the end of the Civil War in 1865 liberated the huge potential of a national market from coast to coast, connecting old cities and new frontier towns, opening up the prairies for the development of corn and cattle. Packaging solved the problem of how to convey perishable products vast distances without them spoiling; branding ensured recognition for products manufactured in a distant city and, it was hoped, would secure repeat purchases from satisfied customers. As in Britain, patent medicines were early out of the starting gate and tobacco followed around mid-century: bales were 'branded' by burning the maker's name into wooden packages with a hot iron.

And then the floodgates opened. For example, the breakfast cereal industry figured out how to print, fold and fill cardboard boxes mechanically in the late 1870s; Quaker Oats (with their trademark icon of a Quaker man) and John and William Kellogg in Battle Creek, Michigan, took advantage. Henry J. Heinz, from selling bottled horseradish from a wheelbarrow in Pittsburgh in the late 1860s, had developed many more than his fabled '57 Varieties' of condiments and preserved foods by the end of the century. Joseph Campbell canned his vegetables, condiments and soups, and the Anheuser-Busch brewery in St Louis began to distribute widely its bottled, pasteurized beers, of which Budweiser became the most famous. John S. Pemberton, an Atlanta pharmacist, in 1886 started selling in soda fountains a concoction of syrup, carbonated water, coca leaves and cola nuts. An Atlanta businessman, Asa Candler, bought the Coca-cola name and formula two years later and, in the 1890s, began bottling it.[20]

In both Britain and America the soap men were among the earliest and most profligate branders and advertisers. The consumption of soap in Britain increased from about 3.5 lb a head per annum to 17 lb during the course of the nineteenth century and the population nearly tripled. The potential for innovative soap sellers was huge. Soap itself became easier to make and more appealing to use, contributing to its greater popularity. Soapboilers had typically blended oils or fats – most usually tallow (rendered beef fat) and cooking grease – with water and lye (an alkali obtained by filtering water through wood ashes), resulting in a chemical change known as saponification. Scents and perfumes could be added as optional extras. Two French chemists revolutionized soap making in the early nineteenth century. One, Nicholas Leblanc, discovered that a suitable alkali (sodium carbonate – caustic soda or soda ash) could be made from common salt, greatly increasing the supply. The other, Michel Eugène Chevreul, laid the basis for the scientific analysis of fats and soaps with his investigations into the chemical nature of fats, glycerine and fatty acids.

At the Great Exhibition of 1851, the year of Lever's birth, 103 soap manufacturers displayed their wares, including a wide variety of soaps with names like honey, mottled, Castile, Windsor, potash or white curd. Some of the big names in the field – A. and F. Pears and John Knight of London, Joseph Crosfield of Warrington and R. S. Hudson of West Bromwich – were already well established; others, such as Joseph Watson and Sons of Leeds or William Gossage and Sons of Widnes, were just getting started. They all had their local niches and did not advertise aggressively or impinge much on neighbours' markets. Aside from a limited commerce in tablet toilet soap, they mainly sold long bars to grocers, who sliced them up for customers by the pound, and the soaps tended to be retailed by variety rather than as proprietary articles. Lever was going to change all that.[21]

At the time he decided to specialize in soap selling in 1884, Lever's leading sales for a decade had been of a soap called 'Lever's Pure Honey Soap'. Now he thought he needed something different. He consulted W. P. Thompson, a Liverpool trade mark and patent agent, who suggested half a dozen alternatives, among which 'Sunlight' stood out (though, ironically, later in life he remarked that 'The ideal trade mark for advertising is one of three letters such as "Lux"'[22]). Lever's son explained the rationale for the adoption of the brand name:

> Any other wholesale grocer could market a soap and call it 'Pure Honey', 'Honey' being only a fanciful name and one commonly applied to a type of soap the colour of which was suggestive of honey. Soaps in those days were supplied by manufacturers in bars and stamped with the name of the grocer who sold it, and possibly with the name of the maker as well, but Lever's idea was to establish a soap which would be of unrivalled quality, and which under a registered name could be advertised and sold universally.... It had to be a name easy to remember, easy to pronounce, and one which could be upheld in a court of law if an imitator came along, and, in order to overcome the obstacles which the Trade-marks Act very properly erected, it had not to be descriptive of the article, or refer to quality, or be geographical.[23]

'Sunlight' early on passed the test. Twice in 1886 Lever sought the legal protection offered by the Trade Marks Registration Act of 1875 and successfully sued imitators who had tried to pass off their own products as Sunlight.[24]

Joseph Watson and Sons of Leeds made a vegetable soap for him that he labelled 'Sunlight Self-washer' because of its easy lather. But, because of difficulties in completely saponifying vegetable oils, this class of soaps sweated drops of unpleasant-smelling, rancid oil on the surface. Most customers opted for the thirty-odd other Sunlight brands instead, like Sunlight XXX, Sunlight XX, Sunlight Mottled and Sunlight Brown. Self-washer was withdrawn until, as Lever related, a woman with a broad Lancashire accent said to him, 'I mun ha' some more of yon stinking soap.' He thought that if practical housewives preferred it because of its superior washing properties, in spite of its rancidity (which was only on the outer skin, and soon disappeared with use), then it might be a winner.[25]

When he began manufacturing for himself in the Warrington soap works he and his chemists set to work on overcoming the rancidity, and succeeded thanks to a combination of the right blend of ingredients – 41.9 per cent copra oil or palm kernel oil, 24.8 per cent tallow, 23.8 per cent cotton oil, 9.5 per cent resin, plus a mixture of many perfumes, including oil of rosemary – and packaging in parchment.[26] 'I was the first to advertise extensively a tablet soap although makers had produced tablet soaps prior to my commencement in the soap business in 1884, but they had not pushed them and they were little known,' Lever later wrote. 'Then their tablets were wrapped with ordinary common paper and the sweating of the soap destroyed the paper. I adopted vegetable parchment and a carton. The result was I lifted Sunlight Soap into a class by itself where it has remained ever since.' Quite apart from helping resolve the practical problems of sweating soaps, the cartons made very sound commercial sense. He had to absorb their cost himself in the beginning, so that his soap would be competitive in the shops; but once he had established brand loyalty, he could ignore competitors' attempts to undercut him.[27]

It was his background as a grocer, he claimed, that gave him crucial insights here. Manufacturers liked to market in bulk; individual packaging cost them money. All they needed to do was persuade the wholesale grocer to buy their product on a regular basis, the wholesaler could sell to the retailer, and the retailer could scoop out or measure a pound of this or dish out a dozen of that to the customer from barrels, crates or boxes – or, indeed, cut off a bar of soap from a long block in the manner of slicing cheese or ham. The customer had no idea whether she was being served goods from X or Y factory and, the theory went, did not care.

For the grocer, however, a pre-measured small packet saved him trouble. In the long term it devalued his skills, because stacking shelves was less challenging than learning how to weigh, to bag, to store in optimum conditions, to blend tea and to cure ham, but that was not taken into consideration. Lever appreciated that the packet held advantages for the manufacturer too, since it allowed him to advertise and the customer to see what she was buying. She could be assured of a fixed measure and a stable quality, and then choose to select Sunlight or some other brand on a regular basis. Predictable quality was significant, since one of the greatest health drives of the nineteenth century was against adulterated and diluted food and drink. As the package now had the manufacturer's name on it, he had a vested interest not only in exhorting consumers to avoid imitations but also in ensuring adequate standards to uphold his reputation.[28]

Lever always emphasized this as a key factor in his success. Soap was cheap compared with the cost of labour, he reasoned, so efforts to cheapen it still further with filler ingredients like silicate of soda were unnecessary. Competitors using such adulterants might undercut him on price by a penny a pound, but as a washerwoman's wages amounted to 3s 6d a day, and she would at most use 2 lb of soap a day, paying a slightly higher price for a superior and easier-to-use product did not significantly increase the overall cost.[29] 'The name Lever on Soap is a Guarantee of Purity and Excellence' was a constantly reiterated theme in his advertising. If anyone could prove him wrong, he offered his famous '£1,000 GUARANTEE OF PURITY ON EVERY BAR'.[30] He never had to pay up.

Many of Lever's best ideas came from the United States, which he called 'the El Dorado of commercial prosperity'.[31] 'I am certain that if there is any body of people who understand the art of salesmanship and the advertising of domestic articles,' he wrote, 'it is the Americans.'[32] He filled his publication *The Lancashire Grocer*, which he started in 1885 as a house organ for the Lever and Co. grocery business, with articles reprinted from American journals.[33] He copied the notion of wrapping in vegetable parchment from the Americans. The paternity of the carton is unclear. It may have been his or he may have borrowed it in the general transatlantic cross-fertilization of ideas. What seems certain is that Lever was the first to introduce both practices to Britain, and where he led others were obliged to follow.[34]

In America, William Procter and James Gamble began manufacturing and selling soap and candles in Cincinnati in 1837, and they took out their first newspaper ads to distributors a year later. The Civil War enormously boosted their sales, both because they supplied the Union army with candles and also allegedly because women running the household while their men were away had less time to manufacture their own soap from left-over fats and ashes. But their big breakthrough, like Lever's, came with a single soap, Ivory, and like Lever's 'stinking soap', there is a creation story drawing on consumer insight. The company first perfected Ivory, a vegetable soap like Sunlight, in 1878, and trademarked its name the year after. One day, the story goes, a worker had accidentally mixed in too much air. After the batch was sold, orders came pouring in for more of the 'floating soap', which was so much easier to find in the washing tub. A commissioned chemist certified that Ivory contained only 0.56 per cent impurities, which sounded impressive enough for people used to contaminated and adulterated foodstuffs and household products for P and G to use it as their most famous slogan in all their Ivory ads: '99 and 44/100 percent pure – it floats.'[35]

We live in an age of advertisement

After the production, branding and packaging came the advertising. Under Harley T. Procter, P and G combined product research and a barrage of marketing and advertising techniques, including posters, ads on streetcars, the distribution of samples and the inducement of premiums. But first and foremost came ads in print. The first Ivory advert appeared in a religious weekly, *The Independent*, in 1882, and by the 1890s the company was taking full-page ads in the new national magazines such as *Good Housekeeping, Harper's Monthly* and *Ladies' Home Journal*.[36] Images of mothers, children, families and home predominated.

'We live in an age of advertisement,' said Lord Randolph Churchill back in Britain, 'the age of Holloway's Pills, of Colman's Mustard, and of Horniman's pure tea.'[37] As manufacturers sought to exploit expanding national markets and as advertising agencies (modelled on American lines) first put in an appearance, familiar advertising images and slogans came to plaster billboards, tramcars, railway stations and along railway tracks. 'Advertisements are turning England into a sordid and disorderly spectacle from sea to sea,' complained some letter writers to *The Times* in 1892. 'Fields and hillsides are being covered with unwonted crops of hoardings ... Night succeeds day only to be utilized for the electrical announcement that "Messrs. So-and-so's soap is the best".'[38]

The government had helped remove artificial blockages by abolishing stamp duties on newspapers in 1855 and duties on paper in 1861.[39] Lever, addressing W. E. Gladstone at the opening of the Gladstone Hall in Port Sunlight in 1891, acknowledged his debt:

> It was in April 1853 that you removed the duty on soap, and thereby made the manufacture on a large and scientific scale possible. It was in 1861 that you removed the duty from paper, and so gave to the country its greatest boon, a free and cheap Press. With a duty on paper, a cheap Press was impossible, and therefore also a large circulation. Without a large circulation it would be useless to advertise, and whilst at present this art is little understood, and often looked at askance as something that is undignified and appertaining to the charlatan, the Press, next to duty-free paper, owes most to the advertisers, and the day is coming when advertising will take its place as a useful and beneficial art, and when it will be recognized that it is a necessity, in continuous, persistent and successful advertising, that the quality of the articles advertised be irreproachable.[40]

In a symbiotic relationship, advertising aided and kept pace with the expansion in number and girth of newspapers and magazines, and national newspapers in turn – devoting the bulk of their space to adverts – were indispensable for the selling of increasingly branded, national products. Technological progress in the 1870s in reproduction and colour printing, especially the introduction of offset lithography, precipitated the greater use not only of colourful packaging and displays in shops but also of pictorial ads in magazines in the 1880s, and enabled the age of the colour poster to begin and then, in the 1890s, to blossom.[41]

The soap men's extensive use of contemporary paintings in their advertising is a case in point. As the owner rather than the painter generally held the power to reproduce paintings, it was quite easy for sentimental Victorian scenes of women and children to be adapted to promote products, often with a bar of soap or a slogan slipped in. Most notoriously, Thomas Barratt used Sir John Everett Millais's *A Child's World*, retitled *Bubbles* and reproduced at considerable expense in an elaborate chromolithograph with a printed gilt frame, to promote Pears' soap in 1888. Lever followed suit with W. P. Frith's *New Frock* to sell Sunlight, much to the artist's chagrin. In both cases the soap makers subverted the intended message: the bubble as a symbol of transience is self-explanatory, and against the entry in the 1889 Royal Academy exhibition catalogue for the *New Frock* Frith had written a phrase from Ecclesiastes, 'Vanitas vanitatum, omnia vanitas.' The soap makers, on the other hand, refocused attention on the material here and now, Lever empathizing with the girl's delight in keeping herself and her frock 'So clean'.[42] The Marxist intellectual Georg Lukács was later to suggest that the commodity transgresses the boundary between culture and commerce, money and art. The soap posters exemplified this in spectacular fashion, taking art from the high cultural realm and reproducing it as a form of commodity mass spectacle.[43] According to Barratt, his poster 'dissipated the delusion that art was lowering itself by an alliance with commerce'.[44] Post-war American pop artists were to repay the compliment by representing the humble commodity as art; Andy Warhol's depiction of Campbell's soup cans is the iconic example.

Medicine, chocolate and soap manufacturers were among the foremost advertisers. Thomas Holloway and Thomas Beecham, followed by his son Joseph, dominated the market for pills and potions. Most of these patent medicines were of doubtful efficacy and teetered on the edge of quackery – indeed, the hyperbolic or fraudulent claims of pill pushers long undermined advertisers' attempts to achieve respectability – but a public hungry for good health nevertheless ensured an insatiable appetite for repeated doses and fixes of 'Carter's Little Liver Pills', 'William Pink's Pills for Pale People' or 'Beecham's Pills, worth a guinea a box'.[45] Holloway was reportedly spending £40,000 a year on ads as early as the 1860s, the Beechams £110,000 by 1890. As one example of Thomas Beecham's ingenuity in filling up and commercializing vacant space, he supplied boatmen at seaside resorts with free sails plastered with his slogans – 'What are the wild waves saying (Try Beecham's pills)' – and slapped ads on bathing machines and boat hulls.[46]

In the world of chocolate, Cadbury's introduced its Cocoa Essence in 1866, and succeeded through a combination of product innovation (it was the first British firm to employ the Van Houten press, imported from the Netherlands, to extract excess and unpalatable oils from the cocoa bean, resulting in a finer, less adulterated, 'absolutely pure' product) and effective branding, packaging and advertising. With the addition of Cadbury's Dairy Milk in 1905 and Bournville Cocoa in 1906, the firm overtook Fry's as Britain's biggest cocoa and chocolate manufacturer.[47] The third of the three big chocolate manufacturers, Rowntree, did not advertise extensively until well into the 1890s. This was mainly because Joseph Rowntree's Quaker principles treated advertising with great suspicion (a legacy of the association with the dubious claims of the patent medicine merchants) and saw it as a rather devious diversion from principles of fair and honest dealing. The Quaker Cadburys did not allow any such scruples to hold them back.

The result was that the gap between Rowntree's and their competitors continued to widen. Therefore they decided to reverse policy and, after it had been on the market for a dozen years, to advertise Elect Cocoa. One sales technique was to mount a 9 ft tin on the back of one of the new-fangled motor cars in 1897 and tour the north of England for three months, attracting much attention. Another was to advertise on a barge during the 1897 Oxford and Cambridge boat race. A third, on the suggestion of S. H. Benson, one of the most innovative advertising agents of the period, entailed placing a coupon in the *Daily Telegraph* that could be exchanged for a penny stamp and a sample of Elect; 138,000 took up the offer. A fourth ruse, again thanks to Benson, was to advertise Elect on London buses, and then to entice female readers of the *Daily Mail* to ride on one of these buses to receive a free tin; 200,000 apparently did so.[48]

The soapboilers loved similar gimmicks. In 1881 Hudson's Soap organized a stagecoach drive using 100 horses, covering the distance from London to York in twelve hours. For Queen Victoria's Diamond Jubilee in 1897 Hudson's published a little book on the kings and queens of England, illustrating each reign with a portrait and a couple of sentences of notable events. The citation next to Victoria read, 'During this reign Hudson's soap was invented.'[49] The flamboyant pioneer for Lever Brothers in Switzerland, F. H. Lavanchy-Clarke, as a prelude to opening an office in Lausanne, organized a washing competition – 'La Fête des blanchisseuses' – on Lake Geneva, Easter Monday 1889. He chartered a couple of steamers to bring the washerwomen from towns around the lake, they washed with Sunlight in front of large crowds, and he gave them a banquet afterwards.[50] The soap men also experimented with prize schemes. From 1887 Lever Brothers' customers received a prize in exchange for a certain number of Sunlight Soap wrappers. By 1897 sales did not appear to justify the outlay, so Lever attempted to wean the public off the schemes by offering 'little better than rubbish': cheap, imitation-leather paper purses and the like. Rivals noticed and stepped up their own prize schemes, and Lever Brothers suffered some loss of custom. In consequence from 1903 they began a renewed wrapper scheme, offering their own soaps in return – with satisfactory results.[51]

Retailers, too, tried gimmicks. Thomas Lipton was one of a number of British entrepreneurs who in the same period established stores and brands that were to become household names. From very modest beginnings in Glasgow, Lipton in 1871 at the age of twenty-one opened his first provision shop, on Stobcross Street, and built a chain of grocery stores across the country. Like Lever, he bought direct from Ireland, cutting out the expense of wholesalers, but much of his expansion can be credited to effective advertising, especially attractive window dressing and shop displays, attentive staff and publicity stunts to keep his name fresh in the public mind. These included purchasing the largest pigs in Glasgow market, stencilling their sides announcing that they were shortly to be slaughtered, sliced and jointed for purchase in a Lipton's store, and parading them through the streets; or, later, acquiring elephants to drag huge cheeses to the opening of a new shop, where the cheeses would be cut, spilling out gold coins for distribution to onlookers; or having processions of Indians and Ceylonese to provide an exotically oriental touch in the marketing of Lipton's teas; or paying thin men to walk around with placards that read 'Going to Lipton's', and fat men 'Coming from Lipton's'.[52]

One method beloved of advertisers and Jesuits alike was to capture the children. In the 1890s purchasers of Sunlight soap received free paper dolls with interchangeable outfits. On other occasions Sunlight and Price's Toilet Soap offered stand-up cardboard sailing ships or pleasure boats, Owbridge's Cough Mixture came up with a cardboard sailor boy dancing on a string, and Beecham's Pills provided a kazoo (comb and paper).[53]

William Woodruff's *The Road to Nab End: A Lancashire Childhood*, his evocative account of growing up in the slums of Blackburn in the early 1920s, contains a vivid description of Mr Manners's classroom at St Philip's School. The walls were sparingly adorned with a stained print of Boadicea, a torn map of the world (the empire prominent in red) and, next to young Billy's seat, a large Lever Brothers' Lifebuoy Soap poster, which depicted a bar of lathered soap, an accusing finger pointing at him, and the slogan 'WHERE THERE'S DIRT, THERE'S DANGER!' Billy worried why Mr Manners seemed to have singled him out in this way, given that he was no dirtier than the rest of the class, but the poster did not encourage him to wash more frequently: 'Washing in such a cold, wet climate didn't come easy with us. I never knew anyone who believed that cleanliness was next to godliness.'

Nevertheless, the family used sufficient quantities of Lifebuoy at home to accumulate the necessary coupons for his first book, a one-volume encyclopædia called *The Wonderland of Knowledge*. This became Billy's most treasured possession as he devoured 'Great Names in English Literature', 'Marvels of Invention' and 'The Romance of Exploration'. The didactic message, spelled out on the title page, was pure Smiles and pure Lever: 'You will learn by the past deeds of Men and Nations what good things to do and what bad things not to do. You will be inspired by the nobility and perseverance of those who rose from humble birth to sway by Thought or Deed the destiny of Man. And what they did, you too may do.'[54]

Targeting and enticing the young, in the hope of manipulating parents at one remove and ensuring a lifetime of brand loyalty, is a staple of the consumer world, as any parent falling victim to Ronald McDonald and the Happy Meal can attest. Lever Brothers were acknowledged experts in the craft and tricks of advertising. Here the stick (DANGER!) there the carrot (coupons!) to lure prospective customers. The opportunity to impart a pull-yourself-up-by-your-own-bootstraps life lesson (Even humble *you* can become great, if you put your shoulder to the wheel!) was an added bonus.

Lever and Barratt were the chief advertisers among the soap makers. Lever shelled out £2 million in his first two decades of making soap, while Barratt was spending £100,000 a year on advertising by the late 1880s.[55] A. and F. Pears, thanks to Barratt, who married into the Pears family and gained control of the firm in 1877, are generally credited with introducing the most brilliant advertising of the late nineteenth century in Britain, using humour and catch phrases ('Good morning! Have you used Pears this morning?') to capture the attention.[56] One advertisement featured an illustration, borrowed from *Punch*, of a dirty tramp writing a letter: 'Two years ago I used your soap, since when I have used no other.'[57] Another, the celebrated 'What! No soap?' advertisement, depicting a tearful bear in a shop lamenting the lack of Pears', turned to memorable advantage a nonsense memory test:

> So she went into the garden to cut a cabbage-leaf, to make an apple-pie; and at the same time a great she-bear, coming up the street, pops its head into the shop. "WHAT! NO SOAP?" So he died, and she very imprudently married the barber; and there were present the Picninnies, and the Joblilies, and the Garcelies, and the Grand Panjandrum himself, with the little round button at top; and they all fell to playing the game of catch as catch can, till the gunpowder ran out at the heels of their boots.[58]

Lever lamented on occasion that it was a laborious business introducing a new product. 'We are more conservative people after all perhaps than the Chinese who I understand prefer to use whatever their grandfathers used rather than the latest production of ever advancing science,' he wrote in 1905.[59] But, he believed, once customers had latched on to a product they were loath to change. That is why he spent so much effort in his early years establishing brand loyalty for his Sunlight Self-washer household or laundry soap. He later recalled that travelling salesmen and customers constantly urged him to diversify, but he followed his own intuition and, with inconsequential exceptions, kept his manufacturing focus narrow and poured his marketing resources into this brand for eight years. Only in 1894 did he bring out a second major brand, Lifebuoy. The third brand, 'Sunlight Flakes', came out in 1899 and was renamed 'Lux' a year later. These soapflakes, 'milled wonderfully fine', also took off thanks to the quality and newness of the product and heavy advertising. Other soap men were not only forced to imitate his advertising methods and appeal to a national market but also to copy his product innovation. Crosfield's, for example, brought out Eureka to rival Lifebuoy, Feather Flakes to match Lux and Glitto to rival Vim.[60]

Lever's attempts to shoulder in on the crowded toilet soap market with Plantol, made entirely from vegetable oils, with Swan (toilet) soap (its slogans 'White floating' and 'A purer soap is beyond the art of soapmaking' clearly modelled on Ivory),[61] and with Refined Toilet Monkey Brand were less successful, however, in spite of his advertising talents. Charles Wilson notes that he succeeded with originality but not with imitative products, because even his advertising skills failed to make much impact on a market overcrowded with established competitors.[62] Refined Toilet Monkey Brand and Vim were two spin-offs in 1904 from Monkey Brand, a scouring soap acquired in 1899 with the purchase of Benjamin Brooke, a Philadelphia-based soap firm.

The head of Benjamin Brooke, Sydney Gross, became a director of Lever Brothers and one of the most important guiding minds in the subsequent development of the company's advertising until his retirement in 1910. According to Lever's son, Gross was expert at picking the right artists for advertisements that were 'pithy, bright and original, and in which humour could be utilized with greater certainty of success than is the case to-day'. Lever said of his good friends Gross and Barrett that they 'have done more between them for the cause of artistic advertising than any other men in the world'.[63] The marketing of Monkey Brand is a fine example of Gross's work and of counter-intuitive advertising. The celebrated depiction of a dressed-up simian under the slogan 'Won't wash clothes' would seem, at first blush, to be the result of a very bad brainstorming session in the advertising department. But it worked. The slogan held the clear implication that it washed everything else – metals, tiles, enamel, glass, marble, paint – and it conveniently distanced the product from Sunlight, which did wash clothes.[64] This is how Lever explained the success of the anthropomorphic ape:

> It was the persistent hammering away at a clean gentlemanly attractive monkey that made Monkey Brand a success. The idea of a monkey in any other hands than those of Mr. Gross would have had exactly the opposite effect. It would have created, as it does when we see it at the Zoo or Menageries, a feeling of repulsion, but the monkey was always made gentlemanly and attractive so that it became a pet.[65]

While Lever increasingly relied on such men because he could not hope to manage all the details himself, he never ceased to have overall oversight of advertising. Throughout his career, as we have seen, Lever micro-managed on a phenomenal scale, firing off an avalanche of observations, instructions and queries to his subordinates, not to mention chunks of soap, shaving cream, shaving sticks, packaging and the like, to show their effectiveness or how well they looked after use. In 1923, for example, he sent a piece of Lifebuoy that he had picked up in the bathroom at The Bungalow to his Special Committee, to demonstrate that the soap had divided so 'clumsily' as to be unsightly. This, he added, was the same with each bar of Lifebuoy that he used in the bath in each of his houses. Quite what he expected his top executives to do with this information – or what they thought of receiving used personal hygiene fragments through the mail – is not recorded.[66]

Frequently he would send examples of advertisements. The page of ads from the *Bolton Evening News* that he sent to one of his staff in 1906 illustrates the importance he placed on position: 'if we had been placed in the top left hand corner instead of in the middle of the right hand half of the page we should have had more prominence'. A rival, Fels Naptha, here and elsewhere always managed to buy a splendid position, 'and I expect it is only by clamour and incessant beating of the drum that they obtain it'.[67] Curiously, by 1915 he had changed his mind about the optimum location. Why, he wrote, do competitors' ads (including once again Fels Naptha) but not Lever Brothers' own appear in the top right-hand corner of the right-hand page of newspapers? 'Can we not specify this position for our advertisements? It is obviously the best as in opening the paper this corner must come more into view than either the corresponding corner of the left hand page or any other position on the page.'[68]

After a visit to the Apollo Theatre in London in 1916, he wrote to his personal assistant that Boot's the Chemist were advertising White Heather in theatre programmes. The clear implication was that Lever Brothers should follow suit.[69] Another thought came to him in 1920 when taking the train to Brighton. From his early days in the business he had advertised widely at railway stations, giving much thought to such intricacies as whether Sunlight ads would be most effective to the right or the left of a booking office.[70] But on this occasion it was the trains themselves that drew his attention. He noted that the third-class railway carriage doors were sporting on the inside advertisements for Wright's Coal Tar Soap, 'and the effect was very strong and startling when going down the platform at Victoria Station with every railway carriage door open'. This was a new phenomenon and the most effective railway advertising he had seen; inevitably, 'I think Lever Brothers ought to get quickly on to it, and see if other Railway Companies are prepared to let their carriage doors' – but only, of course, at the right price.[71]

Value for money was important, but so was maintaining prime site visibility. A case in point in 1920 was Pears' soap, simultaneously losing sales and sites ('which were the lifework of the late Mr. Barratt to acquire'). It appears that Pears had lost the back page of the telephone directory because the cost had become too expensive. This was no good: 'Pears cannot drop out of back pages.' Lever noted the irony that one of the Lever Brothers family, Erasmic soap (part of the recently acquired Crosfield's empire), had moved on to the back page in its place. Allocating kudos to Erasmic but a black mark for Pears, he demanded an explanation as to why this had happened.[72]

Lever was always quick to seize a new opportunity but would not advertise just anywhere. The left-wing *Daily Herald* was an example. It repeatedly tried to encourage Lever Brothers to take out ads, but Lever refused, mingling political prejudice with seller's *nous*.

> [T]hey have openly advocated a policy which is distasteful to the vast majority of people in this country and I am convinced that for an advertiser of household goods to be advertising in a Paper which advocates Bolshevism, Communism, Socialism and all the other anti-civilisationisms, would act rather as a trade repellent than a trade getter [he wrote]. We must understand, of course, that advertising is, after all, what we call 'silent sellers' and just as a Firm is known by the quality of its representatives, so a Firm would be known by the quality of the medium in which it advertises.[73]

A firm would also be known by the depictions on its ads. Take nudes, for example. Scantily clad women in diaphanous clothing, usually safely classical or otherwise historical or 'exotic', bathing or on the point of disrobing, were commonplace in Victorian ads, belying the stereotype of Victorian prudery.[74] But only children were portrayed completely naked. T. J. Barratt had the habit of producing a Christmas *Pears' Annual* featuring a chastely nude young girl, the better to promote pink-skinned, glowing cleanliness, but 'there were generally protests from the Clergy in consequence'. In objecting to a suggested resurrection of the child nude in 1922, Lever wrote:

> There was nothing in the protests in my opinion, but still, we are not pioneers on a question of ethics and if nude figures offend certain people then I think they are not a subject for *Pears' Annual*. That is not my view. We have nothing to do with the maudlin prudishness of the objectors. We want to sell an Annual that is pleasing to the biggest number of people and in addition can sell the biggest amount of Pears' Soap.[75]

Throughout his career Lever continued to follow trends in American advertising. In 1921 he quoted with approval from one American magazine the words of the advertising manager of David Adler and Sons of Milwaukee: 'Truth in advertising is not only an asset but brings business. Untruth in advertising is not only a liability but it does not bring business in any lasting form.' This was the sort of pious, almost platitudinous wisdom that often appealed to him, and that he could use for its practical, moralistic, didactic message. 'I have rarely read anything so true of advertising,' he wrote. 'It might be shortened to a motto in the advertising dept., that truth in advertising is an asset; falsehood in advertising is a liability.'[76]

A magazine advertisement from 1889 featured Britannia introducing the Port Sunlight works as 'The Greatest Show on Earth' to the American showman P. T. Barnum.[77] The manufacturing process, understandably, did not feature in ads. Just as the domestic ads discussed below focusing on mothers, babies and tranquillity by the hearth hid the work involved in scrubbing clothes, even with Sunlight Self-washer, so this advert recast the industrial mashing together of huge quantities of oils, tallow and resin, and the tedium for the workers of each aspect of the creation of the cartoned final product, as a show or entertainment, a wonderful spectacle of industrial and technological progress. Flagrantly misleading sanitization extended to the collecting of raw materials. Speaking about a pamphlet on Plantol, Sydney Gross suggested that 'A pamphlet on Toilet Soap needs picturesque handling, something about the tropic climates in which the materials are produced, the care that is exercised in refining the oils, the flowers that are picked by the women of the South on fields full of colour and beauty'.[78] A vision of paradise would serve to disguise the reality of gruelling toil.

Lever might believe in 'truth in advertising' and boast about how he applied the principle in practice, but, as every advertiser knows, the juxtaposition of an idealized image – the essence of 'soft sell' advertising – is not actively untruthful. If the viewer wished to make an association between images of the perfect family and a particular soap, and make the conscious or unconscious assumption that she and her family too would come close to such perfection in their own private world if they used the product, then it was not for the advertiser to step in and say otherwise.[79] Lever was well able to parse the fine difference between dishonest claims and misleading images. Truth was negotiable, distortion an ally.

Once demand was created, the product had to be made available efficiently. Lever employed an army of travelling salesman (early on called 'District Agents' and later 'Assistant Travellers') to sell his soap. His magazine, *Progress*, produced from 1899 to spread the gospel to shareholders and employees, contained useful tips for his commercial missionaries; for example, 'showing the people that Swan Soap will float is a very good method, and especially where there are children as the latter bother their mothers to buy some'.[80] When he received orders he made sure he could deliver them rapidly. According to Andrew Knox, Lever beat out the competition in London of Watson's of Leeds, manufacturers of Matchless Cleanser soap, because he established a depot there from which he could deliver to wholesalers six times a week, and 'within the hour' if necessary.[81] Overseas, again according to an anecdote related by Knox, Lever relied on energetic salesmen and had little patience with those who failed to deliver. A salesman returned from a trip to Siam (present-day Thailand), admitting that he could make little headway in selling yellow soap. Lever said:

'Well, Mr So-and-So, I've read your report and I see that you can't sell Sunlight Soap in Siam.'

'That's right, sir, it is a blue mottled market.'

'All right then, if you can't sell Sunlight Soap in Siam, I'll have to find someone who can.'[82]

Colin MacDonald, 'the man from the Board' during Lever's dispute with the crofters on Lewis (chapter five), gave the most vivid pen-portrait of Lever the salesman in action – not concerning soap, but fish. Lever was in his late sixties at the time, but as he outlined his plans for harvesting and marketing Hebridean fish he was like 'an evangelist preaching a gospel', MacDonald recounted: 'He all but mesmerised me.' MacDonald's purported verbatim account is as suspect in its details as any other recalled from memory a quarter century after, but it captured something not only of 'the force, the eloquence, the abounding self-assurance' of the man, but also his homely and almost naive phraseology. Lever explained how he would make his own cans for his fish, and had already chosen a label – 'LEWIS CANNED FISH', slanted in red on a white background – from various selections submitted, some 'from men who put R.A. or A.R.A. after their names'. He had experimented with a mock-up in a window of Lews Castle and decided that it was as striking as he had hoped from every angle and even twenty yards away. When it came time to begin selling it, he would send a supply to his corner shops with instructions to make a good window display on the Saturday. He conjectured what might happen next:

John Smith has been busy in the office all the week (or so he tells the wife) and late home every night. On Saturday he goes home to lunch. Conscience-stricken, he tries to make amends.

'Mary, my dear,' says he, 'you've had a dreary week of it. What about a show to-night?'

Poor Mary is overjoyed. What a considerate man is her John! On the way to the theatre they are held up at the corner for a car – the corner where my shop is. The light from the window shows up LEWIS CANNED FISH most attractively. It catches Mary's eye.

'I say, John, what a lovely label! Lewis Canned Fish. I like the look of it…. Just a minute….'

'What is this Lewis Canned Fish?' she asks.

'Madam,' says my salesman. 'It *is* Lewis Canned Fish and very delightful too.'

'Can you recommend it?'

'Thoroughly, madam. I believe it is the best canned fish in the world.'

'Thank you. Will you please send along a tin?'

Back from the show Mary is peckish. That can just asks to be opened. They have Lewis Canned Fish for supper. They have never tasted anything so good. *They lick their fingers.* Nyum nyum!

Monday morning Mrs Smith is in the back green hanging up the washing. Mrs Brown is over the wall on the right.

'Mrs Brown! Do you know! I made the most *wonderful* discovery on Saturday!" – and she lets Mrs Brown into the secret. She also tells Mrs Jones on the left. Each buys a can….

And so the great news spreads and spreads. Within a year – certainly within two years – there is *only one canned fish that counts in the world*, and that is LEWIS CANNED FISH.'[83]

The power of persuasion

Advertising needs to make a rapid impact, communicating crisply and efficiently with a large number of people who will pay it only fleeting attention. An advert is therefore almost always an exercise in simplification, serving up a dumbed down message and drawing on easily recognizable cultural stereotypes.[84] Ads rarely challenge mainstream, consensual, hegemonic values. Even those that ostensibly do so draw on well understood visual and verbal representations to make them legible; and their aim is to sell a product, buttressing a society built on consumption. Thus in soap advertisements the figure, dress, comportment, posture and cleanliness of the characters gave a very clear indication of what was socially acceptable.

Like most advertisers, Lever Brothers primarily targeted women, as the main purchasers and users of their products. In contrast to the fictitious Old Man Evans, Lever tended to be a proponent of 'reason why' ads: the notion that the public needed to be persuaded with logical arguments rather than simply hit over the head with bald, repetitive statements.[85] Many of his early ads in this guise emphasized that Sunlight soap would save women from drudgery. One famous poster, purchased from a Philadelphia soap maker, pondered, 'Why does a woman look old sooner than a man?' The answer was on account of the washing-day toil of pummelling clothes in a steaming, scalding, boiling atmosphere. The solution? Sunlight Soap ('Beware of imitations'! 'Has the largest sale of any soap in the world'!), which cleansed the dirtiest clothing in lukewarm water with very little rubbing ('a girl of 12 or 13 can do a large wash without being tired'), and made 'the white pieces whiter, coloured pieces brighter, and flannels softer than they can be made by washing the old way.'[86]

The ease of the wash was a repeated theme. For example, a magazine advertisement of 1896 depicted Mr and Mrs John Bull admiring a passing motor van, 'SUNLIGHT SOAP' and 'SAVES LABOUR' in bold letters on its side. 'Look, Mary,' says John Bull, 'there's a SUNLIGHT MOTOR VAN going along without horses; that's SAVING LABOUR with a vengeance.' Mrs Bull replies '(emphatically)', 'I don't know anything about the Motor Van saving labour, but I AM CERTAIN THE SOAP DOES.'[87]

A large operation like Lever Brothers, making slender profits on each bar of soap, could prosper only by exploiting the huge potential market of working-class housewives with aspirations to be moderately comfortable. The company's

5 Lever Brothers' advertisement 'Why does a woman look old sooner than a man?'

first booklet, *Sunlight Soap and How to Use it*, was a handy compendium of instructions particularly aimed at these women. Here one could find advice on how to clean pampas grass and feathers, since one would see 'in many working men's houses, the pampas grass in a jar on the Bible in the sitting room and the feathers in the hats of the daughters'.[88] It described one woman worn down by washing clothes. She had tried every soap on the market before she turned to Sunlight, and was astonished at how easy it made washing in comparison. It even improved her love life:

> Her washing is all over and put away before her husband comes home, and after tea they go out for a walk together, a thing they have never been able to do for thirty years.
> It seems like their old 'courting' days, and she never felt so happy before.
> She begins to think that life is worth living after all.[89]

Elsewhere in the booklet, however, in a section devoted to 'hints on washing and cleaning', the time required to make one's whites irreproachable still seemed considerable and the operation finicky. This, for example, was the advice for dealing with table covers:

> Dissolve four tablets of Sunlight Self-washer Soap in six gallons of boiling water, and mix it with one pound of pearlash. Have three earthenware pans or tubs that will hold about eight gallons each; into the first of these put three gallons of the dissolved soap and one pail of cold water; into the second, two gallons of soap and one pail of water; and into the third, one gallon of soap and two pails of water. Well work the cover in each of these three soap liquors, beginning with the strongest, and wring it between each. Stir one tablespoonful of oil of vitriol into a tub containing six pails of cold water. Handle the cover in this spirit water for five minutes then take it out and rinse it in one lot of cold water; this is the proper method for cotton-and-worsted or printed cotton covers.[90]

Lever Brothers continued their domestic advice on a regular basis in the *Sunlight Almanac*, published annually between 1895 and 1900, and in *Woman's World*, a 470 page illustrated book published in 1901, and edited by (to give it a patina of professional validation) an unnamed 'Diplomée of a London Hospital'. In its in-depth exploration of domestic life, *Woman's World* dispensed copious advice to young wives:

> Let a young housewife realize that the most charming ornament of a room is a woman's bright, cheerful and sympathetic face.
> Let the young wife show tact in bearing her own burdens, and not begin the subject of small domestic grievances when her husband comes in after a long and perhaps worrying day. The shortcomings of her servants, the amount of the baker's bill, the short weight sent by the grocer, the trouble she has had because the butcher sent the meat late – all belongs to her own department and should never form the principal item of her conversation.

A wife who … never 'Nags' … will have her reward in the entire trust of her husband.[91]

An advert of 1893 for Sunlight in the *Illustrated Sporting and Dramatic News* read:

[I]f home is to be the very dearest spot on earth it can only be such if the mother or wife brightens it with the sunlight of her cheerful smile. This radiance must be natural, and the genuine fruit of peace, kindness and serenity. When things go right in the kitchen, the laundry and the bath, the good housewife's face is lit up with a loving, smiling calm. This brightness always follows the use of [the right soap].[92]

Another in the same year talked of a mother's special responsibilities in the transmission of knowledge to her daughter, imagining 'one of the most touching moment's in a woman's life' just before her daughter is about to leave for the church to be married:

In those few minutes of waiting the mother lives again in her memory the twenty odd years that have passed since her daughter was born, and asks herself if it were possible to have done more than she has done to secure her daughter's happiness. Ah! my Lady! let your own heart answer that! Does your daughter know what SUNLIGHT SOAP can do? Have you told her that for a few pence, without boiling or bleaching, she can have all her husband's shirts and collars washed at home with SUNLIGHT SOAP and made to look snow white. Does she know that all the house linen, bed linen, table linen, body linen, baby linen, and in fact every kind of linen, can be washed at home with SUNLIGHT SOAP without any inconvenience and fatigue? If you have told her these things, then you have indeed worked for your daughter's happiness.[93]

In many respects these advertising messages drew strongly on and reinforced late Victorian and Edwardian domestic and gendered norms. But, as Lori Loeb points out in her detailed study of turn-of-the-century advertising, ads catered more to an image of woman the consumer than woman the helpless housewife in a male-dominated world. In the tension within Victorian culture between the evangelically inspired duties of frugality, abstinence and otherworldliness and the imperative of a capitalist economy for energetic and conspicuous consumption, advertisers were evidently compelled to favour the latter.[94] Some of the more common images in ads represented women as sensual classical goddesses well aware of their seductive power. As Loeb puts it, 'The late Victorian home in the eyes of advertisers became not a temple of virtue, but a hall of material goods, one that elevated acquisition with classical motifs, which attempted to free the Victorian family from evangelical moral constraints, and which increasingly defined the middle-class ideal in material terms.'[95] And again, 'In keeping with this context, the female presence in Victorian advertisements is frequently commanding and controlling, rather than demure and unassuming. The commercial woman offers a portrait of feminine power, which contradicts a prevalent myth – that the ideal Victorian woman was passive, submissive, and sexually anæsthetic.[96]

If playing to housewives was one of Lever Brothers' key strategies, draping themselves in the flag was another. As an international company, one size would evidently not fit all: for the American market, for instance, Lever turned to American agencies to devise appropriate approaches.[97] But for the domestic and imperial markets the themes of Britishness and the empire could be given full vent, again in common with many other manufacturers. The *"Sunlight" Year Book* for 1899, for example, carried a series of slogans on the bottom of every page, boasting of the soap's royal connections and national and imperial reach and beyond: 'Sunlight Soap, Soapmaker to Her Majesty the Queen … is used from Land's End to John o'Groats … in American log cabins … in Canadian homesteads … by the South African miner … in the Australian bush …'.[98] Robert Opie, collector of advertising and other ephemera, has amassed an impressive collection of ads trading on the British image and making abundant use of Britannia, John Bull, the royal family, the union jack, the armed forces, landmarks of London, British sports, the Boy Scouts and other British 'institutions' such as the police, judges and schoolmasters. For example, a magazine advertisement of 1902 proclaimed, 'Where the British flag flies, DUNLOP TYRES are paramount. A BRITISH invention, made by BRITISH workpeople, with BRITISH capital, for BRITISH cyclists. Avoid all imitations – foreign or otherwise.'[99] A showcard of 1915 hammered home a similar theme: 'Oxo is British. Made in Britain. By a British company. With British capital & British labour.'[100]

During the First World War Lever Brothers too played the patriotic card. Advertisements urged mothers and sweethearts to parcel up a tablet of Sunlight soap in their next package to the front or the fleet, and comforted the nation with the idea that 'while such quality exists, victory is assured'. One poster, depicting a soldier in the trenches, his leg supported by a box of Sunlight, associated the company and its soap with a self-congratulatory sense of British decency. Even if it played well at home, it must have seemed more than a touch ironic from the perspective of the mud and gore of trench warfare:

> The clean, chivalrous fighting instincts of our gallant soldiers reflect the ideals of our business life. The same characteristics which stamp the British Tommy as the CLEANEST FIGHTER IN THE WORLD have won equal repute for British goods. SUNLIGHT SOAP is typically British. It is acknowledged by experts to represent the highest standard of Soap Quality and Efficiency. Tommy welcomes it in the trenches just as you welcome it at home.[101]

As Anne McClintock points out, the way commodities were marketed had important implications for the British imperial mission. No commodity aided more in this process than soap. 'Washing and clothing the savage' was the imperial corollary to 'cleansing the great unwashed' of the British working classes. Her argument, and it is a powerful one, is that missionaries, colonial officials, traders and writers repeatedly accused Africans of lacking domestic culture and proper hygiene. These people evidently needed to be cleansed, clothed and civilized, through violent means if necessary. It was after all, they said, in their own best interests. The drive to subjugate the dirty African body – to scrub away its blackness – thereby served to justify the imposition of alien cultural values and open up the continent to imperial and market forces. In turn, the depiction of this 'civilizing mission' in the imperial kitsch of advertising, on posters and in packaging, helped bring to a wide audience back in Britain the notion of imperialism as benign and altruistic, and to ingrain a cast iron sense of British racial and cultural superiority.[102] The writer John Julius Norwich, speaking of his boyhood in the 1930s, said, 'Empire was all around us, celebrated on our biscuit tins, chronicled on our cigarette cards, part of the fabric of our lives. We were all imperialists then.'[103]

Creating customers[104]

George Orwell famously wrote in *The Road to Wigan Pier* that '*The lower classes smell*.' This is what he and other members of the polite, propertied and genteel ranks had been taught in childhood, and still in the 1930s, he thought, it was the most fundamental of class distinctions, an insurmountable barrier to class unity or equality. Anyone who had grown up in a house with a bathroom and a servant would likely have shared the feeling that 'there was something subtly repulsive about a working-class body':

> You watched a great sweaty navvy walking down the road with his pick over his shoulder; you looked at his discoloured shirt and his corduroy trousers stiff with the dirt of a decade; you thought of those nests and layers of greasy rags below, and, under all, the unwashed body, brown all over (that was how I used to imagine it), with its strong, bacon-like reek…. And even 'lower-class' people whom you knew to be quite clean – servants, for instance – were faintly unappetizing. The smell of their sweat, the very texture of their skins, were mysteriously different from yours.[105]

Orwell was making a broader point about how difficult it would be to overcome ingrained bourgeois prejudices of hatred and fear of the working classes and illustrating the problem by confessing his own feelings of nose-twitching repugnance towards dirt. For him, any sentimental notion 'that dirtiness is healthy and "natural" and cleanliness is a mere fad or at best a luxury' made no sense. With improvements in sanitation, and more and more bathrooms in England's houses, the English, thankfully, were growing visibly cleaner; 'and we may hope that in a hundred years they will be almost as clean as the Japanese'.[106]

His optimism was well placed. During the course of the twentieth century, thanks to the Victorians' sanitary achievements, the provision of water in abundant quantities and the manufacture of affordable soap and washing powders, the British in overwhelming numbers conquered corporeal aromas. As it became possible and fashionable to bathe or shower on a daily basis, change undergarments and socks with almost obsessive frequency, launder clothes with little effort to make them Oh! So fresh!, douse the body with deodorants and antiperspirants, expunge stale breath with mouthwash and breathmints, the lower classes ceased to smell. The British waged a successful war against bodily whiffs and the reek of sweat, against greasy hair and foul breath, and against grimy clothes and stained underwear.

Few today would dispute the positive side of the application of soap, water and other cleansing agents on the habits and health of a nation, nor lament a grubby, earthy past – though the fetishization of bodily hygiene is a sign of how ideas have been transformed. The progression from the 'natural' body, with all its malodorous imperfections, to the preternaturally clean body (as an aspirational standard at least), is not a straightforward story of the inevitable march of civilization. The soap sellers and other cleanliness merchants had a considerable hand in it. They made it their business to persuade each consumer of his or her hygiene problems, of the dangers skulking in the environment and of the need to fix them urgently. Fortunately, the solutions were readily at hand.

Lever Brothers' Lifebuoy, for example, introduced in 1894 and making use of residual oil left over from the manufacture of Sunlight soap, was at first marketed as a disinfectant soap because of the carbolic acid content in its original formula. In the hands of the advertisers its strong hospital smell became an asset, conveying health, safety and sparkling personal cleanliness.[107] 'In a world becoming ever more conscious of the menace of microbes,' as Charles Wilson puts it, 'it was brought before the public as a powerful germicide, and the outbreak of epidemic disease anywhere in the country was often taken as the signal for an intensive local publicity campaign.'[108] One magazine insert of the mid-1890s portrayed through the open door of a well heeled household two contented servants at work, one washing clothes with Sunlight, the other scrubbing the hall floor with Lifebuoy. Sunlight Soap's slogan 'Homes bright, hearts light' supported one door jamb, Lifebuoy's 'Saves life, prevents disease' the other, and inscribed on the pediment was the message 'You need not open the door so frequently for the doctor.'[109] In the United States, Lifebuoy's 'germ-destroying agent', claimed an advert in Harper's Weekly in 1902, tackled any 'taint of typhoid, cholera, or diphtheria floating in the air or concealed in the clothing of the individual'. An Outlook magazine advert from 1904 raised fears with meaningless statistics – 'microbes kill about 15 million human beings a year' – and then allayed them with spurious claims: 'exhaustive experiments by some of the world's greatest scientists proved that Lifebuoy soap destroys the microbes of disease'.[110]

This played on fear, but advertisers after the First World War created new fears: fears of social *faux pas*. The J. Walter Thompson agency created a campaign in 1919 for a deodorant called Odorono, employing the slyly coy headline 'Within the Curve of a Woman's Arm [:] A frank discussion of a subject too often avoided.' People who did not know that they had a problem soon learned that they had. Lever Brothers in 1928 went a step further and named the dreaded 'BO', repositioning Lifebuoy as the protection against this social disgrace.[111] But perhaps the biggest marketing triumph in the advertisers' pursuit of hygiene in the 1920s was for a company called Lambert Pharmacal to convince millions of Americans that they suffered from something medical-sounding called 'halitosis', and that the cure was a daily gargle with their product, Listerine. The condition was invented and the term 'halitosis' borrowed from a clipping one of the senior members of the firm came across in a British periodical. A pharmacist from St Louis had concocted Listerine back in the 1870s and the firm had steadily marketed it as an all-purpose hospital and household antiseptic ever since, with moderate success. But then came the idea to readvertise it as a deodorant rather than a disinfectant.[112] The ad men got to work on this from 1922, producing such classics as 'Often a bridesmaid but never a bride' (1925):

> Edna's case was really a pathetic one. Like every woman, her primary ambition was to marry. Most of the girls of her set were married – or about to be. Yet not one possessed more grace or charm or loveliness than she. And as her birthdays crept gradually toward that tragic thirty-mark, marriage seemed farther from her life than ever…. That's the insidious thing about halitosis (unpleasant breath). You, yourself, rarely know when you have it. And even your closest friends won't tell you.[113]

A succession of ads thereafter, highlighting a variety of social failures because of bad breath, persuaded Ednas everywhere to deploy the only effective remedy: Listerine.

The message seemed to be clear: if one wished to gain or retain a partner, a job, a reputation and self-esteem, one needed to attend to personal hygiene. Sales skyrocketed. This is the classic case of how advertisers could create a demand, with minimal alteration in content, packaging and price. But it was also highly idiosyncratic; in spite of their best efforts, few companies and marketers have succeeded in replicating these spectacular results.[114]

Advertisers, more than any other group of people, made hay with new understandings of human psychology in the twentieth century. Freud, Jung and their acolytes were not going to make their fullest impact until the 1950s – and it is deeply ironic that their potentially revolutionary teachings about the workings of unconscious desires should be harnessed so effectively in the service of consumer capitalism – but at an earlier date advertisers had begun to incorporate the psychology of suggestion into their copy. In the United States a couple of academics provided some intellectual ballast. One was Walter Dill Scott, a psychologist at and later president of Northwestern University, Chicago, in his influential book, *The Psychology of Advertising* (1908). He commented on the marketing of Ivory soap over a quarter of a century,

> These advertisements have created an atmosphere, and when I think of Ivory Soap a halo of spotless elegance envelops it, and I do not think of it merely as a prosaic chunk of fat and alkali. I have had this idea of spotless elegance so thoroughly associated with Ivory Soap by means of these many advertisements that I actually enjoy using Ivory Soap more than I would if the soap had not been thus advertised. The advertising of this soap not only induces me to buy it, but it influences me in my judgment of the soap after I have bought it.[115]

The other was John B. Watson, a behavioural psychologist who abandoned his job at Johns Hopkins University in Baltimore so that he could impart his wisdom in the service of the J. Walter Thompson advertising agency. Watson concluded, on the basis of blindfold tests demonstrating that people could not recognize their preferred brand of cigarette, that appeals to reason did not work; appeals through association would prove more effective.[116]

Edward Bernays, nephew of Freud and the leading American advertising and public relations guru of his generation, produced a book in 1928 called, simply, *Propaganda*. 'The conscious and intelligent manipulation of the organized habits and opinions of the masses is an important element in democratic society,' he began, unapologetically, reflecting a widespread intellectual disdain for the common people's reasoning power. 'Those who manipulate this unseen mechanism of society constitute an invisible government which is the true ruling power of our country.' Advertising agencies, just as much as political parties, perform an essential service: they narrow our choices by attempting to capture our minds for some idea, policy or commodity. This open competition for hearts and minds is preferable to committees of wise men making decisions for us. In a democratic society there is no alternative. Universal education supposedly liberates the ordinary person to rule himself and to take control of his environment. 'But instead of a mind, universal literacy has given him rubber stamps, rubber stamps inked with advertising slogans, with editorials, with published scientific data, with the trivialities of the tabloids and the platitudes of history, but quite innocent of original thought.'

This was not quite as cynical and condescending as it sounded. Later in his book Bernays conceded that the public are not an amorphous mass that can be moulded at will, and that there has to be give-and-take between business and people if a business is to succeed. A business has to explain and present itself in terms the public is willing to accept. Thus an oil corporation should exhibit good labour relations as well as offer satisfactory oil, a bakery should open up its premises so that the public can inspect its standards of hygiene as well as serve up edible bread, and a bank should make sure that its officials are upstanding citizens in public and private as well as effectively look after clients' money.

All of these proponents of the psychology of advertising pointed to the power of suggestion and of association working on the subconscious mind, and many manufacturers began to take note. The classic example is of car manufacturers, drawing on the Freudian notion that an individual's thoughts and deeds act as substitutes for suppressed desires, who might suggest that a man should purchase a top-of-the-line motor to satisfy his wife or impress his colleagues and clients rather than simply to get from A to B more efficiently.[117] Another is of tobacco manufacturers. Persuading a swath of the population to take up the nicotine habit was possibly the ad men's greatest achievement in the 1920s.[118] Smoking a Camel or a Lucky Strike meant buying in to a glamorous lifestyle, they suggested. 'Discrepancy theory' maintains that cigarette ads just like other suggestive ads attempted to implant the notion that Joe Public's leisure practices, material possessions, bathing habits, clothing and accoutrements were miserably inferior to those depicted. Only emulation could make the discrepancy disappear and Joe happier.[119] In a later, cancer-conscious era, tobacco conglomerates tried to defend themselves against the charge of peddling their products to the young, ill informed and vulnerable by claiming that advertising was merely intended to poach market share from rivals, not to recruit fresh converts. Their predecessors in the 1920s did not hide behind such false modesty.

In similar fashion, soap advertisers focused on image by association with feminine glamour and beauty. Lever Brothers' Lux by the mid-1920s was being sold to preserve 'soft, youthful, lovely feminine hands', while another successful J. Walter Thompson campaign of the late 1920s paraded a line-up of Hollywood personalities behind the slogan, 'Nine out of ten screen stars care for their skin with Lux soap.'[120] In 1927 the Association of American Soap and Glycerine Producers established the Cleanliness Institute to promote greater soap consumption, such as by providing teachers with suggestions on how to get their charges hooked on hygiene from an early age, or by talking about how the homemaker could find immense pleasure in caring for her home and her body.[121] For example:

> You 'just hate' the refrigerator job? Don't. It's marvelous exercise, for it brings nearly all your muscles into play. So down on your knees! Think of yourself as kneeling before the altar of beauty and health. Not for one single instant are you a slave to household drudgery. And when you know that the exercise is helping to give you a fine, shapely body, it will become good fun to reach and turn and twist and peer into the refrigerator.[122]

Bernays had particular praise for a successful attempt by Procter and Gamble to tap in to 'the group formation of modern society'. P and G offered a series of prizes for a nationwide competition, held under the auspices of the Art Center in New York City, for sculptures in Ivory soap, open to schoolchildren as well as professional sculptors. The competition appealed to teachers as an educational aid, and mothers at home could use soap shavings and failed efforts for the laundry. All in all, Bernays contended, a number of psychological motives were set in play here: the aesthetic, the competitive, the gregarious, the snobbish, the exhibitionist and the maternal – a fine example of a company using sound psychology and enlightened self-interest to advertise its product.[123]

In much of this advertising for personal and household products, women continued to be the target. In the 1920s advertisers calculated that women bought up to 85 per cent of household products in America. One way to reach this audience was through the new medium of the radio, hence the invention of the soap opera in the 1930s, aimed squarely at a daytime audience of women in the home. Procter and Gamble led the way, sponsoring *The O'Neills*, 'brought to you by Ivory Soap', and *Forever Young*, which reached its audience courtesy of Camay.[124]

Admass

We have been exploring how manufacturers and advertisers sought to market their products during the late nineteenth and early twentieth centuries through a variety of hard sell, soft sell and psychological techniques, actively attempting to shape desire rather than simply meet demand, and sometimes succeeding.[125] The messages they imparted were conflicting. On the surface they appeared to uphold social norms and the separate spheres of gender, but the logic of appealing to the power of women and children as consumers was subtly subversive. Capitalism corroded its own containers. It promised salvation not through conversion but through consumption. The key to Redemption, the solution to all anxieties, could be summed up in one word: buy.[126] As consumer goods and the way in which they were marketed served to construct a sense of self-identity and of status, the only way to cling to and enhance this identity was to continue to purchase – to continue to bolster the culture of consumption and the capitalist system, one purchase at a time.[127]

J. B. Priestley gave a label to the entire culture that he felt was characterized by the ethics of the advertiser: 'Admass'.

This is my name for the whole system of an increasing productivity, plus inflation, plus a rising standard of material living, plus high-pressure advertising and salesmanship, plus mass communications, plus cultural democracy and the creation of the mass mind, the mass man.... Most Americans ... have been *Admassians* for the last thirty years; the English, and probably most West Europeans, only since the War.... you have to be half-witted or half-drunk all the time to endure it.[128]

Attacks on commerce and all its permutations were, of course, centuries old, but indictments of the Admass culture that Lever had helped create were particularly a feature of the inter-war period and after. Cultural critics, right and left, railed against the debasing and homogenization of taste. T. S. Eliot, for instance, feared that standards of art and culture in any mass society organized for profit were bound to be depressed: 'The increasing organization of advertisement and propaganda – or the influencing of masses of men by any means except through their intelligence – is all against them.'[129] More broadly, George Orwell followed in a long line of those appalled by the impact of mass production, decrying:

> the frightful debauchery of taste that has already been effected by a century of mechanisation.... In the highly mechanised countries, thanks to tinned food, cold storage, synthetic flavouring matters, etc., the palate is almost a dead organ....[L]ook at the factory-made, foil-wrapped cheeses and 'blended' butter in any grocer's; look at the hideous rows of tins which usurp more and more space in any food-shop, even a dairy; look at a sixpenny Swiss roll or a twopenny ice-cream; look at the filthy chemical by-product that people will pour down their throats under the name of beer. Wherever you look you will see some slick machine-made article triumphing over the old-fashioned article that still tastes of something other than sawdust.[130]

Countless critics on the left in the twentieth century deplored how ordinary people, thwarted in their attempt to produce a truly democratic society, settled for consumer consolations or the cheap thrills of drink, drugs, porn and mass, mindless entertainment. People traded community spirit, they claimed, for atomized, soulless, unfulfilling affluence, and all the while the fabricated compulsion to keep up with the Joneses was a fraud, since happiness could not be bought and materialism did not enhance a sense of personal well-being.[131] At the same time as the citizen became the customer, the population a market, people degenerated into drones: docile bodies or blind mouths, squawking for more and more morsels, effectively managed and causing little trouble for their capitalist masters, unable to think beyond the 'self-evident' 'common sense' of free-market consumer capitalism.[132]

Economic liberals, on the other hand, celebrated the unfettered agency of the consuming individual. For these proponents of liberal capitalism, commerce was a civilizing force, breaking down provincialism and obscurantism, opening societies to beneficial outside influences and reducing conflict between nations, since societies with vibrant commercial sectors tended to be relatively politically liberal, they argued, and liberal societies did not seek power advantages and territorial conquests at the expense of others. Capitalism, commerce and consumption improved the well-being of more and more people, bringing greater private affluence, creature comforts and increased opportunities for movement (both geographically and up the social scale). Advertising, in spite of its manipulation of emotions, benefited society by creating competition, choice, economic spin-offs and lower prices.[133]

There is no doubt on which side of the fence Lever stood. In a succession of quasi-*non-sequiturs* in a speech in New York in 1923 he outlined his irrepressible optimism about progress and advertising's centrality to it:

> Leagues of Nations may totter and sway, but the eternal principles, which are the fundamentals of honest business, will continue to advance humanity to brotherhood and abolish the artificial barriers between the several nations. Advertising only means keeping up with the times and the big advance in modern business.... Honesty in advertising ... is a cardinal principle in your country and also in mine. Sooner or later the dishonest advertiser disappears. The advertiser of our times is not working for to-day only. He is laying his foundations deep. He is building for those who will follow after him. It should be the same with nations.[134]

It was an audacious claim, offered without the slightest hesitation or qualm about the deleterious aspects of international capitalism. In the tradition of Adam Smith, Richard Cobden and John Bright, Lever believed that it was not supranational organizations but free trade in the humble commodity, honestly advertised, that held the key to the 'brotherhood of man'. It would be difficult to find a greater champion of the art and transcendent significance of selling than the Old Man of Sunlight.

Notes

1 Frederic Wakeman, *The Hucksters* (New York: Rinehart and Co., 1946), p. 23.
2 *Ibid.*, pp. 24–5.
3 UARM, LBC 8104D, Lever to G. Edward Atkinson, 5 November 1923.
4 Quoted by Terry R. Nevett, 'Barratt, Thomas James', in David J. Jeremy (ed.), *Dictionary of Business Biography: A Biographical Dictionary of Business Leaders Active in Britain in the Period 1860–1980*, vol. I (London: Butterworths, 1984), p. 190.
5 Quoted by Asa Briggs, *Victorian Things* (London: Penguin, 1988), p. 326.
6 Michael Schudson, *Advertising, the Uneasy Persuasion: Its Dubious Impact on American Society* (New York: Basic Books, 1984), p. 85; Davis Dyer, Frederick Dalzell and Rowena Olegario, *Rising Tide: Lessons from 165 Years of Brand Building at Procter & Gamble* (Boston, MA: Harvard Business School Press, 2004), p. 40.
7 Nigel Morgan and Annette Pritchard, *Advertising in Tourism and Leisure* (Oxford: Butterworth-Heinemann, 2001), pp. 11, 17; *Ad Age Global*, quoted by Randy Jacobs, 'United Kingdom', in John McDonough and Karen Egolf (eds), *The Advertising Age Encyclopedia of Advertising* (New York: Fitzroy Dearborn, 2003), vol. III, p. 1594.

8 Unilever Global Co. website, www.unilever.com, accessed 30 October 2005.

9 *Guardian*, 7 September 2000, 6 October 2001.

10 Robert Fitzgerald, *Rowntree and the Marketing Revolution 1862–1969* (Cambridge: Cambridge University Press, 1995), pp. 10–14, 19–20, 24, 27; Dyer *et al.*, *Rising Tide*, chap. 4.

11 James Obelkevich, 'Consumption', in Obelkevich and Peter Catterall (eds), *Understanding Post-war British Society* (London and New York: Routledge, 1994), pp. 151–2; Morgan and Pritchard, *Advertising in Tourism and Leisure*, pp. 4–5, 45.

12 Dyer *et al.*, *Rising Tide*, pp. 5, 406–12.

13 Philip Kotler, *Principles of Marketing* (Englewood Cliffs, NJ: Prentice-Hall, 1986 edn), pp. 347–8, quoted by Morgan and Pritchard, *Advertising in Tourism and Leisure*, p. 4.

14 See, for example, Robert Roberts, *The Classic Slum: Salford Life in the First Quarter of the Century* (Harmondsworth: Penguin, 1973), chap. 6; Maud Pember Reeves, *Round about a Pound a Week* (London: Virago, 1979; 1st edn, 1913), chaps 7–10.

15 Robert Opie (ed.), *The Victorian Scrapbook* (London: New Cavendish Books, 2003), pp. 16–20.

16 Gilbert Russell, *Advertisement Writing* (London: Ernest Benn, 1927), p. 38, and Richard B. Franken and Carroll B. Larrabee, *Packages that Sell* (New York: Harper and Bros, 1928), quoted by Rachel Bowlby, *Carried Away: The Invention of Modern Shopping* (New York: Columbia University Press, 2001), pp. 80–1.

17 Torsten H. Nilson, *Competitive Branding: Winning in the Market Place with Value-added Brands* (New York: John Wiley and Sons, 1999), p. 59; Neil McKendrick, 'Josiah Wedgwood and the commercialization of the potteries', in Neil McKendrick, John Brewer and J. H. Plumb (eds), *The Birth of a Consumer Society: The Commercialization of Eighteenth-Century England* (London: Europa Publications, 1982), chap. 3; T. A. B. Corley, 'British entrepreneurs and brand names', and Robin Reilly, 'Wedgwood, Josiah', in *Oxford Dictionary of National Biography* (Oxford: Oxford University Press, 2004; online edn, May 2005, www.oxforddnb.com, accessed 6 June 2005).

18 Sue Shepard, *Pickled, Potted, and Canned: How the Art and Science of Food Preserving Changed the World* (New York: Simon and Schuster, 2000), pp. 226–42.

19 B. W. E. Alford, 'Wills family'; Corley, 'British entrepreneurs and brand names'; and S. D. Chapman, 'Player, John', in *Oxford Dictionary of National Biography*.

20 Dyer *et al.*, *Rising Tide*, pp. 20–1; Juliann Sivulka, *Soap, Sex, and Cigarettes: A Cultural History of American Advertising* (Belmont, CA: Wadsworth Publishing, 1998), pp. 48–51, 73–5; Nilson, *Competitive Branding*, p. 59.

21 Charles Wilson, *The History of Unilever: A Study in Economic Growth and Social Change*, vol. I (London: Cassell and Co., 1954), pp. 9–20; W. J. Reader, *Unilever: A Short History* (London: Unilever House, 1960), p. 8; Richard Lucock Wilson, *Soap through the Ages*, 4th edn (London: Progress Books, 1955), pp. 1–16; Angus Watson, *My Life: An Autobiography* (London: Ivor Nicholson and Watson, 1937), pp. 133–4; A. E. Musson, *Enterprise in Soap and Chemicals: Joseph Crosfield and Sons, Ltd 1815–1965* (Manchester: Manchester University Press, 1965), pp. 100–1.

22 UARM, LBC 5594, Lever to Sir R. Waley Cohen, 7 September 1923.

23 William Hulme Lever [second Viscount Leverhulme], *Viscount Leverhulme* (Boston, MA, and New York: Houghton Mifflin, 1927), p. 38.

24 *Ibid.*, pp. 40–1.

25 UARM, LBC 8362C, Lever to H. F. W. Bousfield, 2 December 1921.

26 Wilson, *Unilever*, p. 31; Andrew M. Knox, *Coming Clean: A Postscript after Retirement from Unilever* (London: Heinemann, 1976), p. 66.

27 UARM, LBC 5594, Lever to Cohen, 31 May 1923.

28 Fitzgerald, *Rowntree and the Marketing Revolution*, pp. 25–6; Roger Scola, *Feeding the Victorian City: The Food Supply of Manchester 1770–1870* (Manchester: Manchester University Press, 1992); F. B. Smith, *The People's Health 1830–1910* (New York: Holmes and Meier, 1979).

29 UARM, LBC 5594, Lever to Cohen, 14 December 1922.

30 For example, Robert Opie, *Rule Britannia: Trading on the British Image* (Harmondsworth: Viking, 1985), p. 68.

31 UARM, LBC 1482, Lever to F. Countway.

32 UARM, LBC 5594, Lever to Cohen, 9 January 1922.

33 Lever, *Leverhulme*, pp. 35–6.

34 Wilson, *Unilever*, p. 29; Ian Campbell Bradley, *Enlightened Entrepreneurs* (London: Weidenfeld and Nicolson, 1987), p. 180.

35 Dyer *et al.*, *Rising Tide*, chaps 1–2; Jennifer Whitson, 'Soap products', p. 1449, and Jack Neff, 'Procter & Gamble Company', p. 1270, in McDonough and Egolf (eds), *Encyclopedia of Advertising*, vol. III.

36 Neff, 'Procter & Gamble Company', p. 1270.

37 Quoted by Thomas Richards, *The Commodity Culture of Victorian England: Advertising and Spectacle 1851–1914* (Stanford, CA: Stanford University Press, 1990), p. 249.

38 W. B. Richmond and Heywood Sumner, disciples of William Morris, in *The Times*, 18–25 November 1892, quoted by Matthew Sweet, *Inventing the Victorians* (London: Faber and Faber, 2001), pp. 44–5.

39 Briggs, *Victorian Things*, p. 325.

40 Quoted by Lever, *Leverhulme*, p. 55.

41 Terry R. Nevett, *Advertising in Britain: A History* (London: Heinemann, 1982), pp. 67, 79, 86; Cyril Sheldon, *A History of Poster Advertising* (London: Chapman and Hall, 1937), pp. 72–3; Briggs, *Victorian Things*, pp. 325–6; Opie, *Rule Britannia*, p. 6.

42 Edward Morris, 'Advertising and the acquisition of contemporary art', in Edward Morris (ed.), *Art and Business in Edwardian England: The Making of the Lady Lever Art Gallery* (Oxford: Oxford University Press, 1992, for National Museums and Galleries on Merseyside; reprinted from *Journal of the History of Collections*, 4:2 (1992)), 195–8; Diana Hindley and Geoffrey Hindley, *Advertising in Victorian England 1837–1901* (London: Wayland Publishers, 1972), pp. 43–4; Sheldon, *History of Poster Advertising*, p. 73; Lever, *Leverhulme*, pp. 43–4; Simon Schaffer, 'A science whose business is bursting: soap bubbles as commodities in classical physics', in Lorraine Daston (ed.), *Things that Talk: Object Lessons from Art and Science* (New York: Zone Books, 2004), pp. 153–6.

43 Anne McClintock, *Imperial Leather: Race, Gender and Sexuality in the Colonial*

Context (New York: Routledge, 1995), pp. 212–13.

44 Quoted by Blanche B. Elliott, *A History of English Advertising* (London: Business Publications, 1962), p. 166.

45 *Ibid.*, pp. 175–6.

46 Nevett, *Advertising in Britain*, p. 98; T. A. B. Corley, 'Beecham, Sir Joseph', in *Oxford Dictionary of National Biography*.

47 I. A. Williams, rev. Robert Fitzgerald, 'Cadbury, George', in *Oxford Dictionary of National Biography*.

48 Fitzgerald, *Rowntree and the Marketing Revolution*, pp. 28, 91–2.

49 Hindley and Hindley, *Advertising in Victorian England*, pp. 42, 105.

50 Lever, *Leverhulme*, p. 71.

51 Wilson, *Unilever*, pp. 40, 52–3.

52 William Blackwood, 'Sir Thomas Lipton 1850–1932', in *The Post-Victorians* (London: Ivor Nicholson and Watson, 1933), pp. 336–8; Nevett, *Advertising in Britain*, p. 97; H. B. Grimsditch, rev. Gareth Shaw, 'Lipton, Sir Thomas Johnstone', *Oxford Dictionary of National Biography*.

53 Lionel Rose, *The Erosion of Childhood: Child Oppression in Britain 1860–1918* (London: Routledge, 1991), p. 163; Hindley and Hindley, *Advertising in Victorian England*, pp. 45–6.

54 William Woodruff, *The Road to Nab End: A Lancashire Childhood* (London: Eland, 2000), pp. 115–17.

55 Nevett, *Advertising in Britain*, pp. 71–4; Morris, 'Advertising and the acquisition of contemporary art', p. 195.

56 Hindley and Hindley, *Advertising in Victorian England*, p. 46.

57 Reproduced by Elliott, *English Advertising*, p. 197.

58 Reproduced by *ibid.*, p. 160.

59 UARM, LBC 4517, Lever to Charles M. Woodford, 28 November 1905.

60 UARM, LBC 162B, Lever to F. D'Arcy Cooper and the Special Committee, 19 October 1923; Wilson, *Unilever*, pp. 55–7; W. Hamish Fraser, *The Coming of the Mass Market 1850–1914* (Hamden, CT: Archon Books, 1981), pp. 205–6.

61 See, for example, illustrations in Lori Anne Loeb, *Consuming Angels: Advertising and Victorian Women* (New York: Oxford University Press, 1994), pp. 64–5.

62 Wilson, *Unilever*, p. 57.

63 Lever, *Leverhulme*, pp. 77–8; Wilson, *Unilever*, pp. 50, 56–7.

64 Hindley and Hindley, *Advertising in Victorian England*, p. 105; *Illustrated London News*, 8:x (1898), quoted by Leonard de Vries, *Victorian Advertisements* (London: John Murray, 1968), p. 98.

65 UARM, LBC 125, Lever to J. H. Hodges, 5 September 1908.

66 UARM, LBC 162B, Lever to Special Committee, 20 April 1923.

67 UARM, LBC 125, Lever to J. H. Hodges, 20 April 1906.

68 UARM, LBC 809A, Lever to John Cheshire, 14 September 1915.

69 UARM, LBC 7353, Lever to H. C. Rushton, 28 November 1916.

70 Wilson, *Unilever*, pp. 28, 32.

71 UARM, LBC 809A, Lever to John Cheshire, 19 August 1920.

72 *Ibid.*, 21 October 1920.

73 *Ibid.*, Lever to John Cheshire, 3 August 1922; see also *ibid.*, 4 December 1922.

74 Loeb, *Consuming Angels*, pp. 62–6.
75 UARM, LBC 8362 C, Lever to H. F. W. Bousfield, 6 November 1922.
76 UARM, LBC 809A, Lever to John Cheshire, 6 September 1921.
77 Opie, *Rule Britannia*, p. 32; Bradley, *Enlightened Entrepreneurs*, p. 183.
78 Quoted by Wilson, *Unilever*, p. 57.
79 Judith Williamson, *Decoding Advertisements: Ideology and Meaning in Advertising* (London and New York: Marion Boyars, 1978), p. 174.
80 Quoted by Wilson, *Unilever*, pp. 42–3.
81 Knox, *Coming Clean*, p. 66.
82 *Ibid.*, p. 88.
83 Colin MacDonald, *Highland Journey* (Edinburgh and London: Moray Press, 1943), pp. 154–6.
84 Paul Rutherford, *Endless Propaganda: The Advertising of Public Goods* (Toronto: University of Toronto Press, 2000), p. 81.
85 Gillian Dyer, *Advertising as Communication* (London: Routledge, 1989), pp. 40–1.
86 Wilson, *Unilever*, p. 41; Watson, *My Life*, pp. 134–5.
87 Opie, *Rule Britannia*, p. 33. See also 'The "Sunlight way of washing"', *Illustrated London News*, 24:v (1890), quoted by de Vries, *Victorian Advertisements*, p. 97.
88 Quoted by Wilson, *Unilever*, pp. 38–9.
89 Quoted by Knox, *Coming Clean*, p. 64.
90 Quoted *ibid.*, pp. 64–5.
91 Quoted *ibid.*, pp. 65–6.
92 *Illustrated Sporting and Dramatic News*, p. 665, quoted by Loeb, *Consuming Angels*, p. 44.
93 Quoted by Loeb, *Consuming Angels*, p. 115. For a similar theme see 'The wedding morning', *Illustrated London News*, 21:i (1893), quoted by de Vries, *Victorian Advertisements*, p. 58.
94 See Brian Lewis, *The Middlemost and the Milltowns: Bourgeois Culture and Politics in Early Industrial England* (Palo Alto, CA: Stanford University Press, 2001), p. 37.
95 Loeb, *Consuming Angels*, p. 45.
96 *Ibid.*, p. 33.
97 J. D. Keeler, 'Lever Brothers Company/Unilever', p. 934, and John McDonough, 'Lintas: worldwide', p. 947, in McDonough and Egolf (eds), *Encyclopedia of Advertising*, vol. II.
98 *The 'Sunlight' Year-Book for 1899* (Port Sunlight: Lever Bros, 1899).
99 Opie, *Rule Britannia*, p. 53.
100 *Ibid.*, p. 56.
101 Bradley, *Enlightened Entrepreneurs*, pp. 194–5; Opie, *Rule Britannia*, p. 68.
102 McClintock, *Imperial Leather*, pp. 209, 226. See also Anandi Ramamurthy, *Imperial Persuaders: Images of Africa and Asia in British Advertising* (Manchester: Manchester University Press, 2003), pp. 7, 24 ff; John M. MacKenzie, 'Introduction', in John M. MacKenzie (ed.), *Imperialism and Popular Culture* (Manchester: Manchester University Press, 1986), p. 8; Joseph Schumpeter, *Imperialism and Social Classes* (New York: Augustus M. Kelley, 1951; 1st edn, 1919), p. 13.

103 *3: The Radio Three Magazine* (November 1982), p. 42, quoted by MacKenzie, *Imperialism and Popular Culture*, p. 8. The impact of empire at home is heavily contested. Bernard Porter, *The Absent-minded Imperialists: Empire, Society, and Culture in Britain* (Oxford: Oxford University Press, 2004), makes a strong case for the shallowness of this imperialist sentiment, discovering widespread popular apathy towards and ignorance of the empire in the inter-war period.

104 To borrow an expression from Peter F. Drucker, *The Practice of Management* (New York: HarperCollins, 1954).

105 George Orwell, *The Road to Wigan Pier* (London: Penguin, 2001; 1st edn, 1937), pp. 119–20.

106 Orwell, *The Road to Wigan Pier*, p. 121.

107 John McDonough, 'Lintas: worldwide', in McDonough and Egolf (eds), *Encyclopedia of Advertising*, vol. II, p. 947; Knox, *Coming Clean*, p. 66.

108 Wilson, *Unilever*, pp. 55–6.

109 Opie, *Rule Britannia*, p. 85.

110 Quoted by Keeler, 'Lever Brothers Company/Unilever', p. 934.

111 Sivulka, *Soap, Sex, and Cigarettes*, pp. 158, 162; Whitson, 'Soap products', p. 1450.

112 Vincent Vinikas, *Soft Soap, Hard Sell: American Hygiene in an Age of Advertisement* (Ames, IA: Iowa State University Press, 1992), pp. xiv–xvi, 27–8.

113 Quoted by Sivulka, *Soap, Sex, and Cigarettes*, p. 160.

114 Vinikas, *Soft Soap, Hard Sell*, pp. xv, 36.

115 Walter Dill Scott, *The Psychology of Advertising: A Simple Exposition of the Principles of Psychology in their Relation to Successful Advertising*, 5th edn (Boston, MA: Small Maynard and Co., 1913), pp. 192–4, quoted by Bowlby, *Carried Away*, p. 97.

116 Sivulka, *Soap, Sex, and Cigarettes*, pp. 113–15, 149.

117 Edward L. Bernays, *Propaganda* (Port Washington, NY: Kennikat Press, 1972; 1st edn, 1928), pp. 9 (first quotation), 10–12, 20 (second quotation), 52, 63–7.

118 Sivulka, *Soap, Sex, and Cigarettes*, p. 166.

119 See Tim Kasser, *The High Price of Materialism* (Boston, MA: MIT Press, 2002).

120 Sivulka, *Soap, Sex, and Cigarettes*, p. 162; Diane Mermigas, 'J. Walter Thompson Company', in McDonough and Egolf (eds), *Encyclopedia of Advertising*, vol. III, p. 1532.

121 Vinikas, *Soft Soap, Hard Sell*, chap. 5.

122 'Kitchen calisthenics', *Houseworking your Way to Good Looks: Five Radio Talks Prepared by Cleanliness Institute* (n.d.), pp. 3–4, quoted by Vinikas, *Soft Soap, Hard Sell*, p. 90.

123 Bernays, *Propaganda*, pp. 57–61.

124 Michele Hilmes, 'Soap opera', pp. 1444–5, and Whitson, 'Soap products', p. 1451, in McDonough and Egolf (eds), *Encyclopedia of Advertising*, vol. III; Vinikas, *Soft Soap, Hard Sell*, p. 98.

125 Richards, *Commodity Culture*, p. 210.

126 Loeb, *Consuming Angels*, p. 102.

127 Rutherford, *Endless Propaganda*, p. 184.

128 J. B. Priestley and Jacquetta Hawkes, *Journey down a Rainbow* (London: Heinemann-Cresset, 1955), pp. 51–2.

129 T. S. Eliot, *The Idea of a Christian Society* (London: Faber and Faber, 1939), pp. 39–40, quoted by Raymond Williams, *Culture and Society 1780–1950* (Harmondsworth: Penguin, 1961), p. 227. See also F. R. Leavis, *Mass Civilisation and Minority Culture* (Cambridge: Minority Press, 1930); Robert S. Lynd and Helen Merrell Lynd, *Middletown: A Study in American Culture* (New York: Harcourt Brace and Co., 1929).

130 Orwell, *Wigan Pier*, pp. 189–90.

131 See Tim Kasser and Allen D. Kanner (eds), *Psychology and Consumer Culture: The Struggle for a Good Life in a Materialistic World* (Washington, DC: American Psychological Association, 2004); Obelkevich, 'Consumption', p. 152.

132 Matthew Hilton, *Consumerism in Twentieth-Century Britain: The Search for a Historical Movement* (Cambridge: Cambridge University Press, 2003), pp. 7–9, 16–17; Rutherford, *Endless Propaganda*, pp. 94–5.

133 Roger Chapman, 'Propaganda', in McDonough and Egolf (eds), *Encyclopedia of Advertising*, vol. III, p. 1295.

134 Quoted by Lever, *Leverhulme*, pp. 306–7.

3

Sunlight for the unwashed

The greatest show on earth

'Even on a really fine day,' Friedrich Engels wrote in 1844, 'Bolton is a gloomy, unattractive hole.'[1] The town into which Lever was born packed 60,000 people into a cluster of straggling streets, dank back alleys and dirty courtyards amidst rashes of factories and warehouses. The stagnant, stinking river Croal, which bisected the town, served as the common sewer. Unadorned chapels and a smattering of similarly uninspired public buildings did little to relieve the eye; only a token display of new, pseudo-Gothic churches made an effort, at least before they were enveloped in grime. Bolton was an unlovely, lethal place. More than a fifth of the population did not survive their first year of life; over a third were dead by age five. Its one saving grace was that it was still small enough that, for those with the leisure and energy, the surrounding countryside was easily within walking distance.[2]

William Hesketh Lever grew up on one of the more prosperous, middle-class streets of this archetypal Coketown, but within spitting distance of dismal poverty and squalor. Such an environment was to have a powerful impact on his thinking. In 1851 Britain was still predominantly a rural country: two-thirds of the population lived in the countryside or in towns of fewer than 10,000 people. By the eve of the First World War, more than three-quarters of people lived in towns of more than 10,000.[3] Everything that Lever attempted to accomplish at Port Sunlight and in his town planning schemes was against the backdrop of this tremendous urban explosion.

Port Sunlight was Lever's contribution to a century-long debate about how to manage the transition to an industrial, urban Britain. The village ranks as probably the most impressive experiment in factory paternalism ever mounted in Britain, the culmination of a ferment of experimentation over the preceding decades. Paternalism is not dead, of course. Major corporations still invest considerable sums in attempting to improve staff morale through a variety of incentive and reward schemes and the inculcation of a feeling of one big happy family. But wholehearted, full-blooded paternalism had its final flourish in the late nineteenth and early twentieth centuries. This variety of paternalism presupposed a firm small enough to be managed by a single boss who could have a face-to-face relationship with his employees. Once the firm grew in size and proliferated its branches, oversight by one man and his family gave way to tiers of professional managers and then, from the 1920s, the multi-divisional corporation. Increasingly the personnel manager's office looked after the company's welfare policies. This 'managerial revolution' was accompanied by broader national changes – the spread of political democracy, the expansion of opportunities to get an education, the growth of the welfare arm of the state – that rendered many of the functions of paternalism obsolete and spelled the end of a relatively quiescent, relatively static work force.[4]

If Port Sunlight was an attempt to do something about labour relations and the bleak state of towns, it was also good advertising copy. It smiled out of Lever Brothers' posters, a radiant, gleaming, sun-blessed idyll. Edwardian commentators were happy to play up to this image: 'It is an agreeable change from the long rows of ugly streets filled with houses of the brick-wall-with-four-holes-in-it pattern, which are passed all the way from Birkenhead to this oasis,'[5] said one; 'a practical achievement unequalled in the annals of industrial Utopias', said another.[6] Journalist Harold Begbie contrasted a northern manufacturing town he saw from his railway carriage on the way back from a visit to Port Sunlight in 1913:

> The air was black with smoke, the roofs were forlorn and melancholy; the whole town lay stretched out in fog and foulness like some cancerous disease … all the time my train waited, a procession of slatternly, white-faced, shawl-hooded women, by threes and twos and ones, was hurrying on its way to the muddied gates and the dejected yard of a factory that was like a ruined prison. I looked at those draggle-tailed women, and thought of the bright-faced girls in blue aprons and caps who make and pack soap in large airy rooms, dine for a few coppers in a great hall hung with beautiful pictures, and after their day's work have the clubs, the gymnasium, the swimming bath, the halls, the museum, and the garden spaces of Port Sunlight for their pleasure and their rest.[7]

Today most of the houses are privately owned and in 1999 Unilever ceded control to a trust, which rents out the rest at market rates.[8] But the game of contrasts can still be played. Port Sunlight's prettiness survives, its faux-quaint buildings and immaculate gardens strikingly different from the surrounding Merseyside sprawl. It retains, as one commentator puts it, 'the slightly unreal homogeneity of a pre-war Hollywood re-creation of an English village'.[9] Leaving the village, in the words of one of the irreverent team of satirists for 'The Framley Examiner', is an enormous shock: 'It's like crashing from Oz back to Kansas; everything seems to drain of colour. And yet, the area around Port Sunlight is not especially unpleasant, unwelcoming, untidy or unloved. It's just the same as 90 per cent of Great Britain: pretty bloody ordinary.'[10]

Happy human machines

The idea of the company village drew its inspiration from a pre-industrial, agrarian world where (in popular imagination at least) squires provided cottages on their estates for their labourers, regaled them with beef and ale from time to time and in return expected them to tug forelocks, doff hats and remember their God-given station in life. A number of pioneering textile manufacturers – Richard Arkwright at Cromford, Derbyshire, from the early 1770s; Jedediah Strutt at Belper and Milford, Derbyshire, from 1778; Samuel Greg at Quarry Bank Mill, Styal, Cheshire, from 1784; Samuel Oldknow at Mellor, near Stockport, from 1793 – who built their water-powered mills on fast-flowing streams in rural locations, sought to adapt the model. In country settings manufacturers often had little choice but to build accommodation for their workers, and for the more imaginative of them therein lay an opportunity to extend their influence outside the factory walls and to milk the maximum amount of deference. Dull economic compulsion, to borrow Marx's phrase, might cause a worker to respond to the factory bell, no matter how poor the pay, how long the hours and how miserable the conditions, but it could not inculcate loyalty, willing obedience or discipline, let alone foster middle-class standards of morality and respectability.

The most notable example of early factory paternalism took place in the Clyde valley in Scotland. David Dale, a Glasgow banker and businessman, and Richard Arkwright, the pioneer of cotton spinning in mills, visited the picturesque Falls of Clyde in 1784. Arkwright realized the potential for a cotton mill on the site. The pair began operation in 1785 at the newly christened New Lanark – but in the same year Arkwright's spinning machinery patent expired, so Dale could soldier on alone without him. It was Dale who developed the monster spinning mills, along with dormitories to house the labour force, which consisted mainly of children plucked from orphanages. He in turn sold up in 1799 to a consortium including Robert Owen, his new son-in-law. Under Owen, as sole manager and leading partner in what came to be the biggest cotton spinning concern in Britain, the paternalist provision came to encompass housing at moderate rents, gardens and allotments, education, free medical services, a store selling food and clothes at cost and social and recreational facilities.

This was not vastly different from other paternalist ventures, such as the worker housing, schools, sick club and co-operative store at the mills of his Unitarian friends, the Strutts, at Belper and Milford. And Owen arrogated to himself the right to discipline his workers by imposing fines for drunkenness and illegitimacy, by inspecting homes and through the use in his mills of the 'silent monitor' – a wooden block suspended above each worker, painted a different colour on each side, the colour recording the worker's conduct the day before, all marked down in a 'book of character'. But Owen went further and attracted more attention, particularly for the progressive approach to education that he tried to implement at New Lanark in two establishments: the New Institution (1812) and the Institution for the Formation of Character (1816). His first major work, *A New View of Society; or, Essays on the Principle of the Formation of Human Character* (1812–13), an unexceptional blend of Enlightenment ideas, called for a series of reforms including a national system of education to prevent poverty, idleness and crime.

It was towards the end of the decade that he began to take substantial steps towards a language of socialism and of communal living. In his *Report to the Committee of the Association for the Relief of the Manufacturing and Labouring Poor* (1817) his solution for the problem of unemployment was to house the poor in self-sufficient pauper colonies ('Agricultural Villages of Unity and Mutual Co-operation'), each colony containing a square surrounded by 1,000–1,500 acres of agricultural land, each square enclosed by accommodation blocks and including a public kitchen and dining room, a school, a lecture room and a library.[11] He was arriving at the conclusion not only that environments needed to be changed to improve the people – a common thread in factory paternalism – but that individualistic capitalism itself was intrinsically flawed and unreformable. Initially he had attracted considerable support in high places, but when he apparently began to attack bedrock institutions like the family, private property and organized religion he seemed like a dangerous and untouchable radical.[12]

The poet Robert Southey was impressed with New Lanark when he visited in 1819, but was sceptical as to whether the lessons from a model factory could be applied to society at large:

> Owen in reality deceives himself. He is part-owner and sole Director of a large establishment, differing more in accidents than in essence from a plantation: the persons under him happen to be white, and are at liberty by law to quit his service, but while they remain in it they are as much under his absolute management as so many negro-slaves. His humour, his vanity, his kindliness of nature (all these have their share) lead him to make these *human machines* as he calls them (and too literally believes them to be) as happy as he can, and to make a display of their happiness. And he jumps to the monstrous conclusion that because he can do this with 2,210 persons, who are totally dependent upon him – all mankind might be governed with the same facility.[13]

In marked contrast to Owen, other leading early factory paternalists adhered closely to the gospel of free-market industrial capitalism. Lever must have been well acquainted with some notable examples on his own doorstep around Bolton. One was the colony built by the Ashworth brothers, Edmund and Henry, Liberal Quakers, next to their cotton mills at Egerton and Turton, on the streams running off the moors to the north of the town. They began by putting up simple cottages to attract a work force, with nothing more extensive in mind. But a bout of fever struck in 1830 and they became more concerned about their tenants' welfare. Evidently, they reasoned, they needed to inspect the houses regularly to guard against filthy, disease-spreading habits. Inspections revealed that large families in small dwellings had to endure 'indelicate' living arrangements, and this insight led to the building of larger, three-bedroom cottages. Schools, a newsroom and a small library followed, and by then the Ashworths had turned themselves into thoroughgoing paternalists.

This was not charity but sound economics. The brothers secured a return of 7 or 8 per cent on the rents of the cottages, only marginally less than a fair rate of profit at the time for manufacturing capital; and, being both employer and landlord, they had more than the usual opportunities for disciplining their workers and workers' families, moulding better, more diligent mill hands from the resistant plebeian clay. Henry Ashworth described in 1833 with evident pride the way in which they visited the houses, examined 'very minutely' the state and cleanliness of the rooms, bedding and furniture and carefully enquired into the condition of the tenants' children, income and habits of life.[14]

Visitors to the colony reacted favourably to 'the order, the regularity, and the cleanliness of both the machinery and work-people',[15] to the well furnished, tidy cottages with their small collections of morally improving books, to the absence of dram shops, pawnbrokers, poaching, trade unions and other signs of moral flaccidity, to the apparent healthiness of the people and to the discouragement of married women with young families from working in the mills. W. Cooke Taylor, a propagandist for the Anti-Corn Law League, discovered in 1842 that surveillance was becoming internalized:

> I was informed by the operatives that permission to rent one of the cottages was regarded as a privilege and a favour, that it was in fact a reward reserved for honesty, industry and sobriety, and that a tenant guilty of any vice or immorality would at once be dismissed. Mr. Ashworth was said to be very strict in enforcing attention to cleanliness, both of house and person, and in requiring the use of separate sleeping apartments for the children of different sexes. It was sufficiently obvious, from the gossip I heard, that public opinion had established a very stringent form of moral police in the village, which superseded the necessity of any other.[16]

A second conspicuous example of extensive paternalism in the same general vicinity was the sewing-cotton and smallware manufacturing enterprise of James and Robert Chadwick at Eagley Mills. This consisted of model cottages, a library and reading room, a bowling green, a cricket pitch, a brass band and a park. A third major example could be found at the Dean Mills, Barrowbridge, in another wooded site by a stream on the edge of the moors north of Bolton. The mill owners, Robert Gardner, his son Richard, and Thomas Bazley, extensive manufacturers across the region, built terraces of model cottages with gardens for around 300 of their hands and later added a bath house and a large building containing a boys' school, library, newsroom, lecture room and 'hall of science'. The workmen established a co-operative provision store. When Prince Albert visited in 1851, the *Illustrated London News* enthused that the 'community of interest between the employer and the employed' was 'perfectly illustrated by the good-will and thoughtful attention of the former to the interest and welfare of their subordinates, and the contentment, steadiness, and affectionate zeal of the latter'. All told, the general harmony indicated 'a well organised community never equalled by the utopias of philosophy'.[17]

Benjamin Disraeli celebrated the Dean Mills in fictional guise in his novel *Coningsby* (1844), and there may be something of the Ashworth brothers in his Mr Millbank in *Coningsby* and in his Mr Trafford in *Sybil* (1845), his other 'Condition of England' novel.[18] Disraeli, following earlier High Tory writers in the same mould like Samuel Taylor Coleridge and Robert Southey, railed against the dehumanizing, impoverishing impact of an ideology grounded in individualism and *laissez-faire* economics, and contrasted modern times unfavourably with a feudal Golden Age built on notions of ordered hierarchy, duty and responsibility. His hope was that an enlightened landed aristocracy, in harness with a revered monarch and a re-energized Anglican Church, could bridge the widening gap between Britain's two nations, the rich and the poor. The natural governors had abdicated, replaced by '*Laissez-faire*, Supply-and-demand, Cash-payment the one nexus of man to man: Free-trade, Competition, and Devil take the hindmost, our latest Gospel yet preached', as Thomas Carlyle famously put it in his essay *Past and Present* in 1843.[19] The solution was for an active, responsible governing class to resume its duties and to provide a decent standard of living and spiritual education for the lower orders. But Disraeli reasoned that if industrial capitalism were here to stay, 'captains of industry' (to borrow another phrase of Carlyle's) could stand in for enlightened aristocrats.

At a time when liberal economic notions had captured the commanding political heights, industrialization was thickening the numbers, power and influence of the middle strata of society and religious Nonconformity was fiercely challenging the sway of the Established Church, such thinking was hopelessly wishful. Nevertheless, High Tory ideas reverberated at the cultural level, particularly in the revival of all things Gothic, a fascination with the Middle Ages in art and literature and the fanciful reincarnation of the chivalric gentleman, assiduously propagated by public schools at least until the First World War. The message was that, since the ruling elite could no longer expect automatic deference simply because they owned many acres of choice real estate, their manifest moral superiority instead would establish their claim to rule.[20]

The irony is that the Bolton paternalist mill owners were not romantic Tories enamoured of Disraelian sentiments. In the troubled 1830s and 1840s, in the context of cyclical slumps in the economy and violent unrest, mill owners were assailed not only by reactionary Tories calling for a return to a mythical Golden Age of rustic simplicity and ordered, landed hierarchy, but also by factory reformers demanding shorter hours, improved conditions and an end to 'wage slavery', and above all by political radicals in the Chartist movement agitating for greater democracy and the overturning of self-interested legislation favouring the propertied classes. These paternalistic mill colonies were attempts by the millocrats or cotton lords, particularly Nonconformists associated with the Anti-Corn Law League, to demonstrate to the naysayers that they were capable of putting their own house in order without the intervention of the state or a radical overhaul of the political system and that they were building an industrial civilization that worked, that spelled progress and that was superior to any possible alternatives.[21]

Lever – fervent capitalist, crusading free trader, Nonconformist Smilesian to the marrow – surely would have had no truck with the high priests of Toryism and the panegyrists of a mythical medieval England? One would think not, but he too did in fact adopt many of the accoutrements of the cult of chivalry and idealized historicism, so pervasively had it drip-dripped through British society. As we have seen, he accepted ennoblement and created coats of arms to match, sent his son to Eton and Trinity College, Cambridge, was an enthusiastic collector of the paintings of the Pre-Raphaelites depicting morally didactic scenes from English history of the Middle Ages, built the replica of the ruins of Liverpool Castle upon the reservoir in Lever Park, constructed the richly Gothic churches at Port Sunlight and Thornton Hough and arranged for his wife and himself to recline in carved stone sepulchres in Christ Church, in the manner of a medieval knight and his lady.

Above all, the houses in his factory village exhibited a variety of supposedly sixteenth- and seventeenth-century facades (albeit concealing thoroughly modern interiors). In this evocation of the ivy-clad, hollyhocked English village of yore, where he could act the squire to his grateful tenantry on special occasions, spreading bonhomie and patting children's heads, there is no doubt that his aim was to create an *ersatz* version of Merrie England with a powerful message that Southey, Coleridge, Carlyle and Disraeli would have understood and applauded. As he put it in 1900, his aim in building Port Sunlight was to 'socialise and Christianise business relations, and get back again in the office, factory, and workshop to that close family brotherhood that existed in the good old days of hand labour'. One had to 'candidly admit that labour has an honest and truthful claim to a share in prosperity, and that, by recognizing such claim, capitalism will gain immensely, whilst the difficulties and responsibilities of management will be enormously reduced'.[22] It was up to the new generation of enlightened plutocrats, he thought, to lead the way.

But if he took on board some of the trimmings of Tory paternalism, he never came close to conceding the foundational Tory point that industrial capitalism was a terrible mistake. Paternalism, in reality, was far too useful and pervasive a concept for any one set of ideologues to be able to claim sole proprietorship. To quote Dennis Hardy's summary of these model communities:

> They usually represented a substantial improvement in environmental standards, but there was no question of challenging the existing system of society. On the contrary, they set out to reinforce those very qualities upon which the future of capitalism would be assured – such qualities as loyalty to employer, retention of a class system, hard and honest labour, disaffection with talk of revolution, respectability, thrift and religious belief. They were paragons of capitalist industrial society – conscious attempts to re-establish the assumed harmony of village life in an industrial setting, this time with the factory and mine-owner usurping the role of the feudal landlord.[23]

As writers and intellectuals agonized over the 'Condition of England' the factory colonies received much attention from those hopeful that they provided the answer. But such model settlements were few in number. The steam engine had largely displaced the waterwheel by the middle of the century, so the need for a rural location next to fast-flowing water became obsolete. Manufacturers overwhelmingly chose to build their factories in towns, close to good transportation links and to markets, where they could rely on housing stock augmented by speculative builders. In the stabilized economy after 1850, with fewer manufacturers hanging on by their fingernails and profit margins becoming a little more comfortable and reliable, more employers could exploit the potential of paternalism, but they did so in a more diffuse and diluted form. Most employers attempted to buy productivity and obedience with the occasional 'treat' for their factory hands, such as a railway trip to the seaside or tea and biscuits up at the mill, rather than anything more extensive.[24]

There were exceptions. Some employers in the second half of the nineteenth century provided company housing, but nothing more, if they needed to attract workers outside established urban centres. The railway works at Crewe are a good example.[25] A number of entrepreneurs continued to build in rural settings if the lure of cheaper land and room to expand outweighed the advantages of the town, and continued to experiment with whole-hog paternalism. The prime mid-century example was Saltaire, in the West Riding of Yorkshire, the creation of Titus Salt. Salt had made a fortune exploiting the possibilities of alpaca wool in his mills in Bradford. After serving as mayor of the town in 1848, witnessing and dealing with the twin traumas of Chartist agitation and the arrival of cholera the following year, he determined on an alternative approach to solving social ills. He started to build a huge mill in the countryside to the north-west of the town in 1851, next to the river Aire and the Leeds and Liverpool Canal and close to excellent road and rail links. Over the next quarter of a century he oversaw the construction of the grid-plan, Italianate terraced housing, chapels, schools, bath and wash houses, almshouses, infirmary, park and institute that make up the village.[26]

Budgett Meakin, a social commentator who wrote a book describing and advocating model factories and villages in 1905, commented, 'Now that our ideals have so far advanced, and we have industrial villages beside which Saltaire is dismal and cramped, there is a tendency to disparage the immense stride marked by its construction over half a century ago.'[27] But in spite of Saltaire's dense concentration of thirty-two houses per acre,[28] it was the mill-colony marvel of its time. Its status today as a UNESCO World Heritage Site is a fair indication of its unrivalled standing in the period between the building of the New Lanark mills (the recipient of a similar accolade) and of the soap and chocolate villages of Port Sunlight and Bournville at the end of the century. And, as in other model communities, paternalism and authoritarianism were inseparable. The proprietor insisted that Saltaire remain teetotal, he allowed no trade unions or political or religious demonstrations and workers lost their houses if they ceased to work for the company.[29]

A handful of bosses attempted plainer imitations of Saltaire, with company housing and a sprinkling of schools, chapels, village halls, libraries and recreation grounds. Examples include the communities attached to John Grubb Richardson's linen mills at Bessbrook, Northern Ireland (from 1846); the Butterley Iron Company's Ironville (1850); Price's Patent Candle Company's Bromborough Pool Village (from 1853), just up the road from the future Port Sunlight; Clark's boot factory at Street, Somerset; Chivers' jam factory at Histon, Cambridgeshire; and W. P. Hartley's jam factory at Aintree, near Liverpool.

In the West Riding the settlements created by Edward Akroyd and by John, Joseph and Sir Francis Crossley stand out. These mill owners were all connected by family and business ties with Titus Salt, were all Congregationalists, Liberals and free-traders too and had also variously served as mayors of Bradford or Halifax. The Crossleys, the world's largest manufacturers of tapestries and Brussels carpets, built their community in the West Hill Park area of Halifax in the 1860s. Akroyd constructed three rows of Gothicized model houses, with shops and allotments, for his worsted mills at Copley, near Halifax, in the late 1840s and another settlement around 1860, which he named Akroydon. This boasted more Gothic houses, to the design of George Gilbert Scott, set around a central park and allotments.[30] Akroyd explained his love of the Gothic in 1862: 'Intuitively this taste of our forefathers pleases the fancy, strengthens house and home attachment, entwines the present with the memory of the past, and promises, in spite of opposition and prejudice, to become the national style of modern, as it was of old England.' A writer in *The Builder* echoed the sentiment a year later: 'Mr. Akroyd is very desirous of keeping up the old English notion of a village – the squire and the parson, as the head and centre of all progress and good fellowship; then the tenant-farmers; and lastly, the working population.'[31]

Similar examples of above-average company housing and facilities were replicated across the Continent and North America, but in his 1905 survey Meakin identified what he deemed to be truly advanced ideals only in a handful of places, including Bournville and Port Sunlight in England, Pullman near Chicago and the Krupp colonies near Essen, in Germany. Pullman, built by George Mortimer Pullman to the designs of Solon Spencer Beman in the early 1880s, comprised more than 1,500 company houses for the workers of the celebrated railway carriage works. It earned a reputation as a world-class showcase of superior-quality worker housing and material welfare, particularly after Pullman exhibited models of it in Paris in 1889 and at the Chicago Exposition in 1893. But already in 1885 Richard Ely, an economist, had written in *Harper's Monthly* that the residents felt as if they were in a 'gilded cage', with their personal liberties curbed. A bitter strike in 1894 badly damaged the town's reputation, and residents and workers vehemently complained about the poky rooms, overcharges in rents, wage deductions and ten-day eviction clauses.[32]

The Krupp engineering and armaments firm established its first colony in the 1860s and went on to build fourteen in total around Essen. The fifth, sixth and seventh colonies, started sequentially at Baumhof, Alfredshof and Altenhof in the 1890s, garnered particular praise for their spaciousness, ample gardens and picturesque dwellings; that at Margarethenhöhe, dating from 1906, most resembled Port Sunlight and Bournville. In common with most of their fellow paternalists, Messrs Krupp were not striving for any radical transformation of society. Far from it: the increasingly elaborate nature of their model villages grew out of a sense that management techniques to pacify the work force needed to keep pace with and provide attractive alternatives to the forward march of trade unionism and socialism.[33]

Duodecimo editions of the New Jerusalem

If the tradition of the company town and the need to attract, retain and control a work force was one line of thought pointing to Port Sunlight, the desire to find an alternative to environmental degradation was another. A combination of fear of revolutionary unrest and of spreading disease, philanthropic impulses, economic self-interest and civic pride had pushed the increasing squalor of the industrial town up to the top of the political agenda for the first time in the 1840s and public health legislation followed in fits and starts. At that time attention focused on northern mill towns; a generation or more later it shifted southward. Social investigators rediscovered poverty on a dramatic scale in the 1880s, particularly in London, and penned shrill tracts about 'the bitter cry of outcast London' or the dire problems besetting 'Darkest England'. Rapid population growth in the cities, spiralling rents, displacement because of slum clearance and the construction of urban railways, and a highly uneven economy creating vast numbers of the casually employed and insufficiently remunerated, all generated fertile conditions for grotesque overcrowding, endemic disease and chronic malnutrition. The fevered imaginations of bourgeois commentators once again detected ripe breeding conditions for domestic discord, drunkenness, crime, disorder, godlessness and sexual immorality. Not only did decency and Christian values seem to be imperilled, in a competitive imperial age it was feared that the nation's health and manly vigour were becoming dangerously enfeebled.[34]

What was to be done? The governmental solution was to construct satisfactory sewers, provide sufficient water and regulate the construction of housing. A succession of statutes – the Torrens Act of 1868, the Cross Act of 1875 and the Public Health Act of 1875 – enabled slum clearance and initiated the building of strings of the famous two-up-two-down terraced bye-law houses that became ubiquitous in towns and cities in the late nineteenth century. But this housing could not keep pace with the urban population explosion and still left many of the older slums and rookeries intact. It was often prohibitively expensive for the underemployed, and at a density of forty houses per acre continued to cram a depressing number of tiny dwellings into a confined area, paving over much of the remaining green space. Usually in narrow, tunnel-back formats to minimize frontage and therefore the cost of roads, paving and sewers, they were frequently dark and gloomy.

The philanthropic solution, such as that organized by the Peabody Trust in London from 1862 – using money provided by George Peabody, an American merchant – was to build solid, clean working-class tenements at affordable rents, while still providing a reasonable return on investment. This small-scale 'five per cent philanthropy' was woefully inadequate to the task at hand, and these 'model' dwellings were necessarily (because they had to turn a profit) too cramped and barrack-like to be a significant improvement. Some municipal authorities, in particular London County Council and Liverpool City Council, built a little housing for cheap rent; but, taken together, philanthropic and council housing still only provided well under 1 per cent of housing stock by 1914.[35]

The better-off could buy clean air and water for themselves by escaping to the suburbs. Suburbanization in its modern guise – detached or semi-detached houses surrounded by patches of garden on winding crescents, the head of the family commuting to work in the city centre each day – had recognizable forebears in eighteenth-century London and by the early nineteenth century in industrializing cities like Manchester, Leeds and Birmingham. But the phenomenon did not come of age and towns and cities begin to separate out on class lines, chromatographically, until after 1850 with the development of improved transportation: first the horse-drawn omnibus, then the suburban and underground railway, the electric tram and finally, by the early twentieth century, the automobile. The suburban house (according at least to the preachings of many a tract, sermon and advice column) promised a separation of home and work, private and public, a haven from the sordidness, corruption, immorality and foul stench of the business and political world, a special place where domestic virtues could be protected, feminine innocence maintained and healthy offspring reared. This cult of domesticity took powerful root in Victorian England. Even labour leaders and trade unionists came to accept the houseproud housewife as the aspirational standard.[36]

At the middling to lower end of the suburban social scale, by the early twentieth century, around London 'the miles and miles of little red houses in little silent streets, in number defying imagination', as the Liberal MP and writer C. F. G. Masterman described it, promised 'a life of Security; a life of Sedentary Occupation; a life of Respectability'. Each of these houses boasted 'its pleasant drawing room, its bow window, its little front garden, its high-sounding title – "Acacia Villa" or "Camperdown Lodge" – attesting unconquered human aspiration'.[37] Add to these 'The Laurels', the home of City clerk Charles Pooter and his wife, Carrie, in George and Weedon Grossmith's *Diary of a Nobody* (1892), the classic gentle satire on this type of lifestyle in the late 1880s. Late nineteenth-century London boasted only one real exception to this monotony – a self-contained, proto-garden suburb that had a reputation for attracting creative and artistic people. In 1876 Jonathan Thomas Carr, a speculative builder, began to lay out a housing estate, Bedford Park, adjoining Turnham Green station, Chiswick. By 1883 there were 490 comfortable middle-class houses in a Queen Anne style, largely the work of E. W. Godwin and Norman Shaw, alongside a church, shops, a club and an inn.[38]

None of these partial and inadequate solutions was good enough for the visionaries. None of them addressed the root causes creating a disordered, dysfunctional society. All of them failed to produce balanced, harmonious, social and economic relations. The visionary solution was to start again: since existing towns were beyond repair, the argument went, the only promising way forward was to build anew. Before we see how Lever fits into the flood of ideas behind the garden city movement, and their partial realization in the subtopias of today, we need briefly to explore these utopian dreams.

At one end of the visionary spectrum were to be found ideas for small, self-sustaining communities based on entirely different social relations and modes of government, often looking back to primitive Christianity, or to the supposed ideals of the monastery, or to tribes living close to nature, or to romanticized distortions of late medieval communes, or to depictions of peasant communities before the imposition of the Norman yoke – all united in the gloriously optimistic belief that poverty, strife and despair were not inevitable and that, given the right circumstances, humanity was perfectible.[39] Gerrard Winstanley, leader of the Diggers or True Levellers during the English Revolution, founder of a short-lived colony at St George's Hill in Weybridge in 1649 and inspiration of many later utopians, put it best: 'Why may we not have our Heaven here (that is, a comfortable livelihood in the Earth) and Heaven hereafter too?'[40]

In nineteenth-century England there were twenty-eight alternative communities, according to Dennis Hardy's calculation – that is, planned communities antithetical to the established order. They ranged from Moravian villages, established in the belief that religious exclusivity was the way to avoid contamination with broader society in preparation for the Kingdom of God, to a variety of agrarian socialist or anarchist settlements preaching communal living and a back-to-the-land philosophy. The sectarian communities, bound by the fervour of religious belief, were the most enduring – just as they were in America, where the Amish, Mennonites, Shakers and Mormons profited from relative religious toleration and vast amounts of space, spectacularly in the case of the Mormons planting Salt Lake City.[41]

The majority of the secular communities in Britain were tiny, of brief duration and far removed from the political and economic struggles of the mainstream labour movement. The most celebrated were the utopian socialist communities inspired by Robert Owen: seven in Britain, plus another three in which Owenites were involved, and at least sixteen avowedly Owenite or Owen-influenced communities in America. The first was New Harmony, Indiana, begun in 1825. It proved a short-lived fiasco, swiftly breaking down into several different factions, and the experiment was virtually dead by the summer of 1827. As Owen himself put it, 'experience proved that the attempt was premature to unite a number of strangers not previously educated for the purpose, who should carry on extensive operations for their common interest, and live together as a common family'. Attempts by himself (at a place he named Harmony Hall at Queenwood, Hampshire) and his disciples to create similar utopian communities elsewhere fared little better, running out of money or collapsing into jealousy and recrimination.[42] But they had dared to dream of something better, and for a time they demonstrated an alternative to industrial capitalism, holding to the belief that private property, religion and the nuclear family were obstacles to human happiness, needing to be abolished and replaced by collective child raising, communal housekeeping and equality of the sexes.[43]

In a celebrated passage, Karl Marx and Friedrich Engels in the *Communist Manifesto* (1848) denounced this 'Critical-Utopian Socialism and Communism' of Owen, and the French writers Charles Fourier, Claude-Henri de Saint-Simon and Étienne Cabet:

Only from the point of view of being the most suffering class does the proletariat exist for them.... [T]hey reject all political, and especially all revolutionary,
action; they wish to attain their ends by peaceful means, and endeavour, by
small experiments, necessarily doomed to failure, and by the force of example,
to pave the way for the new social Gospel.... They, therefore, endeavour, and
that consistently, to deaden the class struggle and to reconcile the class antagonisms. They still dream of experimental realisation of their social Utopias, of
founding isolated "phalanstères", of establishing "Home Colonies", of setting up
"Little Icaria" – duodecimo editions of the New Jerusalem – and to realise all
these castles in the air, they are compelled to appeal to the feelings and purses
of the bourgeois.[44]

The "phalanstère" – the creation of Fourier in a succession of writings,
including *Le Nouveau Monde industriel et sociétaire* (1829) – was a large,
three-wing building on the model of the Palace of Versailles. Each phalans-
tery would, ideally, house 1,620 people (because Fourier had discovered 810
varieties of human nature, each a combination of the twelve basic, God-given
human passions that he was seeking to liberate, and he doubled the number to
include men and women), and at the centre of each building would be dining
rooms, a library, a temple and the *Tour d'Ordre*. Ultimately he envisaged that
phalansteries would serve as building blocks of community solidarity within
model three-ringed, radial cities in the creation of a stateless society.

Phalansteries in practice fared no better than Owenite communities, with
many short-lived ventures, including up to thirty-seven in the United States. A
variation was the Familistère at Guise, northern France, built by Jean-Baptiste-
André Godin, who had made himself wealthy by inventing a cast iron stove.
By 1880 the Familistère housed 1,170 people in a familiar three-wing building
with accompanying community facilities. 'Order, regulations, mechanism,
comfort,' is how the novelist Émile Zola summed up the clash between decent
living standards and the air of surveillance that he noted during a visit, 'but
what about the wish for adventure, the risks of the free and adventurous
life?'

Icaria was the invention of Étienne Cabet. While in exile in London he
published his *Voyages et adventures de Lord William Carisdall en Icarie* (1839),
where he described the utopia of Icaria, run by a benevolent despot, Icar – a
land of minute regulation, cleanliness, symmetry and oppressive good order,
where all property and produce would belong to the people. The capital city,
Icara, was to be circular, with streets on a grid plan, thirty-two identical
houses on each street. Once again, the United States proved to be the testing
ground for these ideas. Once again ventures crashed and burned, but American Icarian communes in some form or another persisted for several decades
in the second half of the nineteenth century.[45]

The Icarias and the phalansteries wrestled with an abiding problem in the quest for perfectibility: how to ensure that imperfect folk, with irrational and deviant traits and desires all their own, conformed to the higher behaviour required. In the absence of a mill owner regulating the lives of his workers, what would be necessary? Already, in desperate contrast to the ideals of equality, co-operation and communalism, the seeds were being planted for the twentieth century's leadership-cult regimes and the great dystopian novels: Yevgeny Zamyatin's *We* (1920), Aldous Huxley's *Brave New World* (1932) and George Orwell's *1984* (1949).[46]

But in addition to inadvertently hinting at the totalitarian potential of their utopias, Fourier and Cabet also pointed to the development of something greater than the isolated community: the far more ambitious, wholly planned town – not a company town, merely serving the needs of one manufacturing concern, but a comparatively large, rationally organized, occupationally diverse settlement. The genealogical line of inspiration here can clearly be traced back to Renaissance dreams of the 'Ideal City' – including Thomas More's *Utopia* (1516), with its fifty-four near-identical, geometrically arranged cities, Johann Valentin Andreae's *Christianopolis* (1619), Tommaso Campanella's *City of the Sun* (1623) and Francis Bacon's *New Atlantis* (1627). These in turn drank deeply from Plato, who described the perfect city-state (in contrast to degenerate Athens) and the marvellous mythical city of Atlantis. Common to most of these visions was the wish to impose a spatial order and harmony, frequently in carefully planned concentric circles, in place of the seemingly random and distressingly messy accretions of time. This physical engineering would somehow, the theory went, more or less automatically translate into universal collective happiness.[47]

The Americans had been planting new towns ever since Jamestown, Virginia, in 1607. Early New England towns attempted to build model Christian communities grouped around common land, and William Penn's plans for the 'Holy Experiment' of Philadelphia (1681–83) went a step further in creating a well ordered town. Having witnessed the plague and the Great Fire in London in the mid-1660s, Penn was concerned to stipulate that 'every house be placed, if the person pleases, in the middle of its plot, as to the breadth way of it, so that there may be ground on each side for gardens, or orchards, or fields, that it may be a green country town, which will never be burnt, and always be wholesome'.[48]

American cities by the nineteenth century were far from ideal or meticulously planned, subsumed by the same problems of overcrowding and urban blight as in Britain. But planners had a new field of endeavour: the British Empire, where white settlers were planting cities from scratch. William Light, the Surveyor General of South Australia from 1836 to 1838, for example, chose the site of the new capital, Adelaide, and produced a celebrated plan surrounding the city with a belt of parkland, introducing the radical notion that green belts should halt the aimless sprawl of a city and that then a second, similarly constrained, city should be begun for overspill populations. Robert Pemberton's plan in *The Happy Colony* (1854) for a settlement, Queen Victoria Town, on a Pacific island – something like a garden city on circular lines – inspired the construction of Canterbury, New Zealand.

Closer to home, author, traveller, social reformer and former MP, James Silk Buckingham, in his *National Evils and Practical Remedies* (1849), pitched the detailed idea of a healthy, environmentally sound town of 10,000, named Victoria, built in concentric squares intersected by radial avenues bearing such optimistic names as Unity, Concord and Faith, with industry on the periphery and surrounded by a green belt. The plan of Benjamin Ward Richardson, a leading London physician, for the 100,000–strong city of Hygiea (*Hygiea, a City of Health*, 1876) was, as its name suggests, a paean to hygiene in an attempt to reduce abysmal urban mortality rates, and included much emphasis on sanitation – hot and cold running water throughout, rubbish chutes, internal chimneys, swimming pools, Turkish baths, as well as the usual schools and libraries.[49]

Somewhere in the middle of the visionary spectrum, again partially realized but mainly frustrated, was a final variation on the alternative community or the ideal planned city: the home colony. This, too, was driven by a strongly anti-urban industrial philosophy, determined to decant the city poor into the countryside. One example was the unfulfilled plans in the 1840s of John Minter Morgan, Christian socialist and enthusiastic campaigner for the co-operative cause, for a Christian commonwealth under the auspices of the Church of England, based on communitarian self-supporting villages for 300 families, surrounded by belts of agricultural land.[50] A critic in the *Illustrated London News* spotted an element of coercion and surveillance in Morgan's scheme:

> It reminds us of Bridewell, or some contrivance for central inspection, not of the sunny or shady lanes in which the rose and honeysuckle-decked cottages of our native land are so happily nestled…. The idea is obviously borrowed from the unsuccessful efforts of the State to correct the people by bridewells, work-houses and prisons – substituting a gentler kind of control for meagre diet, ships, dungeons and fetters.[51]

The idea of planned migration to labour colonies within Britain took on a certain vogue among economists and social reformers in the 1880s and 1890s, borrowing from Continental examples, both as a means to cure underemployment and as perceptions of the crisis of overcrowding in London grew more acute. Co-operative farming communities would lift the poor out of the city slums and substitute lung-expanding, colour-enhancing toil. Some of the schemes were radical in intent, shading into the alternative communities we have already encountered. For example, the Austrian economist Theodore

Hertzka, in his book *Freiland* (1890; translated as *Freeland* in 1892), outlined a plan for democratic colonies combining 'individualism' and 'socialism', and the Brighton-based Russian *émigré* anarchist, Peter Kropotkin, expounded a project in a series of articles written between 1888 and 1890 and later collected together as *Fields, Factories and Workshops* (1898) for self-governing agricultural/artisanal colonies or 'industrial villages'.[52]

Other schemes were more punitive, a way of dealing with or retraining misfits and loafers. For example, William Booth, founder of the Salvation Army, in his *In Darkest England and the Way Out* (1890), proposed a system of colonies to regenerate and redeem what he called the 'submerged tenth' of the population: City Colonies to provide food and shelter in return for work; Farm Colonies as a next step, to supply agricultural or industrial training; and finally shipment to Overseas Colonies in one of the empire's white settlements, where recruits could regain their manhood as productive and respectable members of society. 'Broadly speaking,' Booth wrote, 'your experimental communities fail because your Utopias all start upon the system of equality and government by vote of the majority, and, as a necessary and unavoidable consequence, your Utopias get to loggerheads, and Utopia goes smash.' His colonies, on the other hand, had a 'directing brain' who instilled strict discipline, teetotalism and daily prayer and who demanded 'universal and unquestioning obedience from those at the bottom'. Booth raised £130,000 within two years and planted his first Farm Colony at Hadleigh in Essex. It attracted 325 colonists by the summer of 1892, all engaged in land reclamation, brickmaking and market-gardening. A second Salvation Army colony at Boxted, near Colchester, followed in 1906. John Burns, labour leader and future Liberal Minister, dismissed these and other Christian colonies in 1905 as 'merely doss houses', but Hadleigh was still going strong in the 1920s, sending recruits to new beginnings overseas.[53]

Home colonies of one type or another had the support of many on the moderate left, including labour leaders like Kier Hardy, George Lansbury and Will Crooks, and Fabian socialists like Sidney and Beatrice Webb. But there was a fine line between compulsory colonies designed to punish and hopefully modify the behaviour of the 'work-shy loafer', drunks, the weak-minded and other undesirables and more idealistic training camps intended to teach people necessary skills for the work force. The Fabians came closer to the former, Lansbury to the latter. With the financial support of the American millionaire Joseph Fels, who made his money in manufacturing naphtha soap in Philadelphia, Lansbury and the Poor Law guardians of Poplar, London, established in 1904 two labour colonies for fruit and vegetable growing: one at Laindon, Essex, for 200 men, the other at Hollesley Bay, Suffolk, which grew to 335 residents. They were intended to be co-operative, self-sustaining communities, genuine alternatives to capitalism. But when John Burns, resolutely opposed to all labour colonies, became President of the Local Government Board in the new Liberal government at the end of 1905, he prevented the Poplar board from sending labourers to the colonies for more than sixteen-week stints, which effectively killed off the project.[54]

A shrine for the worship of cleanliness

Most of the visionary schemes proved to be historical dead ends. But they were fertile in ideas for the garden city movement, as we shall see, as was Lever's own solution to the same set of problems. At Port Sunlight Lever replicated the attempts by earlier paternalists to create a happier, fitter, stronger, more productive, less fractious work force and provided a small-scale but replicable answer to urban blight.

When he moved into his first soap factory at Warrington, initial success rapidly encouraged expansion. But the site was hemmed in by the river Mersey, the London and North Western Railway and another firm's pumping station and reservoirs. The owner of the only plot of vacant land spotted his advantage and demanded a prohibitive price. Lever baulked at this and, with William Owen, a local architect, took the train up and down both banks of the Mersey scouting for alternatives. After many months he settled on a marshy greenfield site, which he was to rechristen Port Sunlight, near Bromborough Pool. He was motivated by several factors: the cheapness of the land; the easy access to waterborne transport along the Mersey, but beyond the range of Liverpool Dock and Harbour dues; railway facilities free from the 'tyranny of Railway monopoly' at Warrington; and the ability to spread out on the level, which not only reduced the risks of fire and the cost of handling goods but also provided a better lit, better ventilated, healthier, more systematically organized working environment. He could attract workers from Birkenhead, yet building outside a town encouraged him to provide housing for them. This, too, was to his liking: 'Out in the country with good houses for the workpeople to live in we get a more settled body of workers,' he wrote. 'The children grow up under healthy conditions which guarantees a still further improvement in the workpeople each succeeding generation.'[55]

Over the next quarter of a century Lever Brothers constructed over 800 brick, stone and half-timbered cottages in a range of pseudo English, Dutch, French and Flemish designs stretching from the late medieval through the Jacobean to Queen Anne periods.[56] All the cottages were in blocks surrounded by green space, one block resembling a half-timbered Lancashire manor house, Kenyon Old Hall, another Shakespeare's birthplace at Stratford upon Avon.[57] 'The groups of cottages,' wrote one commentator, ' – varying from two to seven in each – are pretty and dainty, the style of architecture appealing to our strongly pronounced, natural and characteristic love of "home".'[58] In contrast

6 Port Sunlight cottages, Park Road, *c.* 1913

to the forty-an-acre density of bye-law housing and the thirty-two-an-acre at Saltaire, there were no more than seven houses per acre at Port Sunlight.

Lever employed nearly thirty architects or architectural firms, mainly local but with a smattering of London talent, to design the different clusters and phases of houses.[59] But much of the work was his own. In his son's words:

> He was never happier than when seated in front of a plan with a drawing-board, ruler and T-square ready to hand. Architecture was always an absorbing study for him. … With him it was never a case of leaving everything to the architect and settling the bill when the work was finished. Expert advice he wisely sought and freely acknowledged, but the plan and lay-out of Port Sunlight were his own, and so, in the main, were the plans of the works and the buildings in the village, and in many cases of the houses also. The architects he employed all looked upon him as unique amongst their clients. He did not employ them – he collaborated with them.[60]

The dwellings conformed to one of two types: the 'kitchen cottage', which contained a kitchen, a scullery and three bedrooms; and the 'parlour cottage', which added a parlour and a fourth bedroom. Lever Brothers heavily subsidized them through 'prosperity sharing'. In an interview in 1903 with Georges

Benoît-Lévy, the principal organizer of the Association des Cités-jardins de France, Lever divulged some of the thinking behind prosperity sharing, as well as his moralizing intent, father-knows-best attitude and I've-made-my-mind-up-so-that's-final rigidity:

> If I were to follow the usual mode of profit-sharing I would send my workmen and work girls to the cash office at the end of the year and say to them: 'You are going to receive £8 each; you have earned this money; it belongs to you. Take it and make whatever use you like of it. Spend it in the public-house; have a good spree at Christmas; do as you like with your money.' Instead of that I told them: '£8 is an amount which is soon spent, and it will not do you much good if you send it down your throats in the form of bottles of whisky, bags of sweets, or fat geese for Christmas. On the other hand, if you leave this money with me, I shall use it to provide you everything which makes life pleasant, viz. nice houses, comfortable homes, and healthy recreation. Besides, I am disposed to allow profit-sharing under no other form than that form.[61]

Budgett Meakin calculated in 1905 that a cottage that let at 5s a week was worth something like 8s 6d simply to cover costs or, to be commercially viable, 10s 6d.[62] Lever was, it is true, protected from the vagaries of the open market: his rents were guaranteed because they came out of his employees' wages, there was limited depreciation caused by careless occupants, since tenants could be easily ejected, and he improved his work force by offering his model village as bait.[63] Even so, by 1910 the firm had poured more than £350,000 into the venture – for land, buildings, roads, gardens and so on. According to the town planner Patrick Abercrombie, 'The annual cost of the scheme to the firm is some £10,000 a year for interest, which is looked upon as a legitimate charge against the business owing to the increased efficiency and intelligence of workers housed under such invigorating conditions.'[64]

This gives some weight to Lever's claim, repeated *ad nauseam* and not entirely convincingly, that the entire venture was not an act of philanthropy but of shrewd, calculated self-interest. According to the young writer Walter Lionel George, the 'theory is that, though no return is expected from the capital sunk in the village, a more than adequate one is indirectly derived from the health and better work of well-housed and contented workers'.[65] Jervis Babb, president of Lever Brothers in New York in the 1950s, put it bluntly:

> Let us not delude ourselves for a moment that there was anything of the theoretical social reformer in his makeup. He was no impractical idealist seeking to better the lot of the underprivileged out of other people's pockets – his own perhaps least of all. He was a man with an extraordinary ability to spot wealth-creating opportunities. He realized these could best be developed with the cooperation of sturdy, self-reliant working people, living in dignity and comfort. To him, providing good working and living conditions and sharing the wealth he was helping to create were simply good business.[66]

The contrast with the Cadbury village at Bournville is instructive. George Cadbury started building cottages at Bournville in 1879 but began to turn it into something special in 1895. It ranks as one of the great showcase company villages of the period, along with Port Sunlight and the Rowntrees' New Earswick at York (from 1902). Bournville was more than simply a factory paternalist venture, because Cadbury allowed non-employees of the firm to rent and he wished to make a return on his investment. His reasoning was twofold. First, in the words of A. G. Gardiner, his biographer, it was a social experiment whose 'underlying purpose was to show that business success was not only consistent with a high regard for the welfare of the workpeople, but the corollary of it'. Second, it was intended as a seed-plot of ideas: 'It followed that his methods must, to serve this larger purpose, be rooted in sound economics as distinct from sentiment and charity. They must be applicable to industry as a whole, and not a mere quixotic fad of a philanthropist. They must commend themselves to the plain business man.'[67]

Perforce, Cadbury's cottages had to be more modest than Lever's. They were very good by contemporary standards but still rather spartan. Only the better style had a small bathroom with hot and cold running water; the rest had a bath, but sunk in the middle of the kitchen floor under a lid, or in the scullery, covered by a lid which could double as a table, or tippable on end to be stowed in a cupboard when not in use.[68] And although the venture became strong enough to stand on its own two feet, it was not *purely* commercial. Cadbury turned it over to an independent body, the Bournville Village Trust, in 1900, and gave up any financial interest in the village (all future profits were to go towards improvements and expansion); but he made no claim for arrears on the capital that had been tied up in it for many years, and the Cadbury family continued to make contributions to various village institutions such as the infant schools.[69]

Gardens were an essential and compulsory feature of Bournville. They were planted before tenants moved in and rental contracts stipulated what standards needed to be maintained. George Cadbury said in a speech to the Garden City Conference in 1901:

> On Saturday afternoon or summer evening, you may see father and mother and children at work in their gardens. Is not that a delightful occasion for the boys and girls, to be bringing them into contact with Nature, and to love the flowers? One of the most touching things to me is to see the interest and pleasure of town families who come out into the country and who have never before seen the seeds sown and the vegetables grown. [70]

In 1907 he reiterated, 'Largely through my experience among the back streets of Birmingham I have been brought to the conclusion that it is impossible to raise a nation, morally, physically and spiritually in such surroundings, and that the only effective way is to bring men out of the cities into the country and to give to every man his garden where he can come into touch with nature and thus know more of nature's God.'[71]

On this point Lever was in complete agreement. 'A home requires a green-sward and garden in front of it, just as much as a cup requires a saucer or a hat a brim,' he told an international housing conference in Port Sunlight in 1907.[72] Originally the tenants looked after their own front gardens, but they apparently neglected them so much – 'they were used as fowl-runs, and even as dustbins, while the family washing was unblushingly exposed on the palings'[73] – that the prized prettiness of the village was spoilt; so the firm took over the management of the gardens and lawns, leaving allotments for the tenants to hire, if they wished, at 5s a year.[74] As Frederick Law Olmsted, Jr, son of the famous American landscaper, speculated in 1909, the hiring of the necessarily large corps of gardeners cost much more than the workers themselves would have elected to pay, given the choice.[75] The policy oscillated: by the mid-1920s the company had returned to experimenting with tenant initiative – encouraging them through prizes in the form of rent reductions (twelve weeks' rent for first prizes) to look after their own front gardens, plant flowers and display window boxes. Lever's son claimed that it had proved a complete success and that 'The change has greatly enhanced the brightness and beauty of the village.'[76]

7 Lunch hour at the main gate, Port Sunlight works, 1907

By the time W. L. George provided the most comprehensive description of the early Port Sunlight in 1909 the soap works stretched over ninety acres and employed a largely unskilled work force of 3,600 in seventy distinct trades. Males worked a forty-eight-hour week (an eight-hour day, rather than the nine or ten hours standard at many other factories), females forty-five hours. Males clocked on at 7.50 a.m. and finished at 5.30 p.m., females worked from 8.00 a.m. to 5.00 p.m. This was to avoid any hanky-panky: 'It would not be conducive to discipline for the 2,000 men and boys and the 1,600 girls to leave the Works in a confused stream, particularly during the reaction following upon release from work.'[77] Budgett Meakin suggested that the Lever Brothers model was widely followed: 'Where large numbers of girls and men are employed it has been found worth while arranging for them to come and go separately, thus avoiding an unseemly rush for train or tram, or any opportunity for horse-play.'[78] Certainly at Bournville, while George Cadbury 'could not turn the factory into a cathedral … he did at least endeavour to prevent it degenerating into a place of temptation. The corridors are so arranged that girls and boys do not meet on their way to and from the workrooms. Each employee must remain strictly in his or her own department.'[79]

The chances of anything unseemly happening during the lunch hour were limited as well, since males and females ate in different dining halls, the girls

8 Gladstone Hall dining room, Port Sunlight, 1895

in Hulme Hall (which could accommodate 1,800 diners at a time), the men in Gladstone Hall (which catered for 800). The men brought their own food and the canteen staff heated it up for them while maintaining all due decorum with little difficulty: 'the hall is extensively patronized and proceedings are remarkably orderly; the caterer and his assistants have no difficulty in keeping down horseplay, spitting, etc.' The girls could also bring their own food to Hulme Hall, but most of them opted for the meals cooked on site, paying 2*d* for example for a dinner of meat, potatoes and vegetables or 1*d* for a pint of soup and a slice of bread.[80] These were among the earliest experiments in mass catering or 'industrial feeding' in Britain outside the military. The total number of experimenters had reached barely 100 by 1914, but predictably the philanthropic employers, mainly employing female labour, such as Cadbury, Rowntree, Fry of Bristol, Colman of Norwich and Hartley of Aintree, led the way.[81]

George's use of the term 'girl' reflected Lever Brothers' employment practices. 'As soon as a girl marries she is looked upon as a "housekeeper" and debarred from employment in the Works, exceptions being occasionally made for widows and a few special cases,' he wrote. 'It is hardly necessary to emphasise the importance of this rule; the evils that follow in the train of industrial work for married women … are so notorious that it is needless to enlarge upon them, any more than upon the results of such work on the home, upon the health and education of growing children.'[82] He was right: gendered norms and the arguments confining married women to the domestic sphere were so broadly accepted as to need no restating. 'The natural consequence,' an article in a German newspaper noted with approval, 'is that the houses are kept clean, the husbands get proper food and the children keep in good health.'[83] At Bournville, likewise, 'George Cadbury based himself on the simple fact that the duty of a woman who marries is to her children, and that she cannot be in two places at once.'[84]

Visitors to the soap works could reassure themselves that all due proprieties were being met because they were welcome to have a look round. The firm had built special gangways and galleries around each of the departments so that visitors could observe each stage of the production and packaging processes without interfering with them. Sixty thousand people did just that in 1904. As Meakin observed, showing off clean, wholesome conditions was good for business, and a number of other consumer firms made similar arrangements, including Rowntree (chocolate), Pascall (sweets) and Huntley and Palmer (biscuits).[85] Visitors could also observe a pleasing level of time discipline. According to George:

A visit to the Port Sunlight Works certainly shows that no time is wasted; the casual observer cannot conceive of greater activity or expedition, but relations between the workers and their foremen appear to be good, and there is in most of the workshops an atmosphere of good temper and good-will. There is no loitering, partly, no doubt, owing to the military precision of the Factory, partly owing to the zest with which the employees go to work. Rules are evidently not allowed to fall into abeyance; for instance, tobacco chewing is forbidden; if, after a warning, the offence is repeated the offender is dismissed.[86]

To cite but one example of the strict implementation of rules, in 1923 the management came across a case of men playing cards in the office. The person who produced the cards and the head of the department who was with him were sacked, and a youth who stood and watched for a few minutes was suspended for a month. Lever wrote, 'I am pleased to note that the card-playing in the office has been dealt with drastically as is absolutely necessary.'[87]

In spite of such discipline, George reported high levels of contentment among the work force. To be sure, 'the grumbler is not unknown in Port Sunlight, but there would be grumblers in Utopia', but he heard only positive sentiments expressed about Lever and the directors. One indication of cordial labour relations was the lack of strikes at the works. During Lever's lifetime there was, in fact, only going to be one strike confined to Port Sunlight (as opposed to employees in skilled trades holding sympathy strikes in support of their counterparts elsewhere) – a three-week strike in 1920 called by the Warehouse and General Workers' Union because the firm refused to recognize it as the sole negotiating authority for the employees it claimed within its remit and allowed them to join the rival Liverpool Shipping Clerks' Guild as well. It was a strike about union demarcation and had nothing to say about wages or working conditions in the factory.[88]

The company paid union rates. Every shopfloor employee could join the holiday club: an hour's pay per week was deducted, the company contributed forty-eight hours and the employee got a week's holiday at full pay. Almost everyone joined this club, and George reckoned that it was the most successful institution in the village. The Employees' Benefit Fund, instituted in 1904, provided retirement, sickness and widows' pensions with company contributions and no deductions. In terms of old age pensions, every male over sixty-five and female over sixty who had completed more than twenty years' service would receive one-eightieth of the final year's wage multiplied by the number of years of service, to a maximum of £180 a year. This was enough to stave off absolute poverty during old age but not enough to live comfortably, so the level of the pension provided an incentive for the worker to be thrifty and save out of his or her regular earnings.[89] In a public letter to his employees, Lever defended the fund in characteristically robust terms:

> There is no unpleasant taint of pauperising philanthropy in this. … Those who do not do their duty to the Firm will never retain their position long enough to entitle them to a pension or their Widows and Orphans to maintenance – the Firm can do without such members of the Staff, and their place will be taken by those who will do their duty better.[90]

From George's perspective, Port Sunlight was a highly successful experiment in the remoralization of England's toiling classes. Take allotments. Two hundred and fifty men had rented allotments, each producing an average of £4–£5 of fruit and vegetables per year. This was not only a helpful way of eking out wages but it was also a healthy and pleasant way of spending one's leisure hours, keeping clear of more costly amusements. And this lesson could never be inculcated too soon: boys and girls had taken up around 100 plots in the 'Children's Gardens' scheme. Take also the village's public institutions.[91] Now it was true that 'the essential charms of Port Sunlight are found by the fireside' and in 'the peaceful pleasures of the home', but something more than a good cottage was needed to influence the social habits of the people and to teach 'sobriety, cleanliness, and respect for the Law': 'To the low-class music hall we must oppose the theatre; to the drinking den we must oppose the ballroom, the concert hall, and the lecture room.'[92]

This is why Lever built Christ Church, attended by different varieties of Protestant, and the model elementary schools which, after the 1902 Education Act, came under the control of Cheshire County Council. The schools were co-educational but included some segregated lessons, including compulsory woodwork for boys and, George reported, 'Every girl between the ages of eleven and fourteen is taught plain cooking, and also invalid and vegetable cookery, given a thorough knowledge of the dietary that is suitable for infants, of the use of the mangle, and fine laundry work.' The need to influence the social habits of the people is why Lever built the library and museum, with its 700 members and two reading rooms, one for men, one for women (presumably to avoid more of that feared horseplay); the Collegium, a meeting place for the various societies such as the Mutual Improvement Society, for the drills and classes of the Boys' Brigade and for small dances organized by the clubs; and the Auditorium, a large theatre and dance hall. Here, in the winter, the company held very popular weekly dances. Each girl employed at the works was invited twice per season. 'Girls under eighteen are provided with partners by the Company' but those over eighteen were allowed to submit the names of suitable male dance partners to the 'social department', which issued invitations to the men in question, 'unless there be reasons that militate against them'. The decisions were made by the 'social secretary' (the minister of Christ Church) and a committee balanced between foremen and women and regular employees. Veto was allegedly unusual.[93]

The danger lurking behind all of this was paternalism, or 'glorified pauperism': 'It is beyond discussion that a community for which everything is done must deteriorate.' George conceded that the tenants had no voice in the making of the rules or the management of the estate, but was reassured by the fact that the rich array of voluntary associations running the gamut from the Philharmonic Society to the Cycling Club to the Young People's Temperance League to the Mutual Improvement Society (designed 'to promote a truly fraternal spirit among the residents and employees' by way of lectures, social events and poetry readings) – were controlled by the employees and not by Lever or the company directors. The village shop ('the Store') was run by the Employees' Provident Society on co-operative principles and was similarly free from company control.[94]

Sobriety, morality, health and hygiene ranked high on George's list of the village's achievements. The Bridge Inn, the only hostelry in the village, was more a restaurant than a pub. It did serve alcohol, since the residents had voted in a referendum in 1903 to overturn its dry status. Lever respected the result of the poll, in spite of his own preferences. Women had voted too: 'The overwhelming vote in favour of a licence showed that not only the men supported the change, but the women also,' wrote Lever's son, 'and the reason they gave was that they knew their menfolk wanted their glass of beer, and they much preferred that they should have it at the inn in their own village, where they were known, rather than further afield.'[95] But drink, said George, was not a problem in the village: 'The sobriety of the people is remarkable; I passed several "Saturday nights" in the Village without seeing a single drunken man: in how many industrial communities could one do the same?'[96] The Sunlighter did not need to drink: 'He has a comfortable home.'[97]

The village boasted a large gymnasium – 3s 6d a year for men, 2s for girls and boys, implying that the concept of grown women using a gym was rather too absurd to be contemplated – and an open-air swimming pool. The thoroughly modern and clean cottage hospital was free to employees. Everything about the place was, in fact, clean, 'a shrine for the worship of cleanliness', down to the spotless streets, trim gardens and white curtains. Thanks to the bathroom in every cottage and, no doubt, the nature of the product being manufactured, 'The Sunlighter … believes fervently in the gospel of soap and water both for himself and his house.'[98] Because of this hygiene, regular employment, good food and housing, open spaces and exercise, Sunlighters put clear blue water between themselves and other working-class Merseysiders in terms of physical indicators:

> The visitor is struck at once by the generally healthy appearance of the people and especially by the fine physique of the young men; the football team, for instance, is composed of young men in the twenties, and almost all the members of the team are notably taller and heavier than their local antagonists. The appearance of the children is remarkable, for they are usually fat, rosy, and irrepressibly cheerful.

The average annual death rate in the village was 9/100, compared with 20/100 in Liverpool; infant mortality in the first year of life 70/1,000 compared with 140/1,000; only the children at first-rate middle-class schools in Liverpool were taller and heavier.[99]

But it was more than a physical transformation, it was a moral revolution as well: 'no drunkenness, no wife beating, no immorality, no assaults, no deserted wives and children; is all this not an enviable record and a plea for an attempt to improve everywhere the living conditions of the people?'[100] George was suggesting that the standards of Lever and the company and the surveillance by neighbours of neighbours had induced a form of self-discipline and self-policing, the internalization of norms of decent conduct, all adding up to a sedate and tranquil work force. He wrote with approval,

> Standards are certainly wonderfully rigid in the little town; the "oldest inhabitant" could only recall one elopement and in 1907 there was only one illegitimate birth, or about four times less than the average for Great Britain; during the last dozen years only two persons have been involved in what may be called a village scandal. These are truly remarkable facts, and show, in regard to what we know of industrial conditions and of the holocaust of souls that is revealed every day in our police courts, what a revolution has been worked in the habits of the people.[101]

The absolute ruler of the village

In his obituary of Lever, T. P. O'Connor provided a captivating image of the Port Sunlight counting house. Above the rows of hundreds of typists, on an elevated dais, 'stood or walked Lord Leverhulme in solitariness, just like the commander of a great liner on the bridge. He did not speak; he simply looked … Nothing more was necessary than his mere presence to ensure that the great, thundering organization was ploughing its way through its work as surely and steadily as the great liner through the waves of the Atlantic.'[102] Harley Williams recorded a similar thought: 'Through large glass windows to the right and left, the chairman could see his hundreds of clerks stretching out in two long halls, conducting the gigantic business operations, and what was more important as a symbol, they could see him.'[103]

One can cavil at these accounts, because neither of them captures Lever's phenomenal micro-management, focusing instead on the effectiveness of his mere superintendence of the well oiled machine and his delegation to well chosen assistants. But it is a picture of surveillance familiar to readers of Michel Foucault, drawing on Jeremy Bentham's Panopticon and depicted in a wide range of literary and film representations.[104] More subtly, as George suggested, this surveillance and discipline were extended outside the factory gates as Lever sought to mould the moral sensibilities of his workers and their families: through the schools and the church; his insistence that wives keep away from factory work and tend to their duties in the home, reinforcing gendered norms and a cult of domesticity; his provision of rational recreation to fill worker leisure hours in improving ways; and the didactic motive lying behind the Lady Lever Art Gallery.

A German commentator noted in 1904, 'Lever is the absolute ruler of the village built on the private property of the Company, but he wields his sceptre with such kindness and wisdom, that everybody likes to be his subject.'[105] Most commentators were eager to emphasize the benevolence and overlook the despotism. A. R. Sennett in 1905, for example, remarked that 'one has only to visit such a happy community as the dwellers in Port Sunlight to observe that their *status*, their *amour proper*, is a thing apart in the country – a most gratifying contrast to anything to be found in the workers' slums of our great and overgrown hives of industry.'[106] Raffles Davison in 1916 concurred: 'The social reformer sees an object lesson in the value of a pleasant and well-planned community of houses in which individuality is left ample freedom of expression.'[107] And yet, as the secretary of the Bolton branch of the Engineers' union wrote in a letter to Lever in 1919, 'No man of an independent turn of mind can breathe for long the atmosphere of Port Sunlight. That might be news to your Lordship, but we have tried it. The profit-sharing system not only enslaves and degrades the workers, it tends to make them servile and sycophant, it lowers them to the level of machines tending machines.'[108]

As a good Liberal, Lever recognized that 'dependence in any form is not a healthy state',[109] but not only in profit sharing (which we shall return to below), but also in intruding into employee-tenants' personal affairs, he helped ensure that dependence. One of the rules for the regulation of tenancies on the Port Sunlight estate, for example, read, 'An authorized official of the Company may visit any house in Port Sunlight, at any time, for the purpose of seeing that due regard is being paid to order and cleanliness.'[110] Lever made it clear in a letter of 1901 that he would tolerate only clean, well behaved tenants: 'The private habits of an employee have really nothing to do with Lever Brothers, providing the man is a good workman. At the same time a good workman may have a wife of objectionable habits, or he may have objectionable habits himself, which make it undesirable to have him in the village ... it is not a matter of a man being dismissed from his employment but merely being granted or refused a house in the village.'[111]

This sense of dependence and interference seems to have rankled, at least with some. Andrew Knox was another who spoke warmly of Lever's charm and 'great personal magnetism' and who made no secret of his admiration for him. This makes his verdict all the more interesting:

> All this generosity, this pouring out both of money and of spirit, produced for Lever as loyal and enthusiastic a group of workpeople as any man has ever had, but it did not make Port Sunlight into a happy and lively community.... Creature comforts, amusements, sporting facilities were provided very cheaply or for nothing. Help was available in life's difficulties and anxieties. Employment was virtually guaranteed. Port Sunlight offered complete social security. Nevertheless as an experiment in welfare it failed, and it failed because it was

too closely self-contained and it developed a sense of being isolated.

For many years there was no public transport, but the isolation was more psychological than physical, the result of ostracism by the surrounding communities:

> You lived in Port Sunlight and so you must be the son of a workman – a second-class workman, moreover, because he lived under patronage in a tied and subsidized house. Some people in Port Sunlight felt this second-class status so acutely that they gave their postal address as Bebington. It delayed their letters but no doubt it gave them a feeling of respectability.[112]

This is a healthy rejoinder to the usual laudatory takes on Port Sunlight, but Knox was not entirely consistent or logical. He claimed that the sense of inferiority probably did not exist in the early days and grew only gradually; and while Lever was alive the personal affection felt towards him proved to be a strong antidote. The first generation had reason to thank him 'for thirty years of security, comfort and a standard of living which may never be equalled in our present-day Welfare State' (Knox was writing in the mid-1970s); 'And their children look back on the happy days when Port Sunlight was their world and Mr Lever the smiling and exciting godfather of them all.' So why did the good times sour? Knox suggested that the fundamental flaw was in housing people together who worked together and limiting residence to Lever Brothers' employees, but if so it is not clear why the feelings of claustrophobia and emasculation became more acute towards the end of Lever's life.

He posited an additional reason: the rapid growth of the firm and the proliferation of managers, weakening the direct links between boss and employees. Port Sunlight had always been essentially a one-class village (senior managers and directors lived in the nearby countryside or down the road in Rock Ferry, one of Liverpool's fashionable residential suburbs), but status divisions and envy only really began to arrive after Lever's death. Directors ate lunch in one dining room, senior managers in another, ordinary managers in a mess of their own, staff in one canteen, workers in another. If any employee moved up the hierarchy he would eat in a higher canteen, creating estrangements between neighbours. Knox recalled one post-Lever event in particular, when guests above a certain grade at a public dinner sat on a dais and were served chicken and wine; the rest got hotpot and beer.[113]

All this would suggest that the glory years were beginning to fray towards the end of Lever's life, and the real problems set in thereafter. Indeed, Knox recounted that with the arrival of buses from Birkenhead in the late 1920s, scheduled trains stopping at the station (previously it had been merely a 'halt' for workmen's specials) and the spread of motor bikes and even cars, 'It became almost a status symbol to move from the village.' But this was a time when it was possible to escape, either permanently into pleasant houses within commuting distance or simply on excursions, and in that case Port Sunlight was becoming less claustrophobic. At the same time, the growth of the firm meant that an increasingly lower percentage of employees lived in the village, making it less likely that a colleague in factory or office would also be a neighbour. The creation of a 120 acre recreation ground for the firm in Bebington and the establishment of a Staff Training College (in 1917), both open to all the staff and not just the villagers, also helped in the transformation of Port Sunlight from a closed community into a focus of work, sport and social life for a much larger constituency. To top off the contradictions, Knox referred to this period, from the 1920s, post-Lever, as the Golden Age of Port Sunlight.[114]

Whatever the timing, Lever himself recognized the problem. '[M]y own opinion is that the employer ought never to be in the position of landlord to the employee,' he said in a speech in 1917: 'still, if the employer has to choose between being in the position of landlord and the people being badly housed, then the lesser evil is for him to build suitable houses and be landlord; but it is not the right relationship.'[115] According to Knox, he realized in the end 'that a mistake had been made'. On a trip to a Berlin soap works in 1924, which the owners wanted to sell him with the inducement that there was enough vacant land for him to build another company village near by, he said, 'I'd never build a second Port Sunlight. It was a mistake. People who work and live together always quarrel.'[116]

A collection of reminiscences from the mid-1990s gives some anecdotal corroboration of Knox's point for the post-Lever era. Joyce Maddocks, who began as a messenger girl at the works in 1942 at the age of sixteen, wistfully recalled how order was enforced in an age of deference:

> When I started the Company was very paternal both inside the factory and as a tenant living in the village. They were there for you. … There were certain rules and regulations and if kids misbehaved the fathers were hauled up in front of management but when you see the way some of them vandalise now it's not such a bad thing, although it would never work now.

Betty Graham, who worked as a machine operator from 1946, talked of the distinction between tenants and the rest:

> In the printing there were all what you call the "Leverites"; they walked down Greendale and they were home, weren't they? And they were in more or less tied houses and they couldn't do anything, they had to look after their jobs or they were out of the house. … Even if you wanted to do something wrong, stick by your guns regarding a job, they wouldn't join in with you because … [*sic*] I'm not saying they'd get the sack, like, but they wouldn't stick their neck out.[117]

The suspicion that the inhabitants of Port Sunlight were not 'free', and that the village was part of an experiment in social control, has lingered. David

Jeremy, for example, has pointedly and unfavourably contrasted Lever with George Cadbury. Because Cadbury's Bournville was not reserved solely for company employees, if a man lost his job he did not also lose his house. In Port Sunlight, Lever turfed out dismissed employees, usually giving them a month to find new dwellings. His reasoning here was logical – if the sacked worker could still retain his house he would benefit from the unearned subsidy and the village would gradually cease to be for the Lever Brothers work force – but as the consequences of being fired were doubly harsh, the policy was a powerful incentive to good behaviour.[118]

Jeremy charges that Cadbury also respected the balance between employer provision and the freedom of the individual employee and that Lever did not.[119] Cadbury offered unsolicited advice, witness a handbook he distributed to incoming Bournville inhabitants that included recommendations on how long to brew tea (over three minutes); to eat many apples, both raw and cooked; to 'Breathe through the nostrils with the mouth closed, especially at night'; and the suggestion that 'In a truly happy home father or mother will conduct family worship at least once a day when the Bible should be read and a hymn sung.'[120] But Jeremy's allegation is that Lever went much further, turning to religion to counteract any developing socialist sentiment in the village. Lever did indeed act like an Anglican squire in building a new church for the village (at a cost of £25,000), naming it Christ Church, insisting on a surpliced choir, a professional organist and a peal of bells, and appointing the minister (the church was nondenominational, so he felt entitled to contravene the Congregationalist principle that the local congregation choose its own minister).

Nevertheless, the evidence is scanty that he ever perceived socialism in the village as much of a threat or the radicalization of his work force likely, and the suggestion that in 1900 he selected the Rev. Samuel Gamble Walker, a 'Wesleyan Christian Socialist' minister, to disarm the socialists, but then effectively 'muzzled' him, seems unconvincingly devious and is unsupported by evidence. And if this *was* Lever's strategy, it failed, as Jeremy points out. Membership in Christ Church was never particularly impressive, since the villagers could repair to more denominationally orthodox alternatives in the surrounding villages.[121] In addition, Lever and his family never became members of Christ Church, precisely to avoid the imputation that they were directing the church's affairs.[122]

The profit-sharing scheme, as the trade union official remarked above, offered more possibilities for control. One of the problems with 'prosperity sharing' in the shape of subsidizing the village and its amenities was that those employees living outside the village, especially single men and girls, did not benefit. But Lever insisted, for sound business reasons, that he was not going to set up a trust similar to those at Bournville or New Earswick.

Under current arrangements the employees' comfort depended on the firm's prosperity, encouraging them to work harder. Under a trust 'We might have permanent benefits to the men and dwindling trade returns; in brief we should have prosperity-sharing and no adversity-sharing.'[123]

He did, however, institute a 'co-partnership' scheme in 1909, to benefit all his employees, not just Sunlighters, and to improve labour relations. The policy paid an annual dividend to the four different categories of directors, management, salesmen and staff, depending on years of service, out of his profits as Ordinary shareholder. In 1912, for example, the nearly 2,000 co-partners received an average of about £20 each – essentially £40,000 out of Lever's own pocket. This meant that ordinary workers received a lot less: someone on £100 a year could expect between 30s and £5, depending on length of service – no more than a minor adjustment of the wage system. Co-partners had to sign an undertaking not to 'waste time, labour, materials or money in the discharge of his duties, but loyally and faithfully further the interests of Lever Brothers and its associated companies and his fellow co-partners to the best of his skill and ability'. Co-partners could lose their redeemable certificates because of 'neglect of duty, dishonesty, intemperance, immorality, wilful misconduct, flagrant inefficiency, disloyalty to his employers, or a breach of the above-mentioned undertaking'.

His son declared the scheme a success, 'for it instilled into the working lives of the employees a spirit of comradeship', but some of the unions were suspicious, partly because it reinforced individual bargaining between firms and their workers, disrupting the solidarity of the union movement, partly because those who went on strike forfeited their right to co-partnership.[124] A case in point was the dismissal of two Lever Brothers lightermen in London in 1923 for joining an unofficial dockers' strike. Sacking in such circumstances was apparently standard practice, and even if the strike settlement forced the company to take the men back, the co-partnership certificates would 'of course' remain cancelled.[125] None of this amounted to a policy or practice of social control, but it did indicate, in common with most factory paternalists, that the boss's avuncular smile betrayed a glint of steel.

The co-partnership scheme contravened Lever's earlier statements about prosperity sharing, but it was a recognition that something more was needed to inculcate worker loyalty, counter disaffection and improve efficiency, since the village covered an increasingly small portion of his expanding work force. It was a move along a path towards a comprehensive scheme of person management in line with a number of other companies, especially larger, oligopolistic concerns with increasingly corporate structures that enjoyed a greater degree of market stability, less competition and could plan for the future more effectively. These companies were recognizing that they needed to move beyond personal paternalism and that (before the welfare state developed) big businesses had to provide benefits for old age, sickness, infirmity and so on if they were to maintain the right kind of work force.[126]

Lever was not content simply to tend his own pasture or to exhibit his village as a showcase worthy of emulation. His uneasiness about being an absolute ruler locally no doubt added to his concern to provide national solutions to national problems. On the national stage he was a supporter of the New Liberalism and its blend of progressive social policies in the service of a capitalist economy. He was happy to serve the Liberal party in his neighbourhood but entered national politics reluctantly. Elected as an MP for Wirral in the Liberal landslide of 1906, he soon withdrew because he found it impossible to pay full attention to his parliamentary duties: the needs of his business were too pressing and, besides, the tediousness of parliamentary procedure and the slow pace of decision making did not suit his character.

During his brief stint in the House of Commons, however, he spoke in favour of payment of MPs (later taken up by the government; it became law in 1911) and introduced an Old Age Pensions Bill (and a similar measure was propelled through Parliament in 1908 by the Chancellor, David Lloyd George). In his speech introducing the Pensions Bill, Lever took the standard New Liberal line that 'There was an obligation on the part of the State to do for individual citizens what individual citizens could not do for themselves.' Take Betty Jones and her husband, an agricultural labourer, he said. They had never earned more than 16s a week between them and on that measly sum they had raised twelve respectable children, with never enough to set aside for their old age. Now the husband was dead and only Betty's friends and neighbours stood between her and the workhouse. She had more than fulfilled her duty to the state and the state owed her. This was 'mere justice to the great masses of the people' and not, repeating his familiar mantra, benevolence and philanthropy, since they 'were only a system of charity, and charity was the mother of pauperism'; 'the manly independent working man' would have nothing to do with it.[127]

On one of the few other occasions he made a speech in the Commons he spoke out against the idea of imposing an eight-hour day, believing that it was up to employers and trade unions in individual industries to strike a deal, not a role for Parliament.[128] Not that he was opposed to the principle of shorter hours. By the end of the First World War he was publicly advocating a six-hour day, and paid the publisher Stanley Unwin to edit a collection of his talks – *The Six Hour Day and other Industrial Questions* – for publication.[129] His argument in the signature essay was characteristically pragmatic and unsentimental. Working people needed more fulfilling lives, for the sake of themselves and the stability of the nation and to give greater security to the wealthy. Currently:

> Our manufacturing towns are squalid and overcrowded, with ugly dwellings, without gardens. They are unlovely congestions, without beauty or possibility

of refinement, and the great bulk of the workers remain at a relatively low state of betterment. The individual Home is the solid rock and basis of every strong, intelligent race. The more homes there are and the better these homes are, the more stable and strong the nation becomes. Men and women who get up to go to work before daylight and return from that work after dark, cannot find life worth living. They are simply working to earn enough one day to prepare themselves to go to work again the next day. Their whole life is one grey, dull, monotonous grind, and soon their lives become of no more value to themselves or the nation than that of mere machines.[130]

In a speech in the Lords in 1919 he spoke feelingly about his youthful memories:

> Some of you, like myself, may remember the condition of the workers in the late fifties, when, amongst male operatives, you could only see two patterns of legs – the knock-kneed and the bow-legged. That was the result of immature youths being forced to work long and laborious hours in the vitiated atmosphere of mills and foundries.[131]

Working people were quite rightly, he thought, craving and agitating for better conditions. The way to achieve this was not through ca'canny – the restriction of output by workers – but through increased efficiency. He believed that people *could* be paid the same wage to work reduced hours because they would be less fatigued and therefore more productive (this was a lesson reinforced for him by the long hours in wartime munitions factories, which appeared to reduce rather than increase output per worker) and because, crucially, the machinery could be worked in six-hour shifts 'twelve, eighteen, or twenty-four hours per day' (spreading overheads over greater output, reducing costs). And they *should* be paid the same so that there would be adequate demand for the increased volume of goods produced. This could not work everywhere, he claimed: in agriculture, for example, there was little labour-saving machinery to substitute for longer hours; nor would it work for sailors or domestic servants. But where it could be safely adopted, manufacturers would benefit, and needed to be disabused of the myth that low wages and long hours meant cheaper production and higher profits. Leisure increased consumer desires and high wages allowed those desires to be satisfied. Leisure could also be combined with a compulsory two hours a day of education from ages fourteen to thirty: high-school education with physical training from fourteen to eighteen; technical and university education with physical training from eighteen to twenty-four; and military service, training in the duties of citizenship and preparation for membership of village and town councils from twenty-four to thirty.[132]

Some in the labour movement were suspicious about this idea of a six-hour day, seeing it as another attempt to speed up the worker, or another example of benevolent despotism rather than giving workers a share in the control of industry. At a conference of Quaker businessmen, Seebohm Rowntree, the social reformer and scion of the chocolate firm, denounced Lever's idea of three shifts of six hours each as 'monstrous'. Not many directors would be prepared to work such a system, he argued, so why should workers be forced to? Besides, the members of a family might find themselves spread out over the three shifts, which would seriously damage home life.[133] Even Lever's attempts to introduce a two-shift system at Port Sunlight failed, partly because of the difficulties in reorganizing working and social lives for one factory alone.[134]

If the First World War had helped crystallize his ideas on short time, it had also helped clarify his thoughts on women: the 'old idea of women has got to go'. 'This war has discovered Woman,' he said in 1916. Women had beyond doubt proved their usefulness in nursing, munitions and hundreds of other useful occupations. It remained the case that 'the destination and goal of the majority of girls must be the home, marriage, and the household cares that come upon them in their position as mothers of the household', but even these girls needed an education equal to that of the boys if they were to fulfil their duties as the companions and helpmeets of men, and he maintained that co-education was the best way to achieve this equality. Moreover, in arguing for the right of women to practise at the Bar, he maintained that they were perfectly entitled to make that choice over marriage and home keeping and did not deserve to be despised and socially shunned because of it.[135]

He consistently professed to have no qualms about the masses acquiring power. On his trip round the world in the early 1890s he applauded the advent of a moderate Labour government in New Zealand and the approval of a 'one man, one vote' measure by the lower House of the New South Wales parliament; in an address in 1911 he welcomed the prospect of a working-class majority in Parliament in Britain and a working-class Prime Minister (on the grounds that this would complete the working man's education about the limitations on government power); and he was similarly nonchalant about Labour assuming power in 1924 (since as a minority government its scope would be restricted).[136] He believed in trade unions and always paid above union rates and maintained better than union working conditions; but he had no truck with socialism or industrial democracy. He favoured nationalization 'of any practical monopoly such as Railways, Tramcars, Canals, Electric lighting &c,'[137] but in general 'the less a Government interferes with business the better. We have got to work, more work, must work in order to win comfort, welfare, and happiness, whatever may be hoped for from "isms" and whatever faddists may say.'[138]

Life could not be made too easy or it would make a man soft and effeminate. Competition was essential. 'There is no growth, no life, no progress without resistance – merely stagnation,' he wrote in 1915. 'It is the struggle with resistance that makes a man strong, virile and successful. A life without resistance is a life of ease – ignoble and leading to poverty and rags.'[139] Neither God nor nature had any time for equality:

> A man is not an enemy of the human race because, by exercise of foresight, thrift, and intelligence, he has accumulated great wealth. ... It would be as logical, as right, and as reasonable for the consumptives, the weak, the feeble, and the diseased to denounce the healthy and strong as it is for those possessing little or no wealth to denounce the rich and wealthy. And it would be just as effective a cure for consumption, weakness, feebleness, and disease to take steps to reduce the healthy and strong to a state of weakness, feebleness, and disease as it would be a cure for poverty to attempt to constrict the riches of the wealthy.[140]

Like many rich men, he never expressed any qualms about his riches, nor any doubts that he came by his wealth through his own, largely unaided, efforts.

Two sunflowers and a box hedge

The plans, schemes, hopes and dreams of the visionaries outlined above, some of them realized in attenuated forms, most of them not, found their culmination and synthesis in the mind of an unassuming parliamentary stenographer, Ebenezer Howard. George Bernard Shaw later wrote of him that he was 'one of those heroic simpletons who do big things whilst our prominent worldlings are explaining why they are Utopian and impossible.'[141] Howard formulated his ideas during the 1880s and 1890s, when he could draw on the ideal-city schemes of people like James Silk Buckingham, the models provided by Port Sunlight and Bournville, the notions of the agricultural colonists and back-to-the-land enthusiasts and, more diffusely, the anti-industrial propagandizing for a craft-and-community rural life propagated by the likes of John Ruskin, William Morris and the Arts and Crafts movement.

In *To-morrow: A Peaceful Path to Reform* (1898) (republished as *Garden Cities of To-morrow* in 1902) Howard advocated the planned migration of populations and industry to new 'social cities' that would form a compact, healthy, harmonious blend of town and country and a balance of different social and income groups. Public buildings would be placed in the middle, around a public garden, at the centre of a series of concentric circles joined by radial avenues. Commerce, industry, parks and houses (all with gardens) would be allocated to their appropriate zones and circles. Once the town had reached 30,000 people further growth would not be permitted but would continue in similarly designed satellite garden cities beyond a green belt. He imagined hundreds of these communities, all on greenfield sites, all governed by the inhabitants through the principles of co-operation and direct democracy.[142] He borrowed from the American economist Henry George's *Progress and Poverty* (1879) the idea of a tax on land values, so that the value created by the community could be recouped rather than benefiting the landowners in an unearned increment: if development increased land values, the profits should be ploughed back into the community.[143]

Howard attracted the attention of a prominent London lawyer, Ralph Neville, who in 1901 became chairman of his Garden City Association, two years after its inception. Already this was an indication of the way the wind was blowing, because Neville was a Liberal, uninterested in radical change or a co-operative society but all for the pragmatic and cost-effective reduction of social tensions. The Establishment embraced the Association under Neville's tutelage, providing a long list of notables as vice-presidents, including the Countess of Warwick, two peers, the Bishop of London and two other bishops, twenty-three MPs, the economist Alfred Marshall, George Cadbury, Joseph Rowntree, William Lever, H. G. Wells and Cecil Harmsworth, the brother of the newspaper magnate (the *Daily Mail* gave helpful publicity). Lever and Cadbury were particularly important catches, both for their philanthropic reputations and for their wealth. They co-sponsored a conference to promote garden cities at Bournville in September 1901 attended by over 1,500 local government officials concerned about urban problems, and a similar conference was held at Port Sunlight the following year. None of these groups envisaged anything but cautious, practical ways to relieve overcrowding while leaving the structure of society intact.[144]

This flurry of activity led to the formation of the Garden City Pioneer Company in 1902, which bought 3,820 acres of land at Letchworth in north Hertfordshire the following year and established First Garden City Ltd. This meant that a private company was going to implement the experiment, not the elected community representatives, and that company was to be responsible to the shareholders, not the residents – both contrary to Howard's vision. Although Howard himself might see his plans as a step-by-step approach towards land nationalization and an alternative society, leading businessmen could see that it was entirely compatible with the needs of capital. In the process, Howard's vision was sacrificed to reassure investors in the hope of making Letchworth succeed financially. Lever became a director, but after the capital issue failed to raise sufficient amounts he argued strongly that the only way forward was to offer freehold sites for sale to speculative builders at rock-bottom prices. This the board rejected after a stormy meeting in the spring of 1904, so Lever resigned and took no further part in the project.[145]

The architects of Letchworth, Raymond Unwin and Barry Parker, who had designed New Earswick for the workers of Joseph Rowntree's cocoa works, carefully separated residential and industrial land, preserved the best green spaces and constructed comfortable, well lit houses to a high Arts and Craft standard.[146] Letchworth attracted a certain type of Arts and Crafts idealist, and to the dismay of the directors became famous for a motley, outspoken collection of smock-and-sandal-wearing, hat-and-glove-discarding freethinkers, vegetarians, teetotallers, feminists, Esperanto enthusiasts, theosophists, folk-lorists, handicraft workers and (to quote a cartoon of 1909) 'hairy-headed banana munchers', all in pursuit of the simple life.[147] John Betjeman later satirized them in his poem 'Group life: Letchworth':

> Tell me Pippididdledum,
> Tell me how the children are.
>
> …
>
> Sympathy is stencilling
> Her decorative leatherwork,
> Wilfred's learned a folk-tune for
> The Morris Dancers' band.[148]

And George Orwell in *The Road to Wigan Pier* blamed the failure of socialism to catch on in Britain on the type of off-putting 'faddist' one might encounter at Letchworth:

> One sometimes gets the impression that the mere words 'Socialism' and 'Communism' draw towards them with magnetic force every fruit-juice drinker, nudist, sandal-wearer, sex-maniac, Quaker, 'Nature Cure' quack, pacifist and feminist in England. One day this summer I was riding through Letchworth when the bus stopped and two dreadful-looking old men got on to it. They were both about sixty, both very short, pink and chubby, and both hatless. One of them was obscenely bald, the other had long grey hair bobbed in the Lloyd George style. They were dressed in pistachio-coloured shirts and khaki shorts into which their huge bottoms were crammed so tightly that you could study every dimple. Their appearance created a mild stir of horror on top of the bus. The man next to me, a commercial traveller I should say, glanced at me, at them, and back again at me, and murmured, 'Socialists', as who should say, 'Red Indians.'[149]

First Garden City at last began to turn a profit in 1912, the population climbed to 10,000 by 1914 and a distinct community began to develop, but Letchworth failed to achieve the desired mix of social classes because of prohibitive housing costs.[150] Whatever its disappointments, it demonstrated that, where a company held all the land, and in a rural district where there were no restrictive bye-laws, determined individuals could plan and construct a large town from scratch.[151] Likewise Howard's second project, Welwyn Garden City, from 1920, designed in Georgian style by Louis de Soissons, a Canadian Beaux-Arts architect, also counts as a success. But both were for a long time deeply under-capitalized, which made the development painfully slow. Unlike the factory villages, where wealthy employers had the means to invest heavily and not see a return on their investment for many years, and where there was a factory to provide employment and tenants, the difficulty in raising sufficient capital remained the Achilles' heel of the garden city ideal. These financial problems stymied the hope for a proliferation of privately financed new towns.[152]

In formulating his ideas Ebenezer Howard had drawn on a number of American writers and had spent time in Chicago in his younger days. Though he insisted that town designs should vary according to local circumstances, his ideal city did not have any particular place in mind or owe anything to a particularly English idiom. As Standish Meacham notes, this was not true for many of his followers and the implementers of the garden city ideal in England, Unwin and Parker included. The Arts and Crafts idealism of a socialist like Unwin, deploring the late nineteenth-century city, class antagonisms and atomized individualism, looked back to a vision of community or organic unity or virtue – of timeless Englishness – in the hierarchical village of the past, filtering out all that was unpleasant and unwelcome and somehow expecting this to lead in the fullness of time to the socialist harmony of the future. It was a vision of a well ordered England that allowed little space for democracy – in fact was partly a reaction to the *fear* of encroaching democracy.[153]

Unwin was particularly significant for the evolution and implementation of garden city ideas. His next venture after Letchworth was in north London, attracted by the crusading zeal of the social reformer Henrietta Barnett. She owned a house on the edge of Hampstead Heath and anticipated that the Underground railway would soon be extended to Golders Green – and with it an unsightly sprawl of badly built suburb. She began a campaign to extend the Heath and to build a quality suburb; the new Hampstead Garden Suburb Trust as a result purchased 320 acres of land from Eton College, adding eighty acres to the Heath and developing the rest as the garden suburb. Her aim, as she stated in *Contemporary Review*, was to bridge the gap between classes, to preserve the Heath's natural beauty and to give working people an opportunity to 'develop a sense of home life and an interest in nature which form the best security against temptation'.[154] Unwin became consulting architect and surveyor for the suburb.

True believers in the garden city ideal saw this as apostasy, since the Hampstead venture was a dormitory suburb and not a garden city. Garden suburbs were useful in their own way, Howard thought, but antithetical to his principles because they merely controlled the outflow from a town and increased the distance between home and work; they had no self-sustaining industry or corporate life. Unwin defended it on the grounds that improvement of city edges was as necessary as planning new towns and that the new suburb aimed at a socially mixed community. It went on to feature distinguished work by Unwin, Edwin Lutyens and M. H. Baillie Scott, and the overall look was closer to medieval Germany than England. For some it represents one of the finest achievements of twentieth-century British design.[155] Hampstead Garden Suburb, more than anything else, provided an example of 'suburban housing on garden-city lines'. It caught the wave of middle-class imagination but, critics alleged, succeeded only in exacerbating suburban sprawl.[156]

Peter Hall credits Wythenshawe, the City of Manchester's estate for 100,000 people in 25,000 dwellings, 80 per cent of them council houses, as being Britain's third true garden city. It was built from 1927 to 1941 to designs of Barry Parker. Its main inspirer, E. D. Simon, chairman of Manchester City Council's housing committee, called it a 'satellite garden town'. It fulfilled many of the criteria, at least on paper: a green belt, a mixture of industry and residences, an emphasis on well designed single-family housing – but it was not really self-contained because of the numbers who commuted to work in Manchester, and there was no self-government by the community in any Howardian sense.[157]

The garden city ideal inspired a crop of loose, smaller-scale variations on a theme. Some were employer schemes, simulacra of Port Sunlight, Bournville and New Earswick, often with the 'Garden City/Suburb/Village' tag attached. One such was the Hull Garden Suburb, built and owned by the Hull Garden Village Company, nominally independent but in practice largely the work of Messrs Reckitt, a firm of starch and household cleaning product manufacturers.[158] Sir James Reckitt in a speech at the opening ceremony in 1908 made no secret of his anti-revolutionary motivation: 'The only object in view is the betterment of our neighbours, and to enable them to derive advantage from having fresh air, a better house, and better surroundings. I … urge people of wealth and influence to make proper use of their property, to avert possibly a disastrous uprising.'[159]

Some were simply speculative suburban ventures with fanciful names. The cartoonist and author Osbert Lancaster described how, before the First World War, 'rows of quaint and whimsy cottages … appeared in the northern suburbs of London in clusters, which their builders considered themselves justified (by the presence of two sunflowers and a box hedge) in calling garden cities'.[160] Others were co-partnership villages, closer to Howardian ideals. Notably, twelve men in a co-partnership society called Ealing Tenants, consisting mainly of building workers, established a pioneer garden suburb at Brentham from 1901. By 1914 Brentham Garden Suburb had 600 houses, the co-partnership persisted, and this collective ownership of land and houses in terms of its governance came much closer to what Howard had in mind than Letchworth or Hampstead.[161] Liverpool Garden Suburb Tenants Ltd set up the biggest co-partnership venture in 1910. Its first two phases, of 126 Arts and Crafts houses, laid out partly by Unwin, were the only parts of the ambitious scheme of 1,900 houses completed, thanks to the disruption of the Great War.[162]

By 1914 there were Garden City Associations in eleven countries, and the garden city/*cité-jardin*/*Gartenstadt*/*ciudad-jard'n* had a certain vogue on the Continent and in North America in the first decades of the twentieth century. What enthusiasts created from Montreal to Moscow were not the 'social cities' of Howard's imagination but, once again, Port Sunlight-style company villages or pleasant Hampstead-variety garden suburbs on commuter lines, all with decent housing, light, air, space and greenery.[163] One of the more interesting inter-war variations played out in the town of Zlín, Czechoslovakia. This was the work of Tomás Baťa, the creator of the Bata shoe empire, who constructed a garden city on uncompromisingly modernist, functionalist lines, without a hint of Arts and Crafts or rustic vernacular about it, with the intention of creating a contented, healthy work force. Most of the houses were built in prefabricated blocks, but they were individual, family dwellings with their own gardens, conforming to Baťa's slogan: 'Work as a collective, live as an individual.'[164]

The most substantial achievement on garden city lines in America was Radburn, New Jersey (1928–29), built on farmland fifteen miles outside Manhattan. The onset of the Great Depression reduced the scope of the original plans, and in reality it was no more than a bedroom suburb of New York, but it ranks as 'the first community in the world designed to make life compatible with the automobile', separating pedestrians from vehicles by a series of cul-de-sacs, inner parks and pedestrian underpasses. The New Deal promoted more short-lived experimentation, when President Franklin D. Roosevelt's Resettlement Administration began to construct in 1935–36 three garden suburbs for modest-income families: Greenbelt, Maryland, near Washington; Greenhills, Ohio, near Cincinnati; and Greendale, Wisconsin, near Milwaukee, each to be encircled by a farm belt.[165] When the man behind the programme, Rexford G. Tugwell, explained his thinking – 'My idea was to go just outside centers of population, pick up cheap land, build a whole community, and entice people into them. Then go back into the cities and tear down whole slums and make parks of them' – his debt to Howard was clear.[166]

In practice, all of the garden city variations failed to supersede industrial capitalism with co-operation. Small wonder that industrialists and non-radical governments were comfortable with propagating them.[167] And, as we shall see, they did nothing to staunch suburban sprawl. In Britain a group calling themselves the 'New Townsmen', with the principal motivation from C. B. Purdom and F. J. Osborn, authors of *New Towns after the War* (1918), had the idea of reviving a measure of garden-city thinking, this time with the aid of the state in creating satellite towns as an alternative to suburbanization.[168] But only in the aftermath of the Second World War, when faith in planners and progressives was at its height (and given the failure of private schemes like Letchworth and Welwyn and municipal schemes like Wythenshawe to do more than tinker at the edges), was a version of this long-standing dream realized.

Patrick Abercrombie's celebrated *Greater London Plan* of 1944 envisioned not only the reconstruction of those parts of London destroyed by the Luftwaffe, but also a comprehensive plan for the region thirty miles around, advocating a green belt to preserve agriculture and prevent formless sprawl and the decanting of hundreds of thousands of people into purpose-built, self-contained new towns.[169] More than thirty New Towns – places like Stevenage,

Cumbernauld and Milton Keynes – were built over the next three decades, mainly examples of 'Radburn planning' with houses fronting grass and with paths and roads at the rear.[170] They were initially hampered by lack of resources during the post-war austerity years, the corporations overseeing them were rather autocratic and failed to consult the residents, and the years of high unemployment in the 1980s and 1990s meant many of them were rather grim, unlovable places, lacking jobs and amenities. In practice, and with hindsight, they fell well short of any ideal.

Subtopias

Lewis Silkin, the Minister in Clement Attlee's Labour government who introduced the New Towns Act in 1946, later wrote that the creation of the new towns

> set out to show that we in Britain could do something better than the soulless suburbia, ribbon development, single-industry towns, and one-class housing estates of the '30s; that our big cities need not forever go on expanding until all their people were engulfed in a sea of bricks and mortar, cut off from the open countryside; that our obsolete, overcrowded, slum-ridden and bomb-stricken towns could be thinned out and transformed from their Victorian squalor into decent centres of living of which we need no longer be ashamed.[171]

In criticizing suburbanization he was taking aim at the major urban development of the previous several decades, which had completely swamped (but, ironically, was partially stimulated by) the garden city movement. In Edwardian Britain influential people, concerned about demoralized, stunted and potentially disaffected masses in urban slums, latched on to the idea of garden suburbs and town planning as panaceas promising social stability and the extension of the middle-class ideal of the family. Good homes with gardens would provide private family spaces in contrast to the dangerously uncontrolled communal areas of alleys and rookeries. The city seemed to be spreading organically in any case – especially with tramway electrification and workers' concessionary fares on trams and trains – promising an evolutionary decentralization. But letting the market dictate matters could not happen fast enough: a helping hand was needed.

George Cadbury advocated that municipal councils should buy land around every town for the building of belts of garden villages. Lever too argued for municipalities to purchase peripheral land and then offer it free to private builders, since the councils would get a return from their investment because of the rates on the new houses. All this, he thought, would encourage gradual dispersion from the town centre to the suburbs, which would reduce overcrowding and lower downtown rents. High-rise council flats were not the solution:

Believe me ... there is no other way than first dealing with the question of land for houses. All other methods are simply tinkering with the evil we would remedy. Corporations, and notably Liverpool, have built blocks of workmen's dwellings – so-called – and anything more hideous, more undesirable for the rearing of a family, or more wasteful of the public money, it would be impossible to find. The most you can say of them is that they are better than the slums and rookeries they have replaced.[172]

John Sutton Nettlefold, a Conservative industrialist, the chairman of the housing committee in Birmingham, was particularly influential in persuading Birmingham council to call for national legislation to allow municipalities extensive planning powers. Town Planning, a term he coined, was by 1906 replacing the garden city as the practical idea of the moment. The Garden City Association, at a conference in London in 1907, reaffirmed a commitment to independent garden cities in the long term, but called for municipal land purchase and cheap loans to build worker housing. Nettlefold, moving the conference resolution, and in the process seriously distorting Howard's ideas, claimed that 'Town-planning may be shortly described as the application of the Garden City idea to existing cities and their suburbs – the application of business principles to the solution of the Housing problem.' The Association changed its name to the Garden Cities and Town Planning Association. But the Housing, Town Planning, etc., Act, 1909, which enabled local governments to plan town extensions through the zoning of new suburban areas, was non-compulsory, rather timid and, in practice, little used.[173]

Lever was not only a (short-lived) director at Letchworth and a trustee at Hampstead Garden Suburb, but he made key speeches to conferences of housing and municipal authorities about his town-planning ideas. The National Housing Reform Council and the Garden Cities Association in turn made pilgrimages to Port Sunlight.[174] But his principal contribution (beyond the model of Port Sunlight itself) was the funding of the Department of Civic Design at the University of Liverpool, the world's first such centre for the study of town planning. (Cadbury was shortly after to fund a town-planning lectureship at the University of Birmingham, and the first occupant of the position was Raymond Unwin.) The initiative came from Charles Reilly, the Roscoe Professor of Architecture at the university, who described in his auto-biography a characteristic first encounter with Lever at Port Sunlight: 'I was shown into a glass-walled room with endless vistas through the glass of clerks' heads in all directions and with a short red fiery little man with opalescent eyes changing from green to red if you dared to disagree with him, and fair hair standing up on end, sitting at a big desk.'

Reilly claimed that he thought up the idea of a Civic Design department after hearing John Burns, the President of the Local Government Board, fail to mention architecture during a speech on an abortive Housing and Town

Planning Bill in 1908. Reilly wanted planning and architecture to be considered in parallel, and had been given much food for thought through a spate of recent conferences in 1907: a City Beautiful conference in Liverpool and, in London, a Garden City Association conference and an International Housing Congress. Seeking to pioneer a field and build an empire, he approached Lever, the big local benefactor and a man who had practised good architecture and planning at Port Sunlight. Lever was immediately interested. In a letter to the university's vice-chancellor he wrote, 'I have felt for many years that some help is necessary to be given both in educating the public on the matter and also in providing the requisite knowledge available for Towns and Cities in the near future to be able to deal on broad lines with their suburban areas.' Using money from his successful recent libel action against Lord Northcliffe's Associated Newspapers, the upshot was the formation of a Chair in Town Planning and Civic Design, a research fellowship and a journal, the *Town Planning Review*, which returned the favour to Lever by recording many of his own schemes. Stanley Adshead was the first holder of the chair and Patrick Abercrombie (the initial editor of the journal) the second. Together, as two of the leading planners of their generation, they were to have a significant impact on the budding profession – though, interestingly, Lever himself apparently did not avail himself of their talents, trusting more to Thomas Mawson, James Lomax Simpson or his own judgement.[175]

One of Lever's own town-planning schemes involved an attempt to begin something akin to a satellite garden city for Birkenhead. He bought up a number of Wirral estates from 1911. On the land that he accumulated – around 8,000 acres – he built in 1913 a straight, tree-lined, three-carriageway road, three and a half miles long, from the outskirts of Birkenhead to Thornton Hough, cutting the road at right angles with a private drive from Thornton Manor in the direction of Port Sunlight to reduce his commuting time. The centre road was macadamed and intended for cars, the two flanking roads for horse traffic or for macadam to be added when required. He offered to donate the road to the Wirral Rural District Council and to sell at cost to Birkenhead Corporation that part of his estate closest to the town's borders. But after the offer was rejected and the corporation failed to secure the necessary loan, the story goes that the fancy iron gates at each end of this isolated three-line strip in the middle of the countryside were closed, opened only for his own car.[176]

If this was an unappreciated visionary scheme, predicting future domination by the automobile and its need for wide, straight roads, his revamped Port Sunlight and his ideas for Bolton were less concerned with traffic circulation and more with civic monumentalism. The original layout of Port Sunlight curved around a series of depressions, formerly tidal inlets from the Mersey. As the village expanded from its original fifty-six acres (village thirty-two acres, works twenty-four) to 230 acres (village 140, works ninety), he drained

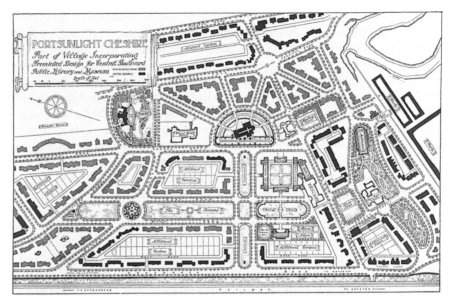

9 Map of Port Sunlight with proposed Beaux-Arts additions, 1911

the pools and basins at considerable expense and filled them in with material excavated from the works site, leaving only one, landscaped, depression, 'The Dell'. This draining and filling made possible a more rigorous plan and shape for the village. Ernest Prestwich, a student at the new Department of Civic Design at Liverpool, won a competition in 1910 to provide a new design. He was inspired both by French École des Beaux-Arts classicist ideas for city centres and by the American City Beautiful movement, whose main architect, Daniel H. Burnham, had produced in 1909 the most celebrated of the numerous City Beautiful plans, the Plan of Chicago, with its lakefront parks and radial-concentric system of boulevards and parkways. Mawson had a hand in adapting Prestwich's design, and significantly he stated his belief in the need for a coalition of the two schools of town planners in Britain: those who created garden cities and suburbs and those who planned great civic centres and processional ways. Port Sunlight created such a fusion. It was a village-size version of the hybrids – monumental centres set in garden cities – to be seen in the designs of Walter Burley Griffin (himself a planner from Chicago) for a new Australian federal capital at Canberra in 1912 and of Edwin Lutyens for New Delhi in 1913.[177]

Lever wished also to impose a Beaux-Arts/City Beautiful town plan on the incrementally grown, haphazard mess that was Bolton. He sketched out his ideas on Ordnance Survey maps of the town and handed them in 1910 to Mawson to work up into something achievable. Between them they concocted

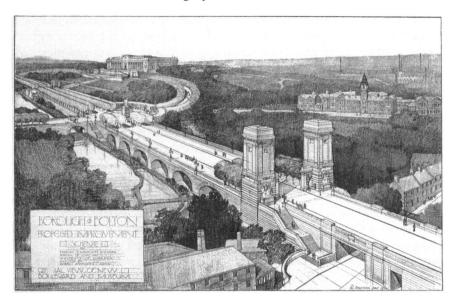

10 The projected causeway, Bolton, 1911

a scheme whose most striking feature was an elevated causeway, largely intended for pedestrians, projecting into Queen's Park, and vaguely modelled on Prince's Street in Edinburgh. A crescent-shaped road off this causeway was to lead up to a huge new art gallery and museum, while boulevards lined with trees and suitably grandiose buildings were to link the causeway with the town hall and the town hall with the parish church. 'These suggestions show Mr. Lever in a new light,' editorialized the *Town Planning Review*; 'he is already well known as a pioneer of Garden Village planning in this country, and we find him here acting as a pioneer of English monumental city planning of a type which has hardly been practised in this country for a century.' The author was presumably thinking of the laying out of Regent Street and Regent's Park in the early nineteenth century, or further back to Edinburgh New Town and Bath in the eighteenth. Mawson, who promoted the ideas vigorously in a series of public lectures, acknowledged that the plan could not be imposed overnight, but argued that the citizens of Bolton had the opportunity to adopt a 'once for all' policy to guide the harmonious development of the future and to cater for the civic graces: 'Circulation, Hygiene, and Beauty'.[178]

There was a wave of interest in this dream of an improbably beautiful Bolton, but nothing came of it. Still, the town council chose Lever as the mayor of Bolton in 1918 (the first time councillors had selected a mayor outside their own ranks) in the hope that he would bring energy, purpose and direction to the goals of post-war planning and to the relief of all the town's accumulated wartime constipations. Lever promised to build his causeway at an estimated cost of £100,000, if the council went ahead with his grand vision. Again it came to nothing. In 1924 the council approved a much less ambitious and more sensible scheme, extending the town hall and building a crescent-shaped building behind it to house municipal and police offices, a sessions house, and a library and art gallery. Lever revived his idea of a causeway, which he again offered to pay for himself, linked to a large public square adjacent to the town hall surrounded by public buildings. The council turned him down once more. For a third time they batted his ideas around, costed them out, looked at the pros and cons and retreated. His plans were simply too extensive and too unpractical. The causeway in particular seemed preposterous: too monumental for pedestrians alone, but if open to traffic an increasing volume of vehicles would be funnelled through the middle of the park.[179]

Returning to the practical and the mainstream, the Housing, Town Planning etc. Act, 1919, generally known as the Addison Act after its sponsor, the Minister of Health, Christopher Addison, came in the wake of the Great War and David Lloyd George's commitment to provide 'homes fit for heroes'. It made central government subsidies available to local councils to build houses. Taking the step that the labour movement had long wanted, that earlier administrations had thought they could and should avoid as unnecessary and expensive (and that most European and North American governments by and large did avoid), government became a major housing provider.

The houses were to be built to standards proposed by a committee chaired by a Liberal MP, Sir John Tudor Walters. As he was a director of Hampstead Garden Suburb, and as Raymond Unwin was the most influential member of his commission, the recommendation for relatively spacious and sunlit English vernacular garden city-style cottages, twelve to an acre (the same limit Lever had recommended in a paper on 'Land for Houses' in 1898),[180] with inside toilets and baths, gardens at front and rear and additional green spaces, came as no surprise. And although levels of subsidies varied considerably over the governments of the 1920s and 1930s, resulting in dips and fluctuations in size and standards, what the government effectively committed itself to during the inter-war years was the planned town extension on garden suburb lines. The private market for middle-class housing similarly lapped up the garden city model (or simply extended the existing patterns of middle-class suburbanization). The explosion of inter-war housing saw the construction of 4.3 million new houses, nearly all of this style: 1.33 million (31 per cent) by local authorities, over 2.5 million (58 per cent) by private enterprise, and the balance by private enterprise with some state assistance. As these suburbs spread, Britain's total urban area increased by 40 per cent.[181]

This was and was not what the garden city pioneers wanted. Social cities had not mushroomed across the land; big cities remained intact and continued their spread, dramatically; co-operative ideals in housing and living failed to flourish. Howard and his supporters had feared the endless outward march of towns and cities, covering over all the available green space and coalescing with other, similar sprawls to create 'conurbations' (a name concocted by the sociologist Patrick Geddes, in his *Cities in Evolution*, 1915). The American architectural critic and urban theorist, Lewis Mumford, wrote, 'Saltaire, Pullman, Port Sunlight, Letchworth are drops in the bucket ... the aim of a garden-city movement must be to change the shape of the bucket itself; that is to say, the frame of our civilization.'[182] That it had failed to do.

And yet, as Stephen Ward points out, local councils and speculative builders were the unanticipated creators of vast acreages of extended towns of reasonable and reasonably cheap garden housing, relieving inner-city congestion and allowing for a more privatized family life with a splash of nature for a much broader segment of the population.[183] J. B. Priestley, in his *English Journey* (1934), lamented how this post-war landscape of suburban housing, bungalows with garages, ring roads, petrol stations, cinemas and cafés, while pointing to increasing affluence, lacked character and flavour. Still, this was where a 'new kind of Englishness' was being invented, as Alison Light puts it, a domesticated Englishness of 'private and retiring people, pipe-smoking "little men" with their quietly competent partners, a nation of gardeners and housewives', the new backbone of the nation.[184] Lever would surely have approved.

Of course garden-city thinking and the bastardized version in garden suburbs and council estates had their critics. The architectural vanguard in the Modern Movement, people like Le Corbusier, Walter Gropius and Mies van der Rohe, went in a very different direction, condemning garden city-style Arts and Crafts housing as quaint, nostalgic and petty bourgeois. Le Corbusier's 'radiant city' (*La Ville radieuse*, 1933), wholly unlike Howard's, was *denser* than contemporary cities, but in glass-and-steel skyscrapers in geometric formations shooting up out of green space intersected by elevated highways. Increasing numbers of British planners, in the early backlash against suburban sprawl, began to take on board modernist ideas in the 1930s – those spread by the Congrès Internationaux de l'Architecture Moderne (CIAM), formed in 1928. The 'international style' – geometrical, unadorned, functional – seemed the way of the future and, although radical in itself, chimed in with municipal governments looking to clear slums and build low-cost multi-storeys on or near the same ground.[185]

In their 1937 book *The Modern Flat* the modernist architects F. R. S. Yorke and Frederick Gibberd contrasted the unappealing landscape of the industrial town with the new suburbs, which they found wanting. Their ideal was the tower block: 'We are making this book because we believe that we shall want to live in a tall building in a park, with common amenities, air, and a view; and that the problem of housing cannot be solved by the provision of millions of little cottages scattered over the face of the country, whether in the garden city manner, or as speculatively built stragglers.'[186] These ideas had a considerable vogue after the Second World War as the Modern Movement found a voice in leading architectural journals and a considerable presence among idealist housing designers seeking to build a new Jerusalem, a utopia, a brave new world for the working people of Britain.

In practice, two-thirds of postwar council houses continued to be of the old 'cottage' style in vast suburban developments and 20 per cent flats of three to five storeys; only 16 per cent were in tower blocks. But it was the tower block that caught the brunt of condemnation when the vision began to fade by the late 1960s. Too much of the new building was shoddy, as municipalities rushed to throw up as much housing as possible as cheaply as possible. A substantial proportion of it degenerated swiftly, and all sorts of social problems seemed to cluster in the neighbourhoods. The idealized vision of the sleek high-rise in the park looked increasingly risible.[187]

Perhaps the harshest critic of Ebenezer Howard was the American writer Jane Jacobs in her furious broadside of 1961, an opening salvo in the battle against the planners. She accused him of failing to avoid the sin of model employers like Lever: paternalism. 'His aim was the creation of self-sufficient small towns, really very nice towns if you were docile and had no plans of your own and did not mind spending your life among others with no plans of their own. As in all Utopias, the right to have plans of any significance belonged only to the planners in charge.' The closest US equivalent to the Howardian ideal city, she claimed, would be a model company town based on profit-sharing run by parent–teacher associations.

But her attack was not because his ideas were realized in practice – they were not – but because his pernicious influence had a powerfully destructive impact on cities. Because of him and followers like Geddes and Mumford, planning orthodoxy in recent decades had turned its back on the city that she admired – the city of vibrant streets and living neighbourhoods and a rich culture and an intermingling of commerce and housing – in favour of segre-gated suburban-type housing in blocks turned inward towards greens and away from the street. The planners, she complained, had between them concocted a sort of Radiant Garden City Beautiful, mashing together Howard's schemes with Le Corbusier's cities of towers in a park and the City Beautiful ideas for the City Monumental: civic and cultural centres along boulevards or parks separated from the rest of the city. Her ideal city, on the other hand, focused on maximizing possibilities for the individual at street level, and keeping the planners in abeyance.[188]

Lewis Mumford did not blame garden-city thinking, but he was unhappy too. He condescendingly described American suburbia in the early 1960s as 'a multitude of uniform, unidentifiable houses, lined up inflexibly, at uniform distances, on uniform roads, in a treeless communal waste, inhabited by people of the same class, the same income, the same age group, witnessing the same television performances, eating the same tasteless pre-fabricated foods, from the same freezers'.[189] In contrast to Europe, where planning, higher petrol prices and more investment in public transport helped to some extent to contain suburban sprawl, America became the quintessential suburban nation. High incomes, cheap land, cheap petrol, cheap balloon-frame housing and massive federal government incentives (federal mortgage insurance, the building of 42,500 miles of toll-free interstate highways from the 1950s to the 1970s and substantial tax breaks), significantly encouraged home ownership in single-family residences. By 1970 America was the first country ever to have more suburbanites than city or country dwellers.[190]

The provision of so much good, inexpensive housing was a considerable achievement. Yet, critics charge, the cost has been enormous. Suburbs, exurbs and edge cities are spewed out by developers heedless of the ecological implications and implicitly contrasting the God-fearing, relatively affluent, largely white and respectable with an imagined mirror image of inner-city hell-holes. As David Harvey puts it, 'Developers offer up this great blight of secure suburban conformity (alleviated, of course, by architectural quotations from Italianate villas and Doric columns) as a panacea for the breakdown and disintegration of urbanity first in the inner city and then, as the deadly blight spreads, the inner suburbs.' Some – 6 million in the United States by the end of the twentieth century – had found the extra security of the gated community, undermining in the process any sense of citizenship or mutual support or solidarity with those beyond the railings.[191]

Inside the 'McMansion', or smaller suburban dream home, one could find the best private realm in the world, in terms of space, utilities and appliances. But, outside, a degraded public realm wholly dependent on the car, with little pedestrian life, little civic identity, few public spaces worth visiting, all connected only by the heavily congested road network – a stunning contrast to the old, mixed-use, walkable American neighbourhood. Andres Duany and Elizabeth Plater-Zybek, who planned Seaside, Florida, in 1981 as a splayed fan of 350 houses around a central square for a well heeled clientele, with a nod towards Raymond Unwin's work at Hampstead, are in a long line of critics passionately calling for a reinvention of healthy growth. For them the new sprawl meant:

> [C]ookie-cutter houses, wide, treeless, sidewalk-free roadways, mindlessly curving cul-de-sacs, a streetscape of garage doors. ... Soulless subdivisions, residential 'communities' utterly lacking in communal life; strip shopping centers, 'big box' chain stores, and artificially festive malls set within barren seas of parking; antiseptic office parks, ghost towns after 6 p.m.; and mile upon mile of clogged collector roads. ... For all of the household conveniences, cars, and

shopping malls, life seems less satisfying to most Americans, particularly in the ubiquitous middle-class suburbs, where a sprawling, repetitive, and forgettable landscape has supplanted the original promise of suburban life with a hollow imitation.[192]

Partly because of, partly in spite of, the efforts of Lever, Howard and all the other dreamers and pragmatists who sought to transform the Victorian city, we have ended up with Subtopia: 'a hollow imitation' of 'the original promise of suburban life'. And in spite of the visions of utopians and of modernists, for whom ordinary folk continue to be a grave and aggravating disappointment, most people who can afford it still see a variation on the theme of a three-bedroom semi built by speculative builders, with a little bit of 'historical' ornamentation tacked on, surrounded by a patch of garden, as the 'Ideal Home'.[193] There is little indication that this will change any time soon, at least while the oil lasts.

Notes

1 Friedrich Engels, *The Condition of the Working Class in England*, trans. and ed. W. O. Henderson and W. H. Chaloner (Palo Alto, CA: Stanford University Press, 1958), p. 51.

2 See Brian Lewis, *The Middlemost and the Milltowns: Bourgeois Culture and Politics in early Industrial England* (Palo Alto, CA: Stanford University Press, 2001), chap. 10.

3 R. J. Morris and Richard Rodger, 'An introduction to British urban history 1820–1914', in R. J. Morris and Richard Rodger (eds), *The Victorian City: A Reader in British Urban History 1820–1914* (London and New York: Longman, 1993), pp. 1–4.

4 David J. Jeremy, *Capitalists and Christians: Business Leaders and the Churches in Britain 1900–1960* (Oxford: Clarendon Press, 1990), pp. 13–17, 414.

5 Harold Edgar Young, *A Perambulation of the Hundred of Wirral in the County of Chester* (Liverpool: Henry Young and Sons, 1909), p. 24.

6 W. L. George, *Labour and Housing at Port Sunlight* (London: Alston Rivers, 1909), p. 210.

7 *Progress*, 14 (1914), 27–8, quoted by David J. Jeremy, 'The enlightened paternalist in action: William Hesketh Lever at Port Sunlight before 1914', *Business History*, 33:1 (January 1991), 72.

8 *Guardian*, 20 May 2004; www.portsunlightvillage.com.

9 Peter Campbell, 'In Port Sunlight', *London Review of Books*, 27:2 (20 January 2005), 28.

10 'The Framley Examiner', *Bollocks to Alton Towers: Fifty Uncommonly British Days Out* (London: Michael Joseph, 2005). For Bill Bryson's take see his *Notes from a Small Island* (Toronto: Minerva Canada, 1996), pp. 191–3.

11 J. F. C. Harrison, *Robert Owen and the Owenites in Britain and America: The Quest for the New Moral World* (London: Routledge and Kegan Paul, 1969), pp.

5–7, 154–60; Gregory Claeys, *Machinery, Money and the Millennium: From Moral Economy to Socialism 1815–1860* (Cambridge: Polity Press, 1987), chap. 2; Edward Royle, *Robert Owen and the Commencement of the Millennium: A Study of the Harmony Community* (Manchester: Manchester University Press, 1998), chap. 1; E. P. Thompson, *The Making of the English Working Class* (London: Victor Gollancz, 1980; 1st edn, 1963), pp. 857–87.

12 See *The Life of Robert Owen, Written by Himself*, vol. I (London: Effingham Wilson, 1857), *passim*.

13 Robert Southey, *Journal of a Tour in Scotland in 1819* (London: John Murray, 1929), reprinted (Edinburgh: James Thin, 1972), p. 39, quoted by Royle, *Robert Owen*, p. 23.

14 See Lewis, *Middlemost and the Milltowns*, pp. 290–4.

15 Timothy Grimshaw, *The Cogitations and Opinions of Timothy Grimshaw Esq.* (Bolton, 1839), p. 76.

16 William Cooke Taylor, *Notes of a Tour in the Manufacturing Districts of Lancashire*, 3rd edn (New York: Augustus M. Kelley, 1968), pp. 30–6.

17 *Illustrated London News*, 25 October 1851.

18 Lewis, *Middlemost and the Milltowns*, p. 518, n. 30.

19 Thomas Carlyle, *Past and Present* (Berkeley, CA, and Los Angeles: University of California Press, 2005; 1st edn, 1843), p. 170.

20 Mark Girouard, *The Return to Camelot: Chivalry and the English Gentleman* (New Haven, CT: Yale University Press, 1981).

21 Lewis, *Middlemost and the Milltowns*, p. 293.

22 *Birkenhead News*, 24 November 1900, quoted by W. L. George, *Engines of Social Progress* (London: Adam and Charles Black, 1907), p. 123.

23 Dennis Hardy, *Alternative Communities in Nineteenth-Century England* (London and New York: Longman, 1979), p. 11.

24 Patrick Joyce, *Work, Society and Politics: The Culture of the Factory in later Victorian England* (Brighton: Harvester Press, 1980); Lewis, *Middlemost and the Milltowns*, pp. 293–5.

25 Martin J. Daunton, *House and Home in the Victorian City: Working-Class Housing 1850–1914* (London: Edward Arnold, 1983), pp. 181–7.

26 Walter L. Creese, *The Search for Environment. The Garden City: Before and After* (Baltimore, MD: Johns Hopkins University Press, expanded edn, 1992; 1st edn, 1966), pp. 30–40; Clive Woods, *Saltaire: History and Regeneration* (Bradford, 2000).

27 Budgett Meakin, *Model Factories and Villages: Ideal Conditions of Labour and Housing* (London: T. Fisher Unwin, 1905), pp. 416–17.

28 Gerald Burke, *Towns in the Making* (London: Edward Arnold, 1971), p. 143.

29 Standish Meacham, *Regaining Paradise: Englishness and the early Garden City Movement* (New Haven, CT: Yale University Press, 1999), p. 13.

30 Meakin, *Model Factories and Villages*, pp. 419–22; Gordon E. Cherry, *Urban Change and Planning: A History of Urban Development in Britain since 1750* (Henley on Thames: G. T. Foulis, 1972), p. 104; Nikolaus Pevsner and Edward Hubbard, *The Buildings of England: Cheshire* (Harmondsworth: Penguin, 1971), p. 116; Young, *Perambulation of the Hundred of Wirral*, pp. 40–1; Burke, *Towns in*

the Making, p. 137; Creese, *Search for Environment*, pp. 15, 20, 23–4, 40–8; Hardy, *Alternative Communities*, pp. 11–12; Daunton, *House and Home*, pp. 181–7.

31 *On Improved Dwellings for the Working Classes* (London: Shaw, 1862), p. 8, and *The Builder*, 14 February 1863, p. 110, quoted by Creese, *Search for Environment*, p. 43.

32 Jon A. Peterson, *The Birth of City Planning in the United States 1840–1917* (Baltimore, MD: Johns Hopkins University Press, 2003), p. 10; Ruth Eaton, *Ideal Cities: Utopianism and the (Un)Built Environment* (London: Thames and Hudson, 2002), p. 133; Creese, *Search for Environment*, pp. 170–1; Stanley Buder, *Visionaries and Planners: The Garden City Movement and the Modern Community* (New York and Oxford: Oxford University Press, 1990), pp. 27–8; Richard Harris, *Unplanned Suburbs: Toronto's American Tragedy, 1900 to 1950* (Baltimore, MD: Johns Hopkins University Press, 1996), pp. 7, 9.

33 Creese, *Search for Environment*, p. 311; Peter Hall, *Urban and Regional Planning* (London and New York: Routledge, 4th edn, 2002), p. 29; Helen Meller, *European Cities 1890–1930s: History, Culture and the Built Environment* (Chichester: John Wiley and Sons, 2001), p. 122.

34 See, for example, Andrew Mearns, *The Bitter Cry of Outcast London* (London: 1883); William Booth, *In Darkest England and the Way Out* (London: 1890); Philip J. Waller, *Town, City and Nation: England 1850–1914* (Oxford: Oxford University Press, 1983); F. B. Smith, *The People's Health 1830–1910* (London: Croom Helm, 1979); Anthony S. Wohl, *Endangered Lives: Public Health in Victorian Britain* (London: J. M. Dent, 1983); David Englander and Rosemary O'Day (eds), *Retrieved Riches: Social Investigation in Britain 1840–1914* (Aldershot: Scolar Press, 1995); Gareth Stedman Jones, *Outcast London* (Oxford: Clarendon Press, 1971).

35 Daunton, *House and Home*, pp. 192–4 and *passim*.

36 See, for example, F. M. L. Thompson (ed.), *The Rise of Suburbia* (New York: St Martin's Press, 1982); Robert Fishman, *Bourgeois Utopias: The Rise and Fall of Suburbia* (New York: Basic Books, 1987); Leonore Davidoff and Catherine Hall, *Family Fortunes: Men and Women of the English Middle Class 1780–1850* (Chicago: University of Chicago Press, 1991).

37 Charles F. G. Masterman, *The Condition of England* (London: Methuen, 1909), pp. 69–70, quoted by Gordon E. Cherry, *Cities and Plans: The Shaping of Urban Britain in the Nineteenth and Twentieth Centuries* (London: Edward Arnold, 1988), p. 62.

38 Margaret Jones Bolsterli, *The Early Community at Bedford Park: 'Corporate Happiness' in the First Garden Suburb* (Oberlin, OH: Ohio University Press, 1972), chaps 1–2; Creese, *Search for Environment*, chap. 4.

39 Hardy, *Alternative Communities*, pp. 3–4; Krishan Kumar, *Utopianism* (Milton Keynes: Open University Press, 1991), p. 29.

40 Quoted by W. H. G. Armytage, *Heavens Below: Utopian Experiments in England 1560–1960* (Toronto: University of Toronto Press, 1961), p. 19.

41 Hardy, *Alternative Communities*, pp. 14–16 and *passim*.

42 Harrison, *Robert Owen*, pp. 163–5, 169, 172–5; Royle, *Robert Owen*, pp. 29–31, 33 (quotation from *New Harmony Gazette*, 23 October 1828), chaps 3–7.

43 Barbara Taylor, *Eve and the New Jerusalem: Socialism and Feminism in the Nine-*

teenth Century (Cambridge, MA: Harvard University Press, 1993).

44 Karl Marx and Friedrich Engels, *Manifesto of the Communist Party* (Moscow: Progress Publishers, 1971), pp. 70–2.

45 Armytage, *Heavens Below*, pp. 184–5, 205–6; Eaton, *Ideal Cities*, pp. 127–8, 132–3 (Zola quotation p. 133), 136; John Carey (ed.), *The Faber Book of Utopias* (London: Faber and Faber, 1999), pp. 208–9, 231.

46 Kumar, *Utopianism*, pp. 26, 62; Eaton, *Ideal Cities*, pp. 159–60; Richard Stites, *Revolutionary Dreams: Utopian Vision and Experimental Life in the Russian Revolution* (New York and Oxford: Oxford University Press, 1989), pp. 187–8.

47 Eaton, *Ideal Cities*, pp. 14–17, 67–8; Kumar, *Utopianism*, pp. 12–16, 20–2.

48 Quoted by Eaton, *Ideal Cities*, p. 92.

49 Cherry, *Urban Change and Planning*, pp. 101–3; Peter Hall and Colin Ward, *Sociable Cities: The Legacy of Ebenezer Howard* (Chichester: John Wiley and Sons, 1998), p. 12; Armytage, *Heavens Below*, pp. 218, 221–3; Eaton, *Ideal Cities*, p. 137; Michael Williams, 'Light, William (1786–1839)' (www.oxforddnb.com/view/article/16646, accessed 29 June 2005), G. F. R. Barker, 'Buckingham, James Silk (1786–1855)', rev. Felix Driver (www.oxforddnb.com/view/article/3855, accessed 29 June 2005), *Oxford Dictionary of National Biography* (Oxford: Oxford University Press, 2004; online edn, May 2005).

50 John G. Corina, 'Morgan, John Minter (1782–1854)' *Oxford Dictionary of National Biography* (www.oxforddnb.com/view/article/19228, accessed 29 June 2005); Armytage, *Heavens Below*, pp. 209–10.

51 *Illustrated London News*, 24 August 1850, quoted by Armytage, *Heavens Below*, p. 221.

52 Buder, *Visionaries and Planners*, chaps 2, 5; Cherry, *Urban Change and Planning*, pp. 105–7; Hardy, *Alternative Communities*, chap. 5.

53 Armytage, *Heavens Below*, pp. 318–21, 324–6 (Booth quotation p. 319, Burns quotation p. 326); José Harris, *Unemployment and Politics: A Study in English Social Policy 1886–1914* (Oxford: Clarendon Press, 1972), pp. 118–27; Dennis Hardy, *Utopian England: Community Experiments 1900–1945* (London: E. and F. N. Spon, 2000), pp. 25–9.

54 John Shepherd, *George Lansbury: At the Heart of Old Labour* (Oxford: Oxford University Press, 2002), pp. 60–2; Hardy, *Utopian England*, p. 24; Thomas Brydon, 'Poor, unskilled and unemployed: perceptions of the English underclass 1889–1914' (MA thesis, McGill University, 2001), pp. 56–61; Harris, *Unemployment and Politics*, pp. 139–43.

55 UARM, LBC 4839, Lever to Walter Hazell, 20 April 1906 (quotations); *Liverpool Echo*, 3 March 1888; William Hulme Lever, *Viscount Leverhulme* (Boston and New York: Houghton Mifflin, 1927), pp. 48–9; Charles Wilson, *The History of Unilever: A Study in Economic Growth and Social Change*, vol. I (London: Cassell and Co., 1954), p. 34.

56 Meacham, *Regaining Paradise*, pp. 36–7.

57 Lever, *Leverhulme*, p. 88.

58 A. R. Sennett, *Garden Cities in Theory and Practice* (London: Bemrose and Sons, 1905), vol. I, pp. 251–2.

59 A 'Unilever Archives Information Sheet' helpfully lists the architects and the

houses they built. The principal architects were Douglas and Fordham, Grayson and Ould, William Owen, William and Segar Owen, James Lomax Simpson, J. Joseph Talbot, and Wilson and Talbot.

60 Lever, *Leverhulme*, p. 86.

61 Quoted by George, *Labour and Housing*, p. 196.

62 Meakin, *Model Factories and Villages*, pp. 428, 437.

63 Angus Watson, *My Life: An Autobiography* (London: Ivor Nicholson and Watson, 1937), pp. 136–7.

64 Patrick Abercrombie, 'Modern town planning in England: a comparative review of "garden city" schemes in England', *Town Planning Review*, 1:1 (April 1910), 35.

65 George, *Engines of Social Progress*, p. 121.

66 Jervis J. Babb, *The Human Relations Philosophy of William Hesketh Lever* (New York: The Newcomen Society in North America, 1952), pp. 9–10.

67 A. G. Gardiner, *Life of George Cadbury* (London: Cassell and Co., 1923), pp. 73, 75.

68 Meakin, *Model Factories and Villages*, pp. 432–3, 439–40.

69 William Ashworth, *The Genesis of Modern British Town Planning* (London: Routledge and Kegan Paul, 1954), pp. 132–3.

70 Meacham, *Regaining Paradise*, p. 26; *The Garden City Conference of Bournville: Report of Proceedings* (London: 1901), p. 43, quoted by Meacham, *Regaining Paradise*, pp. 15–16.

71 Replies to questions of a committee of the Upper House of Convocation on the responsibilities of wealth, 1907, quoted by Gardiner, *Life of George Cadbury*, p. 107.

72 Lord Leverhulme, *The Six-Hour Day and other Industrial Questions* (London: George Allen and Unwin, 1918), p. 182.

73 George, *Labour and Housing*, p. 62.

74 Young, *Perambulation of the Hundred of Wirral*, p. 26.

75 F. L. Olmsted, Jr, 'Through American spectacles: an expert's view of the English garden city schemes', *Garden Cities and Town Planning*, 4:33 (May 1909), 199, quoted by Robert Fishman, *Urban Utopias in the Twentieth Century: Ebenezer Howard, Frank Lloyd Wright, and Le Corbusier* (New York: Basic Books, 1977), p. 60.

76 Lever, *Leverhulme*, p. 89; *Birkenhead and Cheshire Advertiser and Wallasey Guardian* (17 September 1924), in BALS, B920 B LEV, newspaper cuttings on Lever.

77 George, *Labour and Housing*, pp. 22, 42–3 (quotation pp. 42–3).

78 Meakin, *Model Factories and Villages*, p. 57.

79 Gardiner, *Life of George Cadbury*, p. 88.

80 George, *Labour and Housing*, pp. 47–50 (quotation p. 48).

81 John Burnett, *England Eats Out: A Social History of Eating Out in England from 1830 to the Present* (Harlow: Pearson Education, 2004), pp. 110, 112; Meakin, *Model Factories and Villages*, pp. 184–8.

82 George, *Labour and Housing*, p. 44.

83 UARM, LBC 1488, translation of article on Port Sunlight in *Deutscher Reichsanzeiger*, 281 (29 November 1904).

84 Gardiner, *Life of George Cadbury*, p. 82.

85 Meakin, *Model Factories and Villages*, pp. 116–17.
86 George, *Labour and Housing*, pp. 39–40.
87 UARM, LBC 8104D, H. R. Greenhalgh to Lever, 12 July 1923; Lever to Greenhalgh, 13 July.
88 Lever, *Leverhulme*, pp. 226–7.
89 George, *Labour and Housing*, pp. 43, 51–7.
90 *Progress* (February 1905), 42, quoted by Meacham, *Regaining Paradise*, p. 188.
91 George, *Labour and Housing*, pp. 100–4.
92 *Ibid.*, pp. 105–6.
93 *Ibid.*, pp. 109–13, 118, 167–72 (first quotation p. 171, second p. 112).
94 *Ibid.*, pp. 121–3, 131, 184, 207–9.
95 Lever, *Leverhulme*, p. 93.
96 George, *Labour and Housing*, p. 116.
97 *Ibid.*, p. 145.
98 *Ibid.*, pp. 124–5, 147–8, 177 (first quotation p. 177, second p. 148).
99 *Ibid.*, pp. 150–3, 158–60 (quotation pp. 150–1).
100 *Ibid.*, p. 149.
101 *Ibid.*, pp. 178, 180 (quotation).
102 Quoted by *Liverpool Post and Mercury* (8 May 1925), in BALS, B920 B LEV, newspaper cuttings on Lever.
103 Harley Williams, *Men of Stress: Three Dynamic Interpretations: Woodrow Wilson, Andrew Carnegie, William Hesketh Lever* (London: Jonathan Cape, 1948), p. 287.
104 Michel Foucault, *Discipline and Punish: The Birth of the Prison*, trans. Alan Sheridan (London: Penguin, 1977).
105 UARM, LBC 1488, translation of article on Port Sunlight in *Deutscher Reichsanzeiger*, 281 (29 November 1904).
106 Sennett, *Garden Cities*, p. 803.
107 T. Raffles Davison, *Port Sunlight: A Record of its Artistic and Pictorial Aspect* (London: B. T. Batsford, 1916), p. 31.
108 Quoted by Wilson, *Unilever*, p. 150.
109 Quoted by George, *Engines of Social Progress*, p. 126.
110 George, *Labour and Housing*, p. 82.
111 Quoted by Wilson, *Unilever*, p. 151.
112 Andrew M. Knox, *Coming Clean: A Postscript after Retirement from Unilever* (London: Heinemann, 1976), pp. 7–9.
113 *Ibid.*, pp. 9–11.
114 *Ibid.*, pp. 11–14.
115 Lever, *Six-Hour Day*, p. 195 (speech at Sheffield University, 24 September 1917).
116 Knox, *Coming Clean*, pp. 9, 39.
117 David Roberts, *Life at Levers: Memories of Making Soaps at Port Sunlight* (Bebington: Avid Publications, 1995), pp. 17–18, 95.
118 George, *Labour and Housing*, p. 83.
119 Jeremy, *Capitalists and Christians*, pp. 143, 414.
120 Georges Benoît-Lévy, *La Cité-jardin*, II (Paris: 1911), p. 193, quoted by Fishman, *Urban Utopias*, p. 60; 'Residents' handbook and rules', Bournville Village Trust Archives, quoted by Meacham, *Paradise Regained*, p. 29.

121 Jeremy, 'Enlightened paternalist in action', 63–73.

122 John Griffiths, '"Give my regards to Uncle Billy ...": the rites and rituals of company life at Lever Brothers, c. 1900–c. 1990', *Business History*, 37:4 (October 1995), 36.

123 Quoted by George, *Labour and Housing*, p. 203.

124 Lever, *Leverhulme*, pp. 143–8 (quotations pp. 144, 146); J. E. Hodgkin (ed.), *Quakerism and Industry: Being the Full Record of a Conference of Employers, chiefly Members of the Society of Friends, held at Woodbrooke nr. Birmingham 11th–14th April 1918* (Darlington: North of England Newspaper Co., 1918), pp. 113–15; Meacham, *Regaining Paradise*, pp. 32–3; Wilson, *Unilever*, pp. 151–4, 157.

125 UARM, LBC 922, R. A. Hannah to Gen. S. S. Long, 11 July 1923; Long to H. R. Greenhalgh, 12 July; Greenhalgh to Long, 13 July; Lever to Greenhalgh, 17 July.

126 Robert Fitzgerald, *British Labour Management and Industrial Welfare 1846–1939* (London and New York: Croom Helm, 1988), pp. 2–3, 118–27, 131, 247–8.

127 Lever, *Leverhulme*, chaps 14–15; *Parliamentary Debates*, Commons, 4th Ser., vol. 174, cols 470–7. The Jones family lived in a one-bedroom cottage in Thornton Hough, which Lever demolished and replaced. See Lever, *Leverhulme*, p. 103.

128 *Parliamentary Debates*, Commons, 4th Ser., vol. 186, cols 684–6.

129 Stanley Unwin, *The Truth about A Publisher* (London: George Allen and Unwin, 1960), pp. 159–60.

130 Lever, *Six-Hour Day*, p. 5.

131 *Parliamentary Debates*, Lords, 5th Ser., 33, col. 198 (19 February 1919).

132 Lever, *Six-Hour Day*, pp. 6–33; UARM, LBC 809A, Lever to John Cheshire, 20 September 1917; Lever, *Leverhulme*, pp. 199–202.

133 Hodgkin (ed.), *Quakerism and Industry*, pp. 26, 64.

134 Lever, *Leverhulme*, p. 202.

135 Lever, *Six-Hour Day*, pp. 233–5 (speech at prize distribution at girls' side of Bolton School, 7 October 1916).

136 William Hesketh Lever, *Following the Flag: Jottings of a Jaunt round the World* (London: Simpkin Marshall and Co.; Liverpool: Edward Howell, 1893), pp. 90–2, 102–3, 115–18; BALS, A590, 'Bolton Education Society: Education and Common Life, being the presidential address by Sir William Hesketh Lever, Bart, in Bolton Town Hall, 13th October, 1911' (Bolton, 1912), pp. 13–14; *Sunday Times* (Sydney), 20 January 1924, in BALS, B920 B LEV, newspaper cuttings on Lever.

137 UARM, LBC 6187, Lever to Acting Editor, *Financial Times*, 17 June 1912.

138 *Birkenhead and Cheshire Advertiser and Wallasey Guardian*, 17 September 1924, in BALS, B920 B LEV, newspaper cuttings on Lever; Lever, *Leverhulme*, pp. 247–9.

139 'Fast asleep on a gold mine' (address at Mawdsley Street Congregational Church PSA Brotherhood, 5 December 1915), in Sir William Hesketh Lever, *Three Addresses* (Port Sunlight: Lever Brothers, n.d.), pp. 38–9.

140 Lever, *Six-Hour Day*, p. 9. Along the same lines see also pp. 337–41 for his sustained defence of capitalism and attack on socialism in 1918.

141 Hertfordshire Archives and Local Studies, Howard Papers, Eho/F17, quoted by Mervyn Miller, 'Back to the future – the garden city centenary', *Town and Country Planning*, 72:7 (August 2003), 200.

142 Ebenezer Howard, *Garden Cities of To-morrow* (London: Swan Sonnenschein, 1902); Fishman, *Urban Utopias*, pp. 7–8.

143 Mervyn Miller, *Letchworth: The First Garden City* (Chichester: Phillimore, 1989), p. 10; Hardy, *Utopian England*, p. 63; Tristram Hunt, *Building Jerusalem: The Rise and Fall of the Victorian City* (London: Phoenix, 2005), pp. 430–1.

144 Fishman, *Urban Utopias*, pp. 57–63; Robert Beevers, *The Garden City Utopia: A Critical Biography of Ebenezer Howard* (Basingstoke: Macmillan, 1988), p. 79.

145 Buder, *Visionaries and Planners*, pp. 84, 90; Hall and Ward, *Sociable Cities*, pp. 15, 32–6; Meacham, *Regaining Paradise*, pp. 121–2; Creese, *Search for Environment*, pp. 203; Beevers, *Garden City Utopia*, p. 93.

146 Anne Vernon, *A Quaker Business Man: The Life of Joseph Rowntree 1836–1925* (London: George Allen and Unwin, 1958), pp. 146–8; Creese, *Search for Environment*, chap. 8; Miller, 'Back to the future', pp. 201–2.

147 Miller, *Letchworth*, pp. 88, 90.

148 *John Betjeman's Collected Poems* (London: John Murray, 1985), p. 69.

149 George Orwell, *The Road to Wigan Pier* (London: Penguin, 1989; 1st edn, 1937), pp. 161–2.

150 Eaton, *Ideal Cities*, p. 150.

151 Anthony Sutcliffe, *Towards the Planned City: Germany, Britain, the United States and France 1780–1914* (New York: St Martin's Press, 1981), p. 67.

152 Ashworth, *Genesis*, p. 144; Burke, *Towns in the Making*, p. 150; Armytage, *Heavens Below*, pp. 405, 420.

153 Meacham, *Regaining Paradise*, pp. 2–7, 55–6.

154 Quoted by Armytage, *Heavens Below*, p. 381.

155 Meacham, *Regaining Paradise*, chap. 7; Beevers, *Garden City Utopia*, pp. 133–4; Creese, *Search for Environment*, p. 218; Hall, *Urban and Regional Planning*, pp. 33–4.

156 Ashworth, *Genesis*, pp. 146, 160; Hunt, *Building Jerusalem*, p. 447.

157 Hall, *Urban and Regional Planning*, p. 34; Armytage, *Heavens Below*, pp. 421–2; Stephen V. Ward, *Planning and Urban Change*, 2nd edn (London: Sage Publications, 2004), pp. 48–9.

158 Ashworth, *Genesis*, pp. 138–40; Cherry, *Urban Change and Planning*, p. 123; Thomas H. Mawson, *Civic Art: Studies in Town Planning: Parks, Boulevards and Open Spaces* (London: B. T. Batsford, 1911), pp. 287 ff.; Abercrombie, 'Modern town planning', part II, *Town Planning Review*, 1:2 (July 1910), 111–28.

159 Quoted in *Garden Cities and Town Planning*, new ser., vol. III (1908), p. 97, quoted by Ashworth, *Genesis*, pp. 140–1.

160 Quoted by Simon Pepper, 'The garden city', in Boris Ford (ed.), *The Cambridge Cultural History of Britain*, vol. VIII: *Early Twentieth-Century Britain* (Cambridge: Cambridge University Press), p. 102.

161 Aileen Reid, *Brentham: A History of the Pioneer Garden Suburb 1901–2001* (Ealing: Brentham Heritage Society, 2000); Abercrombie, 'Modern town planning', pp. 111–28.

162 Pepper, 'The garden city', pp. 106, 109–10, 114.

163 Hall and Ward, *Sociable Cities*, chap. 6; Sutcliffe, *Towards the Planned City*, p. 41; Meller, *European Cities*, pp. 117–18, 125–7; Suzanne Morton, *Ideal Surroundings: Domestic Life in a Working-Class Suburb in the 1920s* (Toronto: University of Toronto Press, 1995), p. 19; Peterson, *Birth of City Planning*, p. 235; Buder, *Visionaries and Planners*, p. 161.

164 Meller, *European Cities*, pp. 128–45.

165 Peterson, *Birth of City Planning*, pp. 321 (quotation), 323; Ward, *Planning and Urban Change*, pp. 50–2; Buder, *Visionaries and Planners*, pp. 168–9, 174–6.

166 Quoted by Kenneth T. Jackson, *Crabgrass Frontier: The Suburbanization of the United States* (New York and Oxford: Oxford University Press, 1985), p. 195.

167 Meller, *European Cities*, pp. 117–27; Cherry, *Cities and Plans*, p. 75.

168 Ward, *Planning and Urban Change*, p. 48. See also Andrew Saint, 'The new towns', in Boris Ford (ed.), *The Cambridge Cultural History of Britain*, vol. IX: *Modern Britain* (Cambridge: Cambridge University Press, 1992), pp. 147–59.

169 Hall, *Urban and Regional Planning*, pp. 43–4.

170 Buder, *Visionaries and Planners*, pp. 187–98; Saint, 'The new towns', p. 149.

171 Lord Silkin, foreword to Frank Schaffer, *The New Town Story* (London: MacGibbon and Kee, 1970), pp. ix, xiv.

172 'Land for houses', paper delivered to North End Liberal Club, 4 October 1898, in Lever, *Six-Hour Day*, pp. 162–4; Creese, *Search for Environment*, pp. 139–41.

173 Ward, *Planning and Urban Change*, pp. 27–32; Sutcliffe, *Towards the Planned City*, pp. 64, 69–72, 77–8 (quotation p. 78), 81–2; Peterson, *Birth of City Planning*, pp. 238–9.

174 Michael Shippobottom, 'C. H. Reilly and the first Lord Leverhulme', in Joseph Sharples, Alan Powers and Michael Shippobottom (eds), *Charles Reilly and the Liverpool School of Architecture 1904–1933: Catalogue of an Exhibition at the Walker Art Gallery, Liverpool, 25 Oct. 1996–2 Feb. 1997* (Liverpool: Liverpool University Press, 1996), p. 47.

175 C. H. Reilly, *Scaffolding in the Sky: A Semi-architectural Autobiography* (London: George Routledge and Son, 1938), pp. 93 (quotation), 125–7, 130; Myles Wright, *Lord Leverhulme's Unknown Venture: The Lever Chair and the Beginnings of Town and Regional Planning 1908–1948* (London: Hutchinson Benham, 1982), pp. 8, 24, 28, 56–7; Shippobottom, 'C. H. Reilly', pp. 50, 57; Thomas Kelly, *For Advancement of Learning: The University of Liverpool 1881–1981* (Liverpool: Liverpool University Press, 1981), p. 146; University of Liverpool, Special Collections and Archives, Sydney Jones Library: Vice-Chancellors' Papers, Lever to Vice-Chancellor A. W. W. Dale, 25 November 1908; F. E. Hyde Papers, D.116/1, draft Deed of Gift, 1910, between Lever and University of Liverpool; Lever, *Leverhulme*, p. 139.

176 Williams, *Men of Stress*, pp. 330–1; Lever, *Leverhulme*, pp. 298–9.

177 Mawson, *Civic Art*, pp. 280, 284; Mawson, *Bolton As It Is and As It Might Be: Six Lectures Delivered under the Auspices of the Bolton Housing and Town Planning Society* (Bolton: Tillotson and Son; London: Batsford, 1916), p. 13; Pevsner and Hubbard, *Buildings of England: Cheshire*, pp. 305–6; Sutcliffe, *Towards the Planned City*, pp. 182, 184; Peterson, *Birth of City Planning*, *passim*; Cherry, *Cities and Plans*, p. 4; Wright, *Lord Leverhulme's Unknown Venture*, p. 59; Ward, *Planning and Urban Change*, pp. 33–4; Ward, *Planning the Twentieth-Century City: The Advanced Capitalist World* (Chichester: John Wiley and Sons, 2002), p. 75; Helen Meller, *Towns, Plans and Society in Modern Britain* (Cambridge: Cambridge University Press, 1997), pp. 39–40.

178 Thomas H. Mawson, *Bolton (Lancs.): A Study in Town Planning and Civic Art* (Bolton: Tillotson Press [*c.* 1911]); Mawson, *Civic Art*, chap. 3; Mawson, *Bolton As It Is*; *Town Planning Review*, 2:1 (April 1911), 74–5 (quotation), 88.

179 BALS, B711 B MAW, 'Town centre planning', clipping from *Bolton Journal and Guardian*; B920 B LEV, newspaper cuttings on Lever: *Bolton Journal and Guardian*, 15 September 1918, and *Bolton Evening News*, n.d.; Lever, *Leverhulme*, pp. 264–5.

180 Lever, *Six-Hour Day*, p. 165.

181 Ward, *Planning and Urban Change*, pp. 37–40, 44–5; Cherry, *Urban Change and Planning*, pp. 128–9; Ross McKibbin, *Classes and Cultures: England 1918–1951* (Oxford: Oxford University Press, 1998), pp. 72–9, 188–90.

182 Lewis Mumford, 'The fate of the garden cities', *Journal of the A.I.A.* (1927), quoted by Eaton, *Ideal Cities*, p. 151.

183 Ward, *Planning and Urban Change*, p. 47.

184 J. B. Priestley, *English Journey* (London: William Heinemann, 1934), *passim*; Alison Light, *Forever England: Femininity, Literature and Consumerism between the Wars* (London: Routledge, 1991), p. 211; Simon Gunn and Rachel Bell, *Middle Classes: Their Rise and Sprawl* (London: Phoenix, 2003), pp. 68, 80; Meacham, *Regaining Paradise*, pp. 182–3; Hunt, *Building Jerusalem*, pp. 447–53.

185 Eaton, *Ideal Cities*, pp. 199–203, 207–9; Cherry, *Cities and Plans*, p. 5; Fishman, *Urban Utopias*, pp. 9–10; Ward, *Planning and Urban Change*, p. 58; Buder, *Visionaries and Planners*, pp. 148–54.

186 F. R. S. Yorke and Frederick Gibberd, *The Modern Flat* (London: Architectural Press, 1937), p. 16.

187 Miles Glendinning and Stefan Muthesius, *Tower Block: Modern Public Housing in England, Scotland, Wales, and Northern Ireland* (New Haven, CT: Yale University Press, 1994), *passim*.

188 Jane Jacobs, *The Death and Life of Great American Cities* (New York: Vintage Books, 1992; 1st edn, 1961), pp. 17–25 (quotation p. 17).

189 Lewis Mumford, *The City in History: Its Origins, its Transformations, and its Prospects* (New York: Harcourt Brace and World, 1961), p. 486.

190 Peterson, *Birth of City Planning*, pp. 324–5; Andres Duany, Elizabeth Plater-Zyberk and Jeff Speck, *Suburban Nation: The Rise of Sprawl and the Decline of the American Dream* (New York: North Point Press, 2000), pp. 7–9, 18, 43, 95; Jackson, *Crabgrass Frontier*, pp. 219, 244–5, 283–4, 287, 290–5.

191 David Harvey, *Spaces of Hope* (Berkeley, CA, and Los Angeles: University of California Press, 2000), pp. 138, 150, 158; Robert M. Fogelson, *Bourgeois Nightmares: Suburbia 1870–1930* (New Haven, CT: Yale University Press, 2005), pp. 23, 202.

192 Duany *et al.*, *Suburban Nation*, pp. x and xiii (quotations), 12, 41; Creese, *Search for Environment*, pp. 368–9, 371, 375–6.

193 See Tony Chapman and Jenny Hockey, 'The ideal home as it is imagined and as it is lived', in Tony Chapman and Jenny Hockey (eds), *Ideal Homes? Social Change and Domestic Life* (London and New York: Routledge, 1999), pp. 8–9. For a spirited defence of suburbia see Mark Clapson, *Suburban Century: Social Change and Urban Growth in England and the United States* (Oxford and New York: Berg, 2003).

4

Sunlight for savages

What have the Romans done for us?

'Lord Leverhulme brought remote and semi-savage communities to a higher spirit of development than they would have reached by their own unaided efforts,' wrote T. P. O'Connor in his obituary of the Old Man, 'and made them productive agents for the supplies of the world's markets.'[1] This indeed was Lever's boast about his efforts in the Belgian Congo and the South Pacific. But: 'Did he know what it meant to substitute for that innocence of native life his own idea of ordered effort and exploitation?' Harley Williams wondered a generation later, before reaffirming the benefits of the imposition of civilization. '[W]as it wrong to drain their land, free their villages from the anophelene mosquito and the tsetse fly? Could any reasonable person say it was wrong to set them free from fear, disease, malnutrition? … Sunlight indeed is Leverhulme's symbol. He had brought it even to the darkness of the tropical forest.'[2]

A few years later, Jervis Babb, head of Lever Brothers in the United States, eulogized a project 'which well could serve as a model today for the industrial development of backward countries':

> Sunlight was brought to the darkest forests. Steaming swamps were drained; malaria and other diseases stamped out; roads, schools, and hospitals were built; villages were constructed and new meaning and purpose brought into the lives of primitive and aimless savages. Leverville in the Belgian Congo and other villages in Africa and upon islands of the South Pacific were, in their way, akin to Port Sunlight.[3]

Charles Wilson would never have put anything so crudely, but even he believed that, 'Certainly, among the many things he did, few were to have consequences of greater lasting benefit than his bold venture into the Congo.'[4] And Lever's latest biographer, Adam MacQueen, who entitles his chapter on Lever in the Congo 'A good man in Africa', writes simply and uncritically of the Old Man's final expedition to West Africa in 1924, 'Lord Leverhulme looked upon his works, and he saw that they were good.'[5]

The story is not so straightforward. Many first-hand accounts and the researches of labour historians tell a very different tale, impossible to reconcile with the positive spin of empire. My purpose in this chapter is neither to praise nor to bury Caesar. This is not a case for the prosecution. Lever may have meant well but that is really beside the point. Business considerations came first, and these dictated policies and methods that deviated far from the benign picture painted above. Once again, what is most interesting is the context that constricted individual choices: the logic that drove him, his company and comparable companies to follow particular policies at particular times.

Lever and lesser breeds

In the late nineteenth century the notion that, once basic human needs had been satisfied by a growing economy, people could begin to focus on redistribution of wealth and on ethical and moral issues – staples of political economy from Adam Smith to John Stuart Mill – was increasingly displaced in the writings of economists by the belief that people's taste for variety in material matters was limitless. Progress came to mean development, to be measured by the capacity to consume. '[M]*odern* man would henceforth be known by the insatiability of his desires,' in the words of Regenia Gagnier, 'and the indolent races of savages – whether Irish, African, or native American (key examples throughout Victorian political economy) – needed only to be inspired by envy to desire his desires, imitate his wants, to be on the road to his progress and his *civilization*.'[6]

The attempt to create this desire among indolent races ran like a leitmotif through Lever's musings on colonized peoples. It was there as early as 1893, in his published diary account of his first 'jaunt round the world'. In his entries for New Zealand he commented that the government had treated the Maoris exceptionally well because of the stipulation that each acre belonged to them if it had not been alienated to whites by treaty or purchase. However:

> whether the fact that the Maoris were camping out on the land at the time that the white man came makes their claim to absolute ownership stronger than that of the white man, who, coming here, has, by his own exertions and industry, unaided in the slightest degree by the Maoris, given whatever value there may be to the land, is a question to which it must be difficult to find a satisfactory answer.

The Maoris sat in idleness without lifting a finger or bearing any of the burdens of taxation while their lands were being developed and made of value. This was unearned increment with a vengeance.[7]

Lever believed that unproductive land ownership was intolerable. In line with a consistent strand of liberal radical rhetoric from Richard Cobden and John Bright to David Lloyd George that targeted British aristocrats, he despised 'landlordism', the abusive term applied to a system that allowed land to lie fallow or undercultivated (no man was entitled to do 'what he likes with his own'), that enabled the idle to benefit from the exertions of others and that failed to recognize that property had its duties as well as its rights. The remedy at home was graduated land taxation, falling lightly on those (such as himself) whose land was put to proper use and crushingly on the rest. The logic applied equally to land in the undeveloped world. Allowing indigenous peoples to squat inertly on land they called their own made no sense to him, since it stymied any chance of progress and improvement.

To explain where he stood on questions of race requires us to backtrack a little. Modern Western racism is a child of the Enlightenment. To be sure, for centuries beforehand people had found creative ways of using the Bible to persecute or ghettoize Jews (the killers of Christ) or to justify slavery (the Curse of Ham; *Genesis* 9:20–7) or to cleanse the New World of 'savages' and 'heathens' as part of God's plan for the advancement of Christianity and civilization. But this always ran up against the clarity of New Testament teaching that all were of one blood, all had souls and that all could be saved. It was Enlightenment scientific thought that started to shift the discourse towards race, beginning the process of categorizing peoples into physically distinctive racial groups produced, it was generally thought, by differences in climate. Carolus Linnaeus, the Swedish botanist who devised the Linnaean system of plant and animal classification, followed his method to what seemed to be a logical conclusion in his *Systema Naturae* (1735) by dividing humans into Europeans, American Indians, Asians and Africans. He imposed no ranking order but described Europeans as 'acute, inventive' and Africans as 'crafty, indolent, negligent'. The German physiologist and comparative anatomist Johann Friedrich Blumenbach went a step further in his *On the Natural Varieties of Mankind* (1776) by classifying humans, largely according to cranial measurements, into five ideal types: Caucasian, Mongoloid, Malayan, Ethiopian and American. He coined the category 'Caucasian' because he had a rather handsome skull from the Caucasus in his collection; although he resisted placing his races in a hierarchy, he clearly saw the Caucasians as a cut above.

This classification of humans as part of the animal kingdom laid the groundwork for the secular or scientific racism of the nineteenth century. That a superstructure of hierarchical racism would be built on these foundations was not a foregone conclusion. The revival of Evangelical Christianity, the belief that all were born of Adam and that all would be equal in the next world, if not in this, provided a powerful countervailing influence. So did secular Enlightenment thinking premised on 'We, the people', the Rights of Man and *Liberté, Egalité, Fraternité* – the 'all men are created equal' of the American and French Revolutions – potentially at least, because it was going to take some time before the logic of an appeal to the people would become more inclusive, and not simply describe white, propertied males.

But scientific thinking was pushing in the opposite direction, first towards the belief that the races were polygenetic – that is, that they had separate origins – and then, as Charles Darwin's ideas in *On the Origin of Species* (1859) and *The Descent of Man* (1871) gained greater acceptance, that they had indeed evolved from the same source but at different speeds over the millennia, into quasi-species with different physical characteristics and mental aptitudes. And as the Western world entered an era of aggressive nation-state building, often based on exclusionary and/or ethnic principles, and of competitive imperialism, the pseudo-scientific ideas increasingly held sway in the political and cultural realms. One way for elites in the more liberal nations of Europe, which relied on civic rather than ethnic nationalism, to bind their class-divided populations together was through defining the nation against inferior, external others. For some, the contradictions between aspirant egalitarian democracy and modern racism began to seem less glaring, even two sides of the same coin.

Very few across the political spectrum came to doubt that certain races were inferior and that race was a biological fact determined by nature and not a social myth or human artefact. But, broadly speaking, there were two mainstream understandings of race by the turn of the century, both justifying the imperialist mission. Both took for granted a racial hierarchy with Nordic types at the top, black Africans at the bottom, but only one was explicitly racist in its belief in the evolution of a definable typology of distinct races with different capabilities, characteristics and intellects. Lower races were, naturally, for all practicable purposes, subhuman – tameable perhaps, but immutably inferior. For many, these races were doomed to extinction – the laws of nature said so – and that meant that imperialism was a biological imperative. The land of these lower races was up for grabs and proponents at the extreme end of this credo believed it to be acceptable, even necessary, to exterminate them. The most vicious example at the turn of the century was the punishment meted out to the Herero of South West Africa, who rose in rebellion in 1904 against their appalling treatment by German settlers. The German government sent in General Lothar von Trotha to wreak revenge. Von Trotha believed that 'against non-humans one cannot wage war humanely'. He issued the proclamation, 'Inside German territory every Herero tribesman, armed or unarmed, with or without cattle, will be shot.' This was an order for genocide; the Herero were destroyed as a people.

Lever and a spectrum of opinion encompassing humanitarians and British colonial officials shared the alternative interpretation. They believed that backward peoples were immature but teachable and could, over a very long period of time, become civilized. This amounted to racism in practice in that they justified, in a language of 'trusteeship' or 'guardianship', white rule over indigenous populations – based on the uncontentious notion that those who could best work and improve the land should do so – but they did not pretend that such a state of affairs would persist for ever, maintained that these 'children' had a right to humane treatment and even allowed token numbers, who had assimilated rapidly to Western ways, certain rights and positions of trust in the short term.[8]

Again, in *Following the Flag*, Lever gave an early indication of how he viewed the 'children' of the non-developed world. In Honolulu he expressed little surprise at the persistence of native superstitions, given that missionaries had been working on the population for only seventy years, but wondered whether the greater focus should be on people's material needs rather than on the inculcation of Christian beliefs beyond their capacities of comprehension:

> If we really wish to give to native races the blessings of our civilisation and religion, so that they may become a happy and prosperous people, let us first teach them to make for themselves and families the best use of their lands; let us make them into planters, cultivators, and manufacturers of such articles as can be made out of the raw material their lands produce; let us, in short, act as would wise guardians and trustees during the infancy and development of a ward. In this direction there is an enormous field for missionary effort.[9]

The dubious wisdom of the Solomons

Soon after returning from his world trip Lever began to seek ways of securing supplies of coconut and palm oil – the finest quality vegetable oils – for his soaps. It is uncertain whether he needed to or whether this made sound economic sense. Vertical integration – the extension of a manufacturing concern's interests into the production of its raw materials, and/or into shipping those materials or finished products, and/or into the retailing of those products – is a risky strategy because it diverts a business's energies from what it does best and how it made its name. But it becomes logical for a firm to plant or harvest its own raw materials in time of actual or predicted world shortage, which would seriously hamper its manufacturing operations or lead to a spiralling of retail prices, or if other concerns have monopolistic holds on key areas of the raw material market, or if the firm wishes so to increase the world supply of the raw materials in question that manufacturing costs could be reduced.[10] As he explained in a letter in 1904, Lever seems to have been primarily motivated by the first and third of these reasons:

> For many years now this [nut oils] market has been becoming a more and more difficult one. It was for this reason I felt we ought to be doing some pioneer work, with regard to increasing the supply of Coprah [*sic*; the dried kernels of the coconut]. ... The recent use of Coprah Oil for edible purposes increases

our difficulties. There is no corresponding increase in production. To leave the production of Coprah in the hands of natives, who stop producing as soon as they have supplied their limited wants, will not give the world the Coprah it wants. We want the market as much over-done as the Tea-Market is over-done with Tea. ... Tea and Coffee to-day are extremely unprofitable to the grower but extremely profitable to the consumer. We want the same position with regard to Coprah and Palm Kernels, and nothing is being done, as far as I know, in a systematic fashion, in any part of the world to give us this result. ... We are the most interested in this question of any firm in the world, and we have got to make some attempt to relieve the position. Otherwise, what may be represented by £100,000 expenditure now, might cost us many hundreds of thousands a year in the future.[11]

Lever was afraid that competition for the oils, particularly with the arrival on the scene of margarine manufacturers buying the same raw materials, would create shortages. This was scarcely borne out in the short term. In 1902, for example, the price of copra plummeted, which Lever attributed to an abundant corn crop in the United States and to the completion of railways in West Africa easing the transportation of palm oil to the coast.[12]

In the longer term, his case rested on a number of factors. One was that he did not trust native producers, lacking a Western work ethic, to deliver up sufficient quantities of raw materials. When he later moved into the harvesting of oil palms in West Africa, an additional reason was to reduce the content of free fatty acid in the oil so as to maintain the quality of his soaps. This acid increased particularly rapidly if fruit was left lying about for too long (especially if it had been bruised by falling from the tree) or if impurities crept into the extraction process.[13] In the 1920s it was estimated that modern methods extracted all but 2 per cent of the palm oil from the fruit and contained only 5 per cent free fatty acid, whereas the native mortar wasted 10–20 per cent and contained 20–30 per cent free fatty acid.[14]

Another stated factor was his hope to glut the market. This was highly ambitious if he truly believed that Lever Brothers alone could produce sufficient oil to swamp world demand. It was also rather contradictory in terms of the company's best financial interests, because if it were to produce a very large quantity of oil, at a certain point sound business sense would hope that as high a market price could be gained for that oil as possible. In other words, the manufacturing and the commodities sides of the company would come into conflict, the manufacturing wing wanting as low raw materials costs as possible, the commodities branch wanting the maximum return, and it would not make sense for the latter to provide solely for the former if good prices could be gained on the open market, nor for the former to seek a supply only from the latter if cheaper products could be gleaned from more competitive sources. At this point the whole logic of vertical integration tends to break down, and horizontal integration – the manufacturing and commodities components of the multinational acting largely autonomously – takes over. This happened to Lever Brothers in the early 1920s.[15]

Lever's first venture into the raw materials business began in the South Pacific. The Pacific Islands Company, which operated trading networks and exploited scattered copra and other interests across the region, needed an injection of outside capital to mine rich phosphate deposits on Banaba (Ocean Island) and Nauru. In 1902 Lever obliged by purchasing a stake in a revamped version of this company, became a director of the spin-off Pacific Phosphate Company and established Lever Pacific Plantations Ltd. In the years ahead the company dramatically expanded and consolidated its holdings by buying up 300,000 acres of optimal land in the British Solomons for the mass planting of coconuts.[16]

Reshaping the world so that big business could prosper was not pretty, and the South Pacific was no exception. Once the European powers had carved up the region in the late nineteenth century the new colonial governments were expected to be largely self-financing. They could not borrow, so the most efficient way of raising the necessary tax revenue was by encouraging large companies – the Colonial Sugar Refining Company in Fiji, the Société le Nickel in New Caledonia, the Deutsche Handels- und Plantagen-Gesellschaft der Südsee-Inseln zu Hamburg (DHPG) in German Samoa, Lever Brothers and Burns Philp in the British Solomons – to develop a substantial export trade in one of the staple crops. To make this work, administrators had to develop stratagems to pacify the indigenous populations, then to take their land and discourage peasant production, then to get them to labour for the big companies. None of this could be achieved without considerable physical violence and the violation of existing cultures and ways of life.

The British Solomon Islands Protectorate was established in 1893 to keep out the French. According to Doug Munro and Stewart Firth, Charles Morris Woodford, the first Resident Commissioner, pursued in the areas best suited for plantations a ruthless policy known euphemistically as 'pacification', and then alienated huge areas of indigenous land on the pretext that it was 'waste land' and 'quite uninhabited'. Following fashionable racial notions he believed that these islanders were, in any case, a dying race, doomed to be replaced by vigorous, higher, white races. By 1913 he had alienated on freehold or leasehold terms 450,000 acres, mainly of quality coastal land ripe for coconut growing.

Once cleared of their original inhabitants, the plantation sites had to be protected from attack, communications established and a consistent stream of labour found to clear the bush, plant the trees and keep the undergrowth and insects at bay during the six to ten years before the trees bore fruit. As the government was counting on the success of the plantations for a large chunk of its revenues, it was complicit in these activities or (at the very least) compromised in its duty to protect the welfare of the indigenous populations. The role of these populations was, quite simply, to provide menial labour and consume imports, not to participate as producers in the growing cash economy.[17]

Finding that stream of labour was, however, a challenge. Most islanders were involved in cash cropping, which more than catered for their needs, so they could not be recruited for the plantations. On his only trip to the Solomons, during his world tour of 1913–14, Lever noted at one point in his diary:

> The Chief of the native village came out to meet us and we afterwards went into his hut. There I noted a wardrobe, three sewing-machines, chairs, table, gramophone, thermos-flask, and other items of civilization amid general dirt and disorder. Mr. Woodford states that the natives are making so much money out of copra at present that they have no idea what to do with their earnings or profits, and either waste them on useless purchases or hoard them in some hole in the ground. He said he had no doubt this old chief could produce hundreds of pounds hidden away somewhere.[18]

The major source of workers was the Malaitian Islands, deficient in cash-crop possibilities. But once they stepped off the boat in the Solomons the conditions they encountered were little better than those in a labour camp or penal colony. They were housed in corrugated iron sheds, slept on wooden boards and had little social life. They served out two-year contracts, earning £8 a year for fifty-four-hour weeks, could buy goods only at the company store's highly inflated prices and did not receive most of their pay until the end of the contracts, after deductions had been made.[19] Few whites could be tempted to work on the plantations in these remote and often inhospitable places: the only takers were rough Australians who had failed to make good back home and who arrived conditioned by a virulent anti-aboriginal racism. One old hand allegedly advised a newcomer to treat the workers 'as muck. Remember that a white man's the only human being here and that there isn't any other kind.' A. W. Mahaffy, Assistant to the High Commissioner, wrote in 1908 that most of the Australian managers that Lever Brothers employed were:

> for the most part unable to deal with native labour, and it is not surprising when it is remembered that they have every opportunity to manifest their dislike of "niggers" upon some of the most isolated plantations of the firm. ... [I]t is not denied that floggings take place upon the estates, and to put such power into the hands of ignorant and prejudiced persons constitutes a real danger.[20]

He imagined that the conditions on Lever Brothers' plantations were sometimes such as would 'amaze and horrify the proprietor of the model town of Port Sunlight'.[21]

Gross labour abuses, according to Judith Bennett, were particularly bad on the larger plantations of Lever Brothers and those of the Solomon Islands Development Company and the Shortland Islands Plantations Ltd, subsidiaries of the Australian shipping and mercantile company Burns Philp. Ill treatment of labourers through floggings and beatings, even killings, was compounded by a dysentery epidemic in the plantations in 1913–14. This killed nearly 5 per cent of workers, but double that on some plantations, particularly Lever Brothers', thanks to abysmal sanitation and medical care. The Colonial Office began asking questions and bringing prosecutions, and the company started to clean up its act, replacing many managers and overseers with better educated and often family men, employing its own medical superintendent from 1917 and, in 1919, introducing task-work rather than enforcing time discipline. Conditions improved in the 1920s but again worsened in the tougher economic climate during the Great Depression. Plantation overseers were under pressure to produce, and rather than enforcing work discipline through implementing prescribed labour regulations, which lost time and productivity, resorted to many of the old methods like thrashings or forcing labourers to work late at the weekends.[22]

Throughout all this, the plantations failed to reach their full potential. Lever Brothers had planted only 20,000 of its 300,000 acres by the 1920s, yielding not even enough copra to supply the needs of the company mill at Balmain, Sydney, and, over the first three decades, barely breaking even in terms of profits over the capital expended. There were simply too few recruits to expand further, too few lured by the prospect of wages to buy European goods. One attempt to improve matters was for the administration in 1920 to impose a head tax of £1 a year on all able-bodied males aged sixteen to sixty so as to force some of them to take up plantation work, either to avoid paying it (since the plantation owners paid their taxes) or to pay the tax for their relatives back home. Another potential solution to labour shortages would have been to recruit foreign labour. 'I do not see why,' Lever wrote, 'we cannot bring as labourers to these beautiful Islands Hindoos from the teeming millions of India.'

Lever Brothers first made a request for Indian labour in 1909, and both the firm and Burns Philp lobbied repeatedly over the years for Indian or Chinese indentured labour. They were invariably turned down. The Indian government objected, mindful of strong opposition from the growing Indian nationalist movement. The Australian government also objected: its 'White Australia' policy prevented Asian immigration to Papua and other islands within its *cordon sanitaire*, and it feared that coolie labour might give the Solomons an unfair advantage. Lever himself, in his final visit to Australia in 1924, denounced this policy for excluding non-white labour from the Northern Territory. His argument was grounded in economics: white labour was more expensive and not as racially or physically adapted to hot climates, he claimed, so the sugar and cotton plantations were not being developed so that they could compete on world markets. One cartoon portrayed him 'in the guise of a schoolboy being punished by a teacher labelled "Australia" for spilling black ink on a clean white map of the Commonwealth'.

The Colonial Office initially did not mind recruitment of free Asian labour for the Pacific islands, but ruled out indentures, partly following the Indian government's lead but also because of earlier unsuccessful experiments with indentured Chinese labour in the gold mines of the Transvaal in South Africa. (The furore over 'Chinese slavery' had become a major issue in the 1906 British general election.) But, for Lever, indentures were crucial because he wanted a contractual assurance that, if he paid for the passage from India, the Indian worker would labour for the company for a specified time. Partly because of its unsatisfactory experience in the Solomons, the company was later to avoid the problem of an inadequate labour force, first in the Congo by working in cahoots with a more compliant government to conscript unwilling labour, and then in Malaysia, where Unilever successfully established plantations in the midst of an abundant local work force. [23]

Save us from the Exeter Hall crowd

Lever's attempts to extract raw materials from elsewhere in the British Empire were even less successful, principally because British thinking had evolved around the concept of trusteeship. Edmund Burke had outlined the idea in 1783 with India in mind: 'all political power which is set over men, being wholly artificial, and for so much a derogation from the natural equality of mankind at large, ought to be some way or other exercised ultimately for their benefit … such rights … are all in the strictest sense a *trust*; and it is in the very essence of every trust to be rendered accountable'. [24]

The fortunes of the idea of trusteeship fluctuated wildly over the course of the nineteenth century and had limited purchase in the period after the Indian Mutiny of 1857 and during the late nineteenth-century 'Scramble for Africa'. They revived after 1905, principally under Liberal governments whose avowed intent was to protect Africans not only from the abuses of people like King Leopold of the Belgians in the Congo and Cecil Rhodes in southern Africa but also from 'the soap boilers of the world'. [25] Even so, the wish to promote white settler self-government resulted in some spectacular contradictions in policy, notably the abnegation of duties towards blacks in South Africa in 1909–10 when the white minority was accorded self-rule. Still, the Colonial Office during this period generally attempted to prevent practices of forced and indentured labour and flogging, and refused monopoly concessions to European companies, even well respected ones like Lever Brothers.

In West Africa, where climate and disease militated against white settlement, both the Colonial Office and colonial governors preferred a 'pro-African' and anti-settler policy of protecting African land rights, favouring 'native produc-tion' and 'rule through chiefs'. This indirect rule was to be carried out as cheaply as possible, with handfuls of colonial administrators – depending heavily on a public school and Oxbridge sense of self-assuredness and effortless superiority – overseeing millions of Africans.[26] As R. L. Antrobus, Assistant Under-Secretary at the Colonial Office, summed it up, administration was 'first of all and chiefly in the interests of the inhabitants of the Territories; and secondly in accordance with the views of people in this country (and not a small and interested section of them [the merchants] represented in Parliament).'[27]

The rationale was not simply humanitarian, since African–European collaboration was proving quite successful in bringing palm products to market and it seemed that the extension of peasant production in cocoa, groundnuts and cotton would pay similar dividends.[28] A. G. Hopkins suggests three important reasons why most colonial powers limited foreign concessions. First, because peasant production was proven and reasonably effective – West African trade quadrupled in value in the dozen years before 1914 – and setting up plantations would generate friction over land rights and labour recruitment, making the colonies more difficult to govern. The public-school men who ran the colonies tended to be conservative, paternalistic and resistant to change or anything that might stir up the existing social structures through which they worked. Second, because the few plantations established – for example, the limited concessions granted by the French in Ivory Coast and Dahomey, and by the Germans in Togo and the Cameroons – were far from a roaring success, generally lacking capital, labour and a close knowledge of local tropical conditions. And third, because commercial rivals mounted campaigns of opposition to the potential creation of local monopolies.[29]

Lever contemplated establishing palm oil plantations in West Africa in the early days of his quest for secure raw materials, but did not pursue the idea very far because of British government opposition. The only real progress he made against British resistance to his demands for freehold or long-lease land was in Sierra Leone, where the indigenous authorities in the Yonnibanna district, sanctioned by the Sierra Leone government, gave a twenty-one-year lease on 300 square miles. Here a processing factory went into production in 1914, seven years after his opening overtures in Sierra Leone, with independent African collectors supplying the fruit. But the experiment failed within little over a year because the pericarp yield was poor compared with that from equatorial palms and because there was no means of coercing the collectors to provide sufficient fruit. Lever Brothers also built mills for crushing palm kernels at Opobo and Apapa (Lagos), Nigeria, in 1910, the intention being to make a considerable improvement on crude and ineffective methods of African extraction. The firm had spent a considerable sum developing a successful depericarping machine for teasing away the pericarp from the nut, and a machine for cracking the nuts. But in the end even the Nigerian ventures failed to work out, since crushing the palm kernels in Europe came to make more sense. As most of the rest of the kernel could be used for by-products like cattle feed once the oil was extracted, it was easier to transport the kernels intact as natural containers – they travelled well and were easy to handle – whereas separated oil and cattle-cake required careful handling and costly packaging.[30]

In the short term, however, he wished to ensure that nobody else in West Africa could build a mill within twenty miles of a Lever Brothers mill. He reasoned that he would have to spend years persuading the Africans to bring fruit to his mill (by paying them a better rate than if they extracted the oil themselves), and once he had achieved this competing mills would rush to take advantage.[31] Edmund Dene Morel, the crusading leader of the Congo Reform Association, thought this reasonable, and was excited at the prospect of a man with Lever's philanthropic reputation – 'a decent, honest and most powerful capitalistic force' – immersing himself in the region. Lever appeared to open up the prospect of capturing much of the palm-kernel-crushing industry, concentrated in Germany, for West Africa. '[T]he man and his schemes interest me immensely,' Morel wrote, 'and I cannot but believe that the ultimate outcome of his commercial courage will be good for British West Africa.'[32] But foreign companies predictably cried foul at the prospect of the government according special privileges to a British company, and the government would only meet Lever half way. There was still some prospect of a meeting of minds in the autumn of 1910, but Lever had already moved on and was negotiating with the more tractable Belgian government.[33]

He returned to the question again after the First World War, seeking land for plantations in Nigeria in 1920, but the Colonial Office still refused, still preferring 'native production' to big business in areas of sparse white settlement.[34] He tried a final time during his trip in 1924, demanding concessions for plantations, a government-guaranteed labour supply and a monopoly on purchases of fruit from Africans at fixed prices. The Governor of Nigeria, Sir Hugh Clifford, led the opposition. To find the labour force required, Clifford would have to find ways of creating a landless proletariat, possible only through deployment of the coercive techniques that the Belgians were using in the Congo. That he was not prepared to do.[35]

This was not a straightforward battle between enlightened officialdom and big business, since many Manchester and Liverpool traders were among Lever's most fervent opponents and he attracted a measure of support from some prominent civil servants. He would presumably have applauded the concept of a 'dual mandate' proposed by Lord Lugard, the former Governor of Nigeria, in his book *The Dual Mandate in British Tropical Africa* (1922) – Britain as a trustee to civilization for the development of resources and to the natives for their welfare – because it did not necessarily preclude an argument that indigenous wishes could be overridden, since they did not understand their own best interests.[36] Lever had no doubt that he knew best. In 1924 he argued, 'The African native will be happier, produce the best, and live under the larger conditions of prosperity, when his labour is directed and organized by his white brother who has all these million years start ahead of him.'[37] He was scathing about humanitarian do-gooders, whom he blamed for creating an unsatisfactory situation in Nigeria:

> I have asked many people I have met how the system came to be adopted and I am told it has been under pressure from certain very worthy and undoubtedly well-meaning individuals and societies in the United Kingdom which I have found generally in my travels in British Colonies are called 'The Exeter Hall crowd'. I think the African native will have every reason to exclaim with the European cynic: – 'Save us from our friends.'[38]

Sunlight in the heart of darkness

Joseph Conrad's searing indictment of European greed in the Congo, *Heart of Darkness*, was based on his travels in the region in the early 1890s when ivory was the focus of colonial lust. The worst was yet to come. Ivory made billiard balls and piano keys, hardly essential to the developing economy of the 'second industrial revolution'. Rubber was different. In the wake of experiments with pneumatic tyres in the late 1880s by a Scottish vet, John Boyd Dunlop, and a French industrialist, Édouard Michelin, it became clear that rubber tyres would drive the new automotive economy, and the hunt for wild rubber was on. King Leopold II of the Belgians had managed to gain diplomatic recognition for his vast private domain, the Congo Free State, eighty times the size of Belgium, in the mid-1880s. His stunningly brutal pursuit of rubber in this territory at the turn of the century left himself fabulously enriched and millions of Africans dead. Adam Hochschild estimates that – from murder, starvation, exhaustion, exposure, disease and failure to reproduce – the population of the Congo dropped by about half, around 10 million, between 1880 and 1920.

Local agents, persuaded that the Africans were so low on the evolutionary scale that they could be treated like beasts, ruled by the *chicotte*, a hippopotamus-hide whip cut into corkscrew strips. They deployed simple but effective means, keeping women and children, elders and chiefs hostage to force the younger males to collect and supply the requisite quantities of rubber. They shot non-compliants *en masse*, severing hands from corpses to prove the efficient use of bullets. Stories began to trickle out from missionaries and traders. In Britain the exposure of this, one of the greatest crimes of modern history, was principally the work of Edmund Dene Morel, on the staff of the Elder Dempster shipping line operating out of Liverpool, which carried cargo to and from the Congo, and Roger Casement, British consul to the Congo. Morel spotted not only that vast quantities of arms shipments were taking place but also that goods sent to Africa were a tiny fraction of raw materials received in exchange. He deduced the existence of slavery. The Foreign Office sent their man in the Congo, Casement, on a trip into the interior in 1903 to investigate. His report, bearing all the weight and authority of a British consular official, outlined the contours of Leopold's rapacious system in stark and chilling detail. It sparked the formation, by Morel, of the Congo Reform Association, the most wide-spread, passionate and effective of all British humanitarian crusades since the heyday of the anti-slavery movement. The campaign helped force Leopold to sell his private empire to the Belgian state in 1908.[39]

Lever's son later wrote of Leopold that he 'undoubtedly possessed a business brain of the first order', and this is his gloss on the man and his regime:

> Under the autocratic rule of King Leopold the Congo Administration devoted its efforts to freeing the country from Arab slave raiding, stamping out intertribal warfare, and preparing the ground for a complete administrative and judicial system, as well as for a network of railway communications, the funds for these purposes being largely provided out of the King's private purse. In 1907 Leopold offered to hand over the Congo to Belgium as soon as it would please his people to accept the gift.[40]

Granted that Lever Brothers' interests in the Congo would have prevented the second viscount from speaking plainly for fear of offending his hosts; but this transformation of a kleptocratic monster into an enlightened, benign fount of generosity is extraordinary.

Lever entered the story in 1910, after Leopold's death and after his failure to make headway in British West African colonies. As late as October of that year he was writing to Morel that he had seen no prospect of success in planting palm trees in West Africa, had never seriously entertained ideas for planta-tions there and that much more favourable conditions existed for planting coconuts in the East Indies.[41] But he must already have been negotiating with Jules Renkin, the Belgian Colonial Minister. The Belgian administration had sent an emissary, Dr Max Horn, to England in 1909 to try and drum up interest from British capitalists, and he and Lever had had conversations. Lever was sceptical at first because of the transportation difficulties involved in extracting palm products from such a vast area of barely penetrable tropical rain forest, but he was curious enough to commission two on-sight investigations, which reported favourably. He and Renkin then entered negotiations.[42]

When it became clear that Lever was angling for concessions of land in the Congo, Morel exhibited a more ambivalent attitude, retreating from his earlier enthusiasm for Lever's involvement in West Africa. He deplored the fact that the Belgian government was leasing land without acknowledging indigenous land ownership, without consulting African chiefs and without any sign of concern for indigenous interests. '[A]s you know,' he wrote to Lever, 'my funda-mental conviction is that his [the native's] future and his happiness depend entirely upon his being able to retain possession of his land and his free unfettered right to buy and sell in the produce thereof.'[43] Over dinner in March 1911 they aired their differences, which Morel described in a letter to the leading Belgian socialist, Émile Vandervelde. Morel was annoyed at Lever for secretly negotiating the kind of deal that he opposed – turning Africans, the owners of the palm trees, into labourers. How, he asked, was Lever going to persuade the Africans to bring him fruit? By force? Lever, 'visibly irritated', replied no: he would buy the fruit at an acceptable price. Why then had the agreement stipulated a minimum wage (twenty-five centimes a day) and not a minimum price? That is how the Belgian government wanted it, Lever insisted.

Lever then stated firmly that the land belonged to whoever could make it blossom, and if he was going to spend vast amounts and could prove his ability to develop it he had a right to it. It was clear that the future that Lever had in mind for the African was as a labourer: 'well paid, well fed, well housed – but a worker, a wage earner, and nothing more'. Morel concluded,

> Lever is a man without education, and without sentiment, a commercial genius, enormously fabulously rich, probably of good heart but also hard, who sees humanity as a vast engine of production without soul or desires or ambitions other than the accumulation of louis d'or[,] authoritarian, rarely contradicted. This man of vast commercial ideas has now launched himself into West Africa, into the Congo, where he can become an enormous force for good or for ill.[44]

Lever expounded his views very clearly in a letter to Morel. Whites, he agreed, had treated blacks abominably: 'The very deplorable fact is that superior human intelligence in the white man has often not only in the Congo but in Tasmania, Australia, New Zealand, Kentucky, Virginia, New England and Canada abused its ability and illtreated and murdered the Native races.' And yet 'This awful fact has not raised the black man to a position to do without intelligent guidance from the white man.' Indeed, 'It would serve no useful purpose for the white man to go and try to reverse the Divine order under which intellect and mental power rules and develops, protects and benefits inferior nations.' Nowhere had blacks shown the necessary organizational skills to use land profitably:

> He has shown no ability in that direction in Liberia nor in Hayti [sic]; he has prospered and prospered marvellously in the United States where he is directed and helped by the white man. ... I do not think you are likely to achieve the happiness of the black man unless you study his capabilities. ... The land of the world, in any part of the world ought to be in the possession of those people who can develop it and its resources. I do not agree therefore with you because I think that whether a man is a Duke or a Nigger he ought to stand the same in the eyes of his fellowmen and be judged by his ability and willingness to make use of God's earth.

Lever drew a parallel with his own Port Sunlight work force in two regards. The first was his experience of workmen who were very able and diligent as rank-and-file workers but who were miserable when promoted to jobs requiring a little thought, and asked to go back to their former jobs. Promoting them beyond their abilities – for them as for Africans – did not increase the sum total of human happiness. The second concerned how he had treated his work force. It was perfectly right and proper to introduce paternalistic schemes of co-partnership and decent housing, not on grounds of 'maudlin sentimentality' but because it was a sensible way to conduct a business. But, just because some other employers sweated and brutalized their labourers, it made no sense to drive the bosses out and turn over the means of production on socialistic lines to the work force, which had no aptitude for running a business; all would be worse off. 'I think that your advocacy of the black man's interest can be made more helpful to the black man if whilst fighting with all your power against brutal and inhuman and inconsiderate treatment for the black man you do not build a halo round the black man and convert him into a kind of being which it will take him hundreds of years of intercourse with the white man to become.'[45]

Morel retorted that his policy, giving a nod to the principles of Henry George, was for the people of the region to develop the land themselves, assisted by technical knowledge and labour-saving appliances. The only possible justification for European control of the area was the imparting of knowledge for Africans' moral and material enrichment. He could not agree that whites should take advantage of Africans' ignorance to take away their land and leave them as hired labourers for all time. 'I hope, and indeed I believe,' he wrote, 'that so long as you are alive to direct it, your Congo enterprise will be for the good of Congo humanity, and compared with the conditions which have existed for so long, the conditions which I feel sure you desire to bring about for the natives will be elysian.' But the principle of vast areas of land passing under the control of a European company was bad, and in other hands could lead to grave evils.[46]

For Lever, if Africa were left to the Africans it would remain undeveloped for centuries,[47] and it was impossible for someone of his mind set to imagine that happiness could exist independently of Western notions of development, civilization and progress. He liked invoking the parallel between the white duke and the black Negro, and returned to it again and again. In 1917, for example, in a letter to one of his directors, H. R. Greenhalgh, he fulminated against a circular from a leading humanitarian campaigner, Sir Thomas Fowell Buxton, who 'does not consider that civilization, the white man, and the feeding of the white man is entitled to any consideration.' He reeled off a familiar defence of imperialism:

It is impossible to develop the Tropics on the lines advocated by Sir Thomas Buxton, and if our ancestors had held these views three centuries ago, when the Pilgrim Fathers landed in New England from the "Mayflower", and had recognized the Red Indians' right to squat on the ground and hunt the buffalo, then the United States could never have existed. The population of the United States would have been as it was in those days, probably a couple of hundred thousand Red Indians, living in tents, who followed the buffalo South in the winter and followed the buffalo North in the summer, at constant war with each other, and the population stationary.

This would have been a mistake in America, it would be a mistake in the tropics and was being considered only because of imperialist guilt: 'the rebound from the cruelties against the black man that called it forth'. He then outlined a similar argument to that expressed to Morel, but couched in more robust terms. The black man ought to be the most valuable asset of the country, and would be if handled properly, 'but not one of the backward races, and least of all the negro, have any organizing ability'. All the Negro did was squat on the land, 'and cannot even work two cabbage patches jointly'. One needed brains and capital, not just labour, to cultivate the soil. Certainly, the native should be made happier, freed from the tyranny, warfare and cannibalism he currently suffered, but not freed to stymie development. Teddy Roosevelt and many others had said the same. Everyone agreed that a white English duke should not be allowed to hold up the land for his own sport, kudos or amusement but had a much greater tolerance for a chief and his tribe doing the same. 'I think the only excuse for the holding up land, whether the man is a duke or a negro, must be that it is being put to the use the Creator intended – for the production of food for the people living on the world.'[48]

A few months later, re-emphasizing both the white man's burden and the mutual self-interest cases for empire, he wrote:

Obviously our only right for existence in the Congo is the development and improvement of the Congo and the native races on sound practical sensible lines. In carrying out this, naturally we do so in a way that will equally benefit the consumer in Great Britain. The two combined make a perfect chain of events which, in my opinion, should be encouraged not only by the Belgian Government but by the British Government.[49]

His ideas did not evolve. In a speech in 1924 at a dinner of the West African trade section of the Liverpool Chamber of Commerce in which he notoriously laid into the guest of honour, Sir Hugh Clifford, the Governor of Nigeria, he repeated the same refrains: 'We are all flesh and blood. ... We are all brothers – so the missionaries tell us,' so the same standards should be applied to natives as to dukes; but they are not, 'all to the disadvantage of the duke (laughter).' Only the white man can organize African land effectively, producing 'a richer harvest for the benefit of the whole world', because the Africans need to be treated like 'children when they are immature and undeveloped'. We have a responsibility to develop our Empire on sound lines, in the best interests of the people, 'without maudlin sentimentality or brutality'; but that can only be done with capital, which requires that businessmen be given security but then left alone to get on with the job.[50]

This was the same refrain repeated over three decades and more. When they heard it at the time of Lever's deal with the Belgians, the Congo Reform Association and the Anti-slavery and Aborigines Protection Society were deeply unhappy. 'The only saving feature,' noted the Rev. John Harris, a leading CRA campaigner, 'is the reputation of Sir William Lever.' He added, 'but unfortunately these concessions will not always be controlled by him, and he is moreover thousands of miles away from the operations of the Company.'[51] Morel was in two minds, but inclined to give Lever the benefit of the doubt. He agreed that the arrangement between the Belgian government and Lever was bad in principle, but in practice it really all depended on Lever, 'who had his past record behind him plus his reputation to lose'. He felt that the CRA had little alternative but to go along with it, since the agreement had already been sealed and even the socialist Vandervelde had given it his blessing. Besides, the agreement stipulated that the land be merely leased for thirty-three years from the Belgian government, which claimed the ownership of all land that was not 'occupied'. Although this ownership would pass to Lever's successors under certain conditions, Morel was fairly confident that neither the enterprise nor the Belgian administration of the Congo would last that long. In addition, Lever had no coercive powers in his concessions; his economic success depended entirely on securing the good-will of the natives through proper treatment. In sum, 'Lever may be a great power for good in the Congo; as I judge the man and the situation, that is his interest, economically, and also his interest from the personal point of view. Personally I should deprecate antagonising him except on clear evidence of wrong-doing.'[52]

The agreement or convention that generated so much disquiet was signed by Lever and the Belgian government on 14 April 1911, with the Belgians anxious to draw in foreign capital and grateful for an enlightened entrepreneur to help salvage their battered reputation. The deal granted concessions to the new Lever Brothers subsidiary, Les Huileries du Congo Belge (HCB), over a vast area – 750,000 ha, or nearly 4,500 square miles – to be selected within five areas, each of 60 km radius, at a rent of twenty-five centimes per hectare. If the company met its production quotas over three and a half decades, it would get to own the 750,000 ha. The regions selected were the Lusanga area at the junction of the Kwenge and Kwilu rivers, centred at the newly coined Leverville; the Bumba area on the main Congo river, with its centre at Alberta

11 Map of the Belgian Congo showing the concession areas of the 1911 Convention

(named after the new Belgian king, Leopold's nephew Albert); the Basoko area on the Congo, centred in Elisabetha (named after the Belgian queen); the Basongo area on the Kasai river, with its centre at Brabanta (named after the Belgian Crown Prince, the Duc de Brabant); and the Ingende area on the Ruki river, with its centre at Flandria (named after the king's younger son, the Comte de Flandre).

Other parts of the convention stipulated that the company pay a minimum wage to its workers and provide a doctor, a hospital and a school in each area. At least half the white staff was to be Belgian and half the trade goods and a third of the machinery and plant were to be from Belgium. The company was permitted to build transportation and telegraph networks within the concessions on the understanding that the government could use them as well – an indication of a weak government getting big business to build its colonial infrastructure for it. The company would set up oil mills in each of the circles within six years (later extended to eleven because of the First World War), each capable of processing at least 6,000 tons of fruit per year. In signing this convention, later ratified by the Belgian parliament, Lever was acting (to borrow Charles Wilson's phrase) 'almost like a sovereign prince'. At the age of sixty he had committed himself to little less than the development of an entire principality.[53]

The idea of granting concessions for gathering was really only intended as an interim measure until Lever could grow large plantations. Only one of the five circles, Lusanga/Leverville, had a sufficient profusion of palms to justify the whole scheme,[54] but Lever estimated in 1913 on his first trip to the Congo that there the palm trees covered 400,000 ha and were 'all healthy and strong, and fruiting as well as they can be expected to do in a wild tangle of bush with palms overcrowding each other'.[55] This was sufficient, as we shall see, to delay large-scale planting, but it was only going to exacerbate the problems of recruiting labour. From the beginning he recognized clearly enough that his success would depend upon management of the Africans. He had 'unbounded confidence' in the Belgian government, he wrote in 1912 to Dr Max Horn; the necessary facilities for transport and the accuracy of the company's machinery were assured; and there was a plentiful supply of trees and native labour: 'it can only now be a question of organisation in securing the right amount of native labour, and European control to ensure success.... Our success will depend upon and be in proportion to the happiness and contentment of the natives, which must be assured.'[56]

One of the problems was that collecting fruit from wild palms was much harder work than from more compact trees in orderly, cleared plantations. The gangly trunk of the oil palm (*elaeis guineensis*) that flourishes in the high-temperature, high-humidity climate of West Africa thrusts upwards 40 ft or more in search of sunlight amidst the dense jungle canopy, and at the top of the trunk cluster reddish-golden bunches, each containing several hundred fruit, each fruit containing a pericarp and a nut. Palm oil – a red liquid – comes from the pericarp, another oil from the kernel of the nut. Since the trees are dispersed and produce only two bunches each year, the cutters first had to hunt for a suitable tree, then clear the brush from around it – two or three skilled woodsmen required a day and a half to deal with each big tree – then one would haul himself up in a sling and cut off a bunch of fruit with a machete.[57]

An American writer and academic, Raymond Buell, described the process in the 1920s in HCB's Elisabetha district. Here the company had planted 1,200 ha, but since it took seven years before a tree began to bear fruit, most of the fruit still came from wild palms. The cutter hacked off between five and eight clusters or 'régimes' of fruit a day, receiving twenty centimes for each régime, plus additional ration money and a quantity of rice if he cut thirty-six régimes a week. All this made for a wage of at least four times the minimum stipulated wage of twenty-five centimes a day plus rations (though, factoring in the increased cost of living, this was scarcely an increase in real terms). A bunch of fruit could weigh up to 60 lb. The cutter had to carry each of these for miles to one of HCB's forty fruit posts within the district.[58] To save time, a woman might do this backbreaking porterage. An HCB doctor explained what this entailed:

> She is supposed to remove from the fruit the hard and fibrous parts, which is a considerable work, and then carry a basket weighing 20 to 30 kilograms to the factory. ...
> To those tasks already mentioned and themselves hard ... there is also a daily walk of 10 to 30 kilometers, half of it with a heavy basket on the head. ... [W]e see old women deformed by illness, women with children on their backs; pregnant women and pre-adolescent girls aging prematurely.[59]

Once the fruit, separated from the frame of the régime, arrived at the mill, it was separated from its shell, the kernels and oil were extracted, the kernels sacked and the palm oil shipped in hundred-gallon drums. HCB had built a native village at each post, generally of brick houses constructed according to government specifications, each with a garden of 10 m by 20 m, each village with a communal garden of 25 ha. About a third of the men had their wives with them and lived one family per hut; the single men shared three to a hut.[60]

Lever had characteristically micro-managed all aspects of the setting up and running of his Congo enterprise. According to his son:

> Not a palm area was selected nor a site chosen, except on his authority; not a building was erected unless the plans had been passed by him, and very often these plans were largely his own; not a piece of plant or machinery nor a craft on the river, from the largest stern-wheeler to the smallest launch or barge, was ordered until he had carefully examined and passed the specifications. In fact, it is no exaggeration to say that the organization which came into being – from the shipping base at the port of Matadi and the administrative headquarters at Kinshasa to the farthest area of Elizabetha, over a thousand miles from the Congo mouth – was his personal creation.[61]

Predictably, on his first trip to the Congo over the winter of 1912–13, he identified two problems that he was determined to resolve. The first was lousy living conditions. He recorded in his dairy on 22 December on board the company's stern-wheeler *Lusanga* that, at a government wooding station *en route* to Leverville:

> The villagers here are undersized – the women especially so. After dark they all crouched round their fires and ate and chattered like so many monkeys. The

huts are low and the entrance is by a small door. I had a pocket electric torch and peered into the gloom, and no respectable dog would have fought for one of these huts as a kennel.

The second, his leitmotif, was poor work habits. On 29 December, on the Kwenge river, he noted:

> The natives at one place swarmed down to the banks of the river with baskets, etc., full of fruit, and received payment in salt. They were the real bush-native, unspoiled by contact with the white man. It was the most interesting sight we have yet seen. All this river fruit-buying is in its infancy, but I do not think we can rely on it as a permanent supply of fruit. We can only depend on our own gathering and cultivation. The fact is the native has few wants: a little salt and a little cloth are his indispensables; after this, beads, brass rods and other luxuries. Chief Womba, at Leverville, can be taken as an example. Twelve months ago he and his people were poor and few in number, and were keen to bring fruit. After twelve months or less of selling fruit he is rich and lazy, has ten wives, and his village is about four times the size it was; but he gathers little or no fruit. The palm-tree is in these parts the banking account of the native, and he no more thinks of going to his bank for money when his wants and ambitions are supplied than a civilized man would. His bank is always open when he wants to draw on it.[62]

This was all very sensible on the part of the Africans, but offensive to the Western work ethic and a problem for the needs of Western capitalism. Lever noted in his diary at one point on this trip, 'natives must be trained to work to time. At present they work when they please.' He did not always adopt the typical European belief in the lazy African:

> They are only children and, like children, they would work by fits and starts. Regularity of habits must be gradually worked up to. The native material is good, willing and anxious to please the white man. ... The native African will be a good workman when better understood. I have only praise for him as far as I can judge. Yet the white man here is always speaking of the 'lazy nigger'. He is a child, and a willing child, but he wants training and handling with patience.[63]

On the qualities of the work force, he wrote in 1924:

> I am a great admirer of the Congo labourer, the best tropical labour [*sic*] in the world, if treated reasonably well. A Captain on one of our steamers some years ago said: – 'Treat 'em kindly, hammer 'em plenty, and dose 'em with quinine after tornado,' and you would never have any trouble with them. You might think that they could dress their wives and children more, but what could paterfamilias do more than the Congo native does if he had three wives and their piccaninnies to maintain on 5d. per day.[64]

Lever's views were a mishmash of sympathy, prejudice and prudery. The Congo male, he said, 'is a particularly intelligent man when he is rightly handled';[65] he 'only requires to be treated with humanity and sympathy to produce the very best results obtainable from any labour'.[66] In 1916 he strongly supported the technical education of intelligent natives, since 'We must work, in my opinion, to achieve success by working with the natives and by the natives, and not, except in the very highest commands, with Europeans or by Europeans.' He contemplated insisting as part of this that white staff take lessons at a Catholic mission to learn the native language, contrary to current practice.[67] And again:

> [T]he education of the native in the Congo is of supreme importance, and ... no good could be done on any sure foundation with reference to the Congo except by the utilization of the native people. We are simply attempting the impossible when we attempt to develope [sic] the Congo along other lines than by carrying the native population with us, advancing them in civilization, increasing their wants, and raising them in the social scale of humanity.[68]

The company would provide the buildings, the Catholic Fathers the teachers. The brightest of the ten-year-olds should be picked out and trained to be bookkeepers, mechanics, joiners and skilled tradesmen, and educated until they were sixteen:

> My reason for this is that it is a well-known fact that the brain of the African ceases to be capable of receiving new impressions when he arrives at the adult stage. ... It is a very curious fact which has often been investigated, but no explanation has been discovered. It has given rise to the statement that African boys are the equal of European boys in facilities for acquiring knowledge up to their 14th year, but from 14 years to 16 there is a great falling away, and that when they arrive at adultism the average African seems to be incapable of receiving fresh impressions.[69]

In spite of his own religious beliefs, Lever gave three pragmatic reasons for conferring on the Catholic Fathers a monopoly over education in the concessions. The first was that:

> If we follow this policy, we can at any time move an intelligent native to the area in which he is most wanted, whereas if some of the natives were Catholic and some Protestant, we might not be able to do this. Civilized men can work Protestant with Catholic, or with Jew and so on, but I doubt very much whether this would be practical with natives. In any case, it would be upsetting to their mentality to know that the white man had many religions. ... None but a European can understand the various differences between Catholic and Protestant. ... It is only a question of slight variations in beliefs, creeds, and doctrines, and these are really perhaps beyond the comprehension of the native in his early stages of development.[70]

The second reason was that the African needed a religion to match his intellect. 'I am sure the Catholic religion is best suited to the mental development of the natives,' he wrote. 'What we British resent in the Catholic religion – the surrender of free thought – is just what suits the native intelligence.' And the third was that 'the Catholic Sisters do independent work for the good of the native women and girls on a better organised basis than is possible for the wives of missionaries to attempt.'[71]

Lever's philosophy was summed up on the cover of a new periodical for the company's African interests, which he suggested during his final journey to the Congo in 1924, featuring a white hand clutching and pulling up a black hand. His son explained that:

> This device of the helping hand aptly symbolized Leverhulme's policy in the Congo. In approaching native problems his mind was singularly free from false sentiment. He had no sympathy with those who patronized the native and adopted towards him a tone of benign superiority, nor with those who looked upon the native as a being to be driven rather than led. His point of view, put simply, was this. In Europe and America there was the white man whose own soil and climate could not furnish certain of his essential needs; in Africa there was the black man living in a land where Nature in her most prodigal mood heaped in profusion the products which the white man needed. The white man possessed organizing ability and capital; the black man, although better adapted physically to the climate of the Tropics, possessed neither organizing ability nor the reserves of capital which accumulated savings bring. 'A native,' Leverhulme once said, 'cannot organize. He cannot even run a wooding post on the river satisfactorily. You have only to compare one run by a native with one run by a European to prove that.' He held, therefore, that both the white man and the black man were essential to the development of Africa.[72]

Lever made no attempt to view the continent through African eyes. How could he? He was merely dipping into a culture and seeing what he wanted to see and what his handlers wanted to show him. On this last visit, in the autumn of 1924, he travelled up the river Congo cocooned in a 'Cabine de Luxe' ('with pate [sic] de foie gras, caviare [sic], and such like diet to "rough it" on'[73]), peering though a wire-gauze netting which allowed views as clear as through glass while letting the air in and keeping the mosquitoes out. What he saw was rosy: 'on the foreshore canoes paddled gracefully, no gondola more so, by black-bronze Hercules with dark-skinned matrons and maidens and chubby piccaninnies all happy and smiling.'[74] Native health had improved dramatically since his last visit: 'Twelve years ago in villages and at wooding posts on the river the sight of so many sick and underfed people was most distressing. To-day one sees healthy people, men, women, and children happy, contented, and well fed.'[75] In November he wrote to a young friend, Myrtle Huband:

> [I]t is all most interesting because it is all so human. It is a business like none other we have. Perhaps Port Sunlight comes nearest to it in social work.
> We have palmeries where the fruit is collected, railways to take same to the mills where Palm Oil and Palm Kernels are produced therefrom, but in addition a large river fleet for conveying oil and kernels to Kinshasa and fruit from riverside palmeries to the mills. But this is all only the business side. We have to build thousands of houses for the natives and these we now build in brick detached

and one house for one family. We have to run a medical service with hospitals, an educational service with schools, a training service in carpentry, engineering etc. We have to erect and repair our own steamers and barges, and we are now adding a maternity and midwifery service for owing to the ignorance of the natives on such matters over one third of the babies die before five years of age. ... We also have to perform all surgical operations, – but I will not weary you with these details but they all greatly add to the interest of our task – no light one.[76]

By this time the company had met the ten-year production target specified in the convention (extended from 1921 because of the First World War), had seven mills at work in the five concessions, collected 54,000 tons of fruit in that year, had built 1,000 km of road and 70 km of railway track, had nineteen steamers and seventy-two barges on the rivers, employed 200 Europeans and 17,000 Africans, had built ten hospitals, plus schools at Alberta and Leverville, and had constructed over 200 houses for Europeans and 500 permanent brick houses for Africans. As a result of the development plan he laid down during his visit, by 1926 there were fifteen hospitals, five schools and 1,200 houses for Africans (who now numbered 23,000 in the work force).[77]

Whether all this was economically worth while is another question. While Lever was alive, only in 1918–19 and from 1924 were palm oil prices high enough for the venture to make a satisfactory profit, and in some years it registered substantial losses. D. K. Fieldhouse argues that HCB was always heavily over-capitalized, that the Congo enterprise was not a sound way to employ Lever Brothers' money and that Lever would have demanded a far higher return from his soap factories.[78] The suggestion is that the whole Congo enterprise was one man's whimsy rather than a sound commercial investment.

Should HCB have moved more aggressively to establish plantations? By 1928 only 2,500 ha had been planted with oil palms, just enough to supplement the wild palms sufficiently to meet the convention quotas in each of the five circles. Only in 1935 did HCB begin a large-scale planting programme of around 66,000 acres over the next decade. Perhaps it had little choice but to work during its first quarter-century with the conditions it discovered within the concessions, since the capital required for major plantations would have been too exorbitant. Clearing the forest, laying down the roads, planting the trees and waiting several years for the first crop would have been very expensive and the profits slow in coming. But Frederick Pedler, a retired Unilever director, argues in his book that the company depended on the natural palmeries for far too long, allowing in particular the Dutch in Sumatra to gain nearly two decades' head start with palm plantations.[79] The significance is that the prospect of better pay and easier working conditions on well managed plantations might have attracted a voluntary work force. As it was, the tool had to be coercion.

That monstrous trade in flesh and blood

In 1913, the year in which Britain recognized the Congo as a Belgian colony and the CRA wound up its work, Morel wrote that 'The wounds of the Congo will take generations to heal. But … the atrocities have disappeared. … The revenues are no longer supplied by forced or slave labour. … A responsible Government has replaced an irresponsible despotism.' To a point he was right. But forced labour, the lynchpin of the system, did remain.[80]

There are certain instructive parallels with the case of the Cadbury's.[81] We have noted the Cadbury family's strong humanitarian reputation as Quakers, Liberals, philanthropists and factory paternalists. It was entirely in character for the *Daily News*, owned by George Cadbury, in 1904 to denounce conditions for Chinese labour in South African mines, labelling it 'Yellow Slavery'. And yet the firm found itself accused of hypocrisy, because nearly half of its cocoa came from slave labour on the plantations of the islands of São Tomé and Principe, owned by Portugal, off the West African coast. The Portuguese government had outlawed slavery but that did not impede slave traders ('labour merchants') from recruiting a steady supply in Portuguese Angola, typically bartering with local chiefs for a specified number in exchange for guns, rum or other goods. Many of the slaves perished on the forced march to the sea. Those who survived were given five-year contracts by a government agent, who thereby technically 'redeemed' them and converted them from slaves into voluntary 'contracted labourers', but they were given no choice in the matter. They were then shipped to the islands. Their contracts were automatically renewed after five years, if they survived the brutal conditions that long; none of them ever returned.

The Cadburys became aware of the situation in 1901, and a succession of reports and investigations over the next few years, commissioned by the company or carried out by journalists such as Henry Nevinson or the Anti-slavery Society, proved beyond doubt that the company's cheap cocoa came courtesy of slaves. The firm's boast in its advertisements that 'Cadbury's Cocoa is nourishing and sustaining, made in Bournville under ideal conditions'[82] at best left much unsaid. But the Foreign Office preferred a softly-softly approach when it came to dealing with its Portuguese ally and for years the Cadburys went along with an unsuccessful strategy of attempting to exert pressure on the Portuguese planters and government through diplomatic channels to put an end to the slave system. It was not until 1909 that the company finally organized a boycott, ended its buying from the islands and looked instead to the Gold Coast for its cocoa supplies. Cynics argued that this was an economically opportune moment to switch horses, not only because new cocoa plantations in the Gold Coast had matured but also because of a substantial fall in the price of cocoa beans.

By then the damage to the Cadburys' reputation was substantial. In only the latest of a series of newspaper accusations, the *Standard*, a Conservative publication eager to take aim at Liberal business interests and the Liberal government, fired a volley in a 1908 editorial:

> It is not called slavery; 'contract labour' they name it now; but in most of its essentials it is that monstrous trade in human flesh and blood against which the Quaker and Radical ancestors of Mr. Cadbury thundered in the better days of England. … And the worst of all this slavery and slave-driving and slave-dealing is brought about by the necessity of providing a sufficient number of hands to grow and pick cocoa on the islands of Principe and Sao Thomé, the islands which feed the mills and presses of Bournville![83]

The company sued for libel. In another epic courtroom battle between Rufus Isaacs (for the Cadburys) and Edward Carson (for the *Standard*) the plaintiffs contended that nobody disputed the facts of slavery but that the newspaper's accusation of hypocrisy was unproven and that it had failed to acknowledge the Cadburys' efforts behind the scenes to effect reforms. The jury agreed, but awarded only 'contemptuous damages' of one farthing – hardly the clear-cut moral victory the company wanted. As Carson put it, 'the jury were disgusted with the plaintiffs for dealing so long in slave-made cocoa'.[84]

The Cadbury case exemplified the broader problem of how big business and colonial governments could find a work force to grow, harvest or extract raw materials or build the colonial infrastructure at a time when overt slavery was no longer acceptable. There were many approaches in practice. The Leopoldian regime in the Congo perhaps constituted the most egregious example of paying lip service to anti-slavery conventions while ruling by the chicotte. Another case was to be found in the river Putumayo region of the north-west Amazon committed under the aegis of the Anglo-Peruvian Rubber Company. Roger Casement, sent by the British government in 1910 to investigate allegations of atrocities there, discovered that the brutality of forced labour was just as bad, if not worse, than in the Congo.[85] More overtly and less controversially, governments resorted to indentured or conscripted labour or military service. The government in French Madagascar, for example, imposed a *corvée* – that is, unpaid labour for a certain number of days each year – while in French West Africa young Africans were drafted into the army or to serve three-year terms in labour brigades engaged in 'public works' projects. Another favourite was taxation, variously by head, hut or house, which generated government revenue and forced Africans into the cash economy to find the money to pay the tax. This was the practice in the French Congo, Portuguese Mozambique and southern Angola, assorted British territories and, as we shall see, the Belgian Congo.[86]

How did colonizers justify forced labour when they supported the freedom of the wage contract back home? As part of the capacious remit of that most flexible of ideologies, the 'civilizing mission'. When the Portuguese had finally abolished slavery in 1878, for instance, they replaced it with a requirement that all Africans must be engaged in useful labour (as defined by their colonial masters), which as we have seen in practice meant imposed lifelong 'contracts'. A committee of 1898 concluded that the state

> not only as a sovereign of semi-barbaric populations, but also as a depository of social authority, should have no scruples in *obliging* and, if necessary, *forcing* these rude Negroes in Africa ... to work, that is to better themselves by work, to acquire through work the happiest means of existence, to civilize themselves through work.[87]

Lever might have couched it in softer language, but he would not fundamentally have disagreed.

In the Congo, too, the African labourer needed to be taught the work ethic. The *Gazette Coloniale* explained why:

> The atrocity stories that are spread around originate in the fact that each white man who works in the Congo has to force the Negro to provide his labour power. ... Those closet colonizers who deplore this state of affairs, implicitly proclaim the immortal right of the blacks to do absolutely nothing. We protest against this view. The idleness of the Negro should not stop us in trying to overcome or to get round it. ... His unwillingness must not cause the non-utilization of the resources of that country. ... Our own workers [in Belgium], who are forced to work for twelve hours or more each day on penalty of starvation, would find it very strange if they should accidentally learn of the absurd protection that some people would provide to the natives of the Congo. The law of work applies to the blacks as well as to ourselves. If they think they do not have to submit to it, we have the right and even the duty to force them to do so.[88]

The logic held that, since Africans could get by without doing the white man's work, there was no natural coercive incentive – the fear of starvation – to compel them to obey 'the law of work'. Therefore it was necessary – even a duty – for the white man to provide an alternative form of coercion, and the natives would appreciate it in the end. A statue was unveiled in Brussels in 1921 for those who had fallen for 'the colonial cause', depicting a black figure begging Belgium to come and develop.[89] And so the rewriting of colonial exploitation as a benign exercise in bringing progress to grateful natives began.

The transfer of power from Leopold to the Belgian government had promised much: the rule of law, overseen by a Colonial Ministry and a Colonial Council; free trade for both Europeans and Africans, allowing unrestricted gathering and selling of produce by the Congolese; the prohibition of Leopoldian-style work quotas and their replacement with wage labour; and the setting up of a Commission Permanente pour la Protection des Indigènes. But this was less of a repudiation of the old system than it implied. The Commission Permanente met only four times between 1908 and 1924. The white personnel managing the new regime scarcely altered from the days of the reign of terror, so there was no sea change in mentalities. The Colonial Ministry in 1909 introduced a plan to encourage investment and growth – the *Programme Générale* – which combined the incompatible goals of getting Africans to participate voluntarily in the colonial economy and the encouragement of huge rubber and palm oil plantations to be run by Europeans, dependent, if need be, on involuntary labour. The concessions policy depended on another incompatible principle, that of 'vacant lands' (*terra nullius* or *terres vacantes et sans maître*) based on a decree of 1885: the fiction that these areas were uninhabited and therefore the colonial authority could use them as it wished.

The need for coerced labour did not abate after the Free State became a colony – in fact, it increased as the labour needs of business and the state grew. The brutality and the horror subsided; there was more emphasis on the 'Noir, l'homme enfant', the Black as child-man who could be educated to be a good, civilized worker, rather than on the beast of burden who could be brutalized at will; but forced recruitment of labour continued to be the norm for road and railway construction, for public works in general and for the mines and other areas of industry.[90] The needs for minerals, palm products and food-stuffs during the First World War prompted substantial increases in tax rates (the significance of which we shall return to in a moment), restrictions on small traders operating independently of the large concerns and the fixing of the price of palm kernels and oil well below what the market dictated. In 1917 local administrators were empowered to compel the inhabitants of certain villages, on threat of flogging or imprisonment, to produce foodstuffs, such as rice, at low prices for military use. All of this promoted semi-disguised forced labour, and it was extended after the war across many parts of the Congo as the Belgian government sought to milk its colony to help pay for the rebuilding of the devastated mother country. In the words of Martin Evans, 'Belgian rule remained in essence one of oppression and exploitation in the Leopoldian mould, albeit without the accompanying atrocities.' Samuel Nelson concurs: 'While the most violent and drastic features of the Free State were softened, the underlying structures and racist mentality of Leopold's empire survived.'[91]

One of the problems in finding willing workers to gather palm fruit was that the Leopoldian regime had reduced the population substantially, another that labouring for wages and for foreign companies in distant compounds, particularly the dangerous and difficult labour of collecting from tall trees, held little appeal. Over the years, since collecting from wild palms over vast areas was a very inefficient, expensive business, wages had to be kept low to keep costs down. The solution? The introduction in July 1914 of a head tax for all males, with supplementary taxes depending on the number of wives, both to be paid in cash. The intention was to force the men to take paid employment in the large concessions and mines, and to force the chiefs – who had most wives – to find substitute workers.

D. K. Fieldhouse explains how this worked in the Elisabetha circle. The local commissioner calculated in 1915 that he could draw on an adult male work force of about 20,000 in the vicinity, so if these men could be recruited as cutters for six-week stints in rotation, HCB would have a steady 2,000 labourers. He therefore set the annual tax rate at twelve francs, which – at the minimum rate of twenty-five centimes a day – could be earned in forty-eight working days. Since the company paid for food and lodging during this period of labour, the Africans could pay all their earnings directly to the government. The local HCB director called for a refinement of this process in 1917. He complained that the tax was collected almost entirely in the first three months of the year, resulting in a fall in the number of cutters in April. He requested that taxes be spread throughout the year, that the colonial authorities increase the tax rate in the palm regions and that they step up pressure on Africans and their chiefs.

The Flandria and Brabanta circles had few palms, needed few workers and did not create a big recruitment headache. Elisabetha required considerable coercive tactics early on, but gradually built up a sustainable labour force, much of it recruited from outside the region. The biggest continuing problem was in Leverville, with its abundant palms and thin population. One of the most effective ways of conscripting men was for local administrators, company officials and Catholic missionaries to put pressure on the chiefs. The chiefs were persuaded to sign up cutters for periods of usually three years, often in return for a share of the wages. Those chiefs who owned slaves could send some of them, and collect all the after-tax income. Fieldhouse notes that when H. R. Greenhalgh visited in 1915, he discovered that nearly all the labour provided by the chiefs in Leverville consisted of slaves, many of them children who were too weak for the work. HCB subsequently stopped the child labour but continued to rely on the slaves, whose contracts were renewed over and over.[92]

Labour recruitment might have been easier if living and working conditions really had come close to the claims of HCB and its admirers. But they did not. For example, a 1916 report on the Leverville circle by a territorial administrator, Gaston Vandebosch, tells of poor living standards and abysmal hygiene at the agricultural posts, and in most cases wages fell short of the minimum specified in the 1911 convention. The cutters, the highest paid, had to supply seven large régimes or eight or nine small régimes daily, if they carried them to the posts themselves (as most did), or ten or eleven régimes if porters did the carrying. David Northrup, in his study of the eastern Congo, relates that at the end of 1918 the HCB work force at Elisabetha stood at 1,400, down from 4,000 in 1915, a greater fall than elsewhere because of an influenza epidemic, probably exacerbated by rock-bottom wages and food allowances. In the early 1920s the workers experienced chronic food shortages since the area was sparsely populated and the company expanded its work force without giving enough attention to how it was going to feed it. The government forced HCB to increase its food allowance from one franc a week to one and three-quarter francs, plus two kilos of rice and half a kilo of fish, which went only part of the way to solving the problem. Local administrators apparently dealt with an ordinance of 1922 requiring employers to make up any shortfall of food in areas of scarcity by forcing other Africans to supply food, another variation on compulsory labour.[93]

Then in 1923 HCB's housing, sanitation and medical services came under attack from high levels of government. The most damning indictment came from a report by Émile Lejeune, the provincial doctor of Congo-Kasai, after a six-day inspection in the Leverville circle. He found that, of the 3,000 employed at the Leverville station, two-thirds were locals (that is, their villages were no more than ten hours away) and a third were *importés*. Lodgings and rations were provided only for the *importés*. A lucky but small minority lived in a camp of brick huts, which would have been good if they had had latrines, kitchens, rubbish ditches and the like; the rest of the *importés* were packed into poor-quality straw shelters; and the locals, the majority, set themselves up in haphazard, dirty, shanty villages in the vicinity of the central stations or the agricultural posts. Most recruits (including many adolescents and some children) were engaged for three-month stretches, but food rations were so woefully inadequate that they lost weight during that period. To compound everything, medical services for the Africans were deplorable. All told, Lejeune thought that HCB was culpable of neglecting its duties at every turn. Small wonder, he believed, that recruits fled at the end of their three-month terms. He noted that colonial administrators were instructed to help HCB recruit but, personally, if he were an administrator, he would not send a single worker to the company.[94]

HCB scrambled to provide a detailed rebuttal of these allegations, stated that over 1,500 new brick houses were about to be built, blamed the failure to find sufficient recruits on blacks' repugnance for work, and called on the government for more vigorous assistance. The colonial governors were not persuaded. It was principally up to HCB, they argued, to treat its labourers better if the company wanted to attract and retain an adequate work force.[95]

Cumulatively these examples give quite a different picture to that painted by Lever's admirers. 'When he found the natives would only work just enough to earn their daily simple needs, instead of attempting coercion he introduced Cinemas!' Mrs Stuart Menzies had commented, by way of contrast, in her panegyric to Lever. 'A ferment of excitement followed; all wanted to work more so as to have enough money to expend on the Cinemas. The result ... was happy workers, and a good part of their wages found its way back into the pocket of the brilliant inventor of the idea.'[96] Frederick Pedler sums up Lever's 1924 trip:

Twelve years had passed since his previous visit, and he was able to see that his dream had come true and that his faith had been rewarded; not, so far, in terms of profit, but in terms of physical development and social welfare. In the five concession centres thriving communities of Africans had been created, with houses, gardens, churches, hospitals, and schools. One of these townships had been named Leverville. The experience lifted up his heart, and his enthusiasm for the Congo knew no bounds.[97]

Maybe they have a point. Maybe the pull factors ('Cinemas!') attracted some Africans to work for HCB. Maybe the evidence accumulated by historians like Marchal and Northrup should not be exaggerated. It does seem that, sporadically, living standards began to improve in the concessions, particularly in HCB's proudest boast, the showcase Leverville centre, the highlight of trips by Lever and most other travelling Europeans.[98] But what is undeniable is that the colonial authorities coerced the Congolese *en masse* to work for HCB and other big business. Of course Lever must have known, but he was too shrewd to talk about it explicitly. He neither condemned nor condoned it, but he needed it: forced labour was built in to the system. And all of his speeches and letters about inculcating the work ethic among Africans clearly indicated his tacit approval. It was good for them. He knew best.

The workers in the concessions and mines were supposed to be protected by labour contracts, but in practice the contracts weighed against them. If they violated them they were fined fifty francs or imprisoned for two months or both, and if they fled a fellow household member could be imprisoned instead.[99] Raymond Buell concluded, 'A man having been virtually compelled to come to work is through penal sanction compelled to stay. The result is not only compulsory labor but involuntary servitude.'[100] Again, making use of the chiefs could be helpful. The doctor quoted above, who worked for HCB from 1927 to 1930, said, 'When I felt that it was necessary to whip someone I ordered a native chief, a decorated chief, to do it because he had that right towards his subjects.'[101]

Buell quoted the administrator of the Yanonge district, protesting in 1925 against the pressure on administrators to assist HCB in recruiting: 'If the Arabs formerly deported slaves for the eastern coast, we do the same thing ourselves, *in the eyes of the natives*, by recruiting "by way of authority," or, in other words, by force, laborers for regions very far from their homes.' This official asked his superior how he was supposed to balance the colonial mission of improving the lot of Africans with the endless instructions to find labour for HCB. Agents like himself were 'daily becoming more and more veritable merchants of men', like the Arab slavers of the past.[102]

In order to keep the native population submitted [*sic*] and working regularly, there is a special group of agricultural agents [said the European chief of an HCB village]. They are responsible for the increase in production. These functionaries, inundated by circulars and letters, which are always unhappy with the slow growth in production, soon exhaust the legal means of forcing natives to work harder. The agricultural agent has become a policeman.

The HCB doctor reiterated the same theme:

> We try to create vital needs that he can only satisfy by earning money, but at the same time, we use pressure, we threaten harassment, and we use methods which are strangely reminiscent of those used by slave traders. ... Blacks will only work under pressure and not to earn money. Some of them flee to the mission, but they are unhappy because they must also work there.[103]

Involuntary labour was no secret: contemporary commentators were quite willing to call a spade a spade in public. For example, an economist, Allan McPhee, published a book in 1926 on the 'economic revolution' in West Africa in which he claimed that plantations simply could not succeed in tropical Africa without a certain amount of compulsion. The British authorities in Sierra Leone had refused to compel the indigenous populations, or allow Lever Brothers to compel them, so the company had been forced to close down its factory at Yonnibanna. This, he wrote, had undoubtedly retarded the development of Sierra Leone, 'and it is conceivable that British West Africa would have been more productive to-day if ruthlessly exploited by capitalist plantations working with forced or indentured labour'.[104] W. G. A. Ormsby-Gore, Conservative MP and Parliamentary Under-Secretary for the Colonies, said in 1926:

> It is perfectly clear that the type of concession which Lord Leverhulme enjoyed in the Congo is out of the question in a British Protectorate, for it involves the provision by the government of labour for the working of the concession. ... There can be no doubt that the system which obtains in the Congo does involve not only monopoly rights but also elements of compulsion; and the trouble with compulsion in any form is that it is only successful in the long run if it is carried out consistently and completely.[105]

The Belgian periodical *Congo* chimed in as well. An article in 1925 by a missionary priest, Hyacinthe Vanderyst, agreed with African claims that the Belgian state and the big companies had stolen the palmeries created by the indigenous population. A second, in 1928, by Lode Achten, a former commissioner of the Kasai district, contended that the territorial dispossession, the more or less obligatory labour, all the *corvées* and all the prohibitions, vexations and harassments had powerfully disrupted and embittered the Africans.[106]

Although the colonial press rubbished Buell as an American belgophobic anti-imperialist, enough discontent built up against the practice of forced labour that, ironically in the year of Lever's death, the Belgian Colonial Ministry ordered its officials to cease the recruitment for private firms by 1928. HCB directors protested vigorously. The Congo had seen extraordinary advances in a short period of time, they said – too short for the natives to appreciate the laws of work, to offer their labour spontaneously and to support loyally the common task of colonization and progress. Accordingly, they maintained in tellingly sugared terms, for several more years 'the natives must be guided and invited by all persuasion possible to lend their services' ('les indigènes doivent être guidés et invités par toute la persuasion possible, à prester leurs services').[107]

They need not have worried, since in practice the government interdiction was often observed more in the breach. For example, Pierre Roex, an administrator in Yahila in 1927, remarked on the ambiguity of his orders. Administrators, he said, were expected to recruit x number of workers for HCB, but without the use of force. Where, he asked, did force begin? Was it absolutely contrary to the spirit of the law to oblige a native 'to lend his services' ('à louer ses services') for six months every two or three years? He thought not.[108]

Besides this imaginative interpretation of instructions by the men on the ground, the government had also recently adopted another means of forcing Africans into the embrace of big business. The problem was that Africans preferred to collect tropical products and sell them to independent traders where possible. Samuel Nelson, in his study of the Mongo people in the inner Congo basin, makes it clear that most of them disliked and tried to avoid the gathering of palm fruit, especially in the concessions of HCB and Sociéte Anonyme Belge pour le Commerce du Haut Congo. Most of them preferred to collect copal resin, derived from a variety of tropical trees and used in the manufacture of lacquers and varnishes, since this was not massively disruptive of traditional relations of production (it could be carried out locally, slotting into traditional peasant economies of the village) and yet it raised cash to pay the taxes. An individual earned between 1.8 and 4.8 francs a day in 1924 collecting copal, compared with maybe eight francs a week at HCB.[109]

A problem for HCB in particular was that, since there was nothing to prevent Africans from trading fruit in the areas of the circles outside HCB's chosen leaseholds, and as it was impossible to tell whether the fruit that they traded with outsiders actually came from within the leaseholds, a developing free market was undermining the convention. Lever himself complained in 1922 that he was pouring in capital to build all the infrastructure stipulated in the convention and that he had to make purchases in Belgium that he could get more cheaply elsewhere, but that, because he lacked a monopoly of the fruit in his concessions, competitors without similar financial burdens were able to pay higher prices for fruit and to draw away native workers from his own operations.[110] The government's solution was to restrict the independent activities of Africans in or close to some of the concessions by means of *contrats tripartites* (tripartite agreements), which came into force in 1924 and were repeatedly renewed until the end of colonial rule in 1960. Buell reported that the agreement in Flandria was negotiated between HCB, the government and seventy-five chiefs, sub-chiefs and notables. The chiefs were given little option but to sign, and in many cases they did not even understand what they were signing, since the transactions were carried out in French.

In practice, the contracts excluded all independent traders from the circles in question and the Africans lost the freedom to sell palm nuts and oil on the open market. The government guaranteed a price for these products, but only one to match a labourer's earnings, whereas on the free market he would make three or four times as much. Another option for HCB, acted upon in Elisabetha, was simply to refuse to buy African-produced oil. The outcome of this collusion in many forms between government and big business was to shut out competition from independent traders and force the Africans to work for low wages. If we look at the application of similar policies to the colony as a whole, all the coercive measures combined succeeded in increasing the wage-earning work force in the Congo nearly tenfold in little over a decade, from 45,000 in 1916 to 427,000 by 1927.[111]

The age of moral consciousness is at hand

When Lever Brothers absorbed the Niger Company in 1920, one of the latter's directors expressed the hope that the standards and record of the Niger Company regarding Africans would be continued. Lever reassured him:

> I have no intention of creating on the Coast of West Africa or anywhere else, any organization that can be other than for the benefit of the natives on the Coast, the Staff, and of the Consumer. My record in the past is open. All our agreements with agents on the Coast contain a clause that any cruelty or ill-treatment of the natives entails instant dismissal without notice. I may say that in the Belgian Congo we have had special commendation from both the Missionaries and from the Government Officials of how greatly we have benefited not only industry but the natives themselves, so that I think you need have no fear under this head.[112]

His appeal for corroboration was to the government and the Church, not to the Africans themselves, and it is not surprising that they should close ranks in mutual self-admiration. A 'colonial trinity' of the Belgian government, large corporations and the Catholic Church is how Georges Nzongola-Ntalaja describes it, bent on a triple mission of political repression, economic exploitation and cultural oppression. In a scathing indictment of this period of colonial rule, he charges this trinity with the wholesale plunder of human and natural resources, accentuating the extraction of raw materials for export over internal development for the benefit of the Congolese and undermining both peasant production and the activities of African traders. The result of the land alienation through monopolies granted to foreign concession companies, combined with the forced labour that drew men from their villages, badly disrupted the patterns and structures of traditional society. Such a massive transformation could not take place without the systematic undermining or destruction of indigenous culture and an overwhelmingly arrogant sense of white, Christian, cultural and intellectual superiority, with African religions, music and art all condemned as inferior, childlike, barbaric and uncivilized.[113] According to one contemporary Belgian author, 'Such wrongs could only cause to be born, in the hearts of the natives, feelings of hate and revolt, feelings which caused them to await patiently the day when they would be stronger.'[114]

The opinions of Africans were rarely solicited, but on his last trip Lever received a sizeable number of petitions from them. One came from twenty-three African staff of the Niger Company and of Messrs John Walkden and Co., calling among other things for better housing and medical services, better overtime and leave pay and the possibility of promotion to higher positions on well defined lines with appropriate salaries and yearly increments. But it is the language of deference and defiance, assertion and submission that is most intriguing, adopting some but not all of the white man's self-serving rhetoric:

> We support the principle of the development of our waste lands in Africa by white capitalists; provided such development cannot be construed to mean alienation or purchase.... We believe in the principle of the allocation of labour and industries for the greater good of humanity at large. And in this connection, we would implore Your Lordship and other commercial and kindred magnates not to overlook the claims of the African whenever legitimate and moral. The simple and childlike Negro is as much a lady as he is a lad. He is a lad on account of his primitive simplicity; he is a lady on account of his womanly defencelessness and his motherly ownership; for he is the natural owner of the immense natural wealth deposited in the bosom and surface of his lands, without the means of protecting them himself, and yet, with the natural right of ownership of them, in just the same sense as a child belongs more peculiarly and morally to his mother than to his father. We require the judicious and moral protection of the great White Race who, on account of that protection, is the foster-father of our wealth; and upon whom the onus of development rests with rights of participation in the enjoyment of same. ... [The Negro] seldom voices his grievances. He is silent, passive, and hence misunderstood; and only a sympathetic and interested observer may divine the wailings of his inner mind. He knows he is poor and handicapped; and on account of this he is for the most part afraid to voice his feelings; and he prefers suffering to extinction ... Your Lordship, we are among those of our race who believe that the age of misunderstanding is over and that the age of moral consciousness is at hand.[115]

Not all Africans waited so patiently for their voices to be heard. Sporadic rebellions against land alienation in different parts of the country took place from 1915 into the 1930s and were stamped out by the army. The Pende uprising of 1931 in the Kwilu region was one of the most serious rural revolts, prompted by a collapse in palm oil prices and the government raising the head and supplementary taxes. The rising occurred after a community at Kilamba refused to provide cutters. The local government agent and an HCB recruiter locked up all the women in retaliation. The Pende erupted, taking particular aim at conditions imposed by HCB and the Compagnie du Kasaï, the two concession companies operating in the area. Well over a thousand died before the revolt was brought under control, with great brutality.[116]

In perhaps the most noteworthy response to the crisis, the Pende uprising caused the veteran socialist Émile Vandervelde to recant. In a speech to the Belgian parliament, analyzing the reasons for the revolt, he recalled his earlier belief that Lever and his philanthropic intentions would be highly beneficial for the colony and for the natives. Those who had visited the Leverville station over the years and come back with glowing descriptions had impressed him. Yet now he was painfully troubled to learn that HCB bore some responsibility for the uprising. Behind 'le décor superbe de Leverville', he wondered, were labourers' working and living conditions and wages so bad in the vast, infrequently visited reaches of the Lusanga concession that this alone could explain their 'invincible répugnance' to entering the region? Eugène Jungers, president of the Court of Appeal at Kinshasa, had recently reported that scarcely any of the cutters at Leverville were there of their own accord: African chiefs or colonial civil servants had forced nearly all of them to work for HCB. This was entirely unsurprising, Jungers suggested. If conditions were fine in their villages, why would natives walk for five or six days to get to work, abandoning their wives and children for six months, to live (for too many of them) in deplorable conditions? One must not forget, Vandervelde concluded, that barely 4,000 of HCB's 20,000 workers lived in 'camps magnifiques'. Plenty of others lived like animals ('comme des bêtes') in miserable huts.[117]

There are some indications that conditions across the various concessions stabilized during the 1930s as the large companies – including the Union Minière du Haut-Katanga (which mined copper in a huge concession area), the Société Internationale Forestière et Minière du Congo (which mined diamonds in the Kasai area), the Kilo-Moto mines and HCB – improved working standards, wages and rations. Roger Anstey, writing in the 1960s, concluded that in these years the Congo came to enjoy a high reputation for the welfare services provided for workers and their families.[118] HCB in particular seemed to be viewed as a model employer. But then, as Jules Marchal, one of the company's most trenchant critics, notes sardonically, '[D]ans le pays des aveugles le cyclope est roi': in the country of the blind the Cyclops is king.[119]

Anstey and fellow writers at the time wanted to believe, following E. D. Morel and other progressive opinion a couple of generations earlier, that a transformation took place, that the European penetration up the river Congo with steamers and guns in order to carry off the most possible loot in their new railways was a thing of the past, replaced by benign, non-coercive commerce and a friendly paternalism. The evidence, at least for the early decades, suggests that this depiction needs to be heavily qualified.

Recently there have been some attempts in Belgium to come to terms with the country's appalling record in Africa. The Royal Museum for Central Africa has led the way, commissioning an investigation in 2002. At that time the museum director, Guido Gryseels, commented, 'We really haven't coped with it, and the revelations came as a real shock. We were brought up knowing that we brought civilization and good to Africa.' As a result of the investigation the museum mounted a temporary exhibition in 2005, 'Memory of Congo: The Colonial Era', which went some way towards accepting the allegations rather than dismissing them as vicious foreign slurs. Belgians are beginning to recover their imperial memory; Lever hagiographers should do the same.[120]

Notes

1 *Daily Telegraph*, 8 May 1925, quoted in *Progress*, 25:168 (July 1925), 143.

2 Harley Williams, *Men of Stress: Three Dynamic Interpretations: Woodrow Wilson, Andrew Carnegie, William Hesketh Lever* (London: Jonathan Cape, 1948), pp. 298, 300, 363.

3 Jervis J. Babb, *The Human Relations Philosophy of William Hesketh Lever* (New York: The Newcomen Society in North America, 1952), pp. 13–14.

4 Charles Wilson, *The History of Unilever: A Study in Economic Growth and Social Change*, vol. I (London: Cassell and Co., 1954), p. 187.

5 Adam MacQueen, *The King of Sunlight: How William Lever Cleaned up the World* (London: Bantam Press, 2004), p. 294.

6 Regenia Gagnier, *The Insatiability of Human Wants: Economics and Aesthetics in Market Society* (Chicago: University of Chicago Press, 2000), pp. 3–4. See also Edward W. Said, *Culture and Imperialism* (New York: Vintage Books, 1994), pp. 167–8.

7 William Hesketh Lever, *Following the Flag: Jottings of a Jaunt round the World* (London: Simpkin Marshall and Co.; Liverpool: Edward Howell, 1893), pp. 71–2.

8 George M. Fredrickson, *Racism: A Short History* (Princeton, NJ: Princeton University Press, 2002), pp. 6–7, 11–12, 43, 46–7, 51–3, 56–61, 64, 66, 102, 104–8; John W. Burrow, *The Crisis of Reason: European Thought 1848–1914* (New Haven, CT: Yale University Press, 2000), pp. 103–4; Elazar Barkan, *The Retreat of Scientific Racism: Changing Concepts of Race in Britain and the United States between the World Wars* (Cambridge: Cambridge University Press, 1992), pp. 2–3, 15–17, 24, 341; Sven Lindqvist, *'Exterminate all the Brutes'* (New York: New Press, 1996), pp. 140–1; Patrick Brantlinger, *Dark Vanishings: Discourse on the Extinction of Primitive Races 1800–1930* (Ithaca, NY: Cornell University Press, 2003); Bernard Porter, *The Lion's Share: A Short History of British Imperialism 1850–1995*, 3rd edn (London and New York: Longman, 1996), pp. 226–7; Michael Mann, *The Dark*

Side of Democracy: Explaining Ethnic Cleansing (Cambridge: Cambridge University Press, 2005), pp. 55, 82, 84–6, 100–6, 180–1 (Trotha quotations p. 104).

9 Lever, *Following the Flag*, pp. 32–3.

10 D. K. Fieldhouse, *Unilever Overseas: The Anatomy of a Multinational 1895–1965* (London: Croom Helm, 1978), p. 449.

11 Lever to R. Barrie, August 1904, quoted by Fieldhouse, *Unilever Overseas*, p. 460.

12 Fieldhouse, *Unilever Overseas*, p. 458.

13 W. J. Reader, *Unilever Plantations* (London: Unilever Ltd, 1961), pp. 12–15.

14 Raymond Leslie Buell, *The Native Problem in Africa* (New York: Macmillan, 1928), vol. II, p. 513.

15 Fieldhouse, *Unilever Overseas*, pp. 449–50, 557–8; Frederick Pedler, *The Lion and the Unicorn in Africa: A History of the Origins of the United Africa Company 1787–1931* (London: Heinemann, 1974), pp. 295–6; Wilson, *Unilever*, p. 186.

16 Lever, *Leverhulme*, pp. 154–8; Judith A. Bennett, *Wealth of the Solomons: A History of a Pacific Archipelago 1800–1978* (Honolulu, HI: University of Hawaii Press, 1987), chap. 6; Fieldhouse, *Unilever Overseas*, pp. 451–65, 492.

17 Doug Munro and Stewart Firth, 'Company strategies – colonial policies', in Clive Moore, Jacqueline Leckie and Doug Munro (eds), *Labour in the South Pacific* (Townsville, QLD: James Cook University of Northern Queensland, 1990), pp. 9–13, 25; Donald Denoon with Marivic Wyndham, 'Australia and the Western Pacific', in Wm Roger Louis (ed.), *The Oxford History of the British Empire*, vol. III: Andrew Porter (ed.), *The Nineteenth Century* (Oxford: Oxford University Press, 1999), pp. 553, 557; Bennett, *Wealth of the Solomons*, p. 125.

18 Quoted by Lever, *Leverhulme*, p. 160.

19 Nigel Randell, *The White Headhunter* (New York: Carroll and Graf, 2003), pp. 275–6; Munro and Firth, 'Company strategies', p. 11.

20 Public Record Office, Colonial Office Confidential Papers 881/11/192, quoted by Randell, *White Headhunter*, p. 275. See also W. P. Jolly, *Lord Leverhulme: A Biography* (London: Constable, 1976), pp. 98–101.

21 Report by Mahaffy, 1908, Western Pacific High Commission Inward Correspondence, General, 830 (in Fiji), quoted by Deryck Scarr, *Fragments of Empire: A History of the Western Pacific High Commission 1877–1914* (Canberra: Australian National University Press; Honolulu, HI: University of Hawaii Press, 1968), p. 269.

22 Judith A. Bennett, '"We do not come here to be beaten": resistance and the plantation system in the Solomon Islands to World War II', in Brij V. Lal, Doug Munro and Edward D. Beechert (eds), *Plantation Workers: Resistance and Accommodation* (Honolulu, HI: University of Hawaii Press, 1993), pp. 138, 140–1, 143, 154–8.

23 Munro and Stewart, 'Company strategies', pp. 11–12, and Margaret Willson, Clive Moore and Doug Munro, 'Asian workers in the Pacific', p. 98, in Moore *et al.* (eds), *Labour in the South Pacific*; Bennett, '"We do not come here to be beaten"', p. 133; Fieldhouse, *Unilever Overseas*, pp. 466, 473–5; Wilson, *Unilever*, p. 163 ('Hindoo' quotation); Lever, *Leverhulme*, p. 308 ('clean white map' quotation); Kevin Grant, *A Civilised Savagery: Britain and the New Slaveries in Africa 1884–1926* (New York and London: Routledge, 2005), chap. 3.

24 Quoted by Ronald Hyam, 'Bureaucracy and "trusteeship" in the colonial empire', in Wm Roger Louis (ed.), *The Oxford History of the British Empire*, vol. IV: Judith M. Brown and Wm Roger Louis (eds), *The Twentieth Century* (Oxford: Oxford University Press, 1999), p. 265.

25 *House of Commons Debates*, 1913, vol. 56, col. 786 (Harcourt, 31 July 1913), quoted by W. K. Hancock, *Survey of British Commonwealth Affairs*, vol. II: *Problems of Economic Policy 1918-1939*, part 2 (London: Oxford University Press, 1940), p. 190.

26 Hyam, 'Bureaucracy and "trusteeship"', pp. 265-8, and Toyin Falola and A. D. Roberts, 'West Africa', p. 517, in Brown and Louis (eds), *The Twentieth Century*; Sally Marks, *The Ebbing of European Ascendancy* (London: Edward Arnold, 2002), p. 153; Porter, *Lion's Share*, pp. 228-9.

27 Quoted by Hyam, 'Bureaucracy and "trusteeship"', p. 267.

28 Hancock, *Survey of British Commonwealth Affairs*, p. 181.

29 A. G. Hopkins, *An Economic History of West Africa* (New York: Columbia University Press, 1973), pp. 210-14; Porter, *Lion's Share*, pp. 193-4, 229-31; Anne Phillips, *The Enigma of Colonialism: British Policy in West Africa* (London: James Currey; Bloomington, IN: Indiana University Press, 1989), chap. 1; Susan M. Martin, *Palm Oil and Protest: An Economic History of the Ngwa Region, South Eastern Nigeria 1800-1980* (Cambridge: Cambridge University Press, 1988), pp. 60-1.

30 Lever, *Leverhulme*, pp. 162-3; Pedler, *The Lion and the Unicorn*, pp. 176, 178, 180; Phillips, *Enigma of Colonialism*, pp. 91-4.

31 London School of Economics, British Library of Political and Economic Science, Morel Papers, F8, File 99, Lever to Morel, 29 August 1910.

32 LSE, Morel Papers, F8, File 99, Morel to Charles Strachey, Colonial Office, 9 September 1910. See also Morel to Strachey, 17 August; Morel to Sir Walter Egerton, 17 August.

33 LSE, Morel Papers, F8, File 99, Strachey to Morel, 20 August; F. Bohn, Compagnie Française de l'Afrique Occidentale, to Monsieur Fontannaz, 2 September; ? to Bohn, 10 September; Egerton to Morel, 25 September; Strachey to Morel, 26 September; Fontannaz to editor of *Liverpool Daily Post and Mercury*, 15 October; Lever to Morel, 19 October.

34 C. C. Wrigley, 'Aspects of economic history', in A. D. Roberts (ed.), *The Cambridge History of Africa*, vol. VII: *From 1905 to 1940* (Cambridge: Cambridge University Press, 1986), p. 106.

35 For the squabble between Leverhulme and Clifford see correspondence in UARM, LBC 662, January 1925; W. P. Jolly, *Lord Leverhulme: A Biography* (London: Constable, 1976), pp. 229-33; Hancock, *Survey of British Commonwealth Affairs*, pp. 188-95.

36 Hopkins, *Economic History of West Africa*, pp. 211, 213; Hyam, 'Bureaucracy and "trusteeship"', p. 268; Grant, *A Civilised Savagery*, pp. 156-8. The fact that Lever was thwarted by British civil servants and governments and so turned towards the more amenable Belgians may appear to give weight to the Cain and Hopkins thesis (P. J. Cain and A. G. Hopkins, *British Imperialism*, 2 vols, London: Longman, 1993) of a dichotomy between a landed/financial 'gentlemanly capitalist' sector based in and around London and provincial bourgeois industrialists. But the diversity of conflicting ideas and interests, and Lever's part battle against,

part collusion with British officialdom and economic strategies throughout his career, provide scant support for this interpretation. See Raymond E. Dumett (ed.), *Gentlemanly Capitalism and British Imperialism: The New Debate on Empire* (London: Longman, 1999), pp. 6–8, 11.

37 Quoted by Roland Oliver and Anthony Atmore, *Africa since 1800*, 2nd edn (Cambridge: Cambridge University Press, 1972), p. 163, quoted by Marks, *Ebbing of European Ascendancy*, p. 153.

38 UARM, LBC 662, Lever to Sir Hugh Clifford, 11 January 1925. Exeter Hall was the centre of the anti-slavery movement in the nineteenth century.

39 Adam Hochschild, *King Leopold's Ghost: A Story of Greed, Terror, and Heroism in Colonial Africa* (London: Macmillan, 2000); Jules Marchal, *E. D. Morel contre Léopold II : l'histoire du Congo 1900–1910* (Paris: Éditions l'Harmattan, 1996), vol. II; Wm Roger Louis and Jean Stengers (eds), *E. D. Morel's History of the Congo Reform Movement* (Oxford: Clarendon Press, 1967); Wm Roger Louis, 'Roger Casement and the Congo', *Journal of African History*, 5:1 (1964), 99–120; Neal Ascherson, *The King Incorporated: Leopold II in the Age of Trusts* (London: Allen and Unwin, 1963), chaps 27–8; Grant, *A Civilised Savagery*, chap. 2.

40 Lever, *Leverhulme*, p. 163.

41 LSE, Morel Papers, F8, File 99, Lever to Morel, 17 October; UARM, LBC 7286, Lever to Morel, 17 October.

42 Lever, *Leverhulme*, p. 164.

43 LSE, Morel Papers, F8, File 100, Morel to Lever, 12 April 1911.

44 *Ibid.*, Morel to Vandervelde, 29 March. The letter is in French with no accents; the translations are mine. The original quotations read: 'visiblement irrite'; 'bien paye, bien nourri, bien loge – mais un travailleur, un salaire, et rien de plus'; and 'Lever est un homme sans education, et sans sentiment, un genie du commerce, enormement fabuleusement riche, probablement bon de coeur mais dur aussi, qui voit l'humanite comme un vast engin de production sans ame ni desires ou ambitions autres que l'accumulation de louis d'or autoritaire, rarement contecarrie [*sic*]. Cet homme aux idees commerciales tres vastes est lance dorenavant dans l'Afrique occidentale, dans le Congo ou il peut devenir une force enorme pour le bien ou pour le mal.' See also Marchal, *E. D. Morel contre Léopold*, pp. 449–50.

45 LSE, Morel Papers, F8, File 100, Lever to Morel, 18 April 1911. For a discussion of how Lever Brothers ads reflected these notions by depicting African males as babies and children and African females as contented slaves for white women, see Anandi Ramamurthy, *Imperial Persuaders: Images of Africa and Asia in British Advertising* (Manchester: Manchester University Press, 2003), pp. 56, 60, 89.

46 LSE, Morel Papers, F8, File 100, Morel to Lever, 19 April.

47 *Ibid.*, Lever to Morel, 27 April.

48 UARM, LBC 8104A, Lever to H. R. Greenhalgh, 8 October 1917.

49 *Ibid.*, Lever to H. R. Greenhalgh, 8 March 1918.

50 *Liverpool Post and Mercury*, 11 July 1924; see also *Bolton Evening News*, 23 March 1925, report on speech to annual meeting of Bolton Infirmary (both in BALS, B920 B LEV, newspaper cuttings on Lever).

51 LSE, Morel Papers, F8, File 100, report by John H. Harris, 'New Congo concessions', 5 December 1911.

52 *Ibid.*, Morel to Travers Buxton (Secretary to the Anti-slavery and Aboriginal Protection Society), 28 February 1912; Catherine Ann Cline, *E. D. Morel 1873–1924: The Strategies of Protest* (Belfast: Blackstaff Press, 1980), pp. 85–7.

53 Lever, *Leverhulme*, pp. 165–9; Fieldhouse, *Unilever Overseas*, pp. 498–504; Wilson, *Unilever*, pp. 168 (quotation), 170.

54 Fieldhouse, *Unilever Overseas*, p. 500.

55 Diary entry, 1 January 1913, quoted by Lever, *Leverhulme*, p. 173.

56 UARM, LBC 7814, Lever to Dr Max Horn, Brussels, 11 June 1912.

57 Pedler, *The Lion and the Unicorn*, p. 3 and facing p. 144; Samuel H. Nelson, *Colonialism in the Congo Basin 1880–1940* (Athens, OH: Ohio University Center for International Studies, Africa Series, 64, 1994), p. 140.

58 Buell, *Native Problem in Africa*, pp. 512–13; Nelson, *Colonialism in the Congo Basin*, pp. 140–2; Jules Marchal, *Travail forcé pour l'huile de palme de Lord Leverhulme* (Borgloon, Belgium: Éditions Paula Bellings, 2001), p. 125.

59 Quoted by Bogumil Jewsiewicki, 'African peasants in the totalitarian colonial society of the Belgian Congo', in Martin A. Klein (ed.), *Peasants in Africa: Historical and Contemporary Perspectives* (Beverly Hills, CA, and London: Sage Publications, 1980), pp. 61–2.

60 Buell, *Native Problem in Africa*, p. 513.

61 Lever, *Leverhulme*, p. 167.

62 Quoted by Lever, *Leverhulme*, pp. 172 (first quotation), 173 (second).

63 Quoted by Jolly, *Lord Leverhulme*, p. 125.

64 UARM, LBC 4506, Lever to Annie and D'Arcy Lever, 12 November 1924.

65 UARM, LBC 7286, Lever to L. H. Moseley, 11 April 1916.

66 UARM, LBC 5677, statement by Lever in Kinshasa on Congo development, 2 December 1924.

67 UARM, LBC 7286, Lever to L. H. Moseley, 11 April 1916.

68 *Ibid.*, Lever to L. H. Moseley, 11 May 1916.

69 UARM, LBC 8104A, Lever to H. R. Greenhalgh, 21 March 1916.

70 UARM, LBC 7286, Lever to L. H. Moseley, 11 April 1916. See also LBC 8104A, Lever to H. R. Greenhalgh, 23 January 1917.

71 UARM, LBC 5677, Lever to Mr Warrington (of Messrs Hazlehurst and Sons, Port Sunlight), 8 November 1924.

72 Lever, *Leverhulme*, pp. 311–12.

73 UARM, LBC 4506, Lever to Annie and D'Arcy Lever, 12 November 1924.

74 UARM, LBC 4271, Lever to Myrtle Huband, 27 October 1924.

75 UARM, LBC 5677, statement by Lever in Kinshasa on Congo development, 2 December 1924.

76 UARM, LBC 4271, Lever to Myrtle Huband, 11 November 1924.

77 Lever, *Leverhulme*, pp. 310–11; Fieldhouse, *Unilever Overseas*, p. 507.

78 Fieldhouse, *Unilever Overseas*, pp. 508–9.

79 *Ibid.*, pp. 512, 517, 523, 525; Reader, *Unilever Plantations*, pp. 18, 21–3; Pedler, *The Lion and the Unicorn*, p. 294; Phillips, *Enigma of Colonialism*, pp. 95, 106; Martin, *Palm Oil and Protest*, pp. 61–3.

80 Hochschild, *King Leopold's Ghost*, pp. 273 (quotation), 278–9.

81 The following account is taken from Lowell J. Satre, *Chocolate on Trial: Slavery,*

Politics, and the Ethics of Business (Athens, OH: Ohio University Press, 2005). See also Grant, *A Civilised Savagery*, chap. 4.

82 Satre, *Chocolate on Trial*, p. 168.

83 *Standard*, 26 September 1908, quoted by Satre, *Chocolate on Trial*, pp. 228–9.

84 Quoted by Satre, *Chocolate on Trial*, p. 175.

85 Angus Mitchell (ed.), *The Amazon Journal of Roger Casement* (London: Anaconda Editions, 1997).

86 Satre, *Chocolate on Trial*, pp. 41–3; Grant, *A Civilised Savagery*, pp. 5, 10, 22–4, 29, chap. 5; W. G. Clarence-Smith, *Slaves, Peasants and Capitalists in Southern Angola 1840–1926* (Cambridge: Cambridge University Press, 1979), pp. 13, 30–2; Paul E. Lovejoy, *Transformations in Slavery: A History of Slavery in Africa*, 2nd edn (Cambridge: Cambridge University Press, 2000), pp. 286–7; Paul E. Lovejoy and Jan S. Hogendorn, *Slow Death for Slavery: The Course of Abolition in Northern Nigeria 1897–1936* (Cambridge: Cambridge University Press, 1993), pp. 285–6; Myron J. Echenberg, 'Paying the blood tax: military conscription in French West Africa', *Canadian Journal of African Studies*, 9:2 (1975), 171–92; Frederick Cooper, 'Conditions analogous to slavery', in Frederick Cooper, Thomas C. Holt and Rebecca J. Scott (eds), *Beyond Slavery: Explorations of Race, Labor, and Citizenship in Postemancipation Societies* (Chapel Hill, NC: University of North Carolina Press, 2000), pp. 107–49; Martin Klein, *Slavery and Colonial Rule in French West Africa* (Cambridge: Cambridge University Press, 1998), pp. 213, 219.

87 Quoted by Satre, *Chocolate on Trial*, p. 42.

88 Quoted by A. M. Delathuy [Jules Marchal], *E. D. Morel tegen Leopold II en de Kongostaat* (Antwerp: EPO, 1985), pp. 57–8, quoted by James Breman, 'Primitive racism in a colonial context', in James Breman (ed.), *Imperial Monkey Business: Racial Supremacy in Social Darwinist Theory and Colonial Practice* (Amsterdam: Vu University Press, 1990), p. 117.

89 Breman, 'Primitive racism in a colonial context', pp. 110, 117, and 'The civilization of racism: colonial and post-colonial development policies', p. 147, in Breman (ed.), *Imperial Monkey Business*; Cooper, 'Conditions analogous to slavery', pp. 124–5.

90 Nelson, *Colonialism in the Congo Basin*, pp. 113–16, 120–1; Breman, 'The civilization of racism', pp. 123–4, 129–30, 132–3, 147–8, 150; Hancock, *Survey of British Commonwealth Affairs*, pp. 178–9. Jules Marchal, a former colonial official in the Congo, has done most to uncover the extent of forced labour after 1910 in a three-volume study: *L'Histoire du Congo 1910–1945*, vol. I: *Travail forcé pour le cuivre et l'or*, vol. II: *Travail forcé pour le rail*, vol. III: *Travail forcé pour l'huile de palme de Lord Leverhulme* (Borgloon, Belgium: Éditions Paula Bellings, 1999–2001). Vol. I has been translated by Ayi Kwei Armah as *Forced Labor in the Gold and Copper Mines: A History of Congo under Belgian Rule 1910–1945*, vol. I (Popenguine, Senegal: Per Ankh, 2003). Marchal estimates, for example, that in the reconstruction of the Matadi–Kinshasa railway alone between 1923 and 1932 (see vol. II) 60,000 involuntary workers were employed, most of them brought in from a considerable distance, and that 7,000 of them died.

91 Martin Evans, *European Atrocity, African Catastrophe: Leopold II, the Congo Free State and its Aftermath* (London and New York: RoutledgeCurzon, 2002), pp. 238–40, 242 (quotation); Nelson, *Colonialism in the Congo Basin*, pp. 114–15

(quotation), 124–6; David Northrup, *Beyond the Bend in the River: African Labor in Eastern Zaire 1865–1940* (Athens, OH: Ohio University Center for International Studies, African Series, 52, 1988), pp. 93, 117–18.

92 Fieldhouse, *Unilever Overseas*, pp. 512–15; Marchal, *Travail forcé pour l'huile de palme*, pp. 22, 119–20 (quoting Ministère des Affaires étrangères, Brussels, African Archives, MOI [Main-d'oeuvre indigène] 362, 1.156, HCB director Dehees to Commissaire générale Alexis Bertrand, 2 October 1917).

93 Vandebosch report in MOI 3602, 1.156, quoted by Marchal, *Travail forcé pour l'huile de palme*, pp. 22–3; Northrup, *Beyond the Bend*, pp. 93–4, 132–8, 163, 165; Marchal, *E. D. Morel contre Léopold*, p. 451.

94 African Archives, AIMO [Affaires indigènes et main-d'oeuvre du gouvernement générale] 1654, HCB 36, rapport Lejeune, quoted by Marchal, *Travail forcé pour l'huile de palme*, pp. 75–81.

95 Marchal, *Travail forcé pour l'huile de palme*, pp. 83–94, 126–8.

96 Mrs Stuart Menzies, *Modern Men of Mark* (London: Herbert Jenkins, 1921), pp. 165–7.

97 Pedler, *The Lion and the Unicorn*, pp. 294–5.

98 Marchal, *Travail forcé pour l'huile de palme*, pp. 167–8.

99 Nelson, *Colonialism in the Congo Basin*, p. 142.

100 Buell, *Native Problem in Africa*, p. 553.

101 Quoted by Jewsiewicki, 'African peasants', p. 60.

102 Letter of 9 September 1925 to District Commissioner, quoted by Buell, *Native Problem in Africa*, p. 542; Marchal, *Travail forcé pour le rail*, p. 207 (quoting Buell in *The Nation*); Northrup, *Beyond the Bend*, p. 133.

103 Quoted by Jewsiewicki, 'African peasants', pp. 62 (first quotation), 61 (second).

104 Allan McPhee, *The Economic Revolution in British West Africa*, 2nd edn (London: Frank Cass and Co., 1971; 1st edn, 1926), p. 198.

105 W. G. A. Ormsby-Gore, *Visit to West Africa*, Cmd 2744 (London, 1926), p. 107, quoted by Buell, *Native Problem in Africa*, p. 543, n. 30.

106 *Congo*, December 1925 and November 1928, quoted by Marchal, *Travail forcé pour l'huile de palme*, pp. 112–17.

107 AIMO 1705, 1. généralités, Maurice Stubbe and Sidney Edkins of HCB to Nicolas Arnold (administrateur général), 8 June 1926, quoted by Marchal, *Travail forcé pour l'huile de palme*, pp. 153–4; Marchal, *Travail forcé pour le rail*, p. 206; Northrup, *Beyond the Bend*, pp. 135–8.

108 AIMO 1651, farde 9.238, enquêtes dans les Uele, etc., affaire Roex, Pierre Roex to Jean Colin, procureur du roi à Kisangani, 29 June 1927, quoted by Marchal, *Travail forcé pour l'huile de palme*, pp. 141–4.

109 Nelson, *Colonialism in the Congo Basin*, pp. 133–4, 138–9.

110 Lever in Brussels, 20 April 1922, conferring with Minister Louis Franck. AI 1401, 1. contrats tripartites, rapport sur les opérations des HCB pendant l'exercise 1920/21, rédigé par Max Horn, 8 May 1922, p. 11, quoted by Marchal, *Travail forcé pour l'huile de palme*, p. 101.

111 Fieldhouse, *Unilever Overseas*, pp. 518–20; Buell, *The Native Problem in Africa*, pp. 528–31; Nelson, *Colonialism in the Congo Basin*, pp. 127–31; Marchal, *Travail forcé pour l'huile de palme*, pp. 103–4, 111, 365.

112 UARM, LBC 7161, Lord Emmott to Lever, 1 October 1920; Lever to Emmott, 4 October.

113 Georges Nzongola-Ntalaja, *The Congo from Leopold to Kabila: A People's History* (London and New York: Zed Books, 2002), pp. 27, 32–3, 38–9; Bogumil Jewsie-wicki, 'Belgian Africa', in Roberts (ed.), *Cambridge History of Africa*, vol. VII, pp. 492–3.

114 G. Van der Kerken, *Les Sociétés bantoues du Congo belge* (Brussels, 1920), quoted by Evans, *European Atrocity*, p. 237.

115 UARM, LBC 5677, letter of twenty-three African employees to Lever, 5 January 1925.

116 Evans, *European Atrocity*, pp. 237–8; Nzongola-Ntalaja, *The Congo from Leopold to Kabila*, p. 52; Fieldhouse, *Unilever Overseas*, p. 515; Marchal, *Travail forcé pour l'huile de palme*, pp. 13 ff, 245 ff.

117 Speech in Chambre des Représentants, 14 June 1932 (*Annales parlementaires*, Chambre 1932, pp. 2063–5), quoted by Marchal, *Travail forcé pour l'huile de palme*, pp. 267–8.

118 Roger Anstey, *King Leopold's Legacy: The Congo under Belgian Rule 1908–1960* (London: Oxford University Press, 1966), pp. 118–20; Robert B. Egerton, *The Troubled Heart of Africa: A History of the Congo* (New York: St Martin's Press, 2002), pp. 169–70.

119 Marchal, *Travail forcé pour l'huile de palme*, p. 364.

120 *Guardian Weekly*, 18–24 July 2002, p. 3; Susan Spano's column in the *Los Angeles Times*, 13 March 2005, p. L7; www.africamuseum.be/museum (accessed 1 September 2005).

Twilight

A storm of exceptional violence

Lever had no doubts about the righteousness of the British cause during the First World War, nor about German malevolence, nor about what needed to be done. He declared 'the War is decided now' only shortly after the Allies had halted the German advance in 1914 and while the trenches were still been dug between the Belgian coast and Switzerland. It was just a matter of time and economic necessity, he said, before the Germans realized they had lost. They would have to sign a treaty depriving themselves of their colonies, their navy and much of their territory in Europe, plus pay an enormous war indemnity to Belgium, France and Serbia, and in consequence 'cease to be a first-rate Power.'[1] More cautious Liberals gradually came round to the idea of a vindictive peace over the course of the war; Lever arrived there rather more quickly.

He had issued a directive in late August 1914 encouraging enlistment: 'the Directors desire to make it known to all employees that they hope and expect that all men between the ages of nineteen and thirty-five will offer their services to their King and Country; the situations of which will be kept open for them against their return.'[2] He passed a medical examination himself and signed up for the Port Sunlight company of the Birkenhead and District Volunteer Training Corps, turned Gladstone Hall into a recruiting office, converted Hulme Hall from an art gallery into first a shelter for Belgian refugees then a Red Cross military hospital, allowed the use of Thornton Manor as a privately maintained Red Cross hospital and served on several wartime governmental and charitable committees.[3]

Lever expressed grave concern at various points during the war about the disruption to trade. 'The trade that has taken us nearly thirty years to build up is being wrecked,' he said of government restrictions on sending soap to neutral Holland or on supplying oils and fats to the company's Dutch affiliates, in the interests of preventing contraband articles reaching Germany.[4] The Germans took over five works of associated companies – three in Germany, one in Brussels, one in Lille. But, whatever the sacrifice, Lever felt that 'we had no course open to us but to take the side of Belgium when Belgian neutrality was invaded', and that now Britain must see it through to the end. 'It would be simply putting serpents' eggs to hatch for our children to make peace with Germany in her present state of mind,' he wrote in early 1917. 'However much peace may be desired, there can be only one peace and that is the unconditional surrender of Germany and Austria.' By early the following year, after seeing the brutal Treaty of Brest-Litovsk imposed by the Germans upon the new Bolshevik regime in Russia, Lever was even less compromising. 'Germany is not to be trusted,' he said. 'She is a dishonest blackguard and I would no more trust a German word or a German signed Treaty than I would trust a devil from hell.'[5]

After it was all over, he struck a note of triumphalism in a New Year's message in *Bubbles*, the Pears company magazine:

> Our enemies are defeated, our brave men and those of our Allies have conquered, and we face the future with 'eyes that gleam of triumph tasted', and hearts that throb with ambitions to make Great Britain and the Empire not only the greatest Empire the world has ever seen, but also the Empire that contains the greatest number of happy men and women, and where Liberty is enthroned in a constitutional monarchy the most democratic in the world, under which each citizen has the fullest opportunity for the attainment of happiness, comfort, and prosperity.[6]

In truth Lever Brothers had done very well out of the war as the company met government and army needs for soap, glycerine and margarine, and it was now poised to take advantage of pent-up demand. It took over the last two big rival British soap companies, Crosfield's and Gossage's, plus Watson's and John Knight of London, but these transactions were dwarfed by the acquisition of the Niger Company. Lever Brothers' factories required nearly a quarter of a million tons of oils and fats a year by 1919. The Niger Company was an attractive proposition partly because of the 100,000 tons of oil seeds it shipped annually. Lever agreed in January 1920 to buy the Niger shares for more than £8 million, without investigation of the chaotic accounts and unaware that the Niger Company had to repay a £2 million overdraft to its bankers. This was bad enough, but in the next few months the post-war bubble burst, and raw materials prices tumbled. Lever Brothers found themselves in deep financial difficulties, with great quantities of overpriced materials on their hands and tremendous debts to pay off. The banks, reluctant to send good money after bad, kept their distance.

For the first time, Lever Brothers stared at the prospect of liquidation. Francis D'Arcy Cooper of the accounting firm Cooper Bros and Co., who managed to negotiate a loan with Barclays Bank, pulled them back from the brink. This agreement forced Lever Brothers to issue debenture stock, to be held by the bank as collateral security, which obliged the firm to pay interest or the principal on set dates, irrespective of profits – or a receiver would be called in. Neither this nor the fact that for the first time another – Cooper – was deciding company policy sat well with Lever, but he had no choice.[7]

In the midst of the Niger crisis Henry Bell, director and general manager of Lloyds Bank, had told Lever that 'a good many of us feel that you have gone ahead too quickly in view of a difficult financial situation. The truth is that there is not enough money to go round and it has to be strictly rationed as, say, sugar or any other commodity.' But Lever resisted pressure to dump the Niger shares, and by 22 August was able to write:

> Yes the credit of Lever Bros. has been strained to provide £8,000,000 but I contend that the fact that the £8,000,000 has been provided has shown our strength. We are like a ship that has gone through a storm of exceptional violence and weathered the storm successfully and like the ship that has done this, our reputation ought now to stand higher than ever. We have been tested in the furnace and stood the test.[8]

Still, the Lever Brothers' directors could not allow the overheating of the company to pass unchallenged. In January 1921 a special committee met for the first time, comprising Lever, his son, Harold Greenhalgh and John McDowell, and its purpose was to ensure that the Old Man made sensible decisions. At the same time the Lever Brothers headquarters moved from Port Sunlight to London, taking over the former De Keyser's Hotel, Blackfriars, and renaming it Lever House. (Unilever House was going to be built on the same spot in the 1930s.) The firm was moving away from personal rule rooted in the north towards the collective leadership of a metropolitan-centred, multinational corporation. Cooper joined the board in 1923 and soon became vice-chairman.[9] He was to become chairman on Lever's death in 1925. According to D. C. Coleman and W. J. Reader, Cooper stands as a classic example of an 'organization man', a professional manager, bringing in order, consolidation and stability after the whirlwind of visionary innovation has moved on or (if it threatened the company with crazy ideas) been moved on. Lever's misjudgements in his last years almost sank Lever Brothers – a typical pattern in successful businesses as the founder comes towards his end and fails to appreciate his own fallibility or potential to err – and the firm needed to take stock and maintain steady state for a while.[10]

While Lever and the company were weathering this crisis and expanding the soap and margarine business, he was deeply involved in his schemes on Harris and Lewis, with accompanying spin-offs in the food business, as we shall see, and was going ahead with major changes to his houses and gardens at Rivington and The Hill. He did not go gentle into that good night. Running a business empire, expanding into Africa and developing houses, gardens and collections would be more than enough to preoccupy most people. But not Lever. As he aged, his pace became even more frenetic, not less. Andrew Knox speculated that he stepped up his mental and physical activities to fill the gap left by his wife's death: 'If there was a demon it was probably loneliness.'[11] Lever's son, too, spoke about the profound loneliness his father experienced after his mother's death, and conjectured that this explains many of his late projects: 'I cannot help feeling that, in many of his added activities, he was seeking a means of escape from thoughts which inevitably forced themselves upon him, unless his mind was occupied – to an even greater extent than before – with problems which demanded nothing less than the whole of the energy and power within him.'[12]

Lever had become increasingly deaf. A slight ailment had worsened into a serious problem around the time of his first trip to the Congo, and it was to be a recurrent theme, in public and private, throughout the rest of his life.[13] He said in a speech in the House of Lords in 1919, for example, that 'I am suffering from the infirmity of defective hearing and consequently I have been dependent upon the papers to-day for the speeches that were given yesterday and I have not completely heard the speeches delivered to-day.' In 1921 he turned down a lunch invitation to meet the Chinese ambassador because 'owing to my deafness I should not be of the slightest use at this luncheon; I could not hear a word'.[14] The *Manchester Guardian* said of him in his obituary, 'You could always detect Bolton when he spoke on the platform in the loud, rather toneless voice of a deaf man.'[15] This hearing impairment no doubt compounded his loneliness.

A young woman called Myrtle Huband, aged nineteen or twenty, wrote to him in 1919:

> I am the little girl who spoke to you last night after the O. P. dinner and asked if you really meant you were lonely – & you said 'yes' – now may I come & cheer you up sometimes? – I'm engaged to a dear boy who has just lost his leg in this dreadful war, & I know he won't mind me coming as he is so good & thoughtful.

She wrote again a week later, 'I just felt oh so sorry for you when you said you were a lonely "little sparrow".'[16] The evidence is fragmentary, consisting of only a handful of letters, but it seems that in the final years of this industrial titan, paradoxically (or maybe inevitably) isolated atop a web of power and sycophancy, he could bestow a fatherly affection on Myrtle, the daughter he never had. He opened doors in accountancy for her new husband, Lieutenant Harold Odling, and frequently had them up to The Hill for dinner with himself and his sister, or invited them to make use of The Bungalow for extended vacations (usually without him). On occasion he signed his letters to her 'Your Uncle', and she in return signed off with expressions like 'My fondest love and very best of wishes'. A few weeks before his death she addressed a letter to 'Dearest & Best', confided 'It is very wonderful to know I can come to you with all my troubles & know I have one dear Sparrow to hear my inmost thoughts &

sympathise,' and signed herself 'Fondest Love. Yrs. As Ever. Myrtle XXX.'[17]

If loneliness was one psychological factor driving the Old Man, another, as he admitted himself, was fear – in spite of the motto he had adopted for his coat of arms, *Mutare vel timere sperno* (I scorn to change or to fear). He wrote to a colleague in 1923:

> I ask myself what has caused me to begin work at 4.30 in the morning during the last two or three years, and to work laborious hours, and to have only one absorbing thought, namely, my own efficiency and the maintenance of my own health for the task I have to perform; and I am bound to confess that it has not been the attraction of the dividends, but fear, mere cowardly fear … the gnawing fear in my heart that Lever Brothers might have to pass their dividends, and that I have placed myself in the position of accepting money from all classes of investors, including widows, spinsters, clergymen and others – all subscribers for Lever Brothers' shares from the confidence they had in the business and myself – who might possibly have to forgo their dividends, which would mean the probable curtailment of what they depended upon for their day to day food, clothing, rent, etc.[18]

Fear begat ruthlessness in the form of weeding out inefficiencies in his operations. It is notable that he expressed more concern for the hardships of investors than for those of the workers he laid off. The reductions began in 1920 after the collapse of the post-war boom (Andrew Knox wrote, 'One Friday night everyone in the office got an envelope – it was either the sack or a reduction in pay. I got the reduction'[19]) and the Port Sunlight work force was reduced by half from 8,000 over the next seven years while still churning out the same amount of goods because of increased efficiencies.[20]

In the spring of 1923 he confessed to H. R. Greenhalgh, 'I received rather a crushing blow when I read your report of the losses the Niger Company were still making and we must not forget the enormous flow of capital which still continues into West Africa.'[21] His response was to instil fear in his work force. He wrote during the same year:

> We have been combing out inefficient men, and too highly paid men, and elderly men, and men past their work, steadily for the last three years and I am confident that this has produced a state of fear in the minds of the remainder that if they were not efficient their turn would come next, and it is this, in my opinion, which has been the cause of the improved efficiency results achieved to-day.[22]

In the summer he predicted the necessity for drastic reductions at the end of the year, pensioning off or dismissing more employees:

> because in a great many cases I am convinced that they have become automatic in the discharge of their duties and have ceased really for many years to render effective service. I want to be full of sympathy for old members of the staff, but we must fulfil our duty to the Shareholders, and I hope that the Shareholders, if ever

I cease to be efficient or to render service, will promptly turn me adrift without any consideration of the fact that as the founder of the business, and therefore the oldest member of the staff, I perhaps might expect as much consideration to be shown to me as circumstances entitle me to.[23]

It was a strange mixture of pragmatic ruthlessness and special pleading. But Lever had already been sidelined to some extent, and the shareholders did not, of course, turn him adrift (nor, unlike for many workers, would the consequences have been dire if they had).

When Augustus John painted Lever's portrait in 1920 he failed to spot the avuncular side displayed to Myrtle, or the loneliness, or the fear, but he did notice the hardness of the Old Man's character clearly enough. The painting is a poor likeness, but John appeared to be suggesting that he had captured 'a deeper truth' of greed, smugness, arrogance and self-satisfaction. Lever certainly thought this was the intent, finding the portrait 'humbling to pride' and 'chastening'. He was so hurt by it that when it arrived at The Bungalow he decided to hide it away in his safe; but as the safe was too small, he roughly cut out the head of the portrait and stuffed that inside instead – a sort of psychological suicide, Harley Williams called it, the rage of Caliban at being confronted with his true self. The story goes that Lever's housekeeper then mistakenly returned the packing case with decapitated portrait to John, who, understandably, took it to be 'the grossest insult I have ever received in the course of my career.'

Lever apologized profusely, but John still took the story to the press and apparently (by his own probably self-servingly exaggerated account) provoked a flurry of angry demonstrations by artists and art students, including the burning of Lever in effigy in Florence. Editorial comment pondered whether a man had a right to do whatever he wanted with his own property (as Lever claimed) or whether, as in the opinion of the *Manchester Guardian*, 'there is something in a work of art which, in the higher equity as distinct from the law, you can not buy'. John proceeded to exhibit the headless portrait after retitling it 'Lord Leverhulme's watch-chain'. The two parts were not stitched back together, and hung in the Lady Lever Art Gallery, until 1954. The join is still visible.[24]

After receiving such a rough ride, one might have expected Lever to be more careful in dealing with his next portraitist. The following year William Orpen painted him in his mayoral robes for Bolton town hall. Preferring a relaxed look, Orpen persuaded Lever to sit down ('itself an achievement, given the subject's cantankerous disposition', notes Orpen's biographer). It was still a full-length portrait, and Orpen charged £2,000. Lever saw it as a three-quarter length, and would only pay accordingly. After a slew of articles, letters and editorials in the press, Orpen settled for £1,575. Lever had saved a drop in the Atlantic but, in his own eyes at least, he had avoided being 'done' – he had got his money's worth, a cardinal virtue.[25]

The northern Venice by the sea

In the midst of these turbulent post-war years, Lever was devoting a considerable portion of his energy and enthusiasm to his new project in the Outer Hebrides. He had briefly visited Stornoway, the main town on Lewis, as a tourist in 1884. The Matheson family had owned Lewis since 1844, when Sir James Matheson, who had made his money in trading tea, opium and other lucrative commodities in China, bought it from the penurious Earl of Seaforth.[26] Lever started negotiating for the purchase of the property – 400,000 acres inhabited by 30,000 people – from Colonel Duncan Matheson in August 1917 and had completed the deal for £143,000 by the following May. During 1919 he bought both South and North Harris from the Earl of Dunmore and Sir Samuel Scott respectively, a further 170,000 acres, for a total of £56,000. Lever now rivalled the Duke of Sutherland as the largest private landowner in Britain.[27]

The property came complete with Lews Castle, a battlemented, faux-feudal creation built by Sir James Matheson in the mid-nineteenth century across the harbour from Stornoway. This was where Lever made his residence and where he did his chief entertaining. He managed to get to the island only for relatively short bursts, when he would inspect the progress of his works and attend to his properties; the rest of the time his sisters acted as hostesses. His invited guests would travel between the castle and several of the fishing and shooting lodges (built by Sir James) spread around the island. At Lews he revelled in a kind of *ersatz* tartanry. He employed a pipe-major in full regimentals to pipe visitors in to dinner, and he had as guests such figures as the popular music hall entertainer Sir Harry Lauder, whose act consisted of Scots jokes and comic or sentimental songs like 'Roamin' in the gloamin'', and Marjory Kennedy-Fraser, a preserver and improver of allegedly Gaelic songs; her daughter Patuffa would play the clarsach (small Celtic harp). He made few (for him) changes to the castle. Beyond refurnishing and installing electricity, central heating, more bathrooms and internal telephones and bells, he merely knocked the drawing room and ballroom into one, adding a specially sprung dance floor. Plans to double the size of the castle did not get off the ground. In the garden, he did no more than build a terraced kitchen-garden, a tennis court and a carriage drive along the waterfront.[28]

The reason he bought Lewis and Harris was, he said, because 'I am conscious that very often after seventy, changes come very suddenly and I am anxious to consider the business first, foremost and all the time.' On Lewis he could be 'at a distance and yet sufficiently near to be reached immediately by cable and in a couple of days by post.'[29] The pleasures of 'a grouse moor, a yacht, or ... a villa in the South of France' had no appeal for him at all; the concept of rest or inactivity was beyond his grasp; the challenge of solving a human problem and developing a new estate was his idea of an enjoyable retirement. Lewis was to be his sandpit, his retirement playground where he could recreate some of his earlier successes and the great passions of his life: the building and organization of an industry from scratch; the civilization of a work force; and a full-scale exercise in town planning.[30]

Fish were central to his vision. 'Did you know,' he asked Colin MacDonald, a civil servant from the Board of Agriculture, 'that, if you take a map, fix one leg of a pair of compasses in the town of Stornoway and describe a circle of a hundred miles radius, within that circle *you have the richest fishing grounds in the whole world*?'[31] Most of the fishing out of Stornoway consisted of drifting for herring. Before the war the herring was then largely pickled and shipped to the Baltic countries. During the war, with trade to those countries disrupted, it was mostly 'freshed' (packed in ice) or kippered for the British market, which was buoyant because of restricted wartime imports. After the war there was little prospect of the Baltic trade reviving significantly, now that Scandinavian suppliers had benefited from the British absence to establish their own industries, so Hebridean fish would have to continue to supply the British mainland. This posed big problems, because any fish landed in Lewis for packing or curing would then have to be loaded, shipped and unloaded again at railheads on the mainland. This cost money and time, which was of the essence for fresh fish. Increasingly skippers might opt for mainland ports. To overcome this difficulty, Lever decided that he would have to cut out all independent operators and middlemen and establish the chain from sea to fishmonger himself.

Thus evolved his vision of a modernized fishing industry to harvest the seas efficiently. The elements included the most modern fleet of trawlers available, staffed by dedicated, wage-earning crews (and not part-timers who would want to return to their crofts at key moments in the growing cycle); aeroplanes flying out to sea to spot shoals of fish and relay the information by wireless to the fishermen; bigger, better and safer harbours, not only in Stornoway but scattered around the coast of the island; ice factories and cold storage to preserve the fish; refrigerated steamers to convey the fresh fish rapidly to the railhead at Fleetwood, Lancashire; canneries to preserve all the rest of the catch; and a chain of high-street fishmongers to complete the process.[32]

In his plan to revolutionize the local economy and culture, his aim 'to show that it was possible to do for Lewis what Samuel Crompton did for Lancashire,'[33] he did not mean to stop just at fish. He would build roads and over a hundred miles of narrow-gauge, hydro-electric-powered light railways to connect the outlying districts to Stornoway more rapidly and to promote both the tweed industry and commercially viable farms. Stornoway itself, a town of 3,000 people, would become a model garden city for five times that number within a decade or so – a Port Sunlight writ large, with modern, convenient and comfortable housing and Beaux-Arts-style axial thoroughfares.[34]

He was egged on in all this by Thomas Mawson, who, as well as preparing designs for the castle grounds and for the replanning of Stornoway, put together

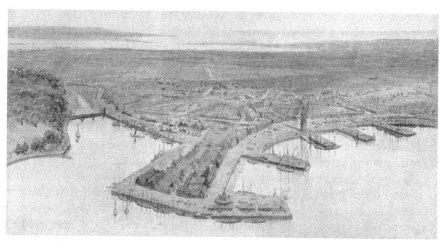

12 'Stornoway of the future': Lever's vision, sketched by Raffles Davison

at Lever's behest a report on the island's natural resources. The report rhapsodized about the economic possibilities. Mawson recommended, among other things, the exploitation of Lewis as a tourist resort, particularly the development of facilities for loch and river fishing; the best ways to extract and use peat for fuel and horticulture, and the conversion of much of the rest of the peat lands into farmland and forest; the creation of an arboricultural business and the afforestation of large chunks of the island for profit, shelter and aesthetic appeal; the development of large-scale co-operative fruit growing, herb growing and beekeeping; the creation of osier beds to build up a basket-making industry; and the setting up of a scientifically controlled experimental garden to research into the growth of such products as New Zealand flax.[35] If he could achieve an unlikely success on the unpromising slopes at Rivington, in defiance of the sceptics, why not fantasize about creating a garden island, in defiance of the biting Atlantic winds and remorseless horizontal rain?

In one respect the Lever project turned out to be supremely successful. He incorporated the retail arm of his fish chain, Mac Fisheries, headquartered in London, in February 1919, and immediately opened his first fishmonger's in Richmond. By offering deals difficult to refuse, he rapidly bought up 400 of the top fishmongers' in the best positions in towns around the country and decked them out in a trademark smart blue-and-white decor. These shops, not remotely dependent on the trade from Harris and Lewis, were supplied by the Mac Fisheries line of trawlers operating out of Fleetwood and from fish markets around the country. He also began to acquire Billingsgate wholesale fish businesses and other allied companies dealing in appropriate food products, such as Angus Watson and Co.'s fish canning business (Skippers sardines and tinned salmon) in Newcastle, the Aberdeen Steam Trawling Company and the Helford Oysterage in Cornwall. A notable addition was Wall's sausages and ice cream. It was then customary to sell sausages in fishmongers', and Wall's had begun selling ice cream after the war because trade in sausages slackened in the summer. They had recently invented the 'Stop me and buy one' tricycle. All this, plus the entire venture in Harris and Lewis, was part of Lever's personal empire. Only in 1922 did he sell Mac Fisheries and the other food suppliers to Lever Brothers.[36]

His grand plans for Lewis, in contrast, constituted the biggest failure of his career, and for three reasons: the resistance of the crofters, the parlous state of his finances after the collapse of the bubble in 1920 and, most significantly, a gross overestimate of the potential of the local fishing industry. The first received most attention in earlier accounts, partly because of some vividly expressed and very quotable opposition. The history of the croft goes back no further than the late eighteenth and early nineteenth centuries, the period of the notorious highland clearances, when commercially minded 'improving landlords' sought to open up their land for the more extensive grazing of livestock and in the process displaced populations. Evicted people made for the lowland towns, emigrated, or moved to land close to the shoreline where they could rent a croft – a thin strip of land on which they could build a black house, grow vegetables and have access to common grazing land. A family could not subsist on a croft and had to supplement their earnings through additional, seasonal employment such as kelping or fishing.

It was a practice that persisted. In the inter-war period, husbands and sons would go line-fishing off the coast of Lewis in the early spring before returning to dig over the crofts and seed the potatoes and corn. They would join the herring fleet in the early summer but be home again by midsummer to harvest the crops. Late autumn they would be off again for more herring fishing. Then home and a period of relative inactivity. The only different note from earlier generations was that many of them belonged to the Fleet Reserve, and would report for a bout of training in a naval base every January. Throughout the year the wives would remain on the crofts, doing most of the everyday work, including digging peat for fuel and carrying it home in creels on their backs, while the daughters would travel with the herring fleets in the summer, all the way from Stornoway round the top of Scotland and down the east coast of England as far as Great Yarmouth, gutting, cleaning and packing the herrings.[37]

The black house was squat and windowless, built of rough stones filled in with earth or rubble, the roof made of sods covered with thatch. It provided a practical solution to a relatively treeless, windswept landscape. 'The only portions of the building where wood is employed are the rafters, doors and partitions,' one commentator noted in the 1920s. 'Low-lying and round-shouldered, it hugs the ground without an angle or a flat surface to catch the wind.' Inside, the space was usually divided into three: a living room, a bedroom and a byre for livestock. In the middle of the living room in the traditional black house was a peat fire, the smoke spiralling upwards towards a hole in the roof or simply percolating through the thatch. More recent variations contained a fireplace and chimney.[38] Halliday Sutherland, a doctor visiting Lewis after the First World War, reported that, while most of those living in the black houses carried head and body lice, the children were healthy, nourished on a wholesome, unadulterated diet of milk, potatoes, dried fish, salt herrings, oatmeal, butter and – very occasionally – meat.[39]

Nevertheless, the lifestyle appalled Lever. He was genuinely shocked that people should be living in such primitive conditions within the United Kingdom – 'they leave the people in houses *not fit for kaffirs!*'[40] If he could civilize savages, he could certainly do the same for Britons. He lacked the breadth of imagination to comprehend that any rational being might choose not to hitch a lift on the capitalist juggernaut, which to him was synonymous with progress; he was quite unable to grasp that some might prefer an alternative way of life to the regular employment, steady income and decent accommodation that he was offering.[41]

Why would they turn him down? It was a question of who was controlling whom, particularly who controlled the pace of work. As one old crofter explained to Dr Sutherland, his black house cost him £20 to build and he was rated at £20. This he and his brother and sister could afford to pay out of the patch of land they owned. 'We live all right.' If they moved into one of Lever's spanking new £400 houses, how could they afford to pay the rates? Not out of the land; 'there would be only one way: to answer a whistle at six in the morning and work for wages in Lever's factory. No damn fear. Poor as I am, I'm master here, and could order you off this croft.'[42] Lever was not dealing with the working classes of Lancashire and Cheshire, who had been trained, bullied and cajoled over the generations of industrialization to answer that factory bell or face the workhouse. He was confronting people who knew little about and cared less for time discipline, clocking on and the supervision of the overseer.

This explanation relies somewhat on caricature, though useful for rhetorical purposes. Many of the Lewis population were used to wage labour – the young women in the curing yards and with the herring fleet, for example – and few objected to earning wages from him by labouring on the roads or constructing his buildings.[43] He also promised not to disturb any crofter who preferred to keep his croft, merely refused to create new ones. And his plan was to modernize native industries, not to impose an outpost of Lancashire. 'I have found that the picture they have in their minds is one of huge iron-works, huge cotton-factories, machine-shops and so on,' he complained in a speech in the Masonic Hall, Stornoway, in June 1919. 'There is not a single word in any of my speeches to justify that idea.'[44]

It was partly the arrogance of a parvenu outsider telling them what to do that rankled. 'At the very moment when we have emerged from the greatest War in history, in the interests of liberty,' said J. L. Sturrock, Liberal MP for Montrose, in the House of Commons in 1919, 'he (Leverhulme) is taking it upon himself to tell these people … that their future lives are to be guided along the lines laid down, not by themselves, not in accordance with the traditions of their ancestors, but according to the dictates of a successful soap-boiler who has happened to buy that island.' But there were practical considerations as well. In the same parliamentary session, the local Liberal MP, Dr Donald Murray, pointed out that the people of Lewis 'are not such simple people as we look'. They had travelled. Some had fought in Flanders, others knew the fishing ports around the coast of Britain and Ireland. They were making an informed choice. 'They know what life is and they have sufficient common sense to know what is best for them,' said Murray, adding, 'I hope industrialisation as we find it today is not the last word in the expression of social life.'[45] Some of them simply did not find Lever's rose-coloured projections for the fishing industry credible – rightly, as it turned out – and wondered what would happen if the fisheries experienced a cyclical slump, the work force was laid off – and had no crofts to fall back on.[46] Or, indeed, what would happen after he died. Even if his successors did not cut and run, would they proceed with the same energy and commitment?[47]

Lever failed to appreciate the psychological significance of the croft and the importance of the rights that the crofters had won. In response to the so-called Crofters' Wars of the 1880s – a combination of land raiding and rent strikes with political lobbying by the Highland Land Law Reform Association – the government set up a Royal Commission into the condition of crofters and cottars, followed by legislation. The Crofters' Holdings (Scotland) Act of 1886, mirroring legislation in Ireland to try and settle the far more troublesome Land Wars there, promised fair rents (to be fixed by a land court), security of tenure (so that tenants could not be booted out at the whim of the landlord, provided they paid the rent), compensation on departure for any improvements to the croft made by the tenant and the right to bequeath the tenancy to a relative. This was an unprecedented statutory incursion into landlords' rights, but it did nothing to assuage the land hunger of the cottars, the descendants of those who had lost their land during the clearances and who could still be found in large numbers in the Hebrides.

A low-level campaign of nocturnal violence and civil disobedience continued, perpetuated by endemic poverty, miserable housing and the demand for land. Beyond policing measures, successive governments attempted to improve matters by assisting emigration, by making limited attempts to develop the local infrastructure and, critically, by setting up the Congested Districts Board in 1897. This board was tasked with alleviating the problems of overpopulation, partly by creating new crofts and enlarging others. But it had a limited budget and had to wait for properties to come on the market because it had no compulsory purchase powers, so in its fifteen-year existence it created just 640 new holdings. Sporadic land raiding by cottars in the Outer Hebrides continued.[48]

The buck passed to the newly created Board of Agriculture for Scotland, which, under the terms of the Small Landholders (Scotland) Act, 1911, designated six Lewis farms for settlement by cottars. Duncan Matheson, the proprietor, had split up two farms under the Congested Districts Board, but stonewalled over further redistribution, and the onset of the First World War froze any further progress. Still, expectations had been raised that the government, armed with its new powers of compulsory purchase of large farms, would deliver. The government had clearly indicated that it favoured some degree of land distribution and gave every indication during the war that it would not only provide houses for heroes but also land for heroes.[49] Many Lewismen who answered their country's call and fought in the trenches or on the high seas were convinced that their country owed them, that their blood sacrifice had added a further moral claim to the land.

Lever did not understand this mountain of expectation: the deep and long-felt yearning for the land and the independence it promised. There was no reason why he could not pursue his schemes and allow the subdivision of the farms at the same time; the two were not incompatible, particularly since (as he frequently pointed out) the land available could meet only a fraction of the demand. If all the remaining large farms were broken up, only around 350 new crofts of about six acres each could be provided, whereas the demand was for 2,000–3,000 new crofts; those unsatisfied would still have to find alternatives, or emigrate. He repeatedly argued that he needed to keep the farms intact to provide sufficient milk for his expanding work force, but this was scarcely true: more milk could easily be shipped in from the mainland at only a marginally additional cost.[50] The deeper reason was that he found the idea of the croft offensive. As he had vowed in 1918 to Sir Robert Greig, Chairman of the Board of Agriculture, he would 'oppose to my last breath and last penny all the attempts to perpetuate the present degrading conditions of the crofter's home and life that is rapidly bringing consumption and enfeeblement on one of the finest races of people the world today possesses.'[51] He was determined to be the arbiter of what was good for the people: not what they wanted but what they *should* want.

Lever had been popular on Lewis when he bought the island. His reputation preceded him and his promises of improvements and prosperity greatly appealed. A rhymester was only half joking when he or she wrote:

I tell you, lad, the place will be
The garden of the west,
The northern Venice by the sea,
With milk and honey blest.
Geraniums growing in the glens,
An' gold-fish in the burns,
An' Sunlight medals for the hens
That show the best returns.[52]

A vulgarian Sassenach in Gaeldom

Civil servants, on the other hand, began to grow concerned at an early date about what Lever was telling them. Thomas Wilson, senior sub-commissioner for the region, wrote to the chairman of the Board of Agriculture in September 1918, after meeting with Lever:

> He has great admiration for the Lewis people, who have done such great and noble service for the Country in the War, and I think feels he should do what he can for them. His whole life, however, has been industrial, and I question if his experience of three months among the Lewis people has taught him their sentiments or desires. He does not realize that they will never feel satisfied until the farms in Lewis are divided into Holdings and given to them. The Lewisman is not by sentiment, tradition or inclination at all inclined to become a Factory-hand, and the present race cannot be satisfied by industrial methods alone … What the Lewis man wants is a small piece of land for a house site, two cows grazing and potato and corn growing.[53]

In order to propagate his ideas, Lever charmed the leading people of the island with a series of dinners and entertainments at Lews Castle, and with a fair degree of success. But this did not prevent parties of disgruntled men, including ex-servicemen, from venting their anger at the lack of progress on land redistribution by recommencing land raiding in March 1919 – that is, squatting on, staking out and planting up land at Tong, Gress and Coll, farms to the north of Stornoway.[54] Lever decided to confront the raiders at a mass open-air meeting at Gress and to try and reason with them. Colin MacDonald, the man from the Board, was in attendance and, though his account is suspiciously melodramatic and no doubt embellished, it captured the flavour. Lever, the *Bodach an t-siapuinn* (wee soap-mannie), standing on an upturned tub in the middle of a thousand listeners, deployed all his superb theatrical and oratorical skills of voice, hand and eye to mesmerize his audience with 'the most graphic word-picture it is possible to imagine – a great fleet of fishing boats – another great fleet of cargo boats – a large fish canning factory (already started) – railways – an electric power station; then one could see the garden city grow – steady work, steady pay, beautiful houses for all – every modern convenience and comfort.' He contrasted their current insecurity and their squalid houses with this new earthly paradise. And he got his hostile audience cheering him, until one of the ringleaders burst the bubble by asking him, in Gaelic, '*Will you give us the land?*' No, said Lever, because my scheme will bring you greater prosperity and happiness. He began word-painting again, and got them cheering him again.

A crofter then spoke, in English, explaining to him that steady work and steady pay might be very desirable for those poor unfortunates in smoky towns, but on Lewis neither was necessary: 'We attend to our crofts in seed-time and harvest, and we follow the fishing in its season – and when neither requires our attention we are free to *rest and contemplate*.' Their houses might be hovels in his eyes, but they were their homes, where '*real human happiness*' could be found. 'Lord Leverhulme! You have bought this island. But you have not bought *us*, and we refuse to be the bond-slaves of any man. We want to live our own lives in our own way, poor in material things it may be, but at least it will be clear of the fear of the factory bell; it will be *free and independent!*'

Lever spoke again after the loud cheering had died down, regained the ear of the crowd, talked about how many of the young men had written to him asking when they could get a job and a new house in Stornoway and leave the croft behind; they wanted a brighter future for themselves, their wives and sweethearts. He left the meeting with the impression that he had won his audience over. MacDonald, correctly, was more sceptical. The land remained an impassable barrier to mutual accommodation. 'I shall *not* compromise,' Lever told him again and again. 'I *must* have control of my factory hands! How can I have that in the case of men who are in the independent position of crofters? … I will *not* compromise. I *must* control.'[55]

The raiders had occupied sixteen of the twenty-two farms on Lewis by the end of the summer. The Scottish Office and Robert Munro, the Scottish Secretary, were caught on the horns of a dilemma, eager to promote Lever's schemes and welcome his influx of capital but sympathetic to the extension of the crofts and aware that it would be politically inexpedient to renege on their commitment to land distribution. Even so, as Nigel Nicolson makes clear, it would be quite wrong to give the impression that Lever was universally viewed as an unwelcome and insensitive interloper rebuffed by the adamantine resistance of the Men of Lewis. Throughout the controversy, support for Lever came from meetings of crofters, official bodies on the island and the *Stornoway Gazette*. Ambivalence was key: admiration for the man, his projects and the construction jobs he had created, balanced against the totemic significance of the croft. And in the meantime, throughout 1919, the work continued on the canning factory, ice factory and power house in Stornoway, the new housing on the perimeter of the town and the building or improvement of roads across the island.[56]

In 1920 the struggle between Lever and the raiders, with the Scottish Office in the middle, continued. Lever took legal proceedings against the raiders and in March obtained the power to call upon the police to evict them. But Munro failed to give assurances that he would not use his powers to release them if they were imprisoned. This was the prelude to Lever's decision, in May, to suspend his works on the island. Public support swung strongly his way and against the raiders, now blaming their selfishness for the loss of his money and jobs. By the start of 1921 Lever seemed to have won. He had had to give some ground, allowing the break-up of farms at Uig and on the west coast. But the raiders had quit Coll and Gress in the autumn (based on vague talk from the government that this would advance their case for land redistribution), and the Scottish Secretary, following the well-nigh universal expression of public opinion on Lewis, had conceded that the government would observe a ten-year moratorium on compulsory land purchases and resettlement in order to give Lever's schemes a chance.

But at that juncture the most significant reasons for the failure of his schemes began to kick in: his financial difficulties and the dive in fish prices. At the mercy of his bankers, and close to bankruptcy, he even had to lay off most of his gardeners, foresters and gamekeepers in January and was only able to recommence his works in a markedly attenuated form by April. After the raiders reoccupied the land in Coll in May, Lever announced the complete shutdown of all his developments on Lewis and that he would be concentrating his efforts on Harris. A number of commentators suspect that he used the renewed raiding merely as a pretext to cover his dignity as he was forced to pull out. Maybe so, and there are obvious reasons why he would steer clear of publicly acknowledging Lever Brothers' financial difficulties. Still, it is not immediately apparent why he would consider capitulation to the raiders a lesser humiliation.[57]

The post-war fishing industry was in trouble. Before the war, salt-cured herring had been the Stornoway staple, but this declined rapidly in the post-war years – it was seen as the poor man's fish, and with an increase of prosperity people deserted it for white fish and for meat – and it never recovered. The war had artificially boosted demand for fish as a source of protein, but the end of the war saw not only renewed competition from other foods but also the dismantling of naval blockades and a return to a free-for-all on the high seas. North Sea and Baltic countries encroached on the British fishing trade; fishing fleets from the east coast of Scotland trawled around Hebridean waters; a trade embargo against the new Soviet Union hit the herring trade; even, it is said, prohibition in America reduced demand for salted herrings, once a standard in saloon bars. The sociologist Arthur Geddes estimated that the island herring catch fell by a half in 1920–21, prices by 60 per cent. Lever's assessment when he made his plans at the top of the market in 1917–18 that pouring money into the fishing industry would reap a rich return came up against the cruel reality that consumption of herring and white fish had fallen off and that the competition for the catch had grown. For the Lewismen this was all the more reason to cling to their crofts.[58]

Amidst his fulminations against the raiders and the Scottish Office, Lever made a rare public concession to underlying economic realities in a speech at the Stornoway Highland Games on 31 August 1921:

> Three years ago it was mutually accepted that our relations would be strictly on a business basis – that there should be no odious taint of philanthropy to lower ourselves in each other's esteem. No one regrets more than myself that the canning factory, the fish products and the ice companies cannot be opened for work. But the conditions of supply and demand in these industries make it impossible to do so. These businesses could only make heavy losses if they operated at present, and we must wait patiently for world markets to be cleared of surplus stocks before prices will adjust themselves to the costs of production.[59]

On reading this, Munro immediately wrote to Lever that the government no longer felt obliged to observe the ten-year moratorium and that it would proceed to implement land resettlement. In the spring of 1922 the Board of Agriculture finally completed the purchase of the farms at Coll, Gress, Tolsta and Orinsay, dividing them into 180 new crofts and enlarging eighty-one existing crofts.[60]

The thesis that market forces defeated Lever is compelling but not entirely satisfactory. It is indeed difficult to imagine that Lever would have pulled the plug on his entire operation on Lewis just because of some small farms that were not essential to his schemes. Logically, for a business brain like his, one might expect the fact to have sunk in that price fluctuations in the fishing industry could not create the stability he needed for his projects, even if the market picked up. And yet there are a number of inconsistencies. He did not abandon fishing. In 1922, when business improved, he could have resumed on Lewis, perhaps in a whittled-down form. But he chose instead to move his operations to the less promising Harris, as we shall see. All this suggests, Nigel Nicolson argues, that the crofting issue was *not* just a cover, and that Lever mistakenly thought it was crucial. In other words, Lever's increasingly unbalanced judgement and pride need to be factored in to any explanation.[61]

Lever half-seriously contemplated restarting his schemes on Lewis as late as the summer of 1923. This shall-I-shan't-I did not endear him to the islanders, particularly since the suspension of his schemes had entailed the loss of several thousand jobs. With the dire state of the fishing industry producing genuine distress and destitution, young islanders once again opted for a traditional remedy: emigration resumed in April 1923, with the first batch of 300 embarking for Canada. Still, Lever's assumption of the title Viscount Leverhulme of the Western Isles in 1922 generated more outrage on the Scottish mainland than on the island, because it rather flattered the people of Harris and Lewis. To the rest it seemed to be entirely presumptuous for the son of a Bolton grocer to take a title rather close to the Lord of the Isles (held by the Prince of Wales) and to trample on the dignity of the clan chiefs of the other Hebridean islands. 'The sway of the vulgarian Sassenach in Gaeldom is increasing,' wrote one commentator. 'As well might a crofter, having bought a bar of Sunlight soap, term himself "of Port Sunlight", as the chairman of the Company having bought one of our 300 islands in the Hebrides style himself "of the Western Isles".'[62]

Lever's attention had switched to Harris, to his home there, Borve Lodge, and to his plans to develop Leverburgh. He had decided to leave Lewis but realized it would be difficult to find a buyer – and besides, he saw the opportunity to make a magnanimous gesture and a political point. In a speech in Stornoway Town Council Chambers on 3 September 1923 he offered Lewis to its people: Lews Castle (to become the town hall), the grounds (to be renamed Lady Lever Park) and the farms and sporting lodges in the parish of Stornoway to be administered by a Stornoway Trust; the farms and lodges on the rest of Lewis to be run by a second trust; and the crofts to be offered as gifts to their tenants. That was the magnanimous gesture. The political point was to the crofters and the outflanked Scottish Office. 'The industrial schemes I had are impossible side by side with crofting,' he wrote to a Bolton friend. 'I think there is nothing that will bring this home to the people better than owning the island themselves and seeing what they can do with the island without industrial employment.'[63]

Only the Stornoway town council took the offer, calculating that there would be sufficient revenue generated from the likes of the farms, the lodges and the gasworks to pay the trust's outgoings. The Lewis district committee rejected the offer for the second trust, because there was no guarantee that the books could be balanced and every prospect that the trust would rapidly become insolvent. And only forty-one out of over 3,000 crofters accepted the gift, mainly because as independent proprietors the owners' rates would fall on them and not the landlord, so they would be financially much worse off, and because they would lose many of the hard-won rights of the tenant crofter, such as the right to compensation for improvements if they quit the croft. Lever, disappointed, put the rest of his estate on the market in lots, only sold a portion (at a low price) and was stuck with the rest until he died.

All of this retreat from Lewis took an emotional toll. He described the day he announced his intention to leave as 'one of the two saddest days in his life, the other being the day he lost his dear wife'. The last time he visited Lewis, in September 1924, was to unveil the war memorial, a great five-storey tower largely designed and built at his own expense. After the ceremony he went with Kenneth Maciver, the son of a close friend, to the canning factory, which had never produced a single can but was now being dismantled for shipment and reinstallation at Leverburgh. This is how Nicolson describes it, presumably drawing on a first-hand conversation with Maciver:

> The two men stood there in the dark, Leverhulme a little ahead of his companion. Maciver suddenly saw the outline of the great shoulders trembling with sobs. Neither said a word to the other. They walked back along the quay, and shook hands at the foot of the gangway. Leverhulme never saw the Hebrides again.[64]

Ozymandias of Bolton

This would be a nice way to end the chapter, on a melancholic note, evoking a hint of regret, a twinge of sympathy for a rich man whose success, by now, we have come to expect. Here is another poignant anecdote for those so inclined. A few months later, on his return from his voyage to West Africa, the ship's captain asked him to choose and read a lesson. He selected *Ecclesiastes* 2:4:

> I made me great works: I builded me houses; I planted me vineyards. ... I made me gardens and orchards, and I planted trees in them of all *kinds of* fruit ... I got *me* servants. ... I gathered me also silver and gold. ... So I was great ... for my heart rejoiced in all my labour. ... Then I looked on all the works that my hands had wrought, and on the labour that I had laboured to do: and, behold, all *was* vanity and vexation of spirit, and *there was* no profit under the sun.

Andrew Knox, the source for this story, interpreted it as the choice not of an arrogant tycoon but of a tired, lonely old man who had recently encountered the failure of one of his ventures for the first time and whose business was only just pulling out of very rough waters.[65] Such an interpretation supports a satisfying narrative trajectory: self-made man builds plutocratic wealth and power but, just before he is consumed by them, remembers the still small voice of God reminding him that all worldly wealth is vanity, vanity: 'What shall it profit a man, if he gain the whole world, and lose his own soul?'[66] In the end riches could not buy happiness, and Lever grasped for the real faith that had hitherto eluded him. (At last, one might suggest, he understood the 'vanitas vanitatum, omnia vanitas' message of W. P. Frith's *New Frock*, which he had erased for passing commercial advantage back in the 1880s (see chapter two).)

Satisfying maybe, but probably quite misleading, and an indication of how biographers, in their hubristic attempts to capture the life, essence and complexities of an individual in a few thousand words of manipulatively crafted prose, are at the mercy of stray wisps of evidence. On that Stornoway quayside Lever did not know it was going to be his last trip to the Hebrides, nor when he chose that passage from *Ecclesiastes* that his time was nearly up. After pulling out of Lewis the previous year he had not remained becalmed in a sea of self-pity for long, nor did he seem to dwell on his failure. He strode ahead with his other projects with full enthusiasm. One of them was Harris. There, said his son, 'Leverhulme's optimism and determination were not merely restored – they were intensified.' There he enjoyed 'some of the happiest hours of his life.'[67]

The population of Harris, at under 5,000, was about a seventh the size of Lewis's, the problem of land congestion less acute, the potential of new crofts less apparent. So, although there was some limited raiding, it never assumed the same proportions as on Lewis and the population tended to be hostile to the raiders and behind Lever. That is why, when he decided to withdraw from Lewis, he applied himself to extending his Harris schemes with gusto. He gave up on Lewis, not on his plans to harvest the Hebridean seas to supply his new fish shops. He had no grand schemes for light railways or Beaux-Arts town planning or fruit farms; simply for developing the fishing and tweed-weaving industries. The landscape was too rugged and barren for anything more adventurous.

He had chosen Obbe on the south coast as the place to build a new harbour, and he renamed it Leverburgh, apparently at the instigation of the locals. It was an unwise choice of site because of the treacherous currents of the rock-strewn approaches, but he overrode local knowledge and warnings, believing that dynamiting some rocks and putting gas beacons on others would suffice. His initial thinking, before he abandoned Lewis, was that while boats out of Stornoway fished the Minch, boats from Obbe would have ready access to Atlantic waters. Both harbours would supply the Mac Fisheries operation at Fleetwood. The harbour never progressed beyond a stone jetty and wooden piers, but close by he also built curing and packing sheds, a kippering house and a refrigeration plant. Several of the buildings were in fact transported from Stornoway after he halted his operations there. He finished off the ensemble with separate dormitories for male and female workers and began to construct a few terraces of housing, a smattering of detached houses for managers and a public building, Hulme Hall.

His most important and lasting legacy was the extension and improvement of the rudimentary road system across Harris. He shared the costs for this with the government, and the wages for labourers were particularly significant during the hard winter of 1923–24 when the fishing and the potatoes failed. On North Harris he attempted to stimulate the tweed industry by building a carding and spinning mill at Geocrab, but the islanders resisted it, insisting that genuine Harris tweed had to be home-spun as well as home-woven.[68]

Lever's whaling operations were no more successful. He bought the whaling station at Bunaveneader on Harris in 1922 from a Norwegian company, plus three Norwegian whaling vessels the following year. After he had extracted the oil for his soap, his initial idea was to make sausages out of the meat, stuff them in cans and ship them to Africa to feed his Congolese work force. 'As whalemeat is rather tough, it will improve the possibilities of mastication,' he wrote to Sir Herbert Morgan in August 1922. 'The native is not an epicure, so long as it is good wholesome food.' After experimentation, he wrote to him again the following year that the meat was hard (too hard, presumably, even for one concerned about African chewing deficiencies) and the watery juice very unpleasant. 'I do not think it would really pay to can it even for Africans.' He decided to smoke the whalemeat instead, and constructed a shed at Leverburgh on Harris for the purpose.[69]

He followed through on his conviction and went so far as to offer samples of this meat during his final trip to the Congo in 1924. He recorded in his diary that after he had watched twenty-five men in a canoe giving a paddling demonstration, and then taking him for a short ride, he 'Treated the crew to a bag of salt and some whalemeat – latter they liked immediately.'[70] On the same trip he wrote to a priest at the Kikwit mission about Leverburgh, 'where I hope to be able to catch and smoke fish and also prepare whale meat salted dried and smoked for the Congo'. He enclosed a cutting on Leverburgh from *The Times*, and commented:

> You will note that the race of Jeremiah prophesying disaster is not yet extinct, and doubt is being thrown on the success of Leverburgh as in the early days doubt was thrown on the success of Leverville. We did not expect success to be achieved immediately at Leverville and similarly we do not expect success to be achieved immediately at Leverburgh in Scotland, but Leverburgh is very favourably situated in Harris ... for fishing in the Atlantic and for getting large quantities of whales from which we get oil for soapmaking and, we hope, whale flesh for sending out to the natives in the Congo. Scientists tell us that the flesh of the whale is more nourishing than beef, and certainly the small supply of whale meat we brought with us has met with a very gratifying reception from those natives we have had the opportunity of giving pieces to as samples.[71]

Eccentric as this sounds, it exemplified Lever's eagerness to fully maximize his resources and to have a free flow of materials and products across his multiple interests. He had two whaling fleets, he extracted the whale oil for his soap, was he going to let the whalemeat go to waste? Selling it on the British market seemed a non-starter, but maybe the Congolese would be more receptive (and would have less choice)? Crazy or visionary? For centuries Europeans had been transporting improbable products vast distances (spices from Asia, tobacco from the New World); Lever was operating in an era of globalization where it was routine to carry commodities like beef, refrigerated or canned, from Argentina to Britain. So whalemeat from the Outer Hebrides to West Africa? Well, why not? At least, so thought Lever; but, as soon as he died, Lever Brothers closed down these operations, a pointed commentary on what D'Arcy Cooper and the other directors thought about the idea.

Lever did not go in for canning at Leverburgh, but wrapped his kippers in cellophane and had reasonable success with them in his fish shops. In the summer of 1924, for the one and only time, his dream of supplying his own fish from his own harbour to his own shops came true, even if it only entailed one refrigerated ship on the run between Leverburgh and Fleetwood and even if it accounted for only a miniscule portion of Mac Fisheries' daily needs.[72] But the dream died with him. D'Arcy Cooper and the other directors closed the works on Harris and sold everything off with insulting rapidity, a clear indication of how fanciful and uneconomic they believed the entire venture to be. The second viscount may have been disposed to continue out of filial loyalty if not conviction, but he did not have the clout or charisma of his father, was sidelined in the direction of Lever Brothers and did not have the personal resources to soldier on alone on Harris because of the substantial death duties that he had to pay on his father's estate.

Looked at in terms of what he set out to achieve – the transformation of a people and their culture – Lever's Hebridean swan song was a dismal failure. He had spent nearly £1.5 million of his own money, according to one estimate, and when all that could be sold was knocked down to the auctioneer's hammer his estate recovered just £55,000. A demolition company, for example, bought for £5,000 the Leverburgh port installations that had cost him a quarter of a million.[73] A number of accounts expatiate elegiacally while surveying the wreckage of his dreams – the abandoned, half-built factory, the derelict narrow-gauge railway, the rusting machinery, the skeletons of works beside the quay, the wreck of a coal steamer.[74] Nigel Nicolson in 1960 commented that there was no memorial to him on Lewis or Harris: 'his work is known only by its ruins. The port of Leverburgh is a waste of concrete foundations; at Geocrab his machinery lies rusting in a corner; the Tolsta road has deteriorated to a cart-track; the remaining bay of the canning-factory is used for spinning wool; even the indestructible Arnish road ends forlornly in a cul-de-sac.' He asked, 'How could £1,400,000 have been spent to so little effect?'[75]

Only fragments of Lever's presence remain today: a few of the managers' houses and Hulme Hall, now part of a school, at Leverburgh; the war memorial at Stornoway, plus a number of semi-detached houses, harbingers of the garden city that never was; the ruins of the whaling station at Bunaveneadar; the so-called Leverhulme Bridge on the 'road to nowhere' – the road to Tolsta, petering out on the moorland, that he started but never finished. Borve Lodge is still there, a private residence. Lews Castle is a shell. It never became the town hall for Stornoway. For a time it was rented out to shooting-and-fishing sportsmen, then became a technical college after the war. Today it lies derelict and boarded up, but there are plans afoot to turn it into 'a high quality hotel with function suites' (shades of Thornton Manor), with a new Lewis museum on the site of the former conservatories.[76]

There is no mention of him in the Stornoway Museum. The name Leverburgh has been removed from road signs on the way in to the village, replaced by the Gaelic name, An t-Ob. The one invocation of his memory on the island is not flattering: artist Will Maclean's 'Memorial to the Heroes of the District' that commemorates the meeting between Lever and the raiders in March 1919. 'The central structure is symbolic of Lord Leverhulme's attempts to fracture the crofting community,' the signboard reads, rather unfairly. 'The earthworks represent the forms of trenches and waves, symbols of the pledges given to ex-servicemen that they would be settled on the land after the Great War.' The visitor is left in no doubt that this was a heroic victory, and that 'the people won the right to the land'.

On Lewis and Harris, as at Rivington, one man's attempts to conquer nature, time and human recalcitrance appear distinctly ephemeral. Roger Hutchinson yields to the understandable temptation to recall Shelley's poem about Ozymandias of Egypt, whose statue lies shattered in the desert, with the legend still legible on the pedestal:

> My name is Ozymandias, king of kings:
> Look on my works, ye Mighty, and despair![77]

This is, of course, unjust. *Si monumentum requiris*, look at the extent of the Unilever empire, walk through Port Sunlight, visit the Lady Lever Art Gallery, or trace the scholarship supported by the Leverhulme Trust with money that he bequeathed. Even his failure paid unexpected dividends. Mac Fisheries and its allied companies were to become part of the Unilever combine. As W. J. Reader puts it, 'Unilever thus found itself with a substantial stake in the food industries as a result of the failure of William Lever's plans to find occupation for himself in retirement: one of the more surprising results of the impact of a strong personality on big business.'[78] He had made himself fishmonger as well as soapboiler to the nation, taking advantage of times and ideologies peculiarly propitious for such a phenomenon to emerge. He left behind a concern with 187,000 shareholders and 85,000 employees (60,000 white, 25,000 black).[79] Not bad for a grocer's boy from Bolton.

So: a tale of local boy made good, after all? In a biography with the avowed intent of normalizing its subject – neither deifying nor demonizing but reducing him to human proportions – this, too, is scarcely a satisfactory ending. Biographers all too easily become mesmerized by their central character. Lever was an extremely interesting man in many respects, living a tremendously energetic life, but he was not somehow 'ahead of his time' (whatever such a logical impossibility may mean). To the contrary, he was deeply embedded in his time, sharing many of its mannerisms, characteristics and prejudices, bounded by its restrictions, permissions and possibilities. As a social historian I have used Lever's life as an entry-point for discussion of a raft of topics as diverse as the 'second consumer revolution', the transition to a corporate economy, the development of advertising, factory paternalism, town planning and suburbanization, colonialism and forced labour in West Africa and the South Pacific, country houses, landscape gardening and art collecting, and even the transformation of crofting and fishing in the Outer Hebrides. The single life has given focus to the social, economic and cultural history of his era, and the larger scope in turn has shown the significance of the particular life and its continuing reverberations up to the present. Placed in context, the Old Man's life and his quest for 'civilization' are so much *more* – and more interesting – than the story of one individual.

Notes

1 UARM, LBC 114, Lever to John Hope, 10 December 1914.
2 Quoted by Mrs Stuart Menzies, *Modern Men of Mark* (London: Herbert Jenkins, 1921), p. 171.
3 William Hulme Lever [second Viscount Leverhulme], *Viscount Leverhulme* (Boston, MA, and New York: Houghton Mifflin, 1927), pp. 185–90.
4 UARM, LBC 118A, Lever to A. P. van Geelkerken (head of Lever's Dutch business in Rotterdam), 23 August 1915, 12 July 1916 (quotation).
5 UARM, LBC 118A, Lever to van Geelkerken, 28 December 1914 (first quotation), 27 February 1917 (second quotation), 7 March 1918 (third quotation).
6 UARM, LBC 8362B, *Bubbles*, 4 (January 1919).
7 Charles Wilson, *The History of Unilever: A Study in Economic Growth and Social Change*, vol. I (London: Cassell and Co., 1954), pp. 250–8; Lever, *Leverhulme*, pp. 224–6.
8 UARM, LBC 7161, Henry Bell to Lever, 4 August 1920; Lever to Barchard, 22 August.
9 D. K. Fieldhouse, *Unilever Overseas: The Anatomy of a Multinational 1895–1965* (London: Croom Helm, 1978), pp. 31–2, 34; Wilson, *Unilever*, pp. 261–2, 269–75; Lever, *Leverhulme*, pp. 222–3, 227–8; Roger Hutchinson, *The Soap Man: Lewis, Harris and Lord Leverhulme* (Edinburgh: Birlinn, 2003), p. 114.
10 D. C. Coleman, 'Historians and businessmen', pp. 27–8, 32, and W. J. Reader, 'Businessmen and their motives', pp. 50–1, in D. C. Coleman and Peter Mathias (eds), *Enterprise and History: Essays in Honour of Charles Wilson* (Cambridge: Cambridge University Press, 1984); W. J. Reader, 'Lever, William Hesketh', in David J. Jeremy (ed.), *Dictionary of Business Biography: A Biographical Diction-ary of Business Leaders Active in Britain in the Period 1860–1980*, vol. III (London: Butterworths, 1985), p. 750.
11 Andrew M. Knox, *Coming Clean: A Postscript after Retirement from Unilever* (London: Heinemann, 1976), p. 45.
12 Lever, *Leverhulme*, p. 179.
13 *Ibid.*, p. 176.
14 *Parliamentary Debates*, Lords, 5th Ser., 33, col. 193 (19 February 1919); UARM, LBC 9485, Lever to Sir Herbert Morgan, 29 April 1921.
15 *Manchester Guardian*, 8 May 1925, in BALS, B920 B LEV, newspaper cuttings on Lever.

16 UARM, LBC 4271, Myrtle Huband to Lever, 3 March, 10 March 1919.
17 See the correspondence in UARM, LBC 4271. The last quotation is in a letter of March 1925.
18 Quoted by Lever, *Leverhulme*, p. 246.
19 Knox, *Coming Clean*, p. 25.
20 Wilson, *Unilever*, pp. 275–6.
21 UARM, LBC 8104D, Lever to Greenhalgh, 26 April 1923.
22 Quoted by W. S. Adams, *Edwardian Portraits* (Secker and Warburg, 1957), p. 170.
23 UARM, LBC 8104D, Lever to Greenhalgh, 13 August 1923.
24 Michael Holroyd, *Augustus John: A Biography*, vol. II: *The Years of Experience* (London: Heinemann, 1975), pp. 98–100 (Lever and John quotations p. 98; *Manchester Guardian* quotation p. 99); Augustus John, *Chiaroscuro: Fragments of Autobiography: First Series* (London: Jonathan Cape, 1952), pp. 150–1; Lever, *Leverhulme*, p. 280; Harley Williams, *Men of Stress: Three Dynamic Interpretations: Woodrow Wilson, Andrew Carnegie, William Hesketh Lever* (London: Jonathan Cape, 1948), pp. 307–9.
25 Bruce Arnold, *Orpen: Mirror to an Age* (London: Jonathan Cape, 1981), p. 395; Lever, *Leverhulme*, p. 283.
26 T. M. Devine, *Clanship to Crofters' Wars: The Social Transformation of the Scottish Highlands* (Manchester: Manchester University Press, 1994), pp. 81–2.
27 Nigel Nicolson, *Lord of the Isles* (Stornoway: Acair, 2000; 1st edn, 1960), pp. 22, 49–51, 122; *Bolton Evening News*, 7 May 1925, in BALS, B920 B LEV, newspaper cuttings on Lever; John R. Gold and Margaret M. Gold, 'To be free and independent: crofting, popular protest and Lord Leverhulme's Hebridean development projects 1917–1925', *Rural History*, 7:2 (1996), 195.
28 Emily Macdonald, *Twenty Years of Hebridean Memories* (Paisley: Alexander Gardner, 1965; 1st edn, 1939), pp. 39, 42–4, 59; Hutchinson, *Soap Man*, pp. 137–8; Nicolson, *Lord of the Isles*, pp. 59–63, 66.
29 UARM, LBC 8104D, Lever to Greenhalgh, 26 April 1923.
30 Lever, *Leverhulme*, pp. 208–211 (quotation p. 208).
31 Colin Macdonald, *Highland Memories* (Edinburgh and London: Moray Press, 1949), p. 154.
32 Hutchinson, *Soap Man*, pp. 90–2; Nicolson, *Lord of the Isles*, chap. 4.
33 *Daily Chronicle* (24 January 1919), quoted by Nicolson, *Lord of the Isles*, p. 76.
34 Gold and Gold, 'To be free and independent', pp. 198–9; Nicolson, *Lord of the Isles*, chap. 5; Lever, *Leverhulme*, pp. 212–13.
35 Thomas H. Mawson, *The Life and Work of an English Landscape Architect: An Autobiography* (New York: Charles Scribner's Sons, 1927), pp. 303–4.
36 Nicolson, *Lord of the Isles*, p. 99; Wilson, *Unilever*, pp. 261–2, 274–5; Hutchinson, *Soap Man*, pp. 114–15.
37 Halliday Sutherland, *The Arches of the Years* (London: Geoffrey Bles, 1933), p. 285; Lever, *Leverhulme*, p. 210.
38 George Gibson, *Caledonian Medical Journal* (August 1924), 208, quoted by Sutherland, *Arches of the Years*, p. 288; Lever, *Leverhulme*, p. 210.
39 Sutherland, *Arches of the Years*, pp. 289–90.

40 Quoted by Arthur Geddes, *The Isle of Lewis and Harris: A Study in British Community* (Edinburgh: Edinburgh University Press, 1955), p. 257.

41 See Macdonald, *Highland Memories*, pp. 149, 151.

42 Sutherland, *Arches of the Years*, p. 291.

43 Nicolson, *Lord of the Isles*, pp. 240–1.

44 Quoted by Nicolson, *Lord of the Isles*, p. 125.

45 *Hansard*, Scottish Estimates, 4 August 1919, quoted by Joni Buchanan, *The Lewis Land Struggle* (Stornoway: Acair, 1996), p. 104.

46 Buchanan, *Lewis Land Struggle*, pp. 120–1; Colin MacDonald, *Highland Journey* (Edinburgh and London: Moray Press, 1943), p. 144; Geddes, *Lewis and Harris*, p. 267.

47 Hutchinson, *Soap Man*, p. 150.

48 Devine, *Clanship to Crofters' War*, pp. 220–1, 228–9, 233–9; Leah Leneman, *Fit for Heroes? Land Settlement in Scotland after World War I* (Aberdeen: Aberdeen University Press, 1989), pp. 1–2.

49 Gold and Gold, 'To be free and independent', p. 194; Leneman, *Fit for Heroes?*, pp. 117–18.

50 Geddes, *Lewis and Harris*, pp. 169–70; Buchanan, *Lewis Land Struggle*, pp. 102–4; Nicolson, *Lord of the Isles*, pp. 130–2.

51 Scottish Record Office, AF/83, Lever to Greig, October 1918, quoted by Buchanan, *Lewis Land Struggle*, p. 98.

52 'R.J.M.', 'A letter from Lewis', first published in the *Glasgow Evening News* and reprinted in *Progress* (April 1918), quoted by Nicolson, *Lord of the Isles*, p. 53.

53 Scottish Record Office, AF83/354, letter of 26 September 1918, quoted by Leneman, *Fit for Heroes?*, pp. 118–19.

54 Leneman, *Fit for Heroes?*, p. 119.

55 MacDonald, *Highland Journey*, pp. 141–9, 157 (first quotation p. 143, second p. 144, third p. 146, fourth p. 149, fifth p. 157).

56 Nicolson, *Lord of the Isles*, pp. 136–51, 178.

57 Buchanan, *Lewis Land Struggle*, pp. 116–23; Hutchinson, *Soap Man*, pp. 165, 167; Geddes, *Harris and Lewis*, pp. 264, 267; Nicolson, *Lord of the Isles*, pp. 151–73; Gold and Gold, 'To be free and independent', pp. 202–3; Leneman, *Fit for Heroes?*, pp. 120–2; Lever, *Leverhulme*, pp. 215–18.

58 Hutchinson, *Soap Man*, pp. 155–8; Louis MacNeice, *I Crossed the Minch* (London: Longman Green and Co., 1938), pp. 40–1; Geddes, *Harris and Lewis*, pp. 263, 265–6; Nicolson, *Lord of the Isles*, pp. 242–5.

59 *Stornoway Gazette*, 9 September 1921, quoted by Nicolson, *Lord of the Isles*, p. 174. See also *The Times*, 2 September 1921, p. 8.

60 Hutchinson, *Soap Man*, p. 168; Nicolson, *Lord of the Isles*, pp. 175–6.

61 Nicolson, *Lord of the Isles*, pp. 178–82.

62 *Ibid.*, pp. 183–91; A. G. Paisley, *Wanderings in the Western Highland and Islands*, preface, quoted by Nicolson, *Lord of the Isles*, p. 188.

63 Lever to George Crowther, 6 September 1923, quoted by Nicolson, *Lord of the Isles*, p. 198.

64 Nicolson, *Lord of the Isles*, pp. 191–205 (first quotation p. 196, quoting A. M. Fletcher; second quotation p. 205); Geddes, *Harris and Lewis*, pp. 275–6; Hutch-

inson, *Soap Man*, pp. 199–215.

65 Knox, *Coming Clean*, p. 79.

66 Angus Watson, *My Life: An Autobiography* (London: Ivor Nicholson and Watson, 1937), p. 170.

67 Lever, *Leverhulme*, p. 221.

68 Nicolson, *Lord of the Isles*, chap. 9; Lever, *Leverhulme*, pp. 220–1.

69 Quoted by Nicolson, *Lord of the Isles*, pp. 219–20.

70 Quoted by Andrew West, 'The history of the ethnography collections of W. H. Lever', in Edward Morris (ed.), *Art and Business in Edwardian England: The Making of the Lady Lever Art Gallery* (Oxford: Oxford University Press, 1992, reprinted from the *Journal of the History of Collections*, 4:2 (1992)), 279.

71 UARM, LBC 5677, Lever to Rev. Father Allard, 27 November 1924. See also LBC 8104F, Lever to Greenhalgh, 31 December 1924.

72 Nicolson, *Lord of the Isles*, p. 228.

73 *Ibid.*, pp. 232–7.

74 Sutherland, *Arches of the Years*, pp. 285, 293; Geddes, *Lewis and Harris*, p. 264.

75 Nicolson, *Lord of the Isles*, p. 242.

76 See the Lews Castle Trust website, www.lews-castle.com (accessed 17 July 2007).

77 Hutchinson, *Soap Man*, p. 227.

78 Reader, 'Lever, William Hesketh', pp. 749–50.

79 Lever, *Leverhulme*, p. 318; Wilson, *Unilever*, p. 290.

Select bibliography

Archival sources

Bolton Archives and Local Studies: Lever Papers; newspaper cuttings on Lever.
London School of Economics, British Library of Political and Economic Science: Morel Papers.
Unilever Archives and Records Management, Port Sunlight: Lever Business Correspondence; Small Deposits Collection.
University of Liverpool, Special Collections and Archives, Sydney Jones Library: Vice-Chancellors' Papers; F. E. Hyde Papers.

Primary sources

Abercrombie, Patrick. 'Modern town planning in England: a comparative review of "garden city" schemes in England', *Town Planning Review*, 1:1 (April 1910); 'Modern town planning', part II, *Town Planning Review*, 1:2 (July 1910).
The Art Collections of the late Viscount Leverhulme: To be Sold by Order of the Executors. New York: The Anderson Galleries, 1926.
Beable, William Henry. *Romance of Great Businesses*. London: Heath Cranton, 1926.
Begbie, Harold ['A Gentleman with a Duster']. *The Mirrors of Downing Street: Some Political Reflections*. London: Mills and Boon, 1920.
Bernays, Edward L. *Propaganda*. Port Washington, NY: Kennikat Press, 1972; 1st edn, 1928.
Birkenhead, Earl of [F. E. Smith]. *Contemporary Personalities*. London: Cassell and Co., 1924.
Booth, William. *In Darkest England and the Way Out*. London: 1890.
Bryson, Bill. *Notes from a Small Island*. Toronto: Minerva Canada, 1996.
Buell, Raymond Leslie. *The Native Problem in Africa*. New York: Macmillan, 1928.
The Bungalow, Rivington: auction catalogue, 1925.
Carlyle, Thomas. *Past and Present*. Berkeley and Los Angeles: University of California Press, 2005; 1st edn, 1843.
Casement, Roger. *The Amazon Journal of Roger Casement*, ed. Angus Mitchell. London: Anaconda Editions, 1997.
Cooke Taylor, William. *Notes of a Tour in the Manufacturing Districts of Lancashire*, 3rd edn. New York: Augustus M. Kelley, 1968.

Crawford, Earl of. *The Crawford Papers: the Journals of David Lindsay twenty-seventh Earl of Crawford and tenth Earl of Balcarres 1871–1940 during the years 1892 to 1940*, ed. John Vincent. Manchester: Manchester University Press, 1984.

Crichton, H. Maitland. *The Romance of Million Making*. London: George G. Harrap and Co., 1931.

Davison, T. Raffles. *Port Sunlight: A Record of its Artistic and Pictorial Aspect*. London: B. T. Batsford, 1916.

Duveen, James Henry. *Collections and Recollections: A Century and a Half of Art Deals*. London: Jarrolds, 1935.

Engels, Friedrich. *The Condition of the Working Class in England*, trans. and ed. W. O. Henderson and W. H. Chaloner. Palo Alto, CA: Stanford University Press, 1958.

'The Framley Examiner', *Bollocks to Alton Towers: Fifty Uncommonly British Days Out* (London: Michael Joseph, 2005).

Gardiner, A. G. *Pillars of Society*. London: James Nisbet, 1914.

George, W. L. *Engines of Social Progress*. London: Adam and Charles Black, 1907.

George, W. L. *Labour and Housing at Port Sunlight*. London: Alston Rivers, 1909.

Grimshaw, Timothy. *The Cogitations and Opinions of Timothy Grimshaw, Esq*. Bolton, 1839.

Hodgkin, J. E., ed. *Quakerism and Industry: Being the full Record of a Conference of Employers, chiefly Members of the Society of Friends, held at Woodbrooke nr. Birmingham 11th–14th April 1918*. Darlington: North of England Newspaper Co., 1918.

Howard, Ebenezer. *Garden Cities of To-morrow*. London: Swan Sonnenschein, 1902.

'In memoriam: William Hesketh Viscount Leverhulme', *Progress*, 25:168 (July 1925).

John, Augustus. *Chiaroscuro: Fragments of Autobiography, First Series*. London: Jonathan Cape, 1952.

Knox, Andrew M. *Coming Clean: A Postscript after Retirement from Unilever*. London: Heinemann, 1976.

The Lady Lever Collection, Port Sunlight: catalogue, 1977.

Lever, Sir William Hesketh. *Three Addresses*. Port Sunlight: Lever Brothers, n.d.

Lever, William Hesketh. *Following the Flag: Jottings of a Jaunt round the World*. London: Simpkin Marshall and Co.; Liverpool: Edward Howell, 1893.

Lever, William Hulme [second Viscount Leverhulme]. *Viscount Leverhulme*. Boston, MA, and New York: Houghton Mifflin, 1927.

Leverhulme, Lord. *The Six-Hour Day and other Industrial Questions*. London: George Allen and Unwin, 1918.

MacDonald, Colin. *Highland Journey*. Edinburgh and London: Moray Press, 1943.

MacDonald, Colin. *Highland Memories*. Edinburgh and London: Moray Press, 1949.

Macdonald, Emily. *Twenty Years of Hebridean Memories*. Paisley: Alexander Gardner, 1965; 1st edn, 1939.

MacNeice, Louis. *I Crossed the Minch*. London: Longman Green and Co., 1938.

McPhee, Allan. *The Economic Revolution in British West Africa*, 2nd edn. London: Frank Cass and Co., 1971; 1st edn, 1926.

Marx, Karl. *The 18th Brumaire of Louis Bonaparte*. Beijing: Foreign Languages Press, 1978.

Marx, Karl and Friedrich Engels. *Manifesto of the Communist Party*. Moscow: Progress Publishers, 1971.

Mawson, Thomas H. *Bolton (Lancs.): A Study in Town Planning and Civic Art.* Bolton: Tillotson Press [*c.* 1911].

Mawson, Thomas H. *Bolton As It Is and As It Might Be: Six Lectures Delivered under the Auspices of the Bolton Housing and Town Planning Society.* Bolton: Tillotson and Son; London: Batsford, 1916.

Mawson, Thomas H. *Civic Art: Studies in Town Planning: Parks, Boulevards and Open Spaces.* London: B. T. Batsford, 1911.

Mawson, Thomas H. *The Art and Craft of Garden Making*, 5th edn. London: B. T. Batsford, 1926.

Mawson, Thomas H. *The Life and Work of an English Landscape Architect: An Autobiography.* New York: Charles Scribner's Sons, 1927.

Meakin, Budgett. *Model Factories and Villages: Ideal Conditions of Labour and Housing.* London: T. Fisher Unwin, 1905.

Mearns, Andrew. *The Bitter Cry of Outcast London.* London: 1883.

Menzies, Mrs Stuart. *Modern Men of Mark.* London: Herbert Jenkins, 1921.

Opie, Robert, ed. *The Victorian Scrapbook.* London: New Cavendish Books, 2003.

Orwell, George. *The Road to Wigan Pier.* London: Penguin, 1989; 1st edn, 1937.

Owen, Robert. *The Life of Robert Owen, Written by Himself,* vol. I. London: Effingham Wilson, 1857.

Parliamentary Debates, Commons, 4th Ser., vols 174, 186. London, 1907.

Parliamentary Debates, Lords, 5th Ser., vol. 33. London, 1919.

Presentation of the Honorary Freedom of the Borough to William Hesketh Lever, Esq. and John Pennington Thomasson, Esq. Bolton, 1902.

Priestley, J. B. *English Journey.* London: Heinemann, 1934.

Priestley, J. B. and Jacquetta Hawkes, *Journey down a Rainbow.* London: Heinemann-Cresset, 1955.

Reeves, Maud Pember. *Round about a Pound a Week.* London: Virago, 1979; 1st edn, 1913.

Reilly, C. H. *Scaffolding in the Sky: A Semi-architectural Autobiography.* London: George Routledge and Son, 1938.

Roberts, David. *Life at Levers: Memories of Making Soaps at Port Sunlight.* Bebington: Avid Publications, 1995.

Roberts, Robert. *The Classic Slum: Salford Life in the First Quarter of the Century.* Harmondsworth: Penguin, 1973.

Schumpeter, Joseph. *Imperialism and Social Classes.* New York: Augustus M. Kelley, 1951; 1st edn, 1919.

Sennett, A. R. *Garden Cities in Theory and Practice*, vol. I. London: Bemrose and Sons, 1905.

The 'Sunlight' Year-Book for 1899. Port Sunlight: Lever Bros, 1899.

Sutherland, Halliday. *The Arches of the Years.* London: Geoffrey Bles, 1933.

Unwin, Stanley. *The Truth about a Publisher.* London: George Allen and Unwin, 1960.

Veblen, Thorstein. *The Theory of the Leisure Class.* Boston, MA: Houghton Mifflin, 1973; 1st edn, 1899.

Wakeman, Frederic. *The Hucksters.* New York: Rinehart and Co., 1946.

Watson, Angus. *My Life: An Autobiography.* London: Ivor Nicholson and Watson, 1937.

Woodruff, William. *The Road to Nab End: A Lancashire Childhood.* London: Eland, 2000.

Yorke, F. R. S. and Frederick Gibberd, *The Modern Flat.* London: Architectural Press, 1937.

Young, Harold Edgar. *A Perambulation of the Hundred of Wirral in the County of Chester.* Liverpool: Henry Young and Sons, 1909.

Secondary sources

Adams, W. S. *Edwardian Portraits.* London: Secker and Warburg, 1957.

Anstey, Roger. *King Leopold's Legacy: The Congo under Belgian Rule 1908–1960.* London: Oxford University Press, 1966.

Archer, Howard. 'The role of the entrepreneur in the emergence and development of UK multinational enterprises', *Journal of European Economic History,* 19:2 (fall 1990).

Armytage, W. H. G. *Heavens Below: Utopian Experiments in England 1560–1960.* Toronto: University of Toronto Press, 1961.

Arnold, Bruce. *Orpen: Mirror to an Age.* London: Jonathan Cape, 1981.

Ascherson, Neal. *The King Incorporated: Leopold II in the Age of Trusts.* London: Allen and Unwin, 1963.

Ashworth, William. *The Genesis of Modern British Town Planning.* London: Routledge and Kegan Paul, 1954.

Babb, Jervis J. *The Human Relations Philosophy of William Hesketh Lever.* New York: Newcomen Society in North America, 1952.

Barkan, Elazar. *The Retreat of Scientific Racism: Changing Concepts of Race in Britain and the United States between the World Wars.* Cambridge: Cambridge University Press, 1992.

Beevers, Robert. *The Garden City Utopia: A Critical Biography of Ebenezer Howard.* Basingstoke: Macmillan, 1988.

Bellini, James. *Rule Britannia: A Progress Report for Domesday 1986.* London: Jonathan Cape, 1981.

Bennett, Judith A. *Wealth of the Solomons: A History of a Pacific Archipelago 1800–1978.* Honolulu, HI: University of Hawaii Press, 1987.

Bennett, Judith A. '"We do not come here to be beaten": resistance and the plantation system in the Solomon Islands to World War II', in Brij V. Lal, Doug Munro and Edward D. Beechert, eds. *Plantation Workers: Resistance and Accommodation.* Honolulu, HI: University of Hawaii Press, 1993.

Blackwood, William. 'Sir Thomas Lipton 1850–1932', in *The Post-Victorians.* London: Ivor Nicholson and Watson, 1933.

Blom, Philipp. *To Have and to Hold: An Intimate History of Collectors and Collecting.* Woodstock and New York: Overlook Press, 2003.

Bolsterli, Margaret Jones. *The Early Community at Bedford Park: 'Corporate Happiness' in the First Garden Suburb.* Oberlin, OH: Ohio University Press, 1972.

Bowlby, Rachel. *Carried Away: The Invention of Modern Shopping.* New York: Columbia University Press, 2001.

Bradley, Ian Campbell. *Enlightened Entrepreneurs*. London: Weidenfeld and Nicolson, 1987.

Brantlinger, Patrick. *Dark Vanishings: Discourse on the Extinction of Primitive Races 1800–1930*. Ithaca, NY: Cornell University Press, 2003.

Breman, James. 'Primitive racism in a colonial context', in James Breman, ed. *Imperial Monkey Business: Racial Supremacy in Social Darwinist Theory and Colonial Practice*. Amsterdam: Vu University Press, 1990.

Breman, James. 'The civilization of racism: colonial and post-colonial development policies', in James Breman, ed. *Imperial Monkey Business: Racial Supremacy in Social Darwinist Theory and Colonial Practice*. Amsterdam: Vu University Press, 1990.

Briggs, Asa. *Victorian Things*. London: Penguin, 1988.

Brooke, Xanthe. '"The art of the home, not of the palace": Lever and his collection of embroidery', in Edward Morris, ed. *Art and Business in Edwardian England: The Making of the Lady Lever Art Gallery*. Oxford: Oxford University Press, 1992.

Brown, Callum G. *The Death of Christian Britain*. London and New York: Routledge, 2001.

Brydon, Thomas. 'Poor, unskilled and unemployed: perceptions of the English underclass 1889–1914'. MA thesis, McGill University, 2001.

Buchanan, Joni. *The Lewis Land Struggle*. Stornoway: Acair, 1996.

Buder, Stanley. *Visionaries and Planners: The Garden City Movement and the Modern Community*. New York and Oxford: Oxford University Press, 1990.

Burnett, John. *England Eats Out: A Social History of Eating Out in England from 1830 to the Present*. Harlow: Pearson Education, 2004.

Burrow, John W. *The Crisis of Reason: European Thought 1848–1914*. New Haven, CT: Yale University Press, 2000.

Cain, P. J. and A. G. Hopkins, *British Imperialism*, 2 vols. London: Longman, 1993.

Campbell, Peter. 'In Port Sunlight', *London Review of Books*, 27:2 (20 January 2005).

Camplin, Jamie. *The Rise of the Plutocrats: Wealth and Power in Edwardian England*. London: Constable, 1978.

Cannadine, David. *The Decline and Fall of the British Aristocracy*. New Haven, CT: Yale University Press, 1990.

Carey, John, ed. *The Faber Book of Utopias*. London: Faber and Faber, 1999.

Chandler, Alfred D., Jr. 'Comparative business history', in D. C. Coleman and Peter Mathias, eds. *Enterprise and History: Essays in Honour of Charles Wilson*. Cambridge: Cambridge University Press, 1984.

Chapman, Tony and Jenny Hockey, eds. *Ideal Homes? Social Change and Domestic Life*. London and New York: Routledge, 1999.

Cherry, Gordon E. *Urban Change and Planning: A History of Urban Development in Britain Since 1750*. Henley on Thames: G. T. Foulis, 1972.

Cherry, Gordon E. *Cities and Plans: The Shaping of Urban Britain in the Nineteenth and Twentieth Centuries*. London: Edward Arnold, 1988.

Claeys, Gregory. *Machinery, Money and the Millennium: From Moral Economy to Socialism 1815–1860*. Cambridge: Polity Press, 1987.

Clapson, Mark. *Suburban Century: Social Change and Urban Growth in England and the United States*. Oxford and New York: Berg, 2003.

Clarence-Smith, W. G. *Slaves, Peasants and Capitalists in Southern Angola 1840–1926*.

Cambridge: Cambridge University Press, 1979.

Cline, Catherine Ann. *E. D. Morel 1873–1924: The Strategies of Protest*. Belfast: Blackstaff Press, 1980.

Cocks, Harry. '*Calamus* in Bolton: spirituality and homosexual desire in late Victorian England', *Gender and History*, 13:2 (August 2001).

Coleman, D. C. 'Historians and businessmen', in D. C. Coleman and Peter Mathias, eds. *Enterprise and History: Essays in Honour of Charles Wilson*. Cambridge: Cambridge University Press, 1984.

Cooper, Fredrick. 'Conditions analogous to slavery', in Frederick Cooper, Thomas C. Holt and Rebecca J. Scott, eds. *Beyond Slavery: Explorations of Race, Labor, and Citizenship in Postemancipation Societies*. Chapel Hill, NC: University of North Carolina Press, 2000.

Creese, Walter L. *The Search for Environment: The Garden City: Before and After*. Baltimore, MD: Johns Hopkins University Press, expanded edn, 1992; 1st edn, 1966.

Darcy, Cornelius P. *The Encouragement of the Fine Arts in Lancashire 1760–1860*. Manchester: Chetham Society, 1976.

Daunton, Martin J. *House and Home in the Victorian City: Working Class Housing 1850–1914*. London: Edward Arnold, 1983.

Daunton, Martin J. '"Gentlemanly capitalism" and British industry 1820–1914', *Past and Present*, 122 (February 1989).

Davidoff, Leonore and Catherine Hall. *Family Fortunes: Men and Women of the English Middle Class 1780–1850*. Chicago: University of Chicago Press, 1991.

De Vries, Leonard. *Victorian Advertisements*. London: John Murray, 1968.

Denoon, Donald with Marivic Wyndham. 'Australia and the Western Pacific', in Wm Roger Louis, ed. *The Oxford History of the British Empire*, vol. III: Andrew Porter, ed. *The Nineteenth Century*. Oxford: Oxford University Press, 1999.

Devine, T. M. *Clanship to Crofters' Wars: The Social Transformation of the Scottish Highlands*. Manchester: Manchester University Press, 1994.

Drucker, Peter F. *The Practice of Management*. New York: HarperCollins, 1954.

Duany, Andres, Elizabeth Plater-Zyberk and Jeff Speck. *Suburban Nation: The Rise of Sprawl and the Decline of the American Dream*. New York: North Point Press, 2000.

Dumett, Raymond E., ed. *Gentlemanly Capitalism and British Imperialism: The New Debate on Empire*. London: Longman, 1999.

Dyer, Davis, Frederick Dalzell and Rowena Olegario, *Rising Tide: Lessons from 165 Years of Brand Building at Procter and Gamble*. Boston, MA: Harvard Business School Press, 2004.

Dyer, Gillian. *Advertising as Communication*. London: Routledge, 1989.

Eaton, Ruth. *Ideal Cities: Utopianism and the (Un)Built Environment*. London: Thames and Hudson, 2002.

Eatwell, Ann. 'Lever as a collector of Wedgwood and the fashion for collecting Wedgwood in the nineteenth century', in Edward Morris, ed. *Art and Business in Edwardian England: The Making of the Lady Lever Art Gallery*. Oxford: Oxford University Press, 1992.

Echenberg, Myron J. 'Paying the blood tax: military conscription in French West Africa', *Canadian Journal of African Studies*, 9:2 (1975).

Egerton, Robert B. *The Troubled Heart of Africa: A History of the Congo.* New York: St Martin's Press, 2002.

Elliott, Blanche B. *A History of English Advertising.* London: Business Publications, 1962.

Englander, David and Rosemary O'Day, eds. *Retrieved Riches: Social Investigation in Britain 1840–1914.* Aldershot: Scolar Press, 1995.

Evans, Martin. *European Atrocity, African Catastrophe: Leopold II, the Congo Free State and its Aftermath.* London and New York: RoutledgeCurzon, 2002.

Falola, Toyin and A. D. Roberts, 'West Africa', in Wm Roger Louis, ed. *The Oxford History of the British Empire*, vol. IV: Judith M. Brown and Wm Roger Louis, eds. *The Twentieth Century.* Oxford: Oxford University Press, 1999.

Fieldhouse, D. K. *Unilever Overseas: The Anatomy of a Multinational 1895–1965.* London: Croom Helm, 1978.

Fishman, Robert. *Urban Utopias in the Twentieth Century: Ebenezer Howard, Frank Lloyd Wright, and Le Corbusier.* New York: Basic Books, 1977.

Fishman, Robert. *Bourgeois Utopias: The Rise and Fall of Suburbia.* New York: Basic Books, 1987.

Fitzgerald, Robert. *British Labour Management and Industrial Welfare 1846–1939.* London and New York: Croom Helm, 1988.

Fitzgerald, Robert. *Rowntree and the Marketing Revolution 1862–1969.* Cambridge: Cambridge University Press, 1995.

Floud, Roderick, Kenneth Wachter and Annabel Gregory. *Height, Health and History: Nutritional Status in the United Kingdom 1750–1980.* Cambridge: Cambridge University Press, 1990.

Fogelson, Robert M. *Bourgeois Nightmares: Suburbia 1870–1930.* New Haven, CT: Yale University Press, 2005.

Foucault, Michel. *Discipline and Punish: The Birth of the Prison*, trans. Alan Sheridan. London: Penguin, 1977.

Fraser, W. Hamish. *The Coming of the Mass Market 1850–1914.* Hamden, CT: Archon Books, 1981.

Fredrickson, George M. *Racism: A Short History.* Princeton, NJ: Princeton University Press, 2002.

Gagnier, Regenia. *The Insatiability of Human Wants: Economics and Aesthetics in Market Society.* Chicago: University of Chicago Press, 2000.

Gardiner, A. G. *Life of George Cadbury.* London: Cassell, 1923.

Geddes, Arthur. *The Isle of Lewis and Harris: A Study in British Community.* Edinburgh: Edinburgh University Press, 1955.

Girouard, Mark. *The Return to Camelot: Chivalry and the English Gentleman.* New Haven, CT: Yale University Press, 1981.

Glendinning, Miles and Stefan Muthesius. *Tower Block: Modern Public Housing in England, Scotland, Wales, and Northern Ireland.* New Haven, CT: Yale University Press, 1994.

Gold, John R. and Margaret M. Gold. 'To be free and independent: crofting, popular protest and Lord Leverhulme's Hebridean development projects 1917–1925', *Rural History*, 7:2 (1996).

Gombrich, E. H. 'Nature and art as needs of the mind: the philanthropic ideals of Lord

Leverhulme 1851–1925', in E. H. Gombrich. *Tributes: Interpreters of our Cultural Tradition.* Ithaca, NY: Cornell University Press, 1984.

Grant, Kevin. *A Civilised Savagery: Britain and the New Slaveries in Africa 1884–1926.* New York and London: Routledge, 2005.

Griffiths, John. '"Give my regards to Uncle Billy ...": the rites and rituals of company life at Lever Brothers *c.* 1900–*c.* 1990', *Business History,* 37:4 (October 1995).

Gunn, Simon. 'The "failure" of the Victorian middle class: a critique', in Janet Wolff and John Seed, eds. *The Culture of Capital: Art, Power and the Nineteenth-Century Middle Class.* Manchester: Manchester University Press, 1988.

Gunn, Simon and Rachel Bell. *Middle Classes: Their Rise and Sprawl.* London: Phoenix, 2003.

Hall, Peter. *Urban and Regional Planning,* 4th edn. London and New York: Routledge, 2002.

Hall, Peter and Colin Ward. *Sociable Cities: The Legacy of Ebenezer Howard.* Chichester: John Wiley and Sons, 1998.

Hamill, John M. 'The Masonic collection at the Lady Lever Art Gallery', in Edward Morris, ed. *Art and Business in Edwardian England: The Making of the Lady Lever Art Gallery.* Oxford: Oxford University Press, 1992.

Hancock, W. K. *Survey of British Commonwealth Affairs,* vol. II: *Problems of Economic Policy 1918–1939,* part 2. London: Oxford University Press, 1940.

Hannah, Leslie. *The Rise of the Corporate Economy.* London: Methuen and Co., 1976.

Hardy, Dennis. *Alternative Communities in Nineteenth-Century England.* London and New York: Longman, 1979.

Hardy, Dennis. *Utopian England: Community Experiments 1900–1945.* London: E. and F. N. Spon, 2000.

Harris, José. *Unemployment and Politics: A Study in English Social Policy 1886–1914.* Oxford: Clarendon Press, 1972.

Harris, Richard. *Unplanned Suburbs: Toronto's American Tragedy 1900 to 1950.* Baltimore, MD: Johns Hopkins University Press, 1996.

Harrison, J. F. C. *Robert Owen and the Owenites in Britain and America: The Quest for the New Moral World.* London: Routledge and Kegan Paul, 1969.

Harvey, David. *Spaces of Hope.* Berkeley and Los Angeles: University of California Press, 2000.

Herries, Amanda. *Japanese Gardens in Britain.* Princes Risborough: Shire Books, 2001.

Hesketh, Phoebe. *My Aunt Edith: The Story of a Preston Suffragette.* Preston: Lancashire County Books, 1992; 1st edn, 1966.

Hilton, Matthew. *Consumerism in Twentieth-Century Britain: The Search for a Historical Movement.* Cambridge: Cambridge University Press, 2003.

Hindley, Diana and Geoffrey Hindley. *Advertising in Victorian England 1837–1901.* London: Wayland Publishers, 1972.

Hochschild, Adam. *King Leopold's Ghost: A Story of Greed, Terror, and Heroism in Colonial Africa.* London: Macmillan, 2000.

Hoffmann, W. G. '100 Years of the Margarine Industry', in J. H. van Stuyvenberg, ed. *Margarine: An Economic, Social and Scientific History 1869–1969.* Toronto: University of Toronto Press, 1969.

Holroyd, Michael. *Augustus John: A Biography*, vol. II: *The Years of Experience*. London: Heinemann, 1975.

Hopkins, A. G. *An Economic History of West Africa*. New York: Columbia University Press, 1973.

Hunt, Tristram. *Building Jerusalem: The Rise and Fall of the Victorian City*. London: Phoenix, 2005.

Hutchinson, Roger. *The Soap Man: Lewis, Harris and Lord Leverhulme*. Edinburgh: Birlinn, 2003.

Hyam, Ronald. 'Bureaucracy and "trusteeship" in the colonial empire', in Wm Roger Louis, ed. *The Oxford History of the British Empire*, vol. IV: Judith M. Brown and Wm Roger Louis, eds. *The Twentieth Century*. Oxford: Oxford University Press, 1999.

Impey, Oliver. 'Lever as a collector of Chinese porcelain', in Edward Morris, ed. *Art and Business in Edwardian England: The Making of the Lady Lever Art Gallery*. Oxford: Oxford University Press, 1992.

Ingham, Geoffrey. 'British capitalism: empire, merchants and decline', *Social History*, 20:3 (October 1995).

Israel, Kali. *Names and Stories: Emilia Dilke and Victorian Culture*. New York: Oxford University Press, 1999.

Jackson, Kenneth T. *Crabgrass Frontier: The Suburbanization of the United States*. New York and Oxford: Oxford University Press, 1985.

Jacobs, Jane. *The Death and Life of Great American Cities*. New York: Vintage Books, 1992; 1st edn, 1961.

Jeremy, David J., ed. *Dictionary of Business Biography: A Biographical Dictionary of Business Leaders Active in Britain in the Period 1860–1980*, vols I and III. London: Butterworth, 1984–85.

Jeremy, David J. *Capitalists and Christians: Business Leaders and the Churches in Britain 1900–1960*. Oxford: Clarendon Press, 1990.

Jeremy, David J. 'The enlightened paternalist in action: William Hesketh Lever at Port Sunlight before 1914', *Business History*, 33:1 (January 1991).

Jewsiewicki, Bogumil. 'African peasants in the totalitarian colonial society of the Belgian Congo', in Martin A. Klein, ed. *Peasants in Africa: Historical and Contemporary Perspectives*. Beverly Hills, CA, and London: Sage Publications, 1980.

Jewsiewicki, Bogumil. 'Belgian Africa', in A. D. Roberts, ed. *The Cambridge History of Africa*, vol. VII: *From 1905 to 1940*. Cambridge: Cambridge University Press, 1986.

Jolly, W. P. *Lord Leverhulme: A Biography*. London: Constable, 1976.

Joyce, Patrick. *Work, Society and Politics: The Culture of the Factory in later Victorian England*. Brighton: Harvester Press, 1980.

Kasser, Tim. *The High Price of Materialism*. Boston, MA: MIT Press, 2002.

Kasser, Tim and Allen D. Kanner, eds. *Psychology and Consumer Culture: The Struggle for a Good Life in a Materialistic World*. Washington, DC: American Psychological Association, 2004.

Kelly, Thomas. *For Advancement of Learning: The University of Liverpool 1881–1981*. Liverpool: Liverpool University Press, 1981.

Kidson, Alex. 'Lever and the collecting of eighteenth-century British paintings', in Edward Morris, ed. *Art and Business in Edwardian England: The Making of the*

Lady Lever Art Gallery. Oxford: Oxford University Press, 1992.

Klein, Martin. *Slavery and Colonial Rule in French West Africa*. Cambridge: Cambridge University Press, 1998.

Kumar, Krishan. *Utopianism*. Milton Keynes: Open University Press, 1991.

The Lady Lever Art Gallery, Port Sunlight. Liverpool: Bluecoat Press, 1996, for National Museums and Galleries on Merseyside.

Leneman, Leah. *Fit for Heroes? Land Settlement in Scotland after World War I*. Aberdeen: Aberdeen University Press, 1989.

Levy, Adrian and Cathy Scott-Clark. *The Stone of Heaven: Unearthing the Secret History of Imperial Green Jade*. Boston, MA: Little Brown and Co., 2001.

Lewis, Brian. *The Middlemost and the Milltowns: Bourgeois Culture and Politics in Early Industrial England*. Palo Alto, CA: Stanford University Press, 2001.

Light, Alison. *Forever England: Femininity, Literature and Consumerism between the Wars*. London: Routledge, 1991.

Lindqvist, Sven. *'Exterminate all the Brutes'*. New York: New Press, 1996.

Loeb, Lori Anne. *Consuming Angels: Advertising and Victorian Women*. New York: Oxford University Press, 1994.

Louis, Wm Roger. 'Roger Casement and the Congo', *Journal of African History* 5:1 (1964).

Louis, Wm Roger and Jean Stengers, eds. *E. D. Morel's History of the Congo Reform Movement*. Oxford: Clarendon Press, 1967.

Lovejoy, Paul. E. *Transformations in Slavery: A History of Slavery in Africa*, 2nd edn. Cambridge: Cambridge University Press, 2000.

Lovejoy, Paul E. and Jan S. Hogendorn. *Slow Death for Slavery: The Course of Abolition in Northern Nigeria 1897–1936*. Cambridge: Cambridge University Press, 1993.

McClintock, Anne. *Imperial Leather: Race, Gender and Sexuality in the Colonial Context*. New York: Routledge, 1995.

McDonough, John and Karen Egolf, eds. *The* Advertising Age *Encyclopedia of Advertising*, vol. III. New York: Fitzroy Dearborn, 2003.

McKendrick, Neil. 'Josiah Wedgwood and the commercialization of the potteries', in Neil McKendrick, John Brewer and J. H. Plumb, eds. *The Birth of a Consumer Society: The Commercialization of Eighteenth Century England*. London: Europa Publications, 1982.

MacKenzie, John M., ed. *Imperialism and Popular Culture*. Manchester: Manchester University Press, 1986.

McKibbin, Ross. *Classes and Cultures: England 1918–1951*. Oxford: Oxford University Press, 1998.

McMillan, Nora. 'Lever and his shell collection', in Edward Morris, ed. *Art and Business in Edwardian England: The Making of the Lady Lever Art Gallery*. Oxford: Oxford University Press, 1992.

MacQueen, Adam. *The King of Sunlight: How William Lever Cleaned up the World*. London: Bantam Press, 2004.

Macquoid, Percy. 'Furniture of the XVII and XVIII centuries: Sir W. H. Lever's collection', *Country Life* (28 October, 4 November 1911).

Mangan, J. A. and James Walvin, eds. *Manliness and Morality: Middle Class Masculinity in Britain and America 1800–1940*. Manchester: Manchester University Press, 1987.

Mann, Michael. *The Dark Side of Democracy: Explaining Ethnic Cleansing.* Cambridge: Cambridge University Press, 2005.

Marchal, Jules. *E. D. Morel contre Léopold II : l'histoire du Congo 1900–1910*, vol. II. Paris: Éditions l'Harmattan, 1996.

Marchal, Jules. *L'Histoire du Congo 1910–1945*, vol. I: *Travail forcé pour le cuivre et l'or*, vol. II: *Travail forcé pour le rail*, vol. III: *Travail forcé pour l'huile de palme de Lord Leverhulme.* Borgloon, Belgium: Éditions Paula Bellings, 1999–2001. Vol. I has been translated by Ayi Kwei Armah as *Forced Labor in the Gold and Copper Mines: A History of Congo under Belgian Rule 1910–1945*, vol. I. Popenguine, Senegal: Per Ankh, 2003.

Marjoribanks, Edward. *The Life of Lord Carson*, vol. I. Toronto: Macmillan, 1932.

Marks, Sally. *The Ebbing of European Ascendancy.* London: Edward Arnold, 2002.

Martin, Susan M. *Palm Oil and Protest: An Economic History of the Ngwa Region, South Eastern Nigeria 1800–1980.* Cambridge: Cambridge University Press, 1988.

Matthew, H. C. G. and Brian Harrison, eds. *Oxford Dictionary of National Biography.* Oxford: Oxford University Press, 2004.

Mawson, David. 'T. H. Mawson, 1861–1933: landscape architect and town planner', *Journal of the Royal Society of Arts*, 5331:132 (February 1984).

Mayhall, Laura E. Nym. *The Militant Suffrage Movement: Citizenship and Resistance in Britain 1860–1930.* Oxford: Oxford University Press, 2003.

Meacham, Standish. *Regaining Paradise: Englishness and the early Garden City Movement.* New Haven, CT: Yale University Press, 1999.

Meller, Helen. *Towns, Plans and Society in Modern Britain.* Cambridge: Cambridge University Press, 1997.

Meller, Helen. *European Cities 1890–1930s: History, Culture and the Built Environment.* Chichester: John Wiley and Sons, 2001.

Miller, Mervyn. *Letchworth: The First Garden City.* Chichester: Phillimore, 1989.

Miller, Mervyn. 'Back to the future: the garden city centenary', *Town and Country Planning*, 72:7 (August 2003).

Morgan, Nigel and Annette Pritchard, *Advertising in Tourism and Leisure.* Oxford: Butterworth Heinemann, 2001.

Morris, Edward. 'Advertising and the acquisition of contemporary art', in Edward Morris, ed. *Art and Business in Edwardian England: The Making of the Lady Lever Art Gallery.* Oxford: Oxford University Press, 1992.

Morris, R. J. and Richard Rodger, eds. *The Victorian City: A Reader in British Urban History 1820–1914.* London and New York: Longman, 1993.

Morton, Suzanne. *Ideal Surroundings: Domestic Life in a Working-Class Suburb in the 1920s.* Toronto: University of Toronto Press, 1995.

Muensterberger, Werner. *Collecting: An Unruly Passion: Psychological Perspectives.* Princeton, NJ: Princeton University Press, 1994.

Mumford, Lewis. *The City in History: Its Origins, its Transformations, and its Prospects.* New York: Harcourt Brace and World, 1961.

Munro, Doug and Stewart Firth. 'Company strategies – colonial policies', in Clive Moore, Jacqueline Leckie and Doug Munro, eds. *Labour in the South Pacific.* Townsville, QLD: James Cook University of Northern Queensland, 1990.

Musson, A. E. *Enterprise in Soap and Chemicals: Joseph Crosfield and Sons, Ltd 1815–1965.* Manchester: Manchester University Press, 1965.

Nelson, Samuel H. *Colonialism in the Congo Basin 1880–1940*. Athens, OH: Ohio University Center for International Studies, Africa Series, 64, 1994.

Nevett, Terry R. *Advertising in Britain: A History*. London: Heinemann, 1982.

Nicolson, Nigel. *Lord of the Isles*. Stornoway: Acair, 2000; 1st edn, 1960.

Nilson, Torsten H. *Competitive Branding: Winning in the Market Place with Value-added Brands*. New York: John Wiley and Sons, 1999.

Northrup, David. *Beyond the Bend in the River: African Labor in Eastern Zaire 1865–1940*. Athens, OH: Ohio University Center for International Studies, African Series, 52, 1988.

Nzongola-Ntalaja, Georges. *The Congo from Leopold to Kabila: A People's History*. London and New York: Zed Books, 2002.

Obelkevich, James. 'Consumption', in James Obelkevich and Peter Catterall, eds. *Understanding Post-war British Society*. London and New York: Routledge, 1994.

Opie, Robert. *Rule Britannia: Trading on the British Image*. Harmondsworth: Viking, 1985.

Pedler, Frederick. *The Lion and the Unicorn in Africa: A History of the Origins of the United Africa Company 1787–1931*. London: Heinemann, 1974.

Pepper, Simon. 'The garden city', in Boris Ford, ed. *The Cambridge Cultural History of Britain*, vol. VIII: *Early Twentieth Century Britain*. Cambridge: Cambridge University Press, 1992.

The Pergola: The Birth, Decline and Spectacular Renaissance of a Unique Edwardian Extravaganza. London: Corporation of London, n.d.

Perkin, Harold. *The Rise of Professional Society: England since 1880*. London and New York: Routledge, 1989.

Peterson, Jon A. *The Birth of City Planning in the United States 1840–1917*. Baltimore, MD: Johns Hopkins University Press, 2003.

Pevsner, Nikolaus and Edward Hubbard. *The Buildings of England: Cheshire*. Harmondsworth: Penguin, 1971.

Phillips, Anne. *The Enigma of Colonialism: British Policy in West Africa*. London: James Currey; Bloomington, IN: Indiana University Press, 1989.

Porter, Bernard. *The Lion's Share: A Short History of British Imperialism 1850–1995*, 3rd edn. London and New York: Longman, 1996.

Porter, Bernard. *The Absent-minded Imperialists: Empire, Society, and Culture in Britain*. Oxford: Oxford University Press, 2004.

Pugh, Martin. *State and Society: A Social and Political History of Britain 1870–1997*, 2nd edn. London: Edward Arnold, 2000.

Ramamurthy, Anandi. *Imperial Persuaders: Images of Africa and Asia in British Advertising*. Manchester: Manchester University Press, 2003.

Randell, Nigel. *The White Headhunter*. New York: Carroll and Graf, 2003.

Reader, W. J. *Unilever: A Short History*. London: Unilever House, 1960.

Reader, W. J. *Unilever Plantations*. London: Unilever Ltd, 1961.

Reader, W. J. *Imperial Chemical Industries: A History*, vol. I: *The Forerunners 1870–1926*. London: Oxford University Press, 1970.

Reader, W. J. 'Businessmen and their motives', in D. C. Coleman and Peter Mathias, eds. *Enterprise and History: Essays in Honour of Charles Wilson*. Cambridge: Cambridge University Press, 1984.

Reid, Aileen. *Brentham: A History of the Pioneer Garden Suburb 1901–2001*. Ealing: Brentham Heritage Society, 2000.

Richards, Jeffrey. '"Passing the love of women": manly love and Victorian society', in J. A. Mangan and James Walvin, eds. *Manliness and Morality: Middle Class Masculinity in Britain and America 1800–1940*. Manchester: Manchester University Press, 1987.

Richards, Thomas. *The Commodity Culture of Victorian England: Advertising and Spectacle 1851–1914*. Stanford, CA: Stanford University Press, 1990.

Rose, Lionel. *The Erosion of Childhood: Child Oppression in Britain 1860–1918*. London: Routledge, 1991.

Royle, Edward. *Robert Owen and the Commencement of the Millennium: A Study of the Harmony Community*. Manchester: Manchester University Press, 1998.

Rubinstein, W. D. *Men of Property: The Very Wealthy in Britain since the Industrial Revolution*. London: Croom Helm, 1981.

Rubinstein, W. D. *Elites and the Wealthy in Modern British History: Essays in Social and Economic History*. Brighton: Harvester Press, 1987.

Rutherford, Paul. *Endless Propaganda: The Advertising of Public Goods*. Toronto: University of Toronto Press, 2000.

Said, Edward W. *Culture and Imperialism*. New York: Vintage Books, 1994.

Saint, Andrew. 'The new towns', in Boris Ford, ed. *The Cambridge Cultural History of Britain*, vol. IX: *Modern Britain*. Cambridge: Cambridge University Press, 1992.

Satre, Lowell J. *Chocolate on Trial: Slavery, Politics, and the Ethics of Business*. Athens, OH: Ohio University Press, 2005.

Scarr, Deryck. *Fragments of Empire: A History of the Western Pacific High Commission 1877–1914*. Canberra: Australian National University Press; Honolulu, HI: University of Hawaii Press, 1968.

Schaffer, Frank. *The New Town Story*. London: MacGibbon and Kee, 1970.

Schaffer, Simon. 'A science whose business is bursting: soap bubbles as commodities in classical physics', in Lorraine Daston, ed. *Things that Talk: Object Lessons from Art and Science*. New York: Zone Books, 2004.

Schudson, Michael. *Advertising, the Uneasy Persuasion: Its Dubious Impact on American Society*. New York: Basic Books, 1984.

Scola, Roger. *Feeding the Victorian City: The Food Supply of Manchester 1770–1870*. Manchester: Manchester University Press, 1992.

Sheldon, Cyril. *A History of Poster Advertising*. London: Chapman and Hall, 1937.

Shepard, Sue. *Pickled, Potted, and Canned: How the Art and Science of Food Preserving Changed the World*. New York: Simon and Schuster, 2000.

Shepherd, John. *George Lansbury: At the Heart of Old Labour*. Oxford: Oxford University Press, 2002.

Shippobottom, Michael. 'Unmatched for drama: Lord Leverhulme's Rivington estate', *Country Life*, 13 September 1984.

Shippobottom, Michael. 'The building of the Lady Lever Art Gallery', in Edward Morris, ed. *Art and Business in Edwardian England: The Making of the Lady Lever Art Gallery*. Oxford: Oxford University Press, 1992.

Shippobottom, Michael. 'C. H. Reilly and the first Lord Leverhulme', in Joseph Sharples, Alan Powers and Michael Shippobottom, eds. *Charles Reilly and the Liverpool School of Architecture 1904–1933: Catalogue of an Exhibition at the Walker Art Gallery, Liverpool, 25 Oct. 1996 –2 Feb. 1997*. Liverpool: Liverpool University Press, 1996.

Sivulka, Juliann. *Soap, Sex, and Cigarettes: A Cultural History of American Advertising*. Belmont, CA: Wadsworth Publishing, 1998.

Smith, F. B. *The People's Health 1830–1910*. London: Croom Helm, 1979.

Smith, Malcolm D. *Leverhulme's Rivington (The Story of the Rivington 'Bungalow')*. St Michael's on Wyre, Lancs.: Wyre Publishing, 1998.

Stedman Jones, Gareth. *Outcast London*. Oxford: Clarendon Press, 1971.

Stites, Richard. *Revolutionary Dreams: Utopian Vision and Experimental Life in the Russian Revolution*. New York and Oxford: Oxford University Press, 1989.

Storry, Mike and Peter Childs, eds. *British Cultural Identities*, 2nd edn. London: Routledge, 2002.

Sutcliffe, Anthony. *Towards the Planned City: Germany, Britain, the United States and France 1780–1914*. New York: St Martin's Press, 1981.

Sweet, Matthew. *Inventing the Victorians*. London: Faber and Faber, 2001.

Taylor, Barbara. *Eve and the New Jerusalem: Socialism and Feminism in the Nineteenth Century*. Cambridge, MA: Harvard University Press, 1993.

Thomas, Angela P. 'Lever as a collector of archaeology and as a sponsor of archaeological excavations', in Edward Morris, ed. *Art and Business in Edwardian England: The Making of the Lady Lever Art Gallery*. Oxford: Oxford University Press, 1992.

Thompson, E. P. *The Making of the English Working Class*. London: Victor Gollancz, 1980; 1st edn, 1963.

Thompson, F. M. L., ed. *The Rise of Suburbia*. New York: St Martin's Press, 1982.

Thompson, F. M. L. *Gentrification and the Enterprise Culture: Britain 1780–1980*. Oxford: Oxford University Press, 2001.

Vernon, Anne. *A Quaker Business Man: The Life of Joseph Rowntree 1836–1925*. London: George Allen and Unwin, 1958.

Vinikas, Vincent. *Soft Soap, Hard Sell: American Hygiene in an Age of Advertisement*. Ames, IA: Iowa State University Press, 1992.

Waller, Philip J. *Town, City and Nation: England 1850–1914*. Oxford: Oxford University Press, 1983.

Ward, Stephen. V. *Planning the Twentieth-Century City: The Advanced Capitalist World*. Chichester: John Wiley and Sons, 2002.

Ward, Stephen. V. *Planning and Urban Change*, 2nd edn. London: Sage Publications, 2004.

Weiner, Martin J. *English Culture and the Decline of the Industrial Spirit 1850–1980*. Cambridge: Cambridge University Press, 1981.

West, Andrew. 'The history of the ethnography collections of W. H. Lever', in Edward Morris, ed. *Art and Business in Edwardian England: The Making of the Lady Lever Art Gallery*. Oxford: Oxford University Press, 1992.

Williams, Harley. *Men of Stress: Three Dynamic Interpretations: Woodrow Wilson, Andrew Carnegie, William Hesketh Lever*. London: Jonathan Cape, 1948.

Williams, Raymond. *Culture and Society 1780–1950*. Harmondsworth: Penguin, 1961.

Williamson, Judith. *Decoding Advertisements: Ideology and Meaning in Advertising*. London and New York: Marion Boyars, 1978.

Willson, Margaret, Clive Moore and Doug Munro. 'Asian workers in the Pacific', in Clive Moore, Jacqueline Leckie and Doug Munro, eds. *Labour in the South Pacific.* Townsville: James Cook University of Northern Queensland, 1990.

Wilson, Charles. *The History of Unilever: A Study in Economic Growth and Social Change*, vol. I. London: Cassell and Co., 1954.

Wilson, Richard Lucock. *Soap through the Ages*, 4th edn. London: Progress Books, 1955.

Wohl, Anthony S. *Endangered Lives: Public Health in Victorian Britain*. London: J. M. Dent, 1983.

Wood, Lucy. 'Lever's objectives in collecting old furniture', in Edward Morris, ed. *Art and Business in Edwardian England: The Making of the Lady Lever Art Gallery.* Oxford: Oxford University Press, 1992.

Woods, Clive. *Saltaire: History and Regeneration.* Bradford, 2000 (guidebook).

Wright, Myles. *Lord Leverhulme's Unknown Venture: The Lever Chair and the Beginnings of Town and Regional Planning 1908–1948.* London: Hutchinson Benham, 1982.

Wrigley, C. C. 'Aspects of economic history', in A. D. Roberts, ed. *The Cambridge History of Africa*, vol. VII: *From 1905 to 1940.* Cambridge: Cambridge University Press, 1986.

Index

Abercrombie, Patrick 112, 134, 137
Aberdeen Steam Trawling Company 208
Achten, Lode 186
Addison, Christopher 140
Adler, David and Sons 71
Adshead, Stanley 137
advertising 56–86
    critics and proponents 85–6
    gimmicks 66–7
    human psychology, and 81–3
    themes 67, 74, 76–9
African and Eastern Trade Corporation 12
Akroyd, Edward and Akroydon 101–2
Albert, Prince Consort 98
Andreae, Johann Valentin 107
Anheuser-Busch (beer) 60
Anstey, Roger 190
Antrobus, R. L. 164
Appert, Nicholas 59
Arkwright, Richard 5, 95
Ashworth, Edmund and Henry 96
Asquith, Herbert Henry 29
Associated Newspapers 10, 130, 137
Atkinson, Robert 33

Babb, Jervis 112, 154
Bacon, Francis 107
Baillie Scott, M. H. 132
Barnett, Henrietta 132
Barratt, Thomas J. 56, 65, 68, 70–1
Baťa, Tomáš 134
Beckham, David and Victoria 46
Bedford Park, Chiswick 104
Beecham, Thomas 59, 65
Begbie, Harold 16, 94

Belgian Congo 154, 167–91
Bell, Henry 201
Bellini, James 4, 7–8
Beman, Solon Spencer 102
Bennett, Judith 161
Bennett, Richard 41
Benoît-Lévy, Georges 111–12
Benson, S. H. 66
Bentham, Jeremy and 'Panopticon' 120
Bernays, Edward 82–4
Betjeman, Sir John 131
Birkenhead 94, 110, 122, 137
Blumenbach, Johann Friedrich 156
Bolton, Lancs. 8–9, 28–30, 46, 93, 96–8,
    137–9
Booth, William 109
Borve Lodge, Harris 24, 216, 220
Bournville 101–2, 113–16, 124, 129–30,
    179–80
Boxted farm colony, Colchester 109
Brentham Garden Suburb 133
Bright, John 86, 156
Brooke, Benjamin (soap maker) 69
Brunner, John and Roscoe 11
Brunner Mond and Co. 11, 39
Bryant and May (safety match) 58
Buckingham, James Silk 108, 129
Buell, Raymond 173–4, 185–8
Bungalow (The) see Roynton Cottage
Burke, Edmund 163
Burnham, Daniel H. 138
Burns, John 109–10, 136
Burns Philp 160–2
Butterley Iron Company 101
Buxton, Thomas Fowell 169–70

Cabet, Étienne, 105–7
Cadbury, George 113, 115–16, 124, 130, 135–6, 179
Cadbury's (chocolate) 65–6, 116
 slavery, and 179–80
 see also Bournville
Calvert, Albert 42
Campanella, Tommaso 107
Campbell, Joseph (soup) 60
Candler, Asa (Coca-cola) 60
Carlyle, Thomas 1, 98–9
Carnegie, Andrew 1, 25, 44
Carr, Jonathan Thomas 104
Carson, Sir Edward 10, 41, 180
Casement, Roger 166–7, 180
Cescinsky, Herbert 40
Chadwick, James and Robert 97
Chesterton, G. K. 20
Chevreul, Michel Eugène 60
'Chinese slavery' scandal 163, 179
Chivers' (jam) 101
Christ Church, Port Sunlight 15, 20, 99, 118, 124
Churchill, Lord Randolph 64
City Beautiful movement 137–8, 142
Civic Design, Dept. of, University of Liverpool 25, 136–8
Clark's (boots) 101
Clifford, Sir Hugh 165, 170
Cobden, Richard 86, 155
Coleman, D. C. 201
Coleridge, Samuel Taylor 33, 98–9
Colgate-Palmolive 58
Colman, Jeremiah (mustard) 35, 64, 116
Colonial Office 162–3
 and 'pro-African' policy, 163–5
Colonial Sugar Refining Company, Fiji 160
Congo Free State 166–7
Congo Reform Association 165, 167, 171, 179
Conrad, Joseph 166
Cooke Taylor, William 97
Cooper, Francis D'Arcy 12, 200–1, 219–20
Co-operative Wholesale Society 11
Copley, Yorks. 101
copra and coconut oil 10, 158–62, 167
council housing 103, 133, 135–6, 140–2
crofters and crofting 208–14, 218, 221

Crompton, Samuel 5, 46, 206
Crompton family, Rivington 27–8,
Crooks, Will 109
Crosfield, Joseph (soap maker) 10–11, 61, 69, 71, 200
Crossley, John, Joseph and Sir Francis 101

Dale, David 95
Darwin, Charles 157
Davison, Raffles 121
Dean Mills, Barrowbridge 97–8
Deutsche Handels- und Plantagen-Gesellschaft
 der Südsee-Inseln zu Hamburg (DHPG) 160
Disraeli, Benjamin 98–9
Duany, Andres 143
Dunlop, John Boyd 166
Dunlop (tyres) 78
Dunmore, Earl of 205
Durand, Peter 59
Duveen, James Henry 39–40

Eliot, T. S. 85
Ely, Richard 102
Engels, Friedrich 93, 105–6
Evans, Martin 182
Evans, Rowland 3

factory paternalism 93–108
 see also Bournville; Port Sunlight
Fels, Joseph 109
Fels Naptha 70
Fieldhouse, D. K. 9, 178, 183
Firth, Stewart 160
fishing industry 206, 208–9, 212–15, 218–20
forced labour
 Belgian Congo 181–8, 190–1
 Cadbury's 179–80
 South Pacific 160–3
Ford, Henry 1, 8, 22
Foucault, Michel 120
Fourier, Charles 105–7
Frith, William Powell 65, 217
Fry's (chocolate) 66, 116

Gagnier, Regenia 155
Gamble, James 63

garden cities and suburbs 104, 129–35
Garden Cities and Town Planning
    Association 136
Garden City Association 130, 136–7
Gardiner, A. G. 2, 4, 13, 19, 27, 113
Gardner, Robert 97
Garstang, John 45
Geddes, Arthur 214
Geddes, Patrick 141–2
George, Henry 129, 169
George, Walter Lionel 112, 115–20
George V 36, 42
Gibberd, Frederick 141–2
Gladstone, William Ewart 2, 64
Godin, Jean-Baptiste-André 106
Godwin, E. W. 104
Gombrich, E. H. 44–5
Gorer, Edgar 41
Gossage, William (soap maker) 10–11, 61,
    200
Graham, Betty 123
Greater London Plan (1944) 134
Greenhalgh, Harold R. 169, 183, 201, 203
Greg, Samuel 95
Greig, Sir Robert 211
Griffin, Walter Burley 138
Gropius, Walter 141
Gross, Sydney 69, 72
Grossmith, George and Weedon 104
Gryseels, Guido 191

Hadleigh farm colony, Essex 109
Hall, Peter 133
Hall i' th' Wood, Bolton 26, 28, 40–1, 45–6
Hampstead Garden Suburb 132–3, 136,
    140, 143
Hardy, Dennis 100, 105
Hardy, Kier 109
Harmsworth, Cecil 130
Harris *see* Lewis and Harris
Harris, Rev. John 171
Hartley, W. P. (jam) 101, 116
Harvey, David 143
Hearst, William Randolph 33, 44
Heinz, Henry J. (condiments) 59–60
Helford Oysterage, Cornwall 208
Herero of South West Africa 157
Herries, Amanda 35

herring industry *see* fishing industry
Hertzka, Theodore 108–9
Hill (The), Hampstead 24, 26–7, 39, 41,
    52n.99, 201–2
Hochschild, Adam 166
Hollesley Bay labour colony 109
Holloway, Thomas 65
Hopkins, A. G. 164, 193n.36
Horn, Dr Max 167, 173
Horniman, John 59
housing, planning statutes 103, 136, 140
Howard, Ebenezer, 129–34, 136, 141–2, 144
Huband, Myrtle 177, 202–4
Hudson, R. S. (soap maker) 10, 61, 66
Huileries du Congo Belge, les (HCB)
    171–8, 183–90
Hull Garden Suburb 133
Huntley and Palmer (biscuits) 116
Hutchinson, Roger 4, 221
Huxley, Aldous 107

Icaria 106
Imperial Chemical Industries (ICI) 11–12
Isaacs, Rufus 10, 180

J. Walter Thompson advertising agency
    81–3
Jacobs, Jane 142
Jamestown, Virginia 107
Japanese gardens 35
Jeremy, David 123–4
John, Augustus 204
Jones, Rev. Dr J. D. 2
Jurgens (margarine) 10, 12

Kellogg, John and William (cereal) 60
Kennedy-Fraser, Marjory 205
Kidson, Alex 39
Knight, John (soap maker) 10, 61, 200
Knox, Andrew 14, 72, 121–3, 201–3, 217
Kropotkin, Peter 109
Krupp colonies, Essen 102

labour colonies 96, 108–10
Lady Lever Art Gallery 2, 40–6, 120, 204
Laindon labour colony 109
Lambert Pharmacal 81
Lancaster, Osbert 133

Lansbury, George 109
Lauder, Sir Harry 205
Lavanchy-Clarke, F. H. 66
Leblanc, Nicholas 60
Le Corbusier 141–2
Lejeune, Émile 184
Leopold II of the Belgians 163, 166–7, 172, 181–2
Letchworth 130–4, 141
Lever, Eliza 8, 24
Lever, Elizabeth Ellen, née Hulme, 8, 14–15
Lever, James 8, 20, 24
Lever, James Darcy 14, 50n.43
Lever, William Hesketh, Viscount Leverhulme
  collections 38–46
  family 8–9, 14–15
  First World War, and 199–200
  garden city movement, and 130, 135–6
  homes and gardens 24–38, 41, 46, 201–2, 205, 216, 220
  personality 1–2, 4, 12–19, 24, 73, 121, 168, 202–3
  politics, and 126–9
  racial beliefs, and 155, 157–8, 163, 165–71, 175–7
  religion, and 8, 14, 20–3, 217
  town planning, and 136–40, 206
  see also advertising; Belgian Congo; Lever and Co.; Lever Brothers; Lewis and Harris; Port Sunlight; Rivington
Lever, William Hulme, 2–3, 7, 14–21, 26, 28, 31, 38, 40, 42–3, 61, 69, 111, 114, 119, 125, 167, 174, 177, 202, 218
Lever and Co. (wholesale grocer) 8–9
Lever Brothers
  acquisitions and mergers 9–12, 188, 200, 208
  advertising 66–81, 83
  Belgian Congo, and 167, 171
  financial crisis 200–1, 203–4, 208, 214
  packaging 62–4
  soap brands 9, 57–8, 61, 68–9, 80, 83
  South Pacific, and 160–2
  West Africa, and 163–5
  see also Huileries du Congo Belge, les
Lever Pacific Plantations Ltd 10, 160
Lever Park 28–9, 31, 38

'Liverpool Castle', and 31–2, 99
Leverburgh, Harris 216–20
Lewis and Harris 24, 26, 28, 201, 205–21
Lews Castle 19, 24, 26, 205, 212, 216, 220
Light, William 107
Lindsay, David 37
Linnaeus, Carolus 156
Lipton, Thomas (grocer), 12, 66–7
Listerine 81
Littler, Ralph 28–9
Liverpool Garden Suburb 133
Lloyd George, David 2, 16, 126, 140, 156
Loeb, Lori 77–8
Longfellow, Henry Wadsworth 24–5
Lugard, Lord 165
Lukács, Georg 65
Lutyens, Edwin 132, 138

Mac Fisheries 10, 207–8, 218, 220–1
McClintock, Anne 78–9
McCullough, George 42
MacDonald, Colin 73–4, 206, 212–13
McDowell, John 201
Maciver, Kenneth 216–17
Maclean, Will 221
McPhee, Allan 186
MacQueen, Adam 3, 50n.43, 154
Maddocks, Joyce 123
Magee, John 37
Mahaffy, A. W. 161
Maoris 155
Marchal, Jules 185, 190, 196n.90
margarine industry 10–12, 58, 159, 200–1
Margarine Union/Margarine Unie 12
Marjoribanks, D. C., Lord Tweedmouth 41
Marshall, Alfred 130
Marx, Karl 5, 95, 105–6
Masterman, C. F. G. 104
Matheson, Col. Duncan 205, 211
Matheson, Sir James 205
Mawson, Edward Prentice 35
Mawson, Thomas Hayton 2, 25–7, 31–5, 42, 137–9, 206–7
Meacham, Standish 132
Meakin, Budgett 101–2, 112, 115–16
Menzies, Mrs Stuart 4, 184
Michelin, Édouard 166
Millais, Sir John Everett 65

Modern Movement (architecture) 141–2
Mond, Ludwig 11, 39
Moor Park estate, Herts. 24
More, Thomas 107
Morel, Edmund Dene 165–71, 179, 190
Morgan, John Minter 108
Morris, Edward 4, 39
Mouriès, Hippolyte Mège 10
Mumford, Lewis 141–3
Munro, Doug 160
Munro, Robert 213–15
Murray, Dr Donald 210

Nelson, Samuel 182, 187
Nettlefold, John Sutton 136
Neville, Ralph 130
Nevinson, Henry 179
New Earswick 124, 130, 133
New Harmony, Indiana 105
New Lanark 95–6, 101
New Towns 134–5
Nicolson, Nigel 4, 19, 213, 215, 217, 220
Niger Company 10, 12, 188–9, 200–1, 203
Normann, Wilhelm 11
Northcliffe, Lord 10, 56, 137
Northrup, David 183, 185
Norwich, John Julius 79
Nzongola-Ntalaja, Georges 188–9

O'Connor, T. P. 1, 120, 154
Odling, Harold 202
Oldknow, Samuel 95
Olmsted, Frederick Law, Jr 114
Ormsby-Gore, W. G. A. 186
Orpen, William 204
Orrock, James 39–40
Orwell, George 79, 85, 107, 131
Osborn, F. J. 134
Owen, Robert 95–6, 105
Owen, Segar 42
Owen, William 14, 110
Owenite communities 105–6

Pacific Islands Company 160
Pacific Phosphate Company 160
packaging and branding 58–63
palm oil 10, 158–9, 164–5, 167–8, 173–5,
    177–8, 182–3, 186–8, 190

Parker, Barry 130, 132–3
Pascall (sweets) 116
Peabody, George and Peabody Trust 103
Pears, A. and F. (soap makers) 10, 56, 61,
    65, 68, 70–1, 200
Pearson, Weetman 7
Pedler, Friedrich 178, 184–5
Pemberton, John S. (cola) 60
Pemberton, Robert 108
Pende uprising 189–90
Penn, William 107
phalansteries 106
Planters Margarine Co. 10, 12
Plater-Zybek, Elizabeth 143
Player, John (cigarettes) 59–60
Port Sunlight 9–10, 14–15, 45, 93–4, 101–2,
    110–26, 128, 136–8, 199
Prestwich, Ernest 138
Price's Patent Candle Company 101
Priestley, J. B. 84–5, 141
Procter, William and Harley T. 63
Procter and Gamble 58, 63–4, 84
Pullman, George Mortimer 102
Purdom, C. B. 134

race and racial ideas 155–8, 160, 182, 189
Radburn, New Jersey 134–5
Rathbone, Frederick 41
Reader, W. J. 11, 201, 221
Reckitt, Sir James 133
Reilly, Charles 136–7
Renkin, Jules 167
Rhodes, Cecil 2, 163
Richardson, Benjamin Ward 108
Richardson, John Grubb (linen maker)
    101
Richter, Jean Paul 39
Rigby, Edith 36, 53n.124
Rivington estate 24, 26, 27–38, 41, 45, 201,
    207, 221
Rockefeller, John D. 1, 8, 44
Roex, Pierre 187
Rohe, Mies van der 141
Roosevelt, Franklin Delano 134
Roosevelt, Theodore 2, 170
Rowntree, Joseph 66, 130
Rowntree, Seebohm 128
Rowntree's (cocoa) 66, 113, 116, 130

Roynton Cottage 24, 28, 36–8, 41, 202
rubber 166, 180, 182

Saint-Simon, Claude-Henri de 105
Salt, Titus 100–1
Saltaire 100–1, 111, 141
Scott, George Gilbert 101
Scott, Sir Samuel 205
Scott, Walter Dill 82
Seaside, Florida 143
Sennett, A. R. 121
Shaw, George Bernard 129
Shaw, Norman 104
Sierra Leone 164, 186
Silkin, Lewis 135
Simon, E. D. 133
Simpson, James Lomax 24, 31, 33, 137
Simpson, Jonathan 18, 31, 33
Smiles, Samuel 1, 23, 46, 67, 91
Smith, Adam 86, 155
Smith, F. E., Earl of Birkenhead 41
Société le Nickel, New Caledonia 160
Soissons, Louis de 131
Solomon Islands 10, 160–3
Southey, Robert 96, 98–9
Stafford House (Lancaster House) 24
Stornoway, Lewis 205–8, 210, 212–18, 220
Strutt, Jebediah 95
Sturrock, J. L. 210
suburbanization 103–4, 135, 140–4
Sunlight soap 9–10, 58, 61–3, 65–70, 72–4,
     76–8, 80, 216
Sutherland, Duke of 24, 205
Sutherland, Halliday 209

Thompson, F. M. L. 5
Thompson, Francis 29
Thompson, W. P. 61
Thornton Hough, Wirral 24, 99, 137
Thornton Manor 2, 15, 18–19, 24–6, 38, 41,
     46, 137, 199
town planning 107–8, 134–43
Town Planning Review 137, 139
Trade Marks Registration Act (1875) 61
Trotha, Gen. Lothar von 157
Tudor Walters, Sir John 140

Tugwell, Rexford G. 134
Tyerman, John Simpson 45

Unilever 3, 8, 12, 57, 94, 163, 201, 221
United Africa Company 12
Unwin, Raymond 130, 132–3, 136, 140, 143
Unwin, Stanley 2–3, 126

Vandebosch, Gaston 183
Van Den Bergh's (margarine) 10, 12
Vandervelde, Émile 168, 171, 190
Vanderyst, Hyacinthe 186
Veblen, Thorstein 43
Vinolia (soap maker) 10

Wakeman, Frederic 56
Walker, Rev. Samuel Gamble 124
Wanamaker, John 57–8
Ward, Stephen 141
Warhol, Andy 65
Watson, Angus 15, 21
Watson, Angus and Co. (sardines) 208
Watson, John B. 82
Watson, Joseph (soap maker) 10, 61, 72,
     200
Webb, Sidney and Beatrice 109
Wedgwood, Josiah 59
Wells, H. G. 130
Welwyn Garden City 131, 134
whaling industry 10–11, 218–19
Williams, Harley 16, 18–19, 120, 154, 204
Wills, W. D. and H. O. (tobacco) 58–60
Wilson, Charles 3, 5–6, 12, 69, 80, 154, 173
Wilson, Thomas 212
Winstanley, Gerrard 105
Woodford, Charles Morris 160–1
Woodruff, William 67–8
Woolworth, F. W. 57–8
Wright, Myles 26
Wythenshawe 133–4

Yorke, F. R. S. 141–2

Zamyatin, Yevgeny 107
Zlín, Czechoslovakia 134
Zola, Émile 106

Ingram Content Group UK Ltd.
Milton Keynes UK
UKHW021254100523
421521UK00018B/98